BEYOND RELEVANCE

BEYOND RELEVANCE
A Collection of Essays

Edited by
LOUIS F. GORR
University of Maryland

Scott, Foresman and Company
Glenview, Illinois   London

"The Movie Industry and the Film Culture" by Ernest Callenbach. © 1968
by The Regents of the University of California. Reprinted from *Film Quarterly*,
Vol. XXII, No. 1, pp. 1–10, by permission of The Regents and the author.
"The Homosexual Revolution: A Status Report" by Donald J. Cantor. This
article first appeared in *The Humanist*, Fall 1967, and is reprinted by permission.   "A Slight Case of Hubris?" by Lewis Chester, Godfrey Hodgson,
and Bruce Page. From *An American Melodrama: The Presidential Campaign
of 1968* by Lewis Chester, Godfrey Hodgson, and Bruce Page. Copyright ©
1969 by Times Newspapers Ltd. All rights reserved. Reprinted by permission
of The Viking Press, Inc.   "Appalachia: Hunger in the Hollows" by Robert
Coles. From *The New Republic*, Nov. 9, 1968. Reprinted by Permission of
The New Republic, © 1968, Harrison-Blaine of New Jersey, Inc.   "Social
Change and the University" by John J. Corson. Copyright 1970 Saturday Review, Inc. Reprinted from the *Saturday Review*, January 10, 1970, a special
issue produced in cooperation with the Committee for Economic Development,
by permission of the publisher.   "Civil Liberties: The Crucial Issue" by
Justice William O. Douglas. Originally appeared in *Playboy* magazine; copy-
right © 1968 by HMH Publishing Co. Inc. Reprinted by permission of
William Morris Agency, Inc.   "The American Indian: A Portrait in Limbo"
by Peter Farb. Excerpted in part from the book *Man's Rise to Civilization
As Shown by the Indians of North America From Primeval Times to the
Coming of the Industrial State* by Peter Farb. Copyright, ©, 1968 by
Peter Farb. Reprinted by permission of E. P. Dutton & Co., Inc.   "Academic Irresponsibility" by Leslie Fiedler. Originally appeared in *Playboy*
magazine; copyright © 1968 by HMH Publishing Co. Inc. Reprinted by
permission of the author.   "The University Community in an Open Society"
by Edgar Z. Friedenberg. Reprinted by permission from *Daedalus*, Journal
of the American Academy of Arts and Sciences, Boston, Massachusetts, Volume 99, Number 1 (Winter 1970).   "Deep Art and Shallow Art" by
Amy Goldin. Reprinted, with authorial revisions, from *New American Review*,
No. 4, 1968, by permission of the author.   "Notes of a Neolithic Conservative" by Paul Goodman. Reprinted with permission from *The New York
Review of Books*. Copyright © 1970 The New York Review.   "The Student Drive to Destruction" by Louis J. Halle. From *The New Republic*,
Oct. 19, 1968. Reprinted by Permission of *The New Republic* and the author,
© 1968, Harrison-Blaine of New Jersey, Inc.   "Is American Radicalism
Possible?" by Irving Louis Horowitz. This article first appeared in *The*

Picture Credits: Paul S. Conklin; Roger Malloch, Magnum; Catherine Ursillo, Nancy Palmer Agency; Luc Joubert, Courtesy of the Pace Gallery, New York; Fred McDarrah.

For Madeleine and Michaela

Preface

This brief anthology is offered in the belief that the search for relevance has become a hollow cliché. It is founded on the proposition that a too heavy reliance on catchwords has blinded many students to the urgency of the problems with which they seek to deal. Of all books, an anthology can lay claim to the fewest pretensions, but it is hoped that this collection of essays will serve to demonstrate to today's student what it is to go beyond relevance in the search for truth and harmony.

The essays included here present a heterogeneous picture of several aspects of American life and attitudes. They have been arranged into five sections: On Minorities, On Youth, On the University, On Communication and Expression, On Democracy. The essays extend from matters of social outlooks to matters of artistic expression.

The essays herein are not rooted to the present, although they deal with current matters. In a variety of ways, each transcends the present and searches into the future for the necessary answers to its questions. While there is a variety of political views represented, these views are subordinated to the fact that each essay is one which questions established truths and conventional wisdom—whether espoused by the vocal activist or by the "silent majority." In this sense, the essays are radical, since they attempt to penetrate to the core of their respective subjects. Such a radicalism, however, is not one which relies on impressive terminology but one which truly searches out new approaches to old problems.

This anthology is not intended to persuade but rather to provoke. Provocation comes through honest dialogue. For this reason questions have been included at the end of each essay. Whether they are used as points for classroom discussion, student essays, or personal meditation, they will engage the reader more intimately with the subjects of the essays.

For those who desire to read more extensively in the fields suggested by the five sections, a list of further readings has been included at the end of each section. The titles in these lists have been selected because of the quality of their writing and the manner in which they treat their subjects. Possibly these books can be employed in the classroom to provide still further points of view and to open further channels of dialogue.

Many people have been involved in the composition of this anthology. Chief among them are several hundred students of many ages and of many social persuasions. I am indebted to my wife, Madeleine Gorr, for her encouragement, to Jack C. Barnes of the University of Maryland, Verne Reaves and Richard Welna of Scott, Foresman and Company, and Gerry Ogdin. All sins of omission and commission remain, of course, my own.

Louis F. Gorr
College Park, Maryland, 1970

Table of Contents

BEYOND RELEVANCE

I ON MINORITIES

Democracy as professed and democracy as practiced have long been in opposition to one another. One crucial issue of the American 1970's —particularly to members of minority groups—is the reconciliation of these poles to bring the ideals of democracy into action. For it is the minorities in America which suffer most because of the failure of our system to practice its own beliefs.

A "minority" is not merely a numerically small group in relation to a larger group, sometimes called the "majority." After all, there are nearly forty million black Americans. Nor is a minority merely an ethnic, religious, or political group holding different opinions from those of the majority. A minority is a state of mind, a state of mind that is determined to a large extent by the controlling agents of the society. Thus, in the late 1960's, the "silent majority" could be labeled a minority; and all those people who believed they were not heard by the government assumed the outlook of a minority: they rightly considered themselves cheated and oppressed. Blacks and Indians are members of a minority not only because they are "different" or numerically small, but because they are barred from certain opportunities by the prejudice and fear directed at them by others. The minority group in America is thus that entity which does not "fit in." As someone once said: "The man who is poor is poor because he is poor."

American history is rife with the evils of fear, bigotry, intolerance, and oppression—attitudes which threaten minorities as well as the existence of our society itself. The problem America faces is that of assuring all members of our society the fullest benefits of that society, while eliminating all vestiges of oppression and hypocrisy. Through the examination of three kinds of minority states of mind—racial, economic, and sexual—the following essays explore the relationship of oppression and prejudice to the status of minorities, and contribute to a general definition of minorities and how they exist in America.

1

Peter Farb

The American Indian:
A Portrait in Limbo

The quadrennial elections never fail to evoke compassion for "the Vanishing Americans," and this year the tragicomedy is again being played with style. "The poor Indian" is once more the theme of position papers and convention planks. As it did four years ago, the Administration has sent a message to Congress that repeats the aspirations of the Great White Father for his red children: better education, better housing, better health care, better job training. (Since "better" is a relative word, the Great White Father has pinpointed exactly how much "better" he has in mind: a mere 12 per cent increase from last year's incredibly low, fantastically mismanaged budget.) Politicians of both parties are making their usual salutes to the "progress" of the red man in adapting to a white world. Vice President Humphrey states that tuberculosis among Indians declined 55 per cent since 1955—but he neglects to add the fact that the Indian death rate from tuberculosis is still seven times that of the American population as a whole. Perhaps the least politically motivated obeisance to the red man was Senator Robert F. Kennedy's inquiry, just before his assassination, into the shame of Indian education.

The facts about Indian life today assuredly are bleak enough without election-year dramatization. Some 400,000 of the total 550,000 Indians in the United States live on approximately 200 reservations in twenty-six states. The reservations exist as poverty-stricken islands surrounded by an ocean of American bounty. The Indians are generally despised by whites; they are in ill health both physically and mentally, almost without political power, inarticulate in their attempts to win respect for their heritage. The amazing thing is not that they have managed to survive at all, but that they still possess patience about the white man's latest aspirations for them this election year. They hang on to a little piece of the future, but every year their grip slips a bit more. For this is their life today:

2

Housing. About 90 per cent of Indians live in tin-roofed shacks, leaky adobe huts, brush shelters, and even abandoned automobiles. Approximately 60 per cent of Indians still haul their drinking water, frequently from more than a mile away and often from contaminated sources.

Income and jobs. Indian unemployment ranges between 40 and 75 per cent in comparison with about 4 per cent for the nation as a whole. On one reservation in Utah I visited this summer, less than 25 per cent of the eligible work force had jobs—and most of these were employed by their own tribal organization. The average red family lives on $30 a week, while average white and black families earn at least $130 a week.

Health. The average age of death for an Indian today is forty-three years, for a white sixty-eight years. Death from dysentery is forty times greater among Indians than whites; influenza and pneumonia death rates are twice as high; middle-ear infections are so widespread that on some reservations a quarter of the children have suffered permanent hearing loss. Trachoma, an infectious eye disease that often causes blindness, is virtually nonexistent in the United States—except on the reservations. A survey made a few years ago on the San Carlos Apache Reservation in Arizona showed that 61 per cent of the children between the ages of five and eighteen were afflicted.

Education. Indian education is the worst of any minority group. The Indian completes about five years of schooling—whereas all other Americans average 11.2 years. It is not only the quantity of education the Indian is deprived of but the quality, for the saddest fact of all is that the longer he stays in school, the farther behind his achievement falls in comparison with white children.

In Idaho's Blackfoot school district, for example, three-fourths of the students in the elementary school are Indian, yet every teacher is white. Speaking any Indian language is prohibited and nothing is taught of Indian culture. In the last few years there have been nearly fifteen suicides by the school children. One out of every five junior-high students was found to be sniffing glue. When Senator Robert Kennedy visited the district this past spring, he asked the principal whether Indian culture and traditions were taught. He was informed, "There isn't any history to this tribe"—although the grandfathers of these children had played an important role in the history of the West. When the Senator asked if there were any books in the library where the children could read about Indian culture, he was shown *Captive of the Delawares*, which had a picture on the cover of a white child being scalped by an Indian.

The Indian can probably survive the bad housing, lack of jobs, dismal health conditions, and poor education—but not the implication that he is irrelevant to American culture. For once the Indians are deprived of the last bit of the culture that has sustained them, they will disappear into the faceless American poor. Yet, the U.S. Bureau of Indian Affairs was founded a century ago with the stated aim to alienate Indian children "from their native culture and language so they could take their place in modern society"—and that has remained an implied aim to this day. A white policy has stripped the Indian of his identity and made him embarrassed about his rich oral literature, his customs and traditions, his native foods and dress. A white education system has turned out imitation whites who succumb to the bleakness of reservation life and the prejudice around them.

"The American Indian today is about to go over the brink—not only of poverty and prejudice, but of moral collapse," says William Byler, executive director of the Association on American Indian Affairs. The Indian has learned that no one wants to listen or to understand when he speaks his thoughts about his own future. He is bewildered by the capricious policies handed down in Washington—first telling him to leave the reservation and get jobs in the cities, next telling him to stay on the reservation and bring industry to it. Some politicians tell him that he is a child who must be protected by the kindly White Father— and other politicians tell him that he is man enough to be cast adrift to sink or swim in the capitalist tide. The result of such confusion is widespread apathy among Indians. They find it difficult to act in concert with other Indians because whites deliberately ripped apart the intricate web of their social and political relationships.

The present plight of the red man is an indication of exactly how far he has fallen from his state of Noble Savage in little more than 450 years. At first, the newly discovered Indians were greatly respected and admired. Columbus brought home six Indians to show Queen Isabella and, dressed in full regalia, they quickly became the curiosities of Spain. Sir Walter Raleigh brought back Indians also and a craze swept Elizabethan England. Shakespeare complained about it in The Tempest: "They will not give a doit [a small coin equal to about half a farthing] to relieve a lame beggar, they will lay out ten to see a dead Indian." The French philosopher Michel de Montaigne talked with Indians who had been brought to the French Court and concluded that the Noble Savage had been found, for the Indian "hath no kind of traffic, no knowledge of letters, no intelligence of numbers, no name of magistrate, nor of politics, no use of services, of riches, or of poverty. . . . The very words that import a lie, falsehood, treason, covetousness, envy, detraction, were not heard among them."

The Noble Savage captivated Europe, but the colonists felt differently about living with red men. When Columbus discovered the Arawak

Indians, who inhabited the Caribbean Islands, he described them as "a loving people, without covetousness. . . . Their speech is the sweetest and gentlest in the world." But in their haste to exploit the abundance of the Americas, the Spaniards set the loving and gentle Arawak to labor in mines and on plantations. Whole Arawak villages disappeared due to slavery, disease, warfare, and flight to escape the Spaniards. As a result, the native population of Haiti, for example, declined from an estimated 200,000 in 1492 to 29,000 only twenty-two years later.

The Puritans in New England were not immediately presented with an Indian problem, for diseases introduced by trading ships along the Atlantic Coast had badly decimated the red populations. Yet, the Puritans failed miserably in their dealings with even the remnant Indians. They insisted upon a high standard of religious devotion that the Indians were unable or unwilling to give. The Puritans lacked any way to integrate the Indians into their theocracy, for they did not indulge in wholesale baptisms (as they charged the French did), nor were any Puritans specifically assigned to missionary tasks.

In 1637, a party of Puritans surrounded the Pequot Indian village and set fire to it after these Indians had resisted settlement of whites in the Connecticut Valley. About 500 Indians were burned to death or shot while trying to escape; the woods were then combed for any Pequots who had managed to survive, and these were sold into slavery. The whites devoutly offered up thanks to God that they had lost only two men; when the Puritan divine Cotton Mather heard about the raid, he was grateful to the Lord that "on this day we have sent six hundred heathen souls to hell."

The Indian came to be regarded as a stubborn animal that refused to acknowledge the obvious blessings of white civilization. Hugh Henry Brackenridge, a modest literary figure of the young nation, expressed the changed attitude when he wrote in 1782 of ". . . the animals, vulgarly called Indians." Rousseau's Noble Savage was laid to rest officially in 1790 when John Adams stated: "I am not of Rousseau's Opinions. His Notions of the purity of Morals in savage nations and the earliest Ages of civilized Nations are mere Chimeras." Even that man of enlightened homilies, Benjamin Franklin, observed that rum should be regarded as an agent of Providence "to extirpate these savages in order to make room for the cultivators of the earth."

After the War of 1812, the young United States had no further need for Indian allies against the British, and, as a result, the fortunes of the Indians declined rapidly. Pressure increased to get the Indians off the lands the whites had appropriated from them and, in 1830, Congress passed the Removal Act, which gave the President the right to extirpate all Indians who had managed to survive east of the Mississippi River. It was estimated that the whole job might be done economically at no more than $500,000—the cost to be kept low by persuasion, promises, threats, and the bribery of Indian leaders. When U.S. Supreme Court Justice John Marshall ruled in favor of the Cherokee Indians in a case with wide implications for preventing removal, President Andrew Jackson is said to have remarked: "John Marshall has made his decision, now let him enforce it."

During the next ten years, almost all the Indians were cleared from the East. Some, such as the Chickasaw and Choctaw and Cherokee, went resignedly. The Seminole actively resisted and retreated into the Florida swamps, where they stubbornly held off the United States Army. The Seminole Wars lasted from 1835 to 1842 and cost the United States some 1,500 soldiers and an estimated $20,000,000 (about forty times what Jackson had estimated it would cost to remove all Indians). Many of the Iroquois found sanctuary in Canada. The Sac and Fox made a desperate stand in Illinois against overwhelming numbers of whites, but ultimately their survivors were forced to move, as were the Ottawa, Potawatomi, Wyandot, Shawnee, Kickapoo, Winnebago, Delaware, Peoria, Miami, and many others who are remembered now only in the name of some town, lake, county, or state.

Alexis de Tocqueville, who examined the young United States with a perceptive eye and wrote it all down in his *Democracy in America*, was in Memphis on an unusually cold day when he saw a ragged party of Choctaw, part of the docile thousands who had reluctantly agreed to be transported to the new lands in the West. He wrote:

> The Indians had their families with them, and they brought in their train the wounded and the sick, with children newly born and old men upon the verge of death. . . . I saw them embark to pass the mighty river, and never will that solemn spectacle fade from my remembrance. No cry, no sob, was heard among the assembled crowd; all was silent. Their calamities were of ancient date, and they knew them to be irremediable.

De Tocqueville described with restrained outrage how the Indians were sent westward by government agents: ". . . half-convinced and half-compelled, they go to inhabit new deserts, where the importunate whites will not let them remain ten years in peace. In this manner do the Americans obtain, at a very low price, whole provinces, which the richest sovereigns of Europe could not purchase." He reported that a scant 6,273 Indians still survived in the thirteen original states.

The experience of the Indians west of the Mississippi River was only a sad, monotonous duplication of what had happened east of it—warfare, broken treaties, expropriation of land, rebellion, and ultimately defeat. No sooner were the Eastern Indians dropped down on the plains and prairies than the United States discovered the resources in the West, and miners and settlers were on the move. Emigrant trains rumbled westward, and once again the aim of the frontiersman was to get the Indian out of the way.

The "final extermination" was hastened by epidemics that swept the West and sapped the Indians' power to resist. A mere hundred Mandan out of a population of 1,600 survived a smallpox epidemic (they are extinct today); the same epidemic, spreading westward, reduced the total number of Blackfoot Indians by about half. The majority of Kiowa and Comanche Indians were victims of cholera. The Indians undoubtedly would have been crushed by whites in any event, but the spread of diseases made the job easier.

Up to 1868, nearly 400 treaties had been signed by the U.S. Government with various Indian groups, and scarcely a one had remained unbroken. The Indians were promised new lands, then moved off them to some other place. They were shifted about again and again, as many as five or six times. All of which led the Sioux chief Spotted Tail to ask wearily: "Why does not the Great White Father put his red children on wheels, so he can move them as he will?"

In the last decades of the last century the Indians finally realized that these treaties were real estate deals designed to separate them from their lands. Indians and whites skirmished and then fought openly with ferocity and barbarity on both sides. Group by group, the Indians rose in rebellion only to be crushed—the southern Plains tribes in 1874, the Sioux in 1876, the Nez Percé in 1877, the Ute in 1879, and the Apache throughout much of the 1880s, until Geronimo finally surrendered with his remnant band of thirty-six survivors. The massacre of more than 300 Sioux, mostly women and children and old people, at Wounded Knee, South Dakota, in 1890 marked the end of Indian resistance to white authority.

Humanitarians who attempted to ease the defeat of the Indians felt that the remnant populations should be given the dignity of private property. As a result, Senator Henry L. Dawes of Massachusetts sponsored the Allotment Act of 1887 to salvage some land for the Indians who otherwise might lose everything to voracious whites. When President Grover Cleveland signed the act, he stated that the "hunger and thirst of the white man for the Indian's land is almost equal to his hunger and thirst after righteousness."

The act provided that after every Indian had been allotted land, the remainder would be put up for sale to the public. But the loopholes with which the act was punctured made it an efficient instrument for separating the Indians from this land. The plunder was carried on with remarkable order. The first lands to go to whites were the richest—bottomlands in river valleys or fertile grasslands. Next went the slightly less desirable lands, such as those that had to be cleared before they could produce a crop. Then the marginal lands were taken, and so on, until the Indian had left to him only desert that no white considered worth the trouble to take. Between the passage of the Allotment Act in 1887 and a New Deal investigation in 1934, the Indians had been reduced to only 56,000,000 acres out of the meager 138,000,000 acres that had been allotted them—and every single acre of the 56,000,000 was adjudged by soil conservationists to be eroded. At the same time that the Indians were being systematically relieved of their lands, their birth rate rose higher than the mortality rate, and so there were more and more Indians on less and less land. The Indians did what they had always done: They shared the little they had and went hungry together.

The victory over the Noble Savage—reduced in numbers, deprived of land, broken in spirit, isolated on wasteland reservations—was complete except for one final indignity. That was to Americanize the Indian, to eliminate his last faint recollection of his ancient traditions—in short, to exterminate the cultures along with the Indians. There was not much culture left to eradicate, but at last zealous whites found something. Orders went out from Washington that all male Indians must cut their hair short, even though many Indians believed that long hair had supernatural significance. The Indians refused, and the battle was joined. Army reinforcements were sent to the reservations to carry out the order, and in some cases Indians had to be shackled before they submitted.

Most of the attention of the Americanizers, though, was concentrated on the Indian children, who were snatched from their families and shipped off to boarding schools far from their homes. The children usually were kept at school for eight years, during which time they were not permitted to see their parents, relatives, or friends. Anything Indian—dress, language, religious practices, even outlook on life—was uncompromisingly prohibited. Ostensibly educated, articulate in the English language, wearing store-bought clothes, and with their hair short and their emotionalism muted, the boarding-school graduates were sent out either to make their way in a white world that did not want them, or to return as strangers to their reservation. The Indian had simply failed to melt into the great American melting pot.

He had been remade in the white man's image and then cast adrift or else safely bottled up on reservations. Yet it is apparent to any objective observer that the Indian problem still nags at the American conscience. It seems that whites, both land-hungry settlers and humanitarians, have tried every possible variation in the treatment of the Indian. What, then, is the solution?

Many people concerned about the American Indian are coming to believe that we should simply stop offering the Indian pat solutions. Everything has been tried. The Indians have been herded from reservation to reservation, switched from hunting to agriculture or from agriculture to hunting, moved to cities to work in factories or told instead to make room for factories on their reservations. Indians exist today as the most manipulated people on earth—and yet our Indian policy has produced only failure after failure.

We have never recognized the Indian as someone who has his own historical rights to live and to act as an Indian within the framework of what remains of his culture. It is time that Washington allowed Indians on their own reservations to make their own decisions about their futures. Instead of dismantling the reservations, as some land-hungry Congressmen propose, let us begin by dismantling the U.S. Bureau of Indian Affairs. Indians directly concerned, and many impartial observers of the Indian scene as well, regard BIA as incredibly inefficient and unresponsive to the needs of modern Indians. Most BIA personnel still operate with the nineteenth-century attitudes of the Indian fighters and still regard the Indians as childlike wards of the federal government. BIA is distrusted, and even hated, by most Indians.

A model for a new Indian-Government relationship already exists and has been tested successfully for thirty-five years—the U.S. Soil Conservation Service. SCS is a service agency that provides farmers, ranchers, and timber growers with technical assistance that aids them in deriving the most benefits from various federal and state programs. But the actual policymaking and coordination of the work of many experts are firmly in the hands of some 3,000 soil conservation districts across the nation. Each district is a legal entity whose locally elected boards have the authority to work out constructive plans for their individual problems.

With such a new Indian-Government relationship, the sprawling federal programs in education, housing, employment, and so forth would be coordinated by local people who would adapt the programs to local need. With such a plan, it would be possible to take away the education responsibilities from BIA and place them in the Office of Education; the employment problems of Indians could be better handled by the Department of Labor; a start in decentralization has already been made in taking many health services away from BIA and having them carried on by the Public Health Service. Taking the human resource problems out of BIA leaves it free to concentrate on the land resource, a responsibility for which the U.S. Department of the Interior, of which it is a part, has a long history of competence.

But will the Indian be willing to participate in administering his own future? Promising indications that he will exist on many reservations. The Sioux of South Dakota, as just one example, impressed me this summer by their aggressive concern for taking what is best from American society while holding on to what remains of their own traditions. They are working hard to get the most benefits from the existing federal programs in health, education, welfare, employment, and housing while at the same time seeking to make their voices heard. Among other things, they have organized voter registration drives and elected Indians to school boards for the first time in history.

Clearly, it is time we stopped regarding Indians as living museum pieces with no relevance to America today. Their past and their future, for better or for worse, are intertwined with ours.

QUESTIONS FOR DISCUSSION AND WRITING

1. Does Farb attach an ironical meaning to the terms "Great White Father" (p. 2) and "Noble Savage" (p. 4)? Is there a relationship between Farb's use of these terms and the thesis of the essay? Explain.
2. Is the phrase "final extermination" (p. 7) appropriate to the subject of this essay? Is "final extermination" still a threat to racial minorities? Explain.
3. According to Farb, what are some of the reasons for the persecution of the Indian in America? Is there any similarity between this persecution and the persecution of other minority groups in America? Discuss.
4. What do the details in this essay reveal about the character of American society and its response to racial matters in general?
5. Does "white civilization" have "obvious blessings" (p. 5)? Is it accurate to speak of civilizations in terms of race—white, black, etc.? Would "culture" be a better term to use? Is one kind of "civilization" better or worse than another? Explain.
6. In your opinion, have the American Indians still failed to melt into the "great American melting pot" (p. 8)? What are the reasons for and against such "melting"?
7. If it is true, as many writers assert, that the white man stole America from the Indians, would an equitable, practical, and moral solution be to literally give back the country to the Indians? How could such a transaction be accomplished? What would be the results?

God's Judgment of White America

White America is doomed! Death and devastating destruction hang at this very moment in the skies over America. But why must her divine execution take place? Is it too late for her to avoid this catastrophe?

All the prophets of the past listed America as number one among the guilty nations that would be too proud, and too blind to repent and atone when God's last messenger is raised in her midst to warn her. America's last chance, her last warning, is coming from the lips of the Honorable Elijah Muhammad today . . . accept him and be saved; reject him and be damned!

It is written that White America will reject him; it is also written that White America will be damned and doomed . . . and the prophets who make these prophecies are never wrong in their divine predictions.

White America refuses to study, reflect, and learn a lesson from history; ancient Egypt didn't have to be destroyed. It was her corrupt government, the crooked politicians, who caused her destruction. *Pharaoh* hired *Hebrew* magicians to try and fool their own people into thinking they would soon be integrated into the mainstream of that country's life. Pharaoh didn't want the Hebrews to listen to Moses' message of separation. Even in that day separation was God's solution to the "slaves problems." By opposing Moses, the magicians were actually choosing sides against the God of their own people.

In like manner, modern Negro magicians are hired by the American government to oppose the Honorable Elijah Muhammad today. They pose as Negro "leaders." They have been hired by this white government *(white so-called liberals)* to make our people here think that integration into this doomed white society will soon solve our problem.

The only permanent solution to America's race problem is the complete separation of these twenty-two million ex-slaves from our White Slavemaster, and the return of these ex-slaves to our own land, where we can then live in peace and security among our own people. . . .

The American government is trying to trick her twenty-two million ex-slaves with false promises that she never intends to keep. The crooked politicians in the government are working with the Negro civil rights leaders, but not to solve the race problem. The greedy politicians who run this government give lip-service to the civil rights struggle, only to further their own selfish interests, and their main interest as politicians is *to stay in power.*

In this deceitful American game of power politics, the Negroes (*i.e., the race problem, the integration, and civil rights issues*) are nothing but tools, used by one group of whites called *Liberals* against another group of whites called *Conservatives,* either to get into power, or to remain in power.

Among whites here in America, the political teams are no longer divided into Democrats and Republicans. The whites who are now struggling for control of the American political throne are divided into liberal and conservative camps. The white liberals from both parties cross party lines to work together toward the same goal, and white conservatives from both parties do likewise.

The white liberal differs from the white conservative only in one way: the liberal is more deceitful than the conservative. The liberal is more hypocritical than the conservative.

Both want power, but the white liberal is the one who has perfected the art of posing as the Negro's friend and benefactor; and by winning the friendship, allegiance, and support of the Negro, the white liberal is able to use the Negro as a pawn or tool in this political football game that is constantly raging between the white liberals and white conservatives.

Politically, the American Negro is nothing but a football, and the white liberals control this *mentally dead ball* through tricks of tokenism: *false promises of integration and civil rights.* In this profitable game of deceiving and exploiting the political potential of the American Negro, those white liberals have the willing co-operation of the Negro civil rights leaders. These "leaders" sell out our people for just a few crumbs of token recognition and token gains. These "leaders" are satisfied with *token* victories and token progress because they themselves are nothing but *token* leaders.

According to a *New York Tribune* editorial (dated February 5, 1960), out of eleven million qualified Negro voters, only 2,700,000 actually took time to vote. This means that, roughly speaking, only three million out of eleven million Negroes who are qualified to vote actually take an active part . . . and the remaining eight million remain voluntarily inactive . . . *and yet this small (three million) minority of Negro voters holds the decisive edge in determining who will be the next President.*

If who will be the next President is influenced by only three million Negro voters, it is easy to understand why the presidential candidates of both political parties put on such a false show with the civil rights bill and with false promises of integration. They must impress the three million voting Negroes who are the actual "integration-seekers."

If such a fuss is made over these three million "integration-seekers," what would presidential candidates have to do to appease the eight million non-voting Negroes, if they ever decide to become politically active?

The three million Negro voters are the so-called middle-class Negroes, referred to by the late Howard University sociologist, E. Franklin Frazier, as the "Black Bourgeoisie," who have been educated to think as patriotic "individualists," with no racial pride . . . and who therefore look forward hopefully to the future "integrated-intermarried" society promised them by the white liberals and the Negro "leaders." It is with this hope that the "integration-minded" three million remain an active part of the white-controlled political parties. But it must never be overlooked that these three million "integration-seekers" are only a small minority of the eleven million potential Negro voters.

The eight million non-voting Negroes are in the majority; they are the downtrodden black masses. The black masses have refused to vote, or to take part in politics, because they reject the Uncle Tom approach of the Negro leadership that have been hand-picked for them by the white man.

These Uncle Tom leaders do not speak for the Negro majority; they do not speak for the black masses. They speak for the "Black Bourgeoisie," the brainwashed, white-minded, middle-class minority, who are ashamed of black, and don't want to be identified with the black masses, and are therefore seeking to lose their "black identity" by mixing, mingling, intermarrying, and integrating with the white man.

The race problem can never be solved by listening to this white-minded minority. The white man should try to learn what the black masses want, and the only way to learn what the black masses want is by listening to the man who speaks for the black masses of America. The one man here in America who speaks for the down-trodden, dissatisfied black masses is this same man so many of our people are flocking to see and hear. This same Mr. Muhammad who is labeled by the white man as a black supremacist, and as a racist.

If the three million white-minded Negroes are casting their ballots for integration and intermarriage, what do the non-voting black masses want? Find out what the black masses want, and then perhaps America's race problem can be solved.

Think how the *late* President himself got into office by only a scant margin which was "donated" to him by Negro voters, and think how many governors, and other white politicians hold their seats (*some by less than 5,000 votes*). Only then can you understand the importance these white liberals place on *their* control of the Negro vote!

The white liberals hate the Honorable Elijah Muhammad, because they know their present position in the power structure stems from their ability to deceive and to exploit the Negro, politically as well as economically.

They know that the Honorable Elijah Muhammad's divine message will make our people (1) *wake up,* (2) *clean up,* and (3) *stand up.* They know that once the Honorable Elijah Muhammad is able to resurrect the Negro from this mental grave of ignorance by teaching him the truth about himself and his real enemy, the Negro will then be able to see and think for himself. Once the Negro learns to think for himself, he will no longer allow the white liberal to use him as a helpless football in the white man's crooked game of "power politics."

Let us examine briefly some of the tricky strategy used by white liberals to harness and exploit the political energies of the Negro.

The crooked politicians in Washington, D.C. purposely make a big noise over the proposed civil rights legislation. By blowing up the civil rights issue they skillfully add *false importance* to the Negro civil rights "leaders." Once the image of these Negro civil rights "leaders" has been blown up way beyond its proper proportion, these same Negro civil rights "leaders" are then used by white liberals to influence and control the Negro voters . . . all for the benefit of the white politicians who pose as friends of the Negro.

The white conservatives aren't friends of the Negro either, but they at least don't try to hide it. They are wolves; they show their teeth in a snarl that keeps the Negro always aware of where he stands with them. But the white liberals are foxes, who also show their teeth to the Negro, but pretend that they are smiling. The white liberals are more dangerous than the conservatives; they lure the Negro, and as the Negro runs from the growling wolf, he flees into the open jaws of the "smiling" fox.

The job of the Negro civil rights leader is to make the Negro forget that the wolf and the fox both belong to the same family. Both are canines; and no matter which one of them the Negro places his trust in, he never ends up in the White House . . . but always in the doghouse.

The white liberals control the Negro and the Negro vote by controlling the Negro civil rights leaders. As long as they control the Negro civil rights leaders, they can also control and contain the Negro's struggle, and they can control the Negro's so-called "revolt."

The Negro "revolution" is controlled by these foxy white liberals, by the government itself. But the Black Revolution is controlled only by God.

The Black Revolution is the struggle of the non-whites of this earth against their white oppressors. The Black Revolution has swept white supremacy out of Africa, out of Asia, and is getting ready to sweep

it out of Latin America. Revolutions are based upon *land*. Revolutionaries are the landless against the landlord. Revolutions are never peaceful, never loving, never non-violent, nor are they ever compromising.
Revolutions are destructive and bloody. Revolutionaries don't compromise with the enemy; they don't even negotiate. Like the flood in
Noah's day, revolution drowns all opposition . . . or like the fire in
Lot's day, the Black Revolution burns everything that gets in its path.

America is the last stronghold of white supremacy. The Black Revolution, which is international in nature and scope, is sweeping down upon
America like a raging forest fire. It is only a matter of time before
America herself will be engulfed by the black flames, these black
firebrands.

Whenever an uncontrollable forest fire is roaring down upon the farm-
house, the only way the farmer can fight that forest fire is by building
a *back fire*, a smaller fire that he himself can control. He then uses
this *controlled fire* to fight the fire that is raging beyond his control.

Here in America, the Black Revolution (the "uncontrollable forest
fire") is personified in the religious teachings, and the religious works
of the Honorable Elijah Muhammad. This great man of God can not
in any way be controlled by the white man, and he will not compromise
in any way with the wrongs this government has inflicted upon our
people.

The Negro "revolt" is controlled by the white man, the white fox.
The Negro "revolution" is controlled by this white government. The
leaders of the Negro "revolution" (*the civil rights leaders*) are all subsi-
dized, influenced, and controlled by the white liberals; and all of the
demonstrations that are taking place in this country to desegregate lunch
counters, theaters, public toilets, etc., are just artificial fires that have
been ignited and fanned by the white liberals in the desperate hope
that they can use this artificial revolution to fight off the *real* Black
Revolution that has already swept white supremacy out of Africa, Asia,
and is sweeping it out of Latin America . . . and is even now manifesting itself also right here among the black masses in this country.

Can we prove that the Negro Revolution is controlled by white liberals? Certainly!

Right after the Birmingham demonstration, when the entire world
had seen on television screens the police dogs, police clubs, and fire
hoses brutalizing defenseless black women, children, and even babies,
it was reported on page twenty-six in the May 15 issue of the *New
York Times*, that the *late* President Kennedy and his brother, Attorney
General Robert Kennedy, during a luncheon conference with several
newspaper editors from the State of Alabama, had warned these editors
that they must give at least some *token* gains to the *moderate* Negro
leaders in order to enhance the image of these *moderate* Negro leaders
in the eyesight of the black masses, otherwise the masses of Negroes

might turn in the direction of Negro extremists. *And the late President named the Black Muslims as being foremost among the Negro extremist groups that he did not want Negroes to turn toward.*

In essence, the *late* President told these Southern editors that he was trying to build up the weak image of the Negro civil rights leaders, in order to offset the strong religious image of the Muslim leader, the Honorable Elijah Muhammad. He wasn't giving these Negro leaders anything they deserved; but he was confessing the necessity of building them up, and propping them up, in order to hold the black masses in check, keep them in his grasp, and under his control.

The *late* President knew that once Negroes hear the Honorable Elijah Muhammad, the white liberals will never influence or control or *misuse* those Negroes for the benefit of the white liberals anymore . . . so the *late* President was faced with a desperate situation.

Martin Luther King's image had been shattered the previous year, when he failed to bring about desegregation in Albany, Georgia. The other civil rights leaders had also become fallen idols. The black masses across the country at the grass-roots level had already begun to take their cases to the streets, on their own. The government in Washington knew that something had to be done to get the rampaging Negroes back into the corral, back under the control of the white liberals.

The government propaganda machine began encouraging Negroes to follow only what it called "responsible" Negro leadership, and by "responsible" Negro leaders the government actually meant *Negro leaders who were responsible to the government,* and who could therefore be controlled by the government, and be used by that same government to control their impatient people.

The government knows that the Honorable Elijah Muhammad is responsible only to God, and can be controlled only by God. But this white government of America doesn't believe in God!

Let us review briefly what happened last spring: in May in Birmingham, Negroes had erupted and retaliated against the whites. During the many long weeks when the police dogs and police clubs and the high-pressure water hoses were brutalizing black women and children and babies, and the Birmingham Negroes had called for the government to intervene with Federal troops, the *late* President did nothing but sit on his hands. He said there was nothing he could do. But when the Negroes in Birmingham exploded and began to defend themselves, the *late* President sent in Federal troops, not to defend the Negroes, but to defend the whites against whom the Negroes had finally retaliated.

At this point, spontaneous demonstrations began taking place all over the country. At the grass-roots level Negroes began to talk about marching on Washington, tying up the Congress, the Senate, the White House, and even the airport. They threatened to bring this government to a halt. This frightened the entire white power structure.

The *late* President called in the Negro civil rights leaders, and told

them to bring this "march" to a halt. The Negro civil rights leaders
were forced to tell the *late* President that they couldn't stop the march
because they hadn't started it. It was spontaneous, at the grass-roots
level across the country, and it had no leadership whatsoever.

When the *late* President saw that he couldn't stop the march, he
joined it. He endorsed it; he welcomed it. He became a part of it,
and it was he who put the six Negro civil rights leaders at the head
of it. *It was he who made them the BIG SIX.*

How did he do it? How did *he* gain control of the March on Washington? A study of his strategy will give you a glimpse of the political
genius with which the Kennedy family was ruling this country from
the White House, and how they used the American Negro in all of
their political schemes.

The *late* President *endorsed* the march; that should have been the
tip-off. A few days later in New York City at the Carlyle Hotel, a philan-
thropic society known as the Taconic Foundation, headed by a shrewd
white liberal, Stephen Currier, called a meeting of the six civil rights
leaders in an effort to bring unity of action and purpose among all
the civil rights groups.

After Martin Luther King had been released from his Birmingham
jail cell in May, he traveled from coast to coast in a fund-raising campaign for his Southern Christian Leadership Conference. Roy Wilkins
then began to attack King, accusing him of stirring up trouble, and
after the NAACP would bail out King and the other demonstrators,
then King would capitalize on the trouble by taking up all the money
for his own organization, leaving the NAACP to hold the bag at a
great financial loss.

As King, Wilkins, and the other civil rights leaders began to fight
publicly among themselves over the money they were trying to get
from the white liberals, they were destroying their own leadership image.

The white liberal, Stephen Currier, showed them how they were
destroying themselves by attacks upon each other, and it was suggested
that since most of their division and disagreement stemmed from competition for funds from white liberals, they should unite their fund-raising
efforts. Then they formed the Council for United Civil Rights Leadership, under the pretext that it would be for fund-raising purposes. They
chose the Urban League's Whitney Young as the chairman, and the
white liberal, Stephen Currier, became the co-chairman.

It took the white man to bring these Negro leaders together and
to unite them into one group. He let them select their own chairman,
but he himself became the co-chairman. *This shrewd maneuver placed
the white liberal and the Taconic Foundation in the position to exercise
influence and control over the six civil rights leaders, and by working
through them, control the entire civil rights movement including the
March on Washington.*

(It also put the white liberals in a position to force the Big Six to come out against the recently proposed Christmas Boycott, by threatening to withdraw their financial support from the civil rights drive.)

According to the August 4 edition of the *New York Times,* $800,000 was split up between these six Negro civil rights leaders on June 19 at the Carlyle Hotel, and another $700,000 was promised to be given to them at a later date after the march was over, if everything went well with the march.

Public relations experts were made available to these six big Negroes, and they were given access to the news media throughout the country. The press skillfully projected them as the leaders of the March on Washington, and as soon as the Big Six were looked upon in the public eye as the organizers of the march, and their image became inseparable from the march image, their first step was to invite four white "leaders" to become a part of the march "godhead." This group of leaders would supposedly okay all plans and thereby control the "direction and the mood" of the march.

These four white "leaders" represented the same factions who had put the *late* President in the White House: Catholics, Jews, Labor, and Protestant liberals. When the *late* President had learned that he couldn't stop the march, he not only joined it himself, but he encouraged all of his political bedfellows to join it. This is the way the white liberals took over the March on Washington, weakened its impact, and changed its course; *by changing the participants and the contents, they were able to change the very nature of the march itself.*

Example: If I have a cup of coffee that is too strong for me because it is too black, I weaken it by pouring cream into it. I integrate it with cream. If I keep pouring enough cream in the coffee, pretty soon the entire flavor of the coffee is changed; the very nature of the coffee is changed. If enough cream is poured in, eventually you don't even know that I had coffee in this cup. This is what happened with the March on Washington. The whites didn't integrate it; they *infiltrated* it. Whites joined it; they engulfed it; they became so much a part of it, it lost its original flavor. It ceased to be a Black March; it ceased to be militant; it ceased to be angry; it ceased to be impatient. In fact, it ceased to be a march. It became a picnic, an outing with a festive, circus-like atmosphere. . . . CLOWNS AND ALL.

The government had learned that in cases where the demonstrators are predominantly black, they are extremely militant, and ofttimes very violent. But to the same degree that whites participate, violence most times is decreased. The government knew that in cases wherein blacks were demonstrating all by themselves, those blacks are so dissatisfied, disenchanted, and angry at the white man that they will ofttimes strike back violently regardless of the odds or the consequences. The white government had learned that the only way to hold these black people in check is by joining them, by infiltrating their ranks disguised as integrationists. By integrating their marches and all their demonstrations, and weakening them, in this way only could they be held in check.

The government told the marchers what time to arrive in Washington, where to arrive, and how to arrive. The government then channeled them from the arrival point to the feet of a dead President, George Washington, and then let them march from there to the feet of another dead President, Abraham Lincoln.

The original black militants had planned to march on the White House, the Senate, and the Congress and to bring all political traffic on Capitol Hill to a halt, but the shrewd politicians in Washington, realizing that those *original* black militants could not be stopped, joined them. By joining the marchers, the white liberals were able to lead the marchers away from the White House, the Senate, the Congress, Capitol Hill and *away from victory*. By keeping them marching from the Washington Monument to the Lincoln Monument, marching between the feet of two dead Presidents, they never reached the White House to see the then *living* President.

The entire march was controlled by the *late* President. The government in Washington had told the marchers what signs to carry, what songs to sing, what speeches to make and what speeches not to make, and then told the marchers to be sure to get out of town by sundown . . . *and all of them were out of town by sundown.*

One of the Big Six leaders, John Lewis, chairman of the Student Nonviolent Coordinating Committee, was prevented from making a very militant speech. He wanted to attack the Kennedy administration for its hypocrisy on civil rights.

The speech was censored by the Right Reverend Patrick O'Boyle, the Catholic Archbishop of Washington, D.C. This was a case in which the Catholic Church itself, for whom Reverend O'Boyle speaks, put itself in the position of censoring the legitimate opinion of one of the Big Six Negro civil rights leaders.

The *late* President's shrewd strategy was: If you can't beat them, join them. The *Catholic* President placed his *Catholic* bishop in a strategic position to exercise censorship over any one of the Big Six Negro leaders who tried to deviate from the script in this great "extravaganza" called the March on Washington which the government had controlled right from the very beginning.

So in the final analysis of the march: It would have to be classified as the best performance of the year; in fact it was the greatest performance of this century. It topped anything that Hollywood could have produced.

If we were going to give out Academy Awards in 1963, we would have to give the *late* President an Oscar for the "Best Producer of the Year"; and the four white liberals who participated should get an Oscar for the "Best Actors of the Year" because they really acted like sincere liberals and fooled many Negroes . . . and to the six Negro civil rights leaders should go an Oscar for the "Best Supporting Cast," because they supported the *late* President in his entire act, and in his entire program.

Now that the show is over, the black masses are still without land, without jobs, and without homes . . . their Christian churches are still being bombed, their innocent little girls murdered. So, what did the March on Washington accomplish? Nothing!

The *late* President has a bigger image as a liberal, the other whites who participated have bigger liberal images also, and the Negro civil rights leaders have now been permanently named the BIG SIX (because of their participation in the BIG FIX?) . . . but the black masses are still unemployed, still starving, and still living in the slums . . . and I might add, getting angrier and more explosive every day.

History must repeat itself! Because of America's evil deeds against these twenty-two million Negroes, like Egypt and Babylon before her, America herself now stands before the Bar of Justice. White America is now facing her Day of Judgment, and she can't escape because today God Himself is the Judge. God Himself is now the administrator of justice, and God Himself is to be her divine executor!

Is it possible for America to escape this divine disaster? If America can't atone for the crimes she has committed against the twenty-two million Negroes, if she can't undo the evils she has brutally, mercilessly heaped upon our people these past four hundred years, then America has signed her own doom . . . and our own people would be foolish to accept her deceitful offers of integration into her doomed society . . . at this late date!

How can America atone for her crimes? The Honorable Elijah Muhammad teaches us that a desegregated theater or lunch counter won't solve our problems. Better jobs won't even solve our problems. An integrated cup of coffee isn't sufficient pay for four hundred years of slave labor, and a better job in the white man's factory or position in his business is, at best, only a temporary solution. The only lasting or permanent solution is complete separation on some land that we can call our own.

The Honorable Elijah Muhammad teaches us that the race problem can easily be solved, just by sending these twenty-two million ex-slaves *back to our own homeland* where we can live in peace and harmony with our own kind. But this government should provide the transportation, plus everything else we need to get started again in our own country. This government should provide everything we need in machinery, materials, and finance; enough to last us from twenty to twenty-five years, until we can become an independent people *in our own country*.

If this white government is afraid to let her twenty-two million ex-slaves go back to our country and to our own people, then America must set aside some separate territory here in the Western Hemisphere, where the two races can live apart from each other, since we certainly don't get along peacefully while we are here together.

The size of the territory can be judged according to our own population. If our people number one-seventh of America's total population, then give us one-seventh of this land. We don't want any land in the desert, but where there is rain and much mineral wealth.

We want fertile, productive land on which we can farm and provide our own people with sufficient food, clothing, and shelter. This government must supply us with the machinery and other tools needed to dig into the earth. Give us everything we need for them from twenty to twenty-five years, until we can produce and supply our own needs.

If we are a part of America, then part of what she is worth belongs to us. We will take our share and depart, then this white country can have peace. *What is her net worth?* Give us our share in gold and silver and let us depart and go back to our homeland in peace.

We want no integration with this wicked race that enslaved us. We want complete separation from this race of devils. But we should not be expected to leave America and go back to our own homeland *empty-handed*. After four hundred years of slave labor, we have some BACK PAY coming, a bill owed to us that must be collected.

If the government of white America truly repents of its sins against our people, *and atones by giving us our true share, only then can America save herself!*

But if America waits for Almighty God Himself to step in and force her into a just settlement, God will take this entire continent away from her; and she will cease to exist as a nation. Her own Christian scriptures warn her that when God comes He can give the "entire Kingdom to whomsoever He will" . . . which only means that the God of Justice on Judgment Day can give this entire continent to whomsoever He wills!

White America, wake up and take heed, before it is too late!

QUESTIONS FOR DISCUSSION AND WRITING

1. Do you agree with Malcolm X's observation that "White America is doomed"? Can you think of some specific problems in America today as examples to support this contention? Discuss.
2. What do you learn from this essay/speech about the black American in recent history? Is it an accurate description? Explain.
3. Malcolm X says that "the white liberal . . . has perfected the art of posing as the Negro's friend and benefactor." What is a "white liberal"? Why does Malcolm X distrust and dislike them?
4. Just as many people accused Malcolm X of being a "trouble-maker," so

many people now consider groups such as the Black Panthers as "trouble-makers." Discuss this as a way of viewing social activists. Is it typical of Americans? Explain.

5. It can be argued that this essay is more concerned with "civil liberties" than with what most people nowadays call "civil rights." Do you agree with this argument? What are some differences between the two ideas, "civil liberties" and "civil rights"?

6. Many whites refuse to or cannot part with their prejudices against the black man; and they frequently refuse to treat him as an equal. Yet whites also argue against the desire of some black men to separate themselves from the mainstream of American society. Can you explain such a paradox?

7. Why does Malcolm X deride the "black bourgeoisie"? Is the black bourgeoisie similar in outlook and desire to the white bourgeoisie? Explain.

8. How similar is the position of the black man in America today to that of the red man? Are they equally oppressed? What possibilities might exist for an alliance between these two groups, and what might be the result of such an alliance?

9. If you have read other writings by Malcolm X, discuss how his views of America, whites, and mankind underwent a transformation during his short lifetime. Discuss the significance of this transformation.

Robert Coles

Appalachia: Hunger
in the Hollows

It all started eight years ago in Appalachia, in West Virginia, where the young Catholic Senator from Massachusetts, with his Boston and Harvard accent, had to demonstrate that thoroughly Protestant Americans, suspicious of Easterners and city people and "Romans" (as I hear it put in the hollows) would take to him—which they did. What came after is painful history. I have been working in the Appalachian mountains since 1962, when John Kennedy was trying to get help for the region out of a reluctant Congress. During that year, I spent time in western North Carolina, in Asheville and in the little town of Burnsville, the capital of Yancey County. I came there because I was studying school desegregation as it took place in city after city of the South, but I lingered because I realized there was something else to see, a whole way of life that was part Southern, part old Anglo-Saxon, part rural, and part nothing but itself. Since then I worked closely in Kentucky and West Virginia with the Appalachian Volunteers, an impressive and effective group made up of students from within and without the mountain states and, as the students sometimes put it in moments of self-consciousness, "just plain folks," men and women of all ages from say, Floyd County, Kentucky, or Raleigh County, West Virginia, who have joined the Volunteers because they've had enough of—well, enough of everything that shocked and angered John Kennedy "back then."

That is how I hear it put in the hollows today. Like us, they remember, and perhaps they have more reason to do so: "I can recall him coming here, back then. They brought him up the creek, and I thought the next thing he'd be up the hollow, too. He was a fine-looking man, and you know how he won us all over—I'll tell you. We're used to those politicians coming around here just before election day and promising us this, that and everything, usually everything. You can smell them a mile away. But he didn't do that. He was sort of like us, actually. He didn't try to talk too much. He just looked around, and for a while you didn't know what he was thinking. Then he'd say something, not too long, like 'it's real bad here, I can see, and I'm going to do the best I can, the best I can to help you out.' Something like that was what you could trust—you knew the guy meant it. But he got killed, and his brother, too. He came here just last spring, his brother, and I heard him. He was looking into things for the Senate—it was a 'hearing,' I guess they called it. He came all by himself. The rest of the Senators, they had other things to do. He was like his brother, a fine-appearing man. I never saw so many people turn up, not around here, not in the shadow of these mountains. My wife and I, we said he gave us the greatest talk we'd ever heard in our whole lives. He'd be questioning those county officials—and it was as though you could believe in your country again. He told them they weren't doing their jobs, and that they owed it to America that we all lived better, here in Kentucky and all over. It wasn't only the words. It was you knew he meant it. The guy had real honest-to-goodness feelings inside of him and he didn't go on and on trying to persuade you. He said what needed saying—the same thing we say day after day with no one listening but ourselves. But that was back then in the spring, a long time it seems. First you'd hear people talk about 'back then when President Kennedy was here,' and now it's 'back then in April when Robert Kennedy came to see us.' Now I don't know, I don't know who I want. Neither of them two, I know that. I think I'll vote for Wallace. A lot of people say they will. He's fed up and so are we."

By turns angry, sad, wry, ironic, resigned or stubbornly determined, he is glad to speak his mind and let me know that like a lot of people from all over the country, he feels cheated this year. So, we talk, hour after hour, and I hear his disenchantment—in a way like mine, but also less wordy, less abstract, more concrete, more tied to the particulars of everyday life. He is 41, the father of nine children. He was once a mine worker, but lost his job along with many others about 15 years ago. Now strip mines tear away at the beautiful mountains and leave a legacy of polluted streams, recurrent landslides, destroyed homes and farms and wildlife. "But they get the coal they want, with machines and not our broken backs." He says that angrily, and I'm not the first doctor to whom he has recited the story. Nor is he the first hurt and ailing man I've met in West Virginia or Kentucky.

Even before he was laid off there was trouble, the beginning of serious trouble: "I had a bad cough all the time, like you do when you work down in the mines. After a while you stop thinking about it. You cough like you breathe, on and off all day. Then the cough got real bad and I saw a couple of doctors, company doctors. They gave me medicine to keep the cough down, and I stopped worrying. You can't be a coal miner and worry about what it looks like inside, in your lungs. Then I got hurt, my back. That happens a lot, too—and you either can go back to work or not. I wanted to go back, and I was lucky because I could. I'd still have trouble, but like with the cough, I could keep going. I took some pills when it got bad, but most of the time I showed up first thing in the morning and stuck it out to the end. And I miss those days. Time went fast, and there was money around, enough to pay the bills and live real decent-like and feel like a man, like somebody who was doing at least something with his life.

"Then they mechanized, and they started strip-mining all over with those machines, and we were through, me and all my friends. And ever since it's been the same. We're lucky to be alive each day, that's how I'd put it all together. I've been trying and trying to get on assistance [relief] but they just won't do it, they won't let me by. The doctors, they say I might have some trouble with my lungs and my back, but I was working when I got fired, and I could work now, so far as they're concerned. Hell, you don't have to be a full-fledged cripple to be on assistance, but it's politics, and if I was on the sheriff's good side, that would be fine—I'd have been collecting a check for years; but I'm not, because I got fresh way back and asked them to send the bus up the hollow to pick up my kids. They freeze in the winter walking those two miles to the bus and standing waiting for it. (They don't have the right clothes. We just can't pay for them.) When the courthouse gang heard that, they decided I was real fresh, a real wiseguy. So they said if I was so ungrateful for all that was being done for me—and me not working—then I'd learn to regret it. And I'll tell you, I have."

But he is a proud man. Like hundreds of thousands all over those lovely Appalachian mountains he can find no work, is refused any relief by the county officials, who have near absolute power in the region, and still somehow survives. He grows vegetables. He has a few chickens, and they lay eggs. He goes up the mountains and finds herbs, which he can sell "because they like to cook with them over in the East." And he is always on the lookout for a job, any job, for any length of time: "I can't stand sitting around and doing nothing. You get to hate it. You get to hate yourself. You get to hate everyone around you. I hate my kids growing up like this, seeing me without work. The oldest one, he wants to go to Ohio or Chicago or someplace like that, and get a job in a factory and make some money and then come back here. If I was in better health I'd have done it a long time ago. That's the only answer these days, go to the city for a while and try to make a few bucks. But you hear it's lousy there, 'lousier than you can ever believe' is the way I hear them say. So, they stay for as long as they have to, and then, believe me, they come back here to die. Yes sir. No one born here wants to leave. The tourists say it's pretty, but we *know* it is."

He may be from the oldest American stock, "here from the beginning," but right now he and his family are in this kind of fix: from odd jobs and an occasional gift sent by a brother (who *did* go to Ohio, to Cincinnati and then Dayton) about $750 a year comes in, and that is all, all the money this family of eleven American citizens receives. They grow some food and they cook and preserve some of it for the winter, but they cannot plant nearly enough (on an acre or two of land up along a steep hill) to keep a supply of tomatoes or beans or cucumbers throughout the long winter and spring. Of course to keep them from literally starving to death the rich and powerful American government offers its food stamps, which require even now, after all the inquiries and hearings and struggles of the last year, an expenditure of $22 at a minimum every month—for a family of eleven that can go for weeks without money. Recently the Congress voted an emergency bill that would allow even that minimum to be waived in cases where there is simply no cash to be had. And here is how it all goes, life and largesse and emergency largesse in the Great Society: "Sometimes we can just raise the money, so we can buy the food stamps, and get about $100 worth of food for the month. But we are eleven of us, and it's as expensive to buy food here as any place else. By the third week we're down to nothing, and I'm desperate. They take up collections at the church, and we go borrowing, and with your kin you don't starve to death, no sir. But it's not very good either, I have to admit. For breakfast there's not much I can give the kids. In the winter I have to warm them up. I just have to. So I give them tea, real piping hot. Sometimes they have oatmeal, if there is some, and some biscuits, hot biscuits. Then for supper it depends—if the chickens have left us a few eggs, and if I have some preserves left. The worst time is around January, thereabouts. There's no work. There's no garden. There's nothing but those stamps, if we can raise the money. Then we'll go without supper sometimes, and breakfast, too. Then it's tea and cornbread and oatmeal if we're lucky."

How about the emergency funds that Congress voted, presumably so that no American would starve? It so happens that this family, and dozens others like it I know, failed to learn about that bit of legislative news. They don't read the *Congressional Record* or *The Washington Post*. They don't even read the very fine *Louisville Courier-Journal* or the not-so-fine *Lexington Herald Leader*. They don't have a television set, and for them a trip to town, unless offered by a neighbor, can cost five dollars. So they remain ignorant of the progress in America: "If it hadn't been for the AV [Appalachian Volunteer] who comes here we'd never have known about the new program, the stamps you're supposed to get if you don't have money to buy them. But it's been more trouble instead of less; it's been a heartache, trying to get them to certify us and tell us we're eligible for the 'emergency provision,' they call it. We would have to pay someone almost as much as the stamps cost to get to their office—they don't know about things like that in Washington—but the AV drove us over to town, and then it was what we know: the same old people in the county courthouse, sending you back and forth, back and forth, and delaying and telling you they have to investigate and things like that. Now either you're going through an emergency or you're not. I have to borrow food at the end of every month, and they know it. I have to go begging at church and with my kinfolk down the creek to pay for those stamps every month, and they know it. I should be on public assistance, and they know it. But they get everything federal that comes through here, every bit, every dollar, no matter what the senators meant to do in Washington. It may say on paper that the money is for us, but the money goes to the county people, the people who get all the money that comes in here. And they don't intend to let anyone in on the gravy who isn't right in their pockets. I remember when I asked them to send that school bus nearer. They told me, 'You'll live to be sorry you ever asked.' Well they were right— though from day to day I wonder if I'll live much more, and be sorry about anything. It can't get much worse than it is."

Their home—one like hundreds I have seen, one like many thousands that stand all over the region—can be tactfully described as extremely modest. It is of wood and tarpaper, and stands on cement blocks. The wind blows right through it. There is no central heating, no plumbing. Water comes from a well several miles away. In winter, in the cold, snowy Appalachian winter, a fireplace provides heat, and eleven bodies leave their five beds to huddle near the burning coals. In summer, flies and mosquitoes are undeterred by screens—and a nearby stream has been badly polluted by a stripmine. Yet they all try hard as a family. They sleep close together, rely on one another impressively, and keep a very neat home. An old picture of John Kennedy is on one wall, and beside it a picture of Robert Kennedy talking with some miners: "After he came here, the teacher gave each child who wanted one a copy of the picture. They got a stack of them from the paper."

The teacher is distant kin of theirs and would like to give them all even more, but cannot: "No sir, none of the children get their lunch at school. No sir, they don't. It's up to the principal, who gets the lunches and who doesn't. The well-off kids from town, they bring their money and so they get fed. It don't mean nothing to their parents, a few dollars here or there. But I can't give each of the kids a quarter every day. I don't have it; I don't have one quarter, never mind six of them. So, they just sit there, while the others eat. And they're not the only ones, at least I know that. Sometimes a kid will offer them something he doesn't want to eat, and sometimes my kids are too proud to accept, but sometimes they swallow their pride to get some of that soup they have."

That is the way it is, not only for that one family but for families up and down hollows in several states of these United States. Respectfully, solemnly one listens, hears the stories, sees evidence of and feels the bravery and courage and honesty and dignity. But one also has to notice the wear and tear on body, mind, on spirit, that goes with hunger and idleness; and one has to notice the illnesses that are never treated, the feet that lack shoes, and most painful of all, the children. On my most recent visit, late this summer, I asked a little girl of seven what she'd wish to be if she were given a wish: "Well, I don't know," she answered. Then she had a thought: "Maybe a beaver." I didn't have the nerve to ask her why, but her mother wanted to know, and asked. "A beaver, child?" For a second or two there was silence, and then the answer came, cheerfully spoken: "Well, they have a good time. They can chew all day long on trees, like they was bubblegum, and they always get to eat, and they can stop by a stream and drink from it anytime they want."

Soon, though, I am heading home. On the plane, from Lexington to New York or from Charlestown to Washington the shame and anger live on for a while. The salesmen are all around, full of plans and ready with cash—which the government allows them to write off as expenses. Often there are some government officials aboard, finished inspecting this or that. In hours I will be safely in the university, where I can remind myself how complicated everything is, and how hard it is to change things, and how much better things go in Appalachia or in migrant camps or in Delano or in George Wallace's Lowndes County than, say, Biafra or certainly North Vietnam.

There are other bits of encouragement, too. I can read that the House Committee on Agriculture, headed by the honorable W. R. Poage, from the great state of Texas, and by its own assertion "always concerned about the ability of all Americans to procure adequate food," has done something called a "hunger study"—by sending a letter to the health officers of 256 counties all over the nation. "Do you have any personal knowledge of any serious hunger in your county occasioned by inability of the individual to either buy food or receive public assistance?" The county officers were asked that—and in a chorus they answered, "no." What is more, a Dr. Pollack from the Institute for Defense Analyses (whose purposes are no doubt patriotic) says that those who have observed hunger and malnutrition among thousands of children in every section of the country have been fooled or mistaken: "What the observers are really declaiming is the failure of people to participate in the foodstamp and commodity programs because of lack of understanding or inadequate educational support of these federal programs." And, of course, after extensive hearings by a Senate subcommittee and in response to strong public pressure, the Congress did vote those emergency funds so that, as Mr. Poage said and Dr. Pollack said, penniless Americans can "procure adequate food." Naturally the funds go to county officials, and naturally those are the people (in Mississippi, in Kentucky, in Delano, California) who are on the side of the poor—or so I can try hard to believe, provided that I can forget statements like this one, written by the director of the Big Sandy Area Community Action Program, with offices in the Johnson County Courthouse, Paintsville, Kentucky: "As you probably know, Emergency Food and Medical Services Program has a very limited amount of money. As a result of this, we do not want our office deluged with people who have been promised aid and that aid cannot be forthcoming."

So, that is that. The man who wrote those words also noted that he has only one employee "working the entire Floyd County area," but nearby in Pikesville, a city of about 5,000 people, there are over 40 lawyers working day in and day out—for what? For poor people? For the poor land that has been torn apart, then abandoned to itself, to its own ways: to landslides; to trickles of acid into streams; to huge rocks that fall upon and crush houses? The answer is yes—if the preposition is changed from "for" to "with." The lawyers work with the poor all right: "They come up to you and they say their mumbo-jumbo and before you know it, you've got to leave your home or you'll go to jail." The lawyers work with the land, too; they make sure it is surrendered to strip-mining companies that do what they say they do to the land, strip it, make it as poor as the people left behind after the machines are gone. But as I constantly hear some mountain people put it, year in and year out, "next season may be better." They always add a qualification, though: "if the trickery down in the court house stops." Then they laugh bitterly.

QUESTIONS FOR DISCUSSION AND WRITING

1. This essay relies heavily on the words of other people and is thus similar to an interview. Does this make the essay more convincing than if Coles had used his own words exclusively? Does the essay convince you that the Appalachian poor are an oppressed group? Explain.
2. Previous articles in this section have dealt with discrimination and exploitation of racial minority groups. The Appalachian people, however, are white, pure Anglo Saxons, and, as Coles says, "from the oldest American stock." Why, then, are they discriminated against and oppressed?
3. Like Farb's essay (p. 2), this essay makes use of irony. Coles refers, for example, to the Appalachian Mountains as "lovely." Are they "lovely" in the social or in the economic sense? Comment on the fact that tourists remark on the "quaintness" and "charm" of the area.
4. Explain Coles' use of the words "for" and "with" in reference to the lawyers of Pikesville (p. 29).

5. Have you ever witnessed or experienced the attitudes which Coles discusses in this essay—either those of the poor or those of the bureaucrats? If so, describe them.
6. Many affluent Americans react to the poor by saying that they should simply move to a better area and find a good job. Discuss this argument.
7. One striking aspect of the inhabitants of Appalachia that comes across in this essay is their great dignity and self-respect. How is such dignity maintained under such conditions, do you think? For example, how can a person be in a state of poverty and yet be too proud to accept free food and clothing? How does this relate to the traditional American concept of "rugged individualism"?

Donald J. Cantor

The Homosexual Revolution:
A Status Report

Obscured by the Negro revolution, the homosexual is, almost unnoticed, pursuing and advancing his own revolutionary cause. Like the Negro, and like every other group that has fought to establish its rights, the homosexual first had to discover that he deserved rights, that what he had been told about himself was not true, that his intrinsic merit was the equal of his detractor, that he need not feel guilt and inferiority by definition. The homosexual is achieving this sense of inner worth and is thus becoming able to withstand identification, in some instances even bear notoriety in service of his cause.

There was a time when homosexuality was thought to be a result of excessive debauchery, or a morbid predisposition activated by onanistic practices, or the placement of a male soul in a female body, or vice versa. Others postulated that homosexuality was a congenital abnormality, and some thought the explanation lay in the hormonal composition of the body. Thus, early theory, when coupled with theological condemnation ("Thou shalt not lie with mankind, as with womankind; it is abomination." *Leviticus 18:22;* "for even their women did change the natural use into that which is against nature . . . men with men working that which is unseemly . . . " *Romans 1:26, 1:27*) made the homosexual easy to despise, for not only were his acts sinful but his condition was either freakish or degenerate or both.

The movement for homosexual rights could not, therefore, begin until at least one of these premises was challenged. Freud did just that. Freud maintained that all persons are born with a psychic sexual duality, the capacity to express *both* male and female characteristics. He traced the existence of homosexual tendencies to Oedipal trauma but did not identify such childhood difficulties as the exclusive cause. Today, the bulk of psychiatrists will point to the child's resolution of the Oedipus complex as crucial, but admit the existence of other childhood conflicts as possible causes. In short, most will concede that no one really knows what causes homosexuality.

31

But it was the late Dr. Kinsey's study of the sexual habits of the white American male and female which provided the impetus for the homosexual movement. Kinsey and his researchers concluded that one's sexual direction is conditioned by the effects of initial sexual experiences and the subsequent failure of cultural pressures to alter this direction. Kinsey considered homosexuality to be a capacity inherent in humans, not in some only, and not due to a failure to resolve infantile trauma. He wrote: "The homosexual has been a significant part of human sexual activity ever since the dawn of history, primarily because it is an expression of capacities that are basic in the human animal."

When Dr. Kinsey and his associates set forth their finding that 37 per cent of the white American males have had at least one homosexual experience involving orgasm during their lives, they delivered a body blow to homosexual mythology from which it can never recover, for the stereotyped homosexual—the effeminate, mincing dandy—clearly was not one of every three males, and this meant that the great majority of persons who had expressed homosexual inclinations, looked just like those who despised them. The inferior image, the crucial difference which had made the mythological homosexual ridiculous, and thus easily persecutable, was suddenly labeled false. Kinsey also attacked the old convenient notion of sexual categories, the idea that one was homosexual or heterosexual the way one was American or alien, and showed instead that sexual activity covered a broad spectrum, much of which was a mixture of homosexual and heterosexual, not clearly either. And thus was the purity of the heterosexual sullied. Kinsey forced society to see that, instead of having just heterosexuals and homosexuals, it had many active bisexuals, and many who were potentially so.

Ten years later, in 1958, the Wolfenden Report was issued in London, and the homosexual movement was blessed with a champion of unimpeachable qualification and respectability.

This report by an English parliamentary committee would have been important solely because it recommended that private, adult, consensual homosexual acts be made lawful, but it was infinitely more important because of the caliber of its membership and because of its depth of research. The Wolfenden Report considered the varied arguments against making such acts lawful, i.e., that homosexuality deprives society of children, that homosexuality creates nervous, undependable persons, that homosexuality menaces the health of society, that homosexual behavior threatens the family, and that homosexuals may turn eventually to minors, and rebutted them all. This Report concluded that overpopulation, not underpopulation, was the social danger, that nervous homosexuals are so because of the present law not because of their homosexuality, that homosexuality is no threat to the social health, that homosexuality is no greater threat to the family than heterosexuality, and that, if anything, legalization of private, adult, consensual homosexual acts would decrease homosexual overtures to minors since these would remain unlawful.

The Wolfenden Report, however, served a greater function than the arguments and conclusions it advanced. It occasioned a great parliamentary debate, one which became a national and then an international education. Homosexuality, once a totally unmentionable subject, a contamination even to contemplate, became a topic people actually discussed and thought about and argued over—all without apparent injury.

Since the Wolfenden Report, more has happened to focus on and alleviate the troubles of the homosexual in the United States than in all the years prior.

In 1961, Illinois amended her criminal statutes and now does not make adult, private, consensual homosexual acts a crime.

Last year the criminal law of New York state came close to being similarly revised when a bill was presented to the legislature which would have made adult, private, consensual homosexual acts lawful, but this bill was amended on the floor of the legislature and such acts remain misdemeanors in New York state. But this last minute failure is of far less import than the fact that the attempt was made to liberalize New York law and that it nearly succeeded.

North Carolina amended its sodomy statute in 1965, eliminating a punishment of not less than five nor more than sixty years, and substituting in its place a fine or imprisonment "in the discretion of the court." The eradication of the five year minimum sentence constitutes definite progress. Since the American Law Institute has drafted its Model Penal Code with this recommendation in it, in light of the influence of the Institute and the prestige of its members, there can be little doubt that like amendments will be offered in other states and probably again in New York.

But the true progress of the movement cannot be solely or even primarily gauged by statutory changes, although these changes are the primary goals. Much more crucial at this time are developments within the churches and within the homophile organizations themselves. The churches are important because homosexuality is mainly despised for reasons based upon the religious concept that homosexual acts are sinful. Thus, if the revolution of the homosexual is to succeed, it must reach the churches. This it is doing.

The Methodist Conference and the Congregational Union indicated support of the Wolfenden Report in 1958. In Philadelphia, during November of 1965, a special symposium met to discuss the homosexuality question in its various aspects, many different disciplines being represented. The reason, I was told, for the symposium being convened was that the United Presbyterian Church had felt the need to speak *to* the problem. (Churchmen, I have learned, never speak *of* or *about* a problem, but only *to* it.)

In Hartford, Connecticut, the Greater Hartford Council of Churches has for two years had a committee existent to study homosexuality and devise means by which the church can assist the homosexual, both as a group and as individuals. Great interest in this work has been manifested by other Councils of Churches throughout the United States. Denver has had an active Council of Churches. San Francisco, in 1964, formed the Council on Religion and the Homosexual, its purpose being "To promote a continuing dialogue between the religious community and homosexuals," and, in New York, the George W. Henry Foundation has, since 1948, offered assistance in many different forms to homosexuals in trouble. It has received backing from the Episcopal ministry, in particular, and now has a Connecticut branch which has broad Protestant support. In November, 1966, The National Council of Churches, Department of Ministry, meeting in White Plains, New York, discussed the relation of the church and the homosexual, and in August of 1966, The World Council of Churches, meeting in London, held a seminar on this question.

As to the homophile organizations themselves, they are not only existent and operative, but are becoming vocal and militant. Homophile organizations are no longer content to provide social comraderie and mutual reassurance; they are evolving into organs of protest, media for propaganda and active lobbyists. Their leaders do not shrink from publicity or shun public identification. The Homosexual Law Reform Society of America in Philadelphia has organized public demonstrations and distributed leaflets protesting the exclusion of homosexuals from the armed services. Mr. Clark Polak, Executive Secretary of the Homosexual Law Reform Society, has appeared on radio and television, at symposia, before service organizations, and has spoken to a great diversity of audiences to decry the injustice America inflicts on its homosexuals. When the Florida Legislature contemplated legislation deemed inimical to homosexuals, Richard Inman, President of Atheneum Society of America, Inc., now The Mattachine Society of Florida, Inc., not only propagandized and lobbied, but had articles sympathetic to his cause printed and distributed to all legislators. Homophile organizations have picketed the White House, Pentagon, State Department and the U.S. Civil Service Commission in Washington and the Philadelphia Navy Yard, among others. A survey taken by and of the Florida Mattachine Society indicated 82 per cent of those questioned were in favor of public picketing by homosexuals, and sentiment in other homophile groups in the country appears similarly inclined.

This personal involvement of homosexuals in public advocacy of their view often accomplishes infinitely more than the propagation of those views. It serves the function of exposing the stereotype for the ridiculous nonsense it is. Every time a homosexual leader appears publicly, walks to his seat without swaying, dressed without frills, talking without a lisp, forcing his audience to the realization that they would not realize he was homosexual if he didn't tell them, a great stride is made. These leaders know this and thus seek constantly to address groups of all kinds. Nothing induces a man to feel tolerance more than seeing similarity between himself and the ones previously scorned. Difference is the root of prejudice, and prejudice dies as difference dissipates.

Those who administer the law give further evidence of this new feeling about homosexuality. Prosecutors, in deciding whether to prosecute and on what charge, and judges, in determining how to sentence, are good barometers of current social values. There is an unmistakable tendency today to allow homosexuals to plead guilty to lesser charges than those for which they were arrested and to sentence leniently, often with probation in place of incarceration. A study of the disposition of arrests for felonious homosexual acts in Los Angeles County, in the March, 1966, *U.C.L.A. Law Review*, showed that only .6 per cent (3 defendants of 493) received ultimate felony dispositions. The remainder were all treated as misdemeanor offenders and the great majority received suspended sentences, probation or fines. John Gerassi, in his recently-published book, *The Boys of Boise*, indicates that this trend is not restricted to the larger, supposedly more sophisticated metropolitan centers, but is a present fact of legal life in Boise, Idaho, as well.

There are other extremely important philosophical influences which are having and will continue to have their effect on the law and the relation of the law to the homosexual. One is the opinion that law should not legislate morality, but should rather confine its proscriptions to those areas where acts or omissions have demonstrably injurious social consequences. This is not, of course, a philosophical innovation; the same notion was quite eloquently advanced by John Stuart Mill in his essay *On Liberty,* and by others of note, but its adoption with specific reference to the question of homosexual acts by a Catholic body is of special importance.

When the Commission which produced the Wolfenden Report was created, it requested the view of many different committees representing churches, professions, and other organizations. The late Cardinal Griffin of Westminster commissioned *The Roman Catholic Advisory Committee on Prostitution and Homosexual Offenses and the Existing Law,* and the report of this body, while stating "all directly voluntary sexual pleasure outside of marriage is sinful," nonetheless also stated:

> It is not the business of the State to intervene in the purely private sphere but to act solely as the defender of the common good. Morally evil things so far as they do not affect the common good are not the concern of the human legislator.

This singularly statesmanlike report went further, adding the following particularity.

Attempts by the State to enlarge its authority and invade the individual conscience, however high-minded, always fail and frequently do positive harm. The Volstead Act in the U.S.A. affords the best recent illustration of this principle. It should accordingly be stated clearly that penal sanctions are not justified for the purpose of attempting to restrain sins against sexual morality committed in private by responsible adults. They are, as later appears, at present employed for this purpose in this country and should be discontinued because:

(a) they are ineffectual;

(b) they are inequitable in this incidence;

(c) they involve severities disproportionate to the offense committed;

(d) they undoubtedly give scope for blackmail and other forms of corruption.

The position advanced by this Report gives a rationale for allowing private, adult, consensual homosexual acts to be lawful to those who regard those acts as morally odious, and therein lies its special significance and value. Now the one with moral objections can be approached, and often persuaded, to favor law reform on the fundamental basis of the need to separate theological morality from state power; the cause of the homosexual thus becomes identified with, and understandable to, all those groups whose history contains instances of persecution resulting from the joinder of morality and criminal law.

The second new philosophical position is that sexual acts should not be condemned morally simply because of their nature, but rather that sexual acts, like any acts, are moral or not depending upon the intentions behind them and the effects of them. In an address before the Missionary Society of the Berkeley Divinity School, on November 23, 1964, Dr. Alfred A. Gross, Executive Director of the George W. Henry Foundation, and long-time advocate of homosexual law reform, expounded this view as he has continued to do since.

And in the January, 1967, issue of *The Living Church*, a weekly magazine of the Episcopal Church, The Reverend R. W. Cromey, Vicar of St. Aidan's Church in San Francisco, calling for homosexual law reform as recommended by the Wolfenden Committee, stated:

> I believe that the sex act is morally neutral. There is no sex act which in itself is sinful . . . I also believe that two people of the same sex can express love and deepen that love by sexual intercourse.

Acceptance of this view would necessarily lead to the law reform sought by the homosexual in light of the absence of any valid utilitarian reasons for the present restrictive laws.

The progress made by the homosexual toward equality has been assisted by a rash of plays (*The Toilet, A Taste of Honey, The Sign in Sidney Brustein's Window*), movies (*The Victim, Darling, The Leather Boys*), non-fiction books (*The Homosexual Revolution, In Defense of Homosexuality, The Homosexual in America*), and fiction by such established authors as Jean Genet, Gore Vidal and James Baldwin. In the law of obscene communication, the United States Supreme Court has facilitated the creation and distribution of literature dealing with homosexuality, and especially matter designed especially for homosexuals, by ruling that homosexual materials, including male nudes, are not ipso facto obscene. As the result of *Mishkin v. New York*, decided by the Supreme Court on March 21, 1966, material is obscene if the dominant theme of it taken as a whole appeals to the prurient interest in sex, not of the average man, but rather of the members of any special group—such as homosexuals—for which such material was designed and to which it was primarily disseminated.

The attitudes thus expressed should be contrasted, to be appreciated, with a 1922 Ohio case in which the judge referred to males who commit homosexual acts as "human degenerates" and "sexual perverts," or the 1938 Maine case in which the Maine Supreme Court had this to say:

> The statute (sodomy) gives no definition of the crime but with due regard to the sentiments of decent humanity treats it as one not fit to be named, leaving the record undefiled by the details of different acts which may constitute the perversion.

Contrast it also with the older attitudes manifested in the sodomy statutes of the various states. In fourteen states the forbidden acts, which include acts between males and females as well as between persons of similar sex, are described as "abominable" or as both "abominable" and "detestable." (What does "detestable" add that "abominable" omits?) In seven states the acts are called "infamous." In ten states the phrases "crime against nature" or "against the order of nature" are used adjectivally; in three states "unnatural," "abnormal," or "perverted" are used. The depth and degree of antipathy which once characterized the public view of homosexual acts can be best appreciated when one recalls that no other crimes, including premeditated murder and rape, are so described.

It would be facile and utterly misleading to imply that the American homosexual is on the threshold of victory in his battle for equality. It is still painfully true that every state but Illinois condemns the private, adult, consensual acts of homosexuals as criminal, that in seven states life imprisonment is a possible sentence for such acts, and that in thirty-five other states the maximum penalty is at least ten years. When Sir Cyril Osborne, Conservative Member of Parliament, said during debate,

"I am rather tired of democracy being made safe for the pimps, the prostitutes, the spivs, the pansies, and now, the queers," he may have spoken for a distinct minority in England (a recent Gallup Poll in England showed 60 per cent of those polled favored homosexual law reform), but it is probable that he reflected the opinions of a larger percentage of Americans, though many would not be quite so intense about it.

John Gerassi tells us that only a decade ago a great number of Boiseans thought that homosexuals were communists. But the trend is clear. The opposition to homosexual law reform is progressively diminishing. The large amount of extortion and blackmail which has victimized the homosexual has reached public consciousness and created sympathy, and forced upon the public the realization that these anti-homosexuality laws, even when not strictly enforced, set the stage by their very existence for this extortion and blackmail. People are becoming aware that England is on the verge of making adult, private, consensual homosexual acts lawful, and wondering whether our oldest teacher has yet another lesson for us to learn.

There is a new sense of perspective alive in the land, born at Hiroshima, which has equipped men to appreciate the dimensions of real danger, and has made them less able to view alleged sexual dangers such as homosexuality quite as seriously as once was possible. There is a sense of reappraisal, an unwillingness in an age of incredible change to presume the rightness of doctrine simply because doctrine is and was. Fittingly, sexual mores are getting perhaps the most serious reappraisal, partially because of the pill and intrauterine device, but more, I think, because the sexual dogmas have had the greatest rigidity and least realism. Homosexuality therefore is benefitting, as part of the general field of sexuality, from this rising examination of the old rules governing intercourse out of marriage, abortion, censorship, and divorce.

There is also not a new, but an increased sense of the dignity of man and of man's right to dignity. The goals of the Negro are now national goals to an extent never before even approximated, not because he is Negro but because he is human. The homosexual is being gradually recognized as one seeking similar goals and deserving them.

Where a sexual act is done publicly, it is a nuisance and an invasion of the public's right to public propriety. It deserves punishment. Where a sexual act is committed with a minor, it is an invasion of the minor's right to privacy until he reaches the age of consent. It deserves punishment. Where a sexual act is done through force, duress, or fraud, or under any circumstances where consent is absent, it is an assault and deserves punishment. But where the act is private, between two consenting adults, where there is no victim, where nothing occurs but the physical expression of affection, it should not be punished.

Equality for the homosexual is an ethical imperative and the American people are beginning to realize this.

QUESTIONS FOR DISCUSSION AND WRITING

1. Does this essay expand your notion of what constitutes a "minority" in America? Explain.
2. Cantor says that "There is a new sense of perspective alive in the land, born at Hiroshima, which has equipped men to appreciate the dimension of real danger, and has made them less able to view alleged sexual dangers such as homosexuality quite as seriously as once was possible." Comment on this argument. Does the argument suggest that other minority groups will also eventually become more acceptable? Explain.
3. Cantor remarks that "Nothing induces a man to feel tolerance more than seeing similarity between himself and the ones previously scorned. Difference is the root of prejudice and prejudice dies as difference dissipates." Can this statement be applied to racial prejudices as well as to cultural, social, economic, religious, and sexual prejudices? If the "difference" dissipates, is there also a parallel decrease in uniqueness, individuality, and personal freedom? That is, will the end of prejudice come only when everybody is exactly like everybody else? Or is Cantor's point more subtle? Explain.
4. In a later article in this book, Paul Goodman (p. 265) states that "My homosexual acts have made me a nigger, subject to arbitrary brutality and debased when my outgoing impulse is not taken for granted as a right." Comment on Goodman's statement, relating it to this essay, to the other articles in this section, and to the general question of minority groups in America.
5. Why does Cantor employ stereotypes in this essay? What are some other stereotypes which are applied to homosexuals? Are stereotypes ever a fair and accurate representation of any minority? Explain.
6. Do you think that homosexuality should be controlled by law and legal sanctions? What, if any, is the danger in such control of minorities?

For Further Reading

Cleaver, Eldridge. *Soul on Ice.* New York: Delta Books, 1967. Paperback, 1968.

Daniels, Roger, and Harry H. L. Kitano. *American Racism: Explorations of the Nature of Prejudice.* Englewood Cliffs, N.J.: Prentice-Hall, Inc., 1970. Paperback.

Deloria, Vine, Jr. *Custer Died for Your Sins.* New York: The Macmillan Company, 1969. Paperback, 1970.

Farb, Peter. *Man's Rise to Civilization as Shown by the Indians of North*

America from Primeval Times to the Coming of the Industrial State. New York: E. P. Dutton and Company, Inc., 1968. Paperback, 1969.

Goldstein, Sidney, and Calvin Goldscheider. *Jewish-Americans: Three Generations in a Jewish Community.* Englewood Cliffs, N.J.: Prentice-Hall, Inc., 1968. Paperback.

Grier, William H., and Price Cobbs. *Black Rage.* New York: Basic Books, Inc., Publishers, 1968. Paperback, 1969.

Kitano, Harry H. L. *Japanese-Americans: The Evolution of a Subculture.* Englewood Cliffs, N.J.: Prentice-Hall, Inc., 1969. Paperback.

Malcolm X, and Alex Haley. *The Autobiography of Malcolm X.* New York: Grove Press, Inc., 1966. Paperback.

Masters, R. E. L. *The Homosexual Revolution: A Challenging Expose of the Social and Political Directions of a Minority Group.* New York: Julian Press, 1962.

Moore, Joan W., and Frank G. Mittelbach. *Residential Segregation in the Urban Southwest: A Comparative Study.* Los Angeles: Division of Research, Graduate School of Business Administration, University of California, 1967.

Raab, Earl, and Seymour Lipset. *Prejudice and Society.* New York: Anti-Defamation League of B'nai B'rith, 1959.

II ON YOUTH

In the 1960's, the term "generation gap" achieved a new prominence and a new significance. The gap widened further than it ever had before and demonstrated that youth was an emerging and potent political and social force. The 1970's are witnessing a continuation of this youth revolution, and the youth revolution is forcing a redefinition of many of the traditional values of American society. At the same time, youth itself is being redefined in terms of the ideals—as opposed to the practices—of American democracy.

From the life-styles of dress, self-expression, and rock music to political and social activism, youth is organizing itself as a new entity. It is challenging most of the basic assumptions of the rulers of society: that age means experience, that experience means authority, that authority means progress. The young see poverty rampant in the wealthiest of all nations; they see war in the name of peace; and they see oppression in the name of law. Indeed, youth is questioning the very ability of American society to continue on the course it has taken for several decades. The youth revolution is one alternative to the failure of democracy to practice what it preaches.

The essays included in this section try to show the way it was, the way it is, and the way it will be with youth. They help to define youth, its attitudes, and its values as a newly-emerged force which can carry the nation into the future. It should also be easy to relate these essays to those on minorities in the preceding section—for youth itself is an oppressed group that has openly rebelled and actively begun to change the status quo. The future is now, the young say, and the American present must listen.

Margaret Mead

Youth Revolt:
The Future Is Now

Our present crisis has been variously attributed to the overwhelming rapidity of change, the collapse of the family, the decay of capitalism, the triumph of a soulless technology, and, in wholesale repudiation, to the final breakdown of the Establishment. Behind these attributions there is a more basic conflict between those for whom the present represents no more than an intensification of our existing cofigurative culture, in which peers are more than ever replacing parents as the significant models of behavior, and those who contend that we are in fact entering a totally new phase of cultural evolution.

Most commentators, in spite of their differences in viewpoint, still see the future essentially as an extension of the past. Edward Teller can still speak of the outcome of a nuclear war as a state of destruction relatively no more drastic than the ravages wrought by Genghis Khan, and historians can point out that time and again civilization has survived the crumbling of empires. Similarly, many authorities treat as no more than an extreme form of adolescent rebellion the repudiation of present and past by the dissident youth of every persuasion in every kind of society in the world.

Theorists who emphasize the parallels between past and present in their interpretations of the generation gap ignore the irreversibility of the changes that have taken place since the beginning of the Industrial Revolution. This is especially striking in their handling of modern technological development, which they treat as comparable in its effects to the changes that occurred as one civilization in the past took over from another such techniques as agriculture, script, navigation, or the organization of labor and law.

One urgent priority, I believe, is to examine the nature of change in the modern world, including its speed and dimensions, so that we can better understand the distinctions that must be made between change in the past and that which is now ongoing. To do so, I make

44

distinctions among three different kinds of culture: *post-figurative*, in which children learn primarily from their forebears; *cofigurative*, in which both children and adults learn from their peers; and *prefigurative*, in which adults learn also from their children.

Although it is possible to discuss both post-figurative and cofigurative cultures in terms of slow or rapid change without specifying the nature of the process and to compare past and present situations when the focus is kept on generation relationships and on the type of modeling through which a culture is transmitted, it is only when one specifies the nature of the process that the contrast between past and present change becomes clear.

The primary evidence that our present situation is unique, without any parallel in the past, is that the generation gap is world-wide. The particular events taking place in England, Pakistan, the United States, New Guinea, or elsewhere are not enough to explain the unrest that is stirring modern youth everywhere. Recent technological change or the handicaps imposed by its absence, revolution or the suppression of revolutionary activities, the crumbling of faith in ancient creeds or the attraction of new creeds—all these serve only as partial explanations of the particular forms taken by youth revolt in different countries.

Concentration on particularities can only hinder the search for an explanatory principle. Instead, it is necessary to strip the occurrences in each country of their superficial, national, and immediately temporal aspects. The desire for a liberated form of communism in Czechoslovakia, the search for "racial" equality in the United States, the desire to liberate Japan from American military influence—these are particularistic forms. Youthful activism is common to them all. The key question is this: What are the new conditions that have brought about the revolt of youth around the world?

The first of these is the emergence of a world community. For the first time human beings throughout the world, in their information about and responses to one another, have become a community that is united by shared knowledge and danger. As far as we know, no such single, interacting community has existed within archaeological time. The largest clusters of interacting human groups have always been fragments of a still larger unknown whole, and the idea that all men are, in the same sense, human beings always has been either unreal or a mystical belief.

The events of the past twenty-five years changed this drastically. Exploration has been complete enough to convince us that there are no humanoid types on the planet except our own species. World-wide air travel and globe-encircling TV satellites have turned us into one community, in which events taking place on one side of the earth become immediately and simultaneously available to peoples everywhere else. No artist or political censor has time to intervene and edit as a leader is shot or a flag is planted on the moon. The world is a community, though it still lacks the forms of organization and the sanctions by which a political community can be governed.

Men who are the carriers of vastly different cultural traditions are entering the present at the same point in time. It is as if, all around the world, men were converging on identical immigration posts, each with its identifying sign: YOU ARE NOW ABOUT TO ENTER THE POST-WORLD-WAR-II WORLD AT GATE 1 (GATE 23, etc.). Whoever they are and wherever their particular points of entry may be, all men are equally immigrants into the new era. They are like the immigrants who came as pioneers to a new land, lacking all knowledge of what demands new conditions of life would make upon them. Those who came later could take their peer groups as models. But among the first comers, the young adults had as models only their own tentative adaptations and innovations.

Today, everyone born and bred before World War II is such an immigrant in time as his forebears were in space—a pioneer struggling to grapple with the unfamiliar conditions of life in a new era. Like all immigrants and pioneers, these immigrants in time are the bearers of older cultures, but today they represent all the cultures of the world. And all of them, whether they are sophisticated French intellectuals or members of a remote New Guinea tribe, land-bound peasants in Haiti or nuclear physicists, have certain characteristics in common.

Whoever they are, these immigrants grew up under skies across which no satellite had ever flashed. Their perception of the past was an edited version of what had happened. Their perception of the immediate present was limited to what they could take in through their own eyes and ears and to the edited versions of other men's sensory experience and memories. Their conception of the future was essentially one in which change was incorporated into a deeper changelessness. The industrialist or military planner, envisaging what a computer, not yet constructed, might make possible, treated it as another addition to the repertoire of inventions that have enhanced man's skills. It expanded what men could do, but did not change the future.

When the first atom bomb was exploded at the end of World War II, only a few individuals realized that all humanity was entering a new age. And to this day the majority of those over twenty-five have failed to grasp emotionally, however well they may grasp intellectually, the difference between any war in which, no matter how terrible the casualties, mankind will survive, and one in which there will be no survivors. They continue to think that a war, fought with more lethal weapons, would just be a worse war. Our thinking still binds us to the past—to the world as it existed in our childhood and youth.

We still hold the seats of power and command the resources and the skills necessary to keep order and organize the kinds of societies we know about. We control the educational systems, the apprenticeship systems, the career ladders up which the young must climb. Neverthe-less, we have passed the point of no return. We are committed to life in an unfamiliar setting; we are making do with what we know.

The young generation, however—the articulate young rebels all around the world who are lashing out against the controls to which they are subjected—are like the first generation born into a new country. They are at home in this time. Satellites are familiar in their skies. They have never known a time when war did not threaten annihilation. When they are given the facts, they can understand immediately that continued pollution of the air and water and soil will soon make the planet uninhabitable and that it will be impossible to feed an indefinitely expanding world population. As members of one species in an underde-veloped world community they recognize that invidious distinctions based on race and caste are anachronisms. They insist on the vital neces-sity of some form of world order.

No longer bound by the simplified linear sequences dictated by the printed word, they live in a world in which events are presented to them in all their complex immediacy. In their eyes the killing of an enemy is not qualitatively different from the murder of a neighbor. They cannot reconcile our efforts to save our own children by every known means with our readiness to destroy the children of others with napalm. They know that the people of one nation alone cannot save their own children; each holds the responsibility for all others' children.

Although I have said they *know* these things, perhaps I should say that this is how they *feel*. Like the first generation born in a new country, they listen only half-comprehendingly to their parents' talk about the past. For as the children of pioneers had no access to the landscapes whose memories could still move their parents to tears, the young today cannot share their parents' responses to events that deeply moved them in the past. But this is not all that separates the young from their elders. Watching, they can see that their elders are groping, that they are man-aging clumsily and often unsuccessfully the tasks imposed on them by the new conditions. The young do not know what must be done, but they feel that there must be a better way and that they must find it.

Today, nowhere in the world are there elders who know what the children know, no matter how remote and simple the societies are in which the children live. In the past there were always some elders who knew more than any children in terms of their experience of having grown up within a cultural system. Today there are none. It is not only that parents are no longer guides, but that there are no guides, whether one seeks them in one's own country or abroad. There are no elders who know what those who have been reared within the last twenty years know about the world into which they were born.

True, in many parts of the world the parental generation still lives by a post-figurative set of values. From parents in such cultures children may learn that there have been unquestioned absolutes, and this learning may carry over into later experience as an expectation that absolute values can and should be re-established.

There are still parents who answer such child's questions as why he must go to bed, or eat his vegetables, or learn to read with simple assertions: Because it is *right* to do so, because *God* says so, or because *I* say so. These parents are preparing the way for the re-establishment of post-figurative elements in the culture. But these elements will be far more rigid and intractable than in the past because they must be defended in a world in which conflicting points of view, rather than orthodoxies, are prevalent.

Most parents, however, are too uncertain to assert old dogmatisms. They do not know how to teach these children who are so different from what they themselves once were, and most children are unable to learn from parents and elders they will never resemble. In the past, in the United States, children of immigrant parents pleaded with them not to speak their foreign language in public and not to wear their outlandish foreign clothes. They knew the burning shame of being, at the same time, unable to repudiate their parents and unable to accept simply and naturally their way of speaking and doing things. But in time they learned to find new teachers as guides, to model their behavior on that of more adapted age mates, and to slip in, unnoticed, among a group whose parents were more bearable.

Today, the dissident young discover very rapidly that this solution is no longer possible. The breach between themselves and their parents also exists between their friends and their friends' parents and between their friends and their teachers.

These young dissidents realize the critical need for immediate world action on problems that affect the whole world. What they want is, in some way, to begin all over again. They are ready to make way for something new by a kind of social bulldozing—like the bulldozing in which every tree and feature of the landscape is destroyed to make way for a new community. Awareness of the reality of the crisis (which is, in fact, perceived most accurately not by the young, but by their discerning and prophetic elders) and the sense the young have that their elders do not understand the modern world, because they do not understand their children, has produced a kind of rebellion in which planned reformation of the present system is almost inconceivable.

Nevertheless, those who have no power also have no routes to power except through those against whom they are rebelling. In the end, it was men who gave the vote to women; and it will be the House of Lords that votes to abolish the House of Lords—as also, in the final analysis, nations will act to limit national sovereignty. Effective, rapid evolutionary change, in which no one is guillotined or forced into exile, depends on the cooperation of a large number of those in power with the dispossessed who are seeking power.

These, in brief, are the conditions of our time. These are the two generations—pioneers in a new era and their children—who have as yet to find a way of communicating about the world in which both live, though their perceptions of it are so different. No one knows what the next steps should be. Recognizing that this is so is, I submit, the beginning of an answer.

I believe we are on the verge of developing a new kind of culture, one that is as much a departure in style from cofigurative cultures as the institutionalization of cofiguration in orderly—and disorderly—change was a departure from the post-figurative style. I call this new style "prefigurative," because in this new culture it will be the unborn child, already conceived but still in the womb—not the parent and grandparent—that represents what is to come. This is a child whose sex and appearance and capabilities are unknown, but who will need imaginative, innovative, and dedicated adult care far beyond any we give today.

No one can know in advance what the child will become—how swift his limbs will be, what will delight his eye, whether his tempo will be fast or slow. No one can know how his mind will work—whether he will learn best from sight or sound or touch or movement. But knowing what we do not know and cannot predict, we can construct an environment in which a child, still unknown, can be safe and can grow and discover himself and the world.

Love and trust, based on dependency and answering care, made it possible for the individual who had been reared in one culture to move into another, transforming, without destroying, his earlier learning. It is seldom the first generation of voluntary immigrants and pioneers who cannot meet the demands of a new environment. Their previous learning carries them through. But unless they embody what is new post-figuratively, they cannot pass on to their children what they had acquired through their own early training—the ability to learn from others the things their parents could not teach them.

Parents, in a world where there are no more knowledgeable others to whom they can commit the children they themselves cannot teach, feel uncertain and helpless. Still believing that there should be answers, parents ask how they can tell their children what is right. So some try to solve the problem by advising their children, very vaguely, that they will have to figure it out for themselves. And some parents ask what the others are doing. But this resource of a cofigurative culture is becoming meaningless to parents who feel that the "others"—their children's age mates—are moving in ways that are unsafe for their own children to emulate, and who find that they do not understand what their children figure out for themselves.

It is the adults who still believe that there is a safe and socially approved road to a kind of life they have not experienced who react with the greatest anger and bitterness to the discovery that what they had hoped for no longer exists for their children. These are the parents, the trustees, the legislators, the columnists and commentators who denounce most vocally what is happening in schools and colleges and universities in which they had placed their hopes for their children.

Today, as we gain a better understanding of the circular processes through which culture is developed and transmitted, we recognize that man's most human characteristic is not his ability to learn, which he shares with many other species, but his ability to teach and store what others have developed and taught him. In the past men relied on the least elaborate part of the circular system—the dependent learning by children—for continuity of transmission and for the embodiment of the new. Now, with our greater understanding of the process, we must cultivate the most flexible and complex part of the system: the behavior of adults. We must, in fact, teach ourselves how to alter adult behavior; we must create new models for adults who can teach their children not what to learn, but how to learn, and not what they should be committed to, but the value of commitment.

In doing this we must recognize explicitly that the paths by which we came into the present can never be traversed again. The past is the road by which we have arrived where we are. Older forms of culture have provided us with the knowledge, techniques, and tools necessary for our contemporary civilization.

The freeing of men's imagination from the past depends on the development of a new kind of communication with those who are most deeply involved with the future—the young who were born in the new world. In the past, in cofigurational cultures, the elders were gradually cut off from limiting the future of their children. Now the development of prefigurational cultures will depend on the existence of a continuing dialogue in which the young, free to act on their own initiative, can lead their elders in the direction of the unknown. Then the older generation will have access to the new experiential knowledge, without which no meaningful plans can be made. It is only with the direct participation of the young, who have that knowledge, that we can build a viable future.

Instead of directing their rebellion toward the retrieval of a grandparental utopian dream, as the Maoists seem to be doing with the young activists in China, we must learn together with the young how to take the next steps. Out of their new knowledge—new to the world and new to us—must come the questions to those who are already equipped by education and experience to search for answers. The children, the young, must ask these questions that we would never think to ask, but enough trust must be re-established so that the elders will be permitted to work with them on the answers.

I feel that we can change into a prefigurative culture, consciously, delightedly, and industriously, rearing unknown children for an unknown world. But to do it we must relocate the future.

Here we can take a cue from the young who seem to want instant utopias. They say the future is now. This seems unreasonable and impetuous, and in some of the demands they make it is unrealizable in concrete detail; but here again, I think, they give us the way to reshape our thinking. We must place the future, like the unborn child in the womb of a woman, within a community of men, women, and children, among us, already here, already to be nourished and succored and protected, already in need of things for which, if they are not prepared before it is born, it will be too late. So, as the young say, the future is now.

QUESTIONS FOR DISCUSSION AND WRITING

1. Miss Mead suggests several things that might be responsible for the "revolt of youth around the world." Discuss these causes. Can you suggest other possible causes?
2. Three terms are crucial to the meaning of this essay: "post-figurative," "cofigurative," and "prefigurative." In your own words, define these terms. Can you suggest any other, everyday terms which are synonymous?
3. On p. 48, Miss Mead refers to parents who want to reestablish "post-figurative elements in the culture," and then says that "these elements will be far more rigid and intractable than in the past because they must be defined in a world in which conflicting points of view, rather than orthodoxies, are prevalent." What does this mean? Do you agree? Explain.
4. This essay can be read in the light of the essays in the preceding section on minority groups. For example, do you think that the slogan "the future is now" can be applied to the problems of racism, poverty, war, and other social evils? Explain your answer.
5. Does this essay suggest that any one specific element is the *object* of the youth revolt? Is there more than one object or goal? Explain.
6. Using the examples and details of the essay, explain why and how there could be another and perhaps very different youth revolt in the future.

Richard Poirier

The War Against the Young

The social systems which organize and rationalize contemporary life have always been ingeniously armed for the day when youth would rebel against the essentially pastoral status assigned to it. Despite pamperings until recently unimaginable, despite economic briberies and various psychological coercions, the rebellion has broken out. Predictably, the response to it is a gradual escalation involving a more naked use of the tactics that were supposed to prevent, but which also helped to provoke, the crisis in the first place: patronizations, put-downs, and tongue-lashings, along with offers of a place in the governing system if only the system is left intact and promises that in any case the future itself holds the solution to whatever now seems to be the trouble. If this technique sounds familiar in its mixture of brutality and pacification, in its combination of aggression and absorption, noted by Edgar Frieden-berg in his brilliant analysis of the adult treatment of the adolescent minority,[1] if it sounds vaguely like methods used in other and related domestic and foreign conflicts, then the point is obvious: our society is unfortunately structured, in the prevalent forms of its language and thinking, in ways designed to suppress some of the most vital elements now struggling into consciousness and toward some awareness of their frustrated powers.

This struggle is essentially a cultural one, regardless of the efforts by older people to make political use of it or to place it, unflatteringly, within the terms of traditional politics, particularly cold-war politics. The intellectual weapons used in the war against youth are from the same arsenal—and the young know this—from which war is being waged against other revolutionary movements, against Vietnam, against any effective justice, as distinguished from legislative melodrama, in matters

[1] See, for example, "The Image of the Adolescent Minority" by Edgar Z. Friedenberg in *The Radical Imagination*, ed. Irving Howe (New York: New American Library, 1967).

52

of race and poverty. These weapons, as I've suggested, are by no means crude. They scarcely look at times like weapons at all, and many of the people most adroit in handling them, writers and teachers as well as politicians, aren't even aware that they are directing against youth arguments of a kind used also to rationalize other policies which they consider senseless and immoral. Aside from the political necessities of candidates, why is it that people who can be tough-mindedly idealistic in opposition to our actions in Vietnam or to our treatment of the power-less, talk about youth and think about the rebellion of youth in a manner implicit in the mentality that produces and excuses these other barbari-ties? The reason, I think, is that most people don't want to face the possibility that each of these troubles grows from the same root and can be traced back to the same murky recesses within each of us and within the social organisms to which we have lent ourselves. They prefer isolated and relatively visible sources for such difficulties, along with the illusion that each of them is susceptible to accredited forms of politi-cal or economic cleansing. By contrast, it is the conviction of the most militant young people, and of some older ones, that any solutions will require a radical change in the historical, philosophical, and psychological assumptions that are the foundations of any political or economic system. Some kind of cultural revolution is therefore the necessary prelude even to our capacity to think intelligently about political reformation.

Oddly enough, the young are proved right, in this supposition at least, by the nature of the attacks made against them. I don't mean attacks from the likes of Reagan and Wallace, but those coming from becalmed and sensible men, whose moderation is of a piece with their desire to increase the efficiency of the present system. At work in these attacks are the same tendencies of thought and language that shape the moderate, rationalizing analyses of the other nightmares I've men-tioned. They help us to sleep through them during the night and during most of the day.

Maybe the most prevalent of these tendencies is the insistence on a language that is intellectually "cool," a language aloof from militant or revolutionary vocabularies, which in their exclusion sound excessive, exaggerated, and unserviceable. This cool language is not at all dull or plodding. On the contrary, it's full of social flair; it swings with big words, slang words, naughty words, leaping nimbly from the "way out" to the "way in"—it really holds the world together, hips and squares alike. The best working example is the style of *Time* magazine, and it wasn't surprising in a recent issue to find a piece full of compliments to what were titularly called "Anti-Revolutionaries." With the suave observation that writers like these "who prefer rationality to revolution are by no means conservative," they honored three distinguished com-mentators on youth and other scenes. One of the three, Benjamin

DeMott, a professor of English at Amherst, diversely active as a novelist, critic, and educational innovator, had earlier written an essay in the Sunday New York *Times Magazine* on the style of what he called the "spirit of over-kill" among some of his fellow writers, especially those of the revolutionary fringe like Paul Goodman, Andrew Kopkind, and Susan Sontag.

According to DeMott, the verbal violence of this decade "was" (and I'll get to the significance of this past tense in a moment) "pressed not at new 'enemies' but at old ones already in tatters." Just at a glance one had to wonder why "enemies," new or old, were assigned the un-reality of quotation marks. Has the semblance of negotiations made the war in Vietnam disappear as an "enemy"? Does he mean racial injustice? the horrors of urban life? the smothering effects of educational institutions of which he is himself one of the most active critics? I'm afraid these enemies aren't so easily dispelled. The degree to which they press against DeMott's own "cool" dismissal of them is in fact made evident, with engaging innocence, in the very form of his essay. In order to find a requisite dispassion for his own style, as against what he mistakenly takes for the dominant style of this decade, he must project himself to the end of the century and then look back at us. Like other critics of our violence, he is himself already visiting the famous year 2000, programming for which, as we are cautioned by a number of distinguished economists, sociologists, and technicians, will only be dis-rupted by people who fail to remain politely soft-spoken amid the ac-cumulating squalor, blood, and suffering of their lives.

This peculiar form of address, by which we are asked to hear our present as if it were our past, suggests yet another and more subtle method of repression—the futuristic—now especially popular in the so-cial sciences. A notably unembarrassed practitioner, and yet another writer commended by the article in *Time* magazine, is Zbigniew Brzezin-ski, director of the Research Institute on Communist Affairs at Columbia, recently a member of the Policy Planning Staff of the State Department, and now head of Hubert Humphrey's "task force" on foreign affairs. Also concerned because revolutionary loudmouths and their young ad-herents are incited by the past rather than the future—keep in mind that there is no present, in case you thought it was hurting someone—Brzezinski has published two futuristic position papers in the *New Re-public:* "The American Transition," and more recently, "Revolution and Counterrevolution (But Not Necessarily About Columbia!)." Happily bounding over invisible rainbows, Brzezinski lets us know that, like it or not, we are already becoming a "technetronic society," and any old-fashioned doctrinal or ideological habits—as if ideology wouldn't be inherent in his imagined social systems—will get us into real, perma-nent troubles instead of temporary ones. We'll fail to adapt, that is, to "the requirements of the metamorphic age," and thus miss the chance of creating a "meritocratic democracy" in which "a community of organization-oriented, application-minded intellectuals [can relate] itself more effectively to the political system than their predecessors." We need only stay calm, and admittedly such language is not designed to excite us, since "improved governmental performance, and its increased sensitivity to social needs is being stimulated by the growing involvement in national affairs of what Kenneth Boulding has called the Educational and Scientific Establishment (EASE)."

Deifications have of course always been announced by capitalization. As in religion, so in politics: an "excessive" concern for the present is a sure way of impairing your future. If, in the one case, you might as well surrender your will to God, in the other you might as well surrender it to EASE, or, getting back to DeMott patiently waiting there at the turn of the century, to "the architects of the Great Disengagement," with "their determination to negotiate the defusing of The Words as well as of The Bombs." But I'm afraid it's merely symptomatic of how bad things are now that many of those who want the young and the rebellious to be more quiet follow the advice of Hubert Humphrey: they speak to the young not about the past, not even about the present, but about some future, which, as prognosticators, they're already privileged to know. They are There; the revolutionists are living in the Past. And who is here and now, living, suffering, and impassioned in the present? Apparently no one, except maybe a few of what Brzezinski likes to call the "historical irrelevants."

If the young are inarticulate, if, when they do try to expound their views, they sound foolish, are these, and other examples of adult thinking and writing which I'll get to presently, somehow evidences of superior civilization, something to be emulated, the emanations of a system worth saving from revolution? Such arguments and such uses of language— almost wholly abstracted from the stuff of daily life as it is lived in this year, these months, this week—do not define but rather exemplify the cultural and linguistic crisis to which the young are responding with silence even more than with other demonstrations of their nearly helpless discontent. "Power, or the shadow cast by power, always ends in creating an axiological writing," as the French critic Roland Barth puts it, "in which the distance which usually separates fact from value disappears within the space of a word." To prefer "rationality" to "revolution" is good *Time* magazine language. It can't be faulted except by those who feel, as I do, that a revolution is probably necessary if rationality is to be restored to a society that thinks it has been operating rationally. If the young are "revolutionary," and if this is the reverse of "rational," what, then, is the nature of the rationality they're attacking? Quite aside from science fiction passing for history in the writings we've just looked at, are the practices of the United States government with regard to most issues of race, poverty, the war, the gun laws, or even the postal service rational? Is it rational to vote an increase of money for Vietnam, and on the same hot day in July, cut appropriations for the summer employment of young Negroes and Puerto Ricans, thus helping to encourage a bloody summer at home while assuring one abroad?

These are all, as Brzezinski would point out, complex issues, and according to him, they will not be solved by "historical irrelevants," by those who, with revolutionary fervor, are yearning, as he would have it, for the simplicities of the past and who therefore "will have no role to play in the new technetronic society." But what has decided, since I know no people who have, that we want his "technetronic society," that it is desirable or inevitable? Who decides that it is necessary or even good for certain issues to be construed as complex and therefore susceptible only to the diagnosticians who would lead such a society? Why have certain issues become complex and who is served by this complexity? Why is the life we already lead, mysterious and frightening as it is, to be made even more so by the ridiculous shapes conjured up in Brzezinski's jaw-breaking terminologies? Some issues are not simple, which does not mean that some others are not unnecessarily complex. It is clear to everyone that Vietnam is "complex." But it is equally clear that it need not, for us, have become complex; that it might not even have existed as an issue, except for those members of EASE who helped justify our continued presence there. Maybe the secret is that it is really "easy" to be complex.

The funniest and in a way the most innocent example of this kind of no-thinking passing in sound and cadence for responsible, grown-up good sense is offered by George Kennan. The third figure heralded for his rationality in the *Time* article, Kennan is a renowned historian, a former ambassador to the Soviet Union, and the author of yet another containment policy, this one for youth. Kennan's specialty is what might be called "the argument from experience," easily slipping into "the argument from original sin." "The decisive seat of evil in this world," he tells us in *Democracy and the Student Left*, a just-published debate between him and nearly forty students and teachers, "is not in social and political institutions, and not even, as a rule, in the ill-will or iniquities of statesmen, but simply in the weakness and imperfection of the human soul itself." No one can deny a proposition so general, but surely only someone who likes for other reasons to plead the inescapable complexity of issues could propose such an idea to people wondering how the hell we got into Vietnam or why millions of poor in a country so rich must go hungry every day.

Kennan has, of course, had direct experience with other revolutions and with other people who have ignored the imperfections of the human soul simply by denying its existence. No wonder it often sounds, then,

as if the militant young are merely his chance at last to give a proper
dressing-down to the kind of fellows who brought on the Russian Revolution, his historical analogies being to that extent, at least, more com-
plimentary to the young than Brzezinski's evocation of Luddites and
Chartists. "I have heard it freely confessed by members of the revolutionary student generation of Tsarist Russia," Kennan rather huffily reports,
"that, proud as they were of the revolutionary exploits of their youth,
they never really learned anything in their university years; they were
too busy with politics." Earlier, from Woodrow Wilson at his prissiest,
he describes an ideal "at the very center of our modern institutions
of higher learning": it is a "free place," in Wilson's words, "itself a
little world; but not perplexed, living with a singleness of aim not known
without; the home of sagacious men."

Was it such sagacious men, one must ask, since it surely was not
the rampaging students, who assumed that this ideal place should also
house ROTC units, defense projects, recruiters from Dow Chemical,
and agents of the CIA? An ideal institution freed of *those* perplexities—
which evidently do not bother Mr. Kennan—is precisely what the students have been agitating for. It is not possible to think about learning
now without being, as he pejoratively puts it, "busy with politics." The
university officials and the government have seen to that. But again,
Kennan probably doesn't regard ROTC as a political presence on
campus, and students are "busy with politics" not in the precious hours
wasted on drill and military science, but only while agitating against
these activities, which are mostly useless even from a military point
of view. Out of this mess of verbal and moral assumptions, the finest
and stiffest blossom is the phrase "freely confessed": imagine having
the gall to tell someone outright that as a student you hadn't even
done your assignments while trying to overthrow a corrupt and despotic
government. Doubtless that government also preferred its universities
"not perplexed" by anything related to the conduct of public affairs.

Compared with the futuristic modes of Brzezinski and DeMott, Kennan's mode of argument is at least honest about seeing the present
only as if it were the past. In its rather ancient charm it isn't nearly
so dangerously effective as still other less explicitly theological, less passionate, more academically systematized methods now in vogue for
abridging youthful radicalism or transcendentalism. Consider for example what might be called the tight-contextual method. This is particularly useful in putting assassinations in their place, or rather in no-place
("it was not Dallas that curled a finger round that trigger and pulled
it; it was a sad and sick individual," one informant irrefutably told
me), and in explaining why we cannot withdraw from Vietnam. That
country gets reduced, in this form of argument, to some thousands of
vaguely identified friends whom we cannot desert, even though their
worth is even more difficult to locate than is their presence during com-

bat operations. Of course this kind of analysis works wonders on anything as worldwide and variously motivated as student or youth protest.
Unanswerably the students at Columbia are not the students in Paris
or Czechoslovakia or even Berkeley. Like the leaders in any generation,
the rebellious students are only a small minority of the young, a minority
even of the student bodies they belong to. There are local, very special
reasons not only for the motivations of each group but for each of
the different acts of each group. What is astonishing, however, is that
they all do act, that they are all acting now, that the youth of the
world almost on signal have found local causes—economic, social, political, academic ones—to fit an apparently general need to rebel. So universal and simultaneous a response to scarcely new causes reveals in
the young an imaginative largeness about the interconnection of issues,
an awareness of their wider context, of a world in which what in former
decades would have been a local war is now symptomatic, as is poverty
and the quality of life in our cities, of where the dominant forms of
thinking have taken us. Again, it can be said that the young are in
effect rebelling against precisely the kinds of analysis that are inadequate
to explain what the young are up to. More terrifying than the disorder
in the streets is the disorder in our heads; the rebellion of youth, far
from being a cause of disorder, is rather a reaction, a rebellion against
the disorder we call order, against our failure to make sense of the
way we live now and have lived since 1945.

Yet another form of restrictive or deflationary analysis—and appro-
priately the last I'll consider—is a special favorite of literary critics and
historians as well as politicians: the anti-apocalyptic. Implicit in some
of the methods we've already looked at, this one dampens revolutionary
enthusiasms with the information that history has recorded such efforts
before and also recorded their failure—the Abolitionists, the young
Bolsheviks, the Luddites. All claims to uniqueness are either tarnished
by precedent or doomed to meaninglessness. We've been through it
all, and are now doing the best we can, given—and here we're back
at the borders of Original Sin—our imperfect state of being. In the
treatment of militant youth, this type of argument is especially anxious
to expose any elitist or fascist tinge in the young, with their stress on
a chimerical "participatory democracy" or their infantile assumption that
the worst must be allowed to happen—let us say the election of George
Wallace—if ever the inherent horrors of the "System," and thus the necessities of revolution, are to become apparent to everyone. Some people
do talk this way; some people always have. But only a minority of
the articulate and protesting young lend themselves to anything so politically programmatic. Such arguments are wholly peripheral to the emergence of youth as a truly unique historical force for which there are
no precedents. Youth is an essentially nonpolitical force, a cultural force,
that signals, while it can't by itself initiate, the probable beginnings

of a new millennium, though hardly the one described in the Book of Revelations. If only because of its continuously fluid, continuously disappearing and emerging, membership, it is incapable of organizing itself into shapes suitable to the political alliances that can be made by other, more stable minority groups like the blacks. It has no history; it may never have one, but it is that shared experience of all races which may come finally to dominate our imagination of what we are.

What is happening to the youth of the world deserves the freest imagination, the freest attention that older people are capable of giving. It requires an enormously strenuous, and for most people, probably impossible, intellectual effort. Working within the verbal and conceptual frames—a sadly appropriate word—against which the rebellion of youth is in large part directed, we must try to invent quite different ways of seeing, imagining, and describing. So complicated is the task linguistically that it is possible to fail merely because of the vocabulary with which, from the best intentions, we decide to try. It is perhaps already irrelevant, for example, to discuss the so-called student revolt as if it were an expression of "youth." The revolt might more properly be taken as a repudiation by the young of what adults call "youth." It may be an attempt to cast aside the strangely exploitative and at once cloying, the protective and impotizing concept of "youth" which society foists on people who often want to consider themselves adults. Is it youth or is it the economic and sexual design of adult society that is being served by what Erik Erikson calls the "moratorium," the period when people under twenty-one are "allowed" to discover their identities without at the same time having to assume adult responsibilities? Quite painfully, the young have suddenly made us aware that the world we have been seeing isn't necessarily the world at all. Not only that France wasn't France, but that even the young weren't necessarily that thing we call "young." It is no longer a matter of choice therefore: we must learn to know the world differently, including the young, or we may not know it until it explodes, thus showing forth its true nature, to follow the logic of Marx, only in the act and at the moment of breakdown.

Before asking questions about the propriety and programs of young militants who occupy buildings, burn cars, and fight the police, let's first ask what kind of world surrounds these acts. Let's not conceive of the world as a place accidentally controlled by certain people whose wickedness or stupidity has been made evident by disaster, or as the scene of injustices whose existence was hidden from us. Because to do so implies that we are beguiled rather than responsible even for specific things that we do not know are happening. We're in danger of becoming like the Germans before the war who afterward turned to their children with dismay, then surprise, then amnesia. Such analogies to our present situation, and even more to an anticipated one, are not exact, but neither are they remote.

The world we now live in cannot get any better merely by changing its managers or improving some of its circumstances. It exists as it does because of the way we think about one another and because of our incapacity, so far at least, to learn to think differently. For those who fought in it and who are now the middle generation and parents of the young, World War II gave absolutely the worst kind of schooling. It trained us to think in extraordinarily simplistic terms about politics and history. One might even say that it made people my age strangely apolitical and ahistorical. We were convinced that evil resided in Nazism and Fascism, and that against these nothing less than total victory was acceptable. The very concept of total victory or unconditional surrender was part of a larger illusion that all wickedness was entrenched in certain places, circumstances, and persons, and very subtly these were differentiated from the people or the nations where they found hospitality. The Morgenthau plan had no chance of success, and not simply because it was economically unfeasible in proposing the creation of an agrarian state between the West and the East. It would have had the even more tactically dangerous effect of blaming a *people* for a war. Thereby two embarrassing questions would have been raised: either that the Germans were really a separate kind of people, or if not, that they were like us, and must therefore have had some understandable provocation for acting as they did. And what could that provocation have been if not something for which we too had a responsibility? No—better just talk about the eradication of Nazism and warlords.

Like all wars, World War II blinded us to the conditions at home that required our attention, and so did the cold war that followed: for nearly twenty-five years we looked at foreign devils rather than domestic ills. The consequences were even worse in our thinking, however, or rather in our not thinking, about the true sources and locations of our trouble. They are within ourselves and within the mechanisms of our own society. One reason why those in the parental generation cannot understand the rebellion of the young is that our own "rebellion" was managed for us, while for the young now it is instinctive and invented and unprogrammed. Our protest movement was the war itself, the crusade against Nazism, Fascism, and Japanese imperialism. In many ways our youth didn't matter to the world. I went into the infantry in 1943 at seventeen, fought in Germany, and came out in 1946 imagining that I'd helped cleanse the globe and could therefore proceed to make up for lost personal time at the university, where a grateful government paid my expenses.

If the war absorbed and homogenized the political feelings of the millions like me who are now the parents of people nearly old enough to be drafted for a quite different kind of war, the G.I. Bill of Rights gave us an experience of college and university life different from any before or since. The G.I. Bill was legislation of enormous political and social importance. It allowed the first huge influx into colleges, universities, and later into the academic profession, of people who for financial and social reasons weren't before recognized as belonging to the group which represents youth as our society likes to imagine it—the students. But, given their backgrounds, which made them poignantly anxious to take advantage of an opportunity they never thought available, much less a right, given their age, service experience, sexual maturity, and often marriage, this influx of a new kind of student had a stabilizing rather than a disrupting effect. We were maybe the first really serious mass of students who ever entered the academy, designed up till then, and still designed, to prolong immaturity until the ridiculous age of twenty-one or later.

If we were serious, it was in a bad sense, I'm afraid: we wanted so much to make it that we didn't much question the value of what we were doing. I'm not surprised that so few people my age are radical even in temperament. My fellow academicians who came through the process I've described have fitted all too nicely into the Anglophilic gentility of most areas of academic life, into the death-dealing social manners promoted by people who before the war could afford the long haul of graduate as well as undergraduate education. For how many families did the fact that "my boy" is a professor, especially a professor in English, mean the final completion of citizenship papers? Because that's what most of the proliferation of exams, graduate or otherwise, really add up to. Much more than the reputed and exaggerated effect of television and other media in creating a self-conscious community of the young (effects shared, after all, by people in their thirties and early forties), it is the peculiar nature of World War II and of subsequent schooling experience which separates the older from the younger but still contiguous groups.

In thinking about the so-called generation gap, then, I suggest that people my age think not so much about the strangeness of the young but about their own strangeness. Why is it "they" rather than "we" who are unique? By what astonishing arrogance do people my age propose to themselves the program described recently in the New York *Times* Sunday Book Review by a critic who wrote that during the summer he would support McCarthy and that "beyond that, full-time opposition to radical or reactionary excesses in the arts and criticism strikes me as proper and sufficient activity for a critic. And political enough, too, in its ultimate implications." The ultimate implications are dead center. Dead because what can anyone mean now by an "excess," and from where does one measure it unless, like the person in question, he entertains, as do most of my contemporaries, the paranoiac illusion that he has emerged a representative of True Nature?

Only when the adult world begins to think of itself as strange, as having a shape that is not entirely necessary, much less lovely, only when it begins to see that the world, as it has now been made visible to us in forms and institutions, isn't all *there,* maybe less than half of it—only then can we begin to meet the legitimate anguish of the young with something better than the cliché that they have no program. Revolutionaries seldom do. One can be sick and want health, jailed and want freedom, inwardly dying and want a second birth without a program. For what the radical youth want to do is to expose the mere contingency of facts which have been considered essential. That is a marvelous thing to do, the necessary prelude to our being able, any of us, to think of a program which is more than merely the patching up of social systems that were never adequate to the people they were meant to serve.

Liberal reformers, no matter how tough, won't effect and might even forestall the necessary changes. In our universities, for example, there is no point in removing symptoms and leaving the germs. It is true, as the young have let us know with an energy that isn't always convenient even to sympathizers like myself, that our universities are too often run by fat cats, that renowned professors are bribed by no or little teaching, that a disproportionate amount of teaching is done by half-educated, miserably underpaid, and distracted graduate assistants, that, as a consequence of this imbalance, research of the most exciting kind has very little immediate bearing on curriculum, which remains much as it has for the past fifty years, and that, as Martin Duberman eloquently showed in a recent issue of *Daedalus,* authoritarianism in curriculum and in teaching, not to be confused with being an authority in a subject, is so much a part of our educational system that university students arrive already crippled even for the freedom one is prepared to give them. These conditions exist in a pattern of idiotic requirements and childish, corrupting emoluments not simply because our universities are mismanaged. The mismanagement has itself a prior cause which is to be found in the way most people think about scholarship and its relation to teaching—a question which is a kind of metaphor for the larger one of the relations between the generations: what conditions permit the most profitable engagements between an older mind that is trained and knowledgeable and a younger one anxious to discover itself but preconditioned by quite different cultural circumstances?

These circumstances have, of course, always differed between one generation and another, but never so radically as now. Never before have so many revered subjects, like literature itself, seemed obsolete in any strict compartmental form; never before have the divisions between such subjects as anthropology, sociology, and languages seemed more arbitrary and harmful to intelligent inquiry; and seldom in the history of modern civilization has there been a greater need felt by everyone for a new key to our mythologies, a key that we nervously feel is about to be found. For if we are at a moment of terror we are also at a moment of great expectation and wonder, for which the young have a special appetite. To meet this challenge, the universities need to dismantle their entire academic structure, their systems of courses and requirements, their notion of what constitutes the proper fields and subjects of academic inquiry.

Most people who teach have in their heads some ideal university, and mine would be governed by a single rule: there is nothing that does not need to be studied in class, including, of course, the oddity of studying *in* a class. Everything and everybody, the more randomly selected the better, has to be subjected to questions, especially dumb questions, and to the elicitation of answers. The point is that nothing must be taken for other than "strange," nothing must be left alone. Study the morning paper, study the teacher, study the listless slouching of some students—half-dead already at eighteen. But above all, those working in advanced research sponsored at any university would also let capable students study that research and ask questions about it. And if in fact some things cannot be taught, then that in itself should be the subject of inquiry. The hierarchies that might evolve would be determined on a wholly pragmatic basis: for subjects, by the amount of effort and time needed to make something yield up the dimensions of its mystery; for any way of thinking, by the degree to which it raises a student to eye level with the potentialities of a subject, the degree to which it can tune his ears into it. Above all, the university would be a place where curricula are discovered anew perhaps every year or so. The argument that the demands of an existing student body cannot be allowed to determine policy for succeeding ones would mean the reverse of what it now means: not that changes are difficult to effect, but that they would be effected year after year, if necessary, to meet the combined changes of interest in student and faculty. Given the sluggishness of most people, the results of such a policy would not be nearly as chaotic or exciting as one might imagine. Indeed, what would be hoped for is *more* disruption, and therefore more questioning and answering than one would ever get.

In confronting oppositions from youth as in other matters short of Vietnam, Lyndon Johnson is a genius in that his most decent impulses, and he has some, don't merely serve, aren't merely synchronized with, but are indistinguishable from his often uncanny political instinct for pacifying any opposition, for castrating any force that threatens to move the system off the center track which carried him to power. While demonstrations at Columbia were making Hubert Humphrey sick "deep inside," and Nixon was reportedly saying that if there was a second Columbia he wouldn't have to care *whom* he had to run against, LBJ was proposing that the vote be given to all people between eighteen and twenty-one. But the terrible price of the political logic he so masterfully handles is at once made evident if we ask what many of the young, and not simply the militant ones, would find to vote for in this election. They would be joining the electorate just when it is at last stagnating from our national satisfaction with the mere manipulation and redistribution of the poisons within us. So ingeniously is the center still in control of the manipulative forces that there will not be a turn to the right *within* our political system, not one with any more chance of success than Goldwater, at least, and no one within the system represents the left. The danger sign will be abstention, political indifference, a decision not to care very much who wins, not to participate in a process that affords only a negative choice.

When any large number of people demonstrate their indifference to the choices offered them, they tend to invent others that exist outside the going "democratic" system. They tend to gravitate toward some species of the "participatory democracy" for which the elitist young are most severely criticized. It's fortunate that Johnson's voting-age proposal can't be enacted in time for the young people of eighteen to twenty-one to enter a political imbroglio so contemptibly arranged as this one. It could only further convince them of the necessity for some kind of nondemocratic movement to replace the farce of democracy in which they'd have been asked to take part, and it would allow their critics to assign to them some blame for the consequences of the indifference among the older electorate. The indifference grows on the momentum supplied not by the young but by the nature of our public life. The now not uncommon proposition that our problems are no longer manageable within existing political systems, and that we need an Authority empowered to decide what is best for us, cannot be ascribed merely to youth, Herbert Marcuse, Vietnam, race, violence, or any combination of these. The emerging failure of confidence in our way of managing ourselves and our interests in the world is the consequence of a political process now overwhelmed by the realities it has tried to hide, realities that have grown like cancer cells treated by pain-killers.

Instinctively, the militant young are involved less in a political rebellion, where demands for their "program" would be relevant, than in an attack on the foundations of all of our current political programming. The issues they raise and the issue they personify are essentially anthropological, which brings us to the cultural rather than the political importance of the President's proposal to move the voting age back from twenty-one to eighteen. The importance can be dramatized, with no intention of melodrama, by predicting that within twenty years or so it will be necessary to propose, if not to pass, a voting age of sixteen. Like other mere changes of policy, changes in voting age should not be taken as a sign that we are suddenly to be governed by new or radical modes of thinking. Rather, such reforms signal the accumulated power of forces which our operative modes of thinking have before tried to ignore and which they will now try to make invisible by absorption.

But with the mass of youth—nearly half the population is now under twenty-five—our society is faced with an unprecedented difficulty in the application of this essentially social technique. For when it comes to the young, society· is not simply absorbing a group who, like the Irish or labor, duplicate in their social organization each part of the dominant group. To give something like adult or historic identity to a mass that has up to now been relegated to the position of "youth" means a disruptive change in the concept of human identity, of when that identity is achieved, of what it properly should contribute to history. The time scheme that governs our ideas of adolescence, youth, and maturity has changed many times in history since the sixteenth century—Juliet was fourteen, and early in the eighteenth century the age of consent was ten—but it was adjusted to the convenience of an extraordinarily small ruling minority which was in turn submissive to familial regulations. For the first time in history a change of this kind is being made on demand from a powerful mass of young people freed of familial pieties, and never before has a society worked as strenuously as ours, through a mesh of mythologies, to hold these young people back, in an unmercifully prolonged state of adolescence and of what we call "youth." Especially in the United States, the representative and most talented young—the students—have for generations been forced *not* to take themselves seriously as men and women.

So far, the rebellion has accomplished at least one thing: it has succeeded in demoting "collegiate types" (and the sickly reminiscent values that they injected into later life) from glamour to absurdity. The change is not complete, and it never will be. Whole campuses are holdouts, some quite distinguished ones, like Yale and Stanford, where the prep-school ethos remains dominant, while at others the overwhelming number of young clods makes it difficult for the few students who really are alive even to find one another, much less establish an *esprit* that can irradiate more than a small circle. Still, recent agitations have confirmed some of the advances made by the earlier generation of students under the G.I. Bill and cleared still more room on American campuses for the kind of young person who does want to enter history at eighteen, and who is therefore contemptuous of society's cute and reassuring idea of the collegiate—with Lucille Ball as ideal House Mother. Such historical self-consciousness on the part of university students has been fairly common in Europe and in England, where, as shown by Peter Stansky and William Abrahams in *Journey to the Frontier*, students in the thirties could feel that the "journey" to the Spanish Civil War did not follow but rather began at Oxford and Cambridge. But the differences are obvious, and again, relate to class and family: children of the English upper classes were educated to feel historical, and what distinguished them from lower-class boys was that from boyhood their "careers" *meant* something to the political and historical career of England. Only rarely, and almost exclusively at Harvard, does this phenomenon occur in American universities. Education in American universities has generally been a combination of utilitarian course work and play-acting, "getting ready" to be an adult, even if it meant still getting ready at twenty-two.

The shattering of this pattern has been the work of a complex of forces that include students within the larger power bloc of youth, with its enormous influence on dress and mores, and, perhaps above all, its success in the fields of entertainment. By force of numbers and energy alone, the young have created images which older people are now quite anxious to endow with a sexual-social significance that they before refused to find in the activity of "kids." Put another way, youth has ceased to fulfill the "literary" role which American society has been anxious to assign them. They no longer supply us with a pastoral, any more than the "darkies" do, and this is a serious cultural deprivation for which we have yet to discover a replacement.

Every civilization has to invent a pastoral for itself, and ours has been an idea of youth and of adolescence that has become socially and economically unprofitable, demographically unmanageable, and biologically comic. By a pastoral I mean any form of life that has, by common consent, been secured from the realities of time and history. Some form of pastoral is absolutely essential: it helps stabilize the cycles of individual lives and of civilizations. Its function is an idealizing, simplifying one: it secures certain elemental human attributes from the contaminations of time and of historical involvement. But if the logic of pastoral is to protect certain attributes, its ulterior motive is to keep the human embodiment of these attributes in their proper place, servants rather than participants in daily business where real men really face complex reality.

Insofar as America's imagination of itself can be inferred from literature, from popular entertainment, from fashions, conventions, and educational theory, it can be said that we have used youth as a revenge upon history, as the sacrificial expression of our self-contempt. Youth has been the hero of our civilization, but only so long as it has remained antagonistic to history, only so long as it has remained a literary or mythological metaphor. War, the slaughter of youth at the apparent behest of history, is the ultimate expression of this feeling. The American hatred of history, of what it does to us, gets expressed in a preposterous and crippling idealization of youth as a state as yet untouched by history, except as a killer, and in a corresponding incapacity to understand the demand, now, by the best of the young, to be admitted into it. More hung up on youth than any nation on earth, we are also more determined that youth is not to enter into history without paying the price of that adulteration we call adulthood. To justify what grown-ups have made of our young, virgin, uncontaminated land, it's as if we are compelled to show that what happened was necessary. Exceptions would prove our human culpability for what is otherwise ascribed to history, and so all that is best in our land must either be kept out of history or tarnished by it. Like our natural wonders, youth will be allowed to exist only on condition that it remain, like some natural preserve, outside the processes that transform everything else into waste.

Surely the destination of our assets needn't be so bleak, so inexorable, so neurotically determined. It will now be seen whether or not we are to exhaust our youth, whether or not in its vulnerability, its continually evaporating and exposed condition, it can resist being made grist for the mill. Because youth is not a historically grounded pressure group, aware of its history, jealous of its progress, continuous and evolving. It is rather what we, all of us, sometimes are. I have avoided any precise definition of youth because it refers to the rare human condition of exuberance, expectation, impulsiveness, and above all, of freedom from believing that all the so-called "necessities" of life and thought are in fact necessities. This condition exists most usefully, for the nation and the world, in people of a certain age, specifically in those who have attained the physical being that makes them wonderfully anxious to create life, to shape life, to enter into life rather than have it fed into them. It is the people of this age, members of what Friedenberg calls the "hot-blooded minority," who are in danger of obliteration as representatives of youth. It is impossible for them to remain youth, in any sense that would profit the rest of society, and also enter into history on the hateful terms now offered them by our political, economic, and technological system. Lyndon Johnson knew instinctively what he was up to when, calling for a vote for people of this age, he remarked that they deserved it because they are "adults in every sense."

Fine, if that means we now change our concept of adulthood to include an eighteen-year-old Bob Dylan rather than an eighteen-year-old Nixon, some creep valedictorian. But that isn't what he has in mind. LBJ has not changed his way of thinking about youth, adulthood, or anything else. He has merely responded to this fantastic cultural opportunity the way our leaders respond to any such opportunity for change: they merely make more room in the house with as little inconvenience as possible to the settled inhabitants. All he proposes to do, and this will have some amusing as well as sad consequences, is lift the term youth from those who threatened us with it, and then hold it in reserve for the time, not far off, when it can be quietly left on the narrow shoulders of what we now call adolescents. Some tinkering will be necessary here and there, of course. The Adolescent Clinic at Children's Hospital in Boston chooses the ages thirteen to nineteen for its patients, but those who've seen some of the ten-to-twelve-year-olds who sneak in tell me that if the ranks of adolescence are to be depleted to fill the vacated positions of youth, these in turn will be quickly occupied by Robert Coles's children of crisis. This will seem a facetious prediction to people who like to think they are reasonable.

So, what I'm saying is that if young people are freeing themselves from a repressive myth of youth only to be absorbed into a repressive myth of adulthood, then youth in its best and truest form, of rebellion and hope, will have been lost to us, and we will have exhausted the best of our natural resources.

QUESTIONS FOR DISCUSSION AND WRITING

1. This essay describes several main techniques used against the young by their critics and even by their "friends." What are these techniques and how do they work?
2. At the root of this essay, as often happens, lies a dispute over words, the words "rational" and "revolutionary." Poirier discusses these terms on p. 55. Comment on what Poirier says about them and suggest your own definitions for these two words. For example, are the words really contradictory?
3. What is meant by the word "allowed" (p. 59) in reference to the privileges of the young and how these privileges are obtained? Does the "allowing" of privileges suggest a reason why the young are in rebellion? Explain. Is there also a relationship between "allowing" and the idea of "castrating" which Poirier suggests on p. 63? Explain.
4. What is the meaning of the terms "eighteen-year-old Bob Dylan" and "eighteen-year-old Nixon" (p. 67)? What does each term suggest to you? Why does Poirier refer to the latter type as a "creep valedictorian"?
5. Poirier says that "I suggest that people my age think not so much about the strangeness of the young but about their own strangeness." The implicit question here seems to be: Who is the minority—the young? the old? Explain.
6. Poirier discusses some of the possible effects of lowering the voting age to eighteen. Consider Poirier's opinion and then give your own opinion on this matter.
7. In what ways does Poirier's essay complement, expand, or contradict the ideas expressed in the preceding essay by Margaret Mead?
8. Do you feel that there is a war being waged against the young in America? If so, is the war against *all* young people, or just against some of them? What is Poirier's opinion? What is yours?

Nicholas von Hoffman

Sanctuary in Jail

It used to be that if you had a white-collar job, the absolutely worst thing that could happen was that your kid might call up and say, "Dad, I've only got one phone call so don't get mad and hang up, but I'm in jail."

It used to be that while that was the final disgrace—worse than welfare even—it never happened. White collar people, young or old, were too well drilled to get arrested for anything more than speeding. Still, the horrible thought, the scandal of it, the possible loss of job or financial preferment, the social disapproval kept the idea as a vague, unformed fear in the back of the middle-class brain.

Even the law, merciless mechanism that it may be, took pity on middle-class man in this predicament and the names of juvenile defendants were kept secret. Yet middle-class papa and white-collar mama could never be sure those arrest records were not revealed. So they would shout and implore their young ones to remember, "what it'll do to you if you ever want a job with the government or with a big corporation or if you ever need a security clearance. You'll ruin your future."

Now all of that is changing. Every day thousands of kids are being busted for pot, for the draft, for printing newspapers, for subversive hairstyles, for music, for being young in public. If the trend continues it will be the young person without a jail record who'll have some explaining to do. The new college graduate with a spotless arrest sheet may appear to the personnel manager of the mid-'70s as a maladjusted loner, a deviant who couldn't relate to his peer group, a person who's missed out on his generation's greatest formative experience—pulling time in some joint.

It may be that by the mid-'70s, discharge papers from jail will be as necessary for the young aspirant in life as discharge papers from the armed services were to his father. The penitentiary a person served in could be as important as the name of a man's college. For example, we could have the equivalent of Ivy League pens. Sing Sing may be the Harvard of the future; Leavenworth may be the new Yale.

The first generation of middle-class, professionally-educated felons hasn't found prison particularly appealing. They're pioneers, however, like the first rich people to move into a quaint old slum neighborhood which is in the process of being fashionably restored. The first people have to put up with the poor and unhealthy for a while, with the petty street criminals, until the renewal program is well under way.

Even now, things aren't as bad as they might be. Really disreputable people are seldom found in prisons. With all the raging and carrying on about the Mafia, you have a better chance of winning the Irish Sweepstakes than meeting a member of this much-denounced organization in any penitentiary.

A lot of parents may not see it in this light. Prisons, probably through no fault of their own, have gotten a bad name. They're supposed to be places where the worst sort of people live, jackrollers, bank robbers, car stealers and murderously jealous husbands. Naturally a concerned parent wouldn't want a child emulating such people.

However, the statistics show that most people in these blood-curdling occupations do not live in jails, and those who do have made precious little money from their work; they're scarcely successful enough to trap an intelligent young person into copying them. There's no use denying there is some risk that a person may come under evil influences in jail, but look what can happen if you send a boy to Princeton. He might learn how to drink or smoke dope or behave less than properly toward a girl.

A young man will escape all contact with these three evils if he's sent to any reasonably well-run place of incarceration. In jail he won't be allowed to see violent TV shows or sexy movies. He will also be kept away from people who might teach him how to commit such socially questionable acts as conflict of interest.

He will not meet Justice-designate Haynsworth in any prison. Say what you will against this man's confirmation to the Supreme Court, the fact remains he's never been indicted by any grand jury, he's never been convicted by any court of any crime. That may be his only qualification for his new job, but it's enough to separate him from your son. Rest easy.

In prison, your son or daughter will not learn how to beat a conspiracy rap with a consent decree. This is how some of the automobile manufacturers got out of the accusation that they conspired to suppress the development and installation of anti-pollution devices on cars.

Nothing can be more damaging to a teen-ager without a fully-matured moral sense than to meet and associate with a member of Congress. In prison your child will never meet a member of Congress, or an administrative assistant, or a campaign contributor, or a businessman who wants a congressman to put in a good word with a regulatory agency. Such men are never known to violate the law.

When your child is older, he'll understand that there is nothing wrong with a man sitting in Congress and voting himself hundreds of thousands of dollars in subsidies or special tax concessions. A young person without experience in life has trouble distinguishing between a secret, campaign contribution and a bribe, which is another reason why kids belong in jail.

Behind prison walls things are simpler. They won't have to worry themselves about cyclamate and who arranged it that this stuff could be sold to millions of people for years without anybody being positively sure it was safe. Behind bars they can drink their diet cola and not worry about what people are putting in bread and the milk and the anti-perspirants.

Today's parent shouldn't think of the penitentiary as a place of shame but as a modern monastery where a young person is shielded from Washington law firms, from regulatory agencies, from selling second-hand guns out the back door of the Pentagon, from the cost over-runs, from the delayed kickback (I do you a favor now when I'm in government, you fix me up with a fat job later), from all the perfectly lawful operations which keep their perpetrators out of stir. The worst your boy's going to learn in jail is how to pick a lock or knock over a gas station; there are very few persons in jail for committing more than a couple of murders—what's the Boston Strangler got to boast about in comparison with men who legally can kill us by taking strength from our food, health from our water, and life from our air?

Many people misjudge jails. They think of them as they used to be, full of tough, unappetizing rowdies. Nowadays some of the most admirable people go to jail. The jails are full of our most respected priests, ministers and rabbis, the very persons you want your children to be influenced by. Running around loose your boy might bump into somebody from John W. McCormack's office; in jail he might be lucky enough to share a cell with Father Berrigan.

QUESTIONS FOR DISCUSSION AND WRITING

1. Through satire and irony this essay approaches a problem that is delicate for many people. What is the author's real attitude toward the subject? How does it differ from his apparent attitude?
2. What is von Hoffman's opinion of automobile manufacturers, the Mafia, Clement Haynsworth, and members of Congress? Does the fact that he only briefly mentions these figures detract from the thrust of his comments? Are these people criminals who should be jailed when they break the law? Explain your answer.

3. Does this essay make any comments about what Richard Poirier (p. 52) sees as the "war against the young"? Explain.

4. This same writer recently pointed out that there is a great absurdity in the fact that people who litter the highways are heavily fined while corporations which pour tons of poisonous smoke into the air are given tax credits. Do you agree that this is "absurd"? Explain.

5. Have you ever been in jail, or known someone who was, because of involvement in some kind of social protest? If so, describe the *effect* that being in jail had on you or on that person.

6. In his famous essay "Civil Disobedience," Henry David Thoreau described a night he spent in jail for refusing to pay his tax. Thoreau says, "I could not help being struck with the foolishness of that institution . . . I saw that, if there was a wall of stone between me and my townsmen, there was a still more difficult one to climb or break through before they could get to be as free as I was. I did not for a moment feel confined, and the walls seemed a great waste of money. I felt as if I alone of all my townsmen had paid my tax." In the light of von Hoffman's essay, comment on Thoreau's observations.

Jack Newfield

Hayden-Marat Dylan-Sade:
Defining a Generation

Tom Hayden, the Thomas Jefferson of the New Left, and at twenty-eight the author of two important books, has written:

> What is desperately needed is the person of vision and clarity, who sees both the model society and the pitfalls that precede its attainment, and who will not destroy his vision for short-run gains, but instead, will hold it out for all to see, as the farthest dream and perimeter of human possibility.

Twenty-seven-year-old Bob Dylan, who has put poetry into song, just as Dylan Thomas returned song to poetry, has written:

> Although the masters
> make the rules
> for the wise men and the fools
> I've got nothing, ma, to live up to

Hayden and Dylan personalize the two most important moods and movements of the generation still under thirty: the politics of resistance, and the art of the absurd. Hayden and Dylan are the modern equivalents of Marat, the utopian revolutionary, and Sade, the poet of nihilism; linked by the common outrage against what is, but divided by contradictory visions of how to forge what might be. They are what Emerson called "representative men," and Hegel called "zeitgeists."

Hayden, the seminal architect of SDS (Students for a Democratic Society), left graduate school to become its organizer and has lived, since 1964, with the wretched of Newark. He would agree with Marat when he says, "Against nature's silence I use action. . . . I don't watch unmoved, I intervene and say this and this are wrong. The important thing is to pull yourself up by your own hair, to turn yourself inside out, and see the world with fresh eyes."

Dylan, who abandoned narrow political protest songs in 1964, in order to explore the surreal, the absurd, and the hallucinatory, would agree with Sade, who answered, "Why should you care about the world outside? For me the only reality is imagination, the world inside myself. The revolution no longer interests me."

I know that 75 per cent of the "Now Generation" cares only about fraternities, drive-ins, and football. But that has been true of all generations, including those baptized by the pop sociologists as Beat, Lost, Silent, and Now. Minorities give all generations their characters. Less than one million young people participated in social action during the 1930's, but they are remembered now, not the majority untouched by political passion, or motivated only by commercial ambition. So it is today that the New Left, symbolized by Hayden, and the absurd artists and juke box poets, symbolized by Dylan, will give this generation its historical character. And not the button-down opportunists of the Young Democrats, the jingle-hucksters of Madison Avenue, or the dreamless millions, already programmed for safe jobs, dull marriages, and what Thoreau once called "lives of quiet desperation."

Hayden and Dylan, born one year apart, in the adjacent heartland states of Michigan and Minnesota, are *Zeitgeists* because they have let themselves be vulnerable to the traumas which have most shaped this generation, a generation whose collective biography is inscribed in the names of blood-stained places: the Bay of Pigs, Mississippi, Dallas, Watts, and Vietnam. And because they are both young Americans, *in extremis*, Hayden and Dylan are most repelled by arbitrary authority, the mass media, hypocrisy, status, and compromise. Neither one is a liberal Democrat with a nine-to-five job.

For all its paradoxes, lack of program, and anti-intellectualism, the New Left is the most hopeful political movement in the country because it knows certain crucial things the rest of the country does not yet know.

It knows, for one, that the liberalism of the unions and the ADA (Americans for Democratic Action) is exhausted and without relationship to the new agents of change. It was the ADA's generation of liberals who executed Caryl Chessman, invaded Cuba, sold out the Mississippi Freedom Democrats, sent the state police onto the campus at Berkeley (and Madison and Brooklyn), accepted covert money from the CIA to subsidize their cold war unions and organizations, and made Vietnam a charred monument to their paranoid anti-communism.

The New Left also knows the limits of mere legislation and bureaucratic programs. A poverty program became the patina of the Great Society, but more Americans are on welfare today, and live in slum housing today, than when LBJ was inaugurated. Two civil rights bills have been passed, but Negroes are poorer and more bitter now than ever before. The under-thirty radicals know that *values* and *attitudes* must be changed before new laws do anything more than polish the illusion of reform; they know that justice is more important than Professor Daniel Patrick Moynihan's sacred "stability," and that justice will only emerge from more, not less, conflict.

The New Left knows other things too, that the editors of *Time,* LBJ's cabinet, and Freedom House do not. They know that if the Vietnam war is not wrong, *then nothing is wrong;* that marijuana is pleasurable and does not lead to heroin; that the *New York Times* does not print the truth all the time; that anti-communism is now a greater threat to American democracy than communism; that people riot because they are poor, not because Rap Brown tells them to.

Generations, however, are not defined by their rhetoric or by their abstract insights, but by their deeds and their impact on the general culture. And it is here that the young radicals have made and altered history.

If Christ began with only twelve followers, and Fidel began in the Sierra Maestra with less than fifty, the modern civil rights movement began with the four Negro freshmen who sat-in in Greensboro, North Carolina, on February 1, 1960. If SNCC, the freedom rides, and the Mississippi Summer Project had not flowered from that seed, there would never have been civil rights bills passed in 1964 and 1965, nor a Negro sitting today in the Mississippi State Legislature. If SDS had not organized a march of twenty thousand against the Vietnam war on April 17, 1965, Senators like Fulbright, Kennedy, and McCarthy would not now be so bold in their dissents. If the Free Speech Movement had not challenged Berkeley's computerized bureaucracy, the "Multiversity" would not now be the subject of dozens of symposia. If Tom Hayden, Herbert Aptheker, and Staughton Lynd had not traveled to Hanoi in December of 1965, the courts would never have had a chance to declare the State Department's ban on free travel illegal. If *Ramparts* magazine had not exposed the secret life of the Central Intelligence Agency, God knows what might have happened.

Any generation that has grown up listening to Jack Ruby, CIA recruiters, Eichmann, George Romney, Andy Warhol, Richard Speck, and Lyndon Johnson must have a sense of the absurd. And so it has been that the absurd artists have given the under-thirty generation its second characteristic vision—that of comic-apocalyptic chaos and absurdity. They find it in the songs of Dylan, the Beatles, the Mothers of Invention, and Phil Ochs; in the fiction of Joseph Heller, Thomas Pynchon, J. P. Donleavy, Terry Southern, and Ken Kesey; in films like *Morgan* and *Dr. Strangelove;* in the poetry of Allen Ginsberg, the comedy of Lenny

Bruce; and the cartoons of Jules Feiffer. The immense underground popularity on the campuses of novels like *Catch-22* and *One Flew Over the Cuckoo's Nest* mirror a generation's perception that logic, rules, and order explain less and less about a culture that puts Martin Luther King, Joan Baez, and Ken Kesey in jail—and Lester Maddox, General Hershey, and Ronald Reagan in power. Or a culture that can send 525,000 troops to Asia, but not eighty-two voting registrars to Mississippi.

The only analogies for that are Kesey's novel, where the inmates of a mental hospital are healthier than the guards, or Yossarian, who screams at his colonel in *Catch-22:* "Crazy! What are you talking about? You're the one who's crazy!"

That's how the young feel, when literally the most sensitive and dispassionate adults in the land—Senator Mansfield, Eric Sevareid, James Reston, etc.—emotionally condemn their demonstrations against the war but admit, ever so calmly, that the war is wrong and that dissent (in the abstract) is nice. It is this irony that makes Dylan's lines like, "To live outside the law you must be honest," and "Don't follow leaders, watch the parkin' meter," appear so prophetic. Or Hayden's remark that "It has been the most respected liberals who have caused most of our problems and disillusioned me the most." James Reston sounding like a "good German" is what C. Wright Mills meant by "crackpot realism."

Four years ago a leader of SDS tried to convince me that the Warren Report was a fraud, that the NSA (National Student Association) was being secretly financed by the CIA, that I shouldn't vote for Lyndon Johnson because he would follow the same policy as Barry Goldwater in Southeast Asia, and that a washed-up Late Show actor would soon become governor of the nation's largest state. I told him he was crazy. But it turns out that it is America that is crazy.

"All the lonely people, where do they all come from?" ask the Beatles.

"Not with my life you don't," chant the draft resisters of SDS.

"I can't get no satisfaction," sing the Rolling Stones.

"Burn, Baby, Burn," chant the ghetto children of Malcolm X.

"You don't know what's happening, do you, Mister Jones?" taunts Dylan.

These expressions of rebellion and chaos reflect the deepest feelings of the generation that has grown up absurd, listening to Dean Rusk explain why we are in Vietnam.

Sartre said of blood-sick France, during the Algerian war: "Ours is the age of assassins." And perhaps that is the truest epitaph for this American generation, that before its thirtieth birthday it has witnessed the assassinations of John Kennedy and Malcolm X, and the murder of a nation ten thousand miles away.

QUESTIONS FOR DISCUSSION AND WRITING

1. To whom is this essay addressed? How can you tell?
2. Why does Newfield equate Tom Hayden to Marat and Bob Dylan to de Sade? What are the "politics of resistance" and the "art of the absurd"? Why is today's youth drawn to these forms of expression and to these exponents?
3. Are "the politics of resistance" and the "art of the absurd" always in agreement, or do they sometimes work against each other? Explain.
4. Newfield says that Hayden and Dylan are both "young Americans, *in extremis.*" What does he mean by this?
5. Do you agree with Newfield that a minority of the young people in America will be responsible for leaving their mark on an entire generation and perhaps even on an entire culture? Is it "fair" that such a thing should happen? Explain.
6. In your opinion, do the quotes from the Beatles, the SDS, the Rolling Stones, Malcolm X, and Bob Dylan at the end of the article sum up the world-view of a large portion of the present generation? Explain.
7. What relevance does the slogan "the future is now" have to the ideas expressed in this essay?

Louis J. Halle

The Student Drive to Destruction

> *"We shall destroy because we are a force," observed Arkady. . . .*
> *"Yes, a force is not to be called to account. . . ."*
> *"Allow me, though," began Nikolai Petrovitch. "You deny every-*
> *thing; or, speaking more precisely, you destroy everything. But one*
> *must construct too, you know."*
> *"That's not our business now. The ground wants clearing first."*
> —Turgenev, *Fathers and Sons*

To understand the implications of the students' revolt for the future of our civilization one should place it in its historical setting. As a movement of rejection it represents the nihilism that has been developing for over a century now, to the point where it is at last becoming the dominant intellectual drive of our time.

The word "nihilism" was introduced into the common language in 1862, when Turgenev published his *Fathers and Sons,* a compassionate novel dealing with the gap between the generations. Bazarov, the young nihilist who is its hero, represents the revolt of the new generation against the old, against its whole traditional culture.

By the second half of the nineteenth century that traditional culture was losing such innate authority as it had once had. It was the possession of a ruling élite, expressed in the affectation of high ideals that took no account either of the findings of science or of the impoverished lives of the great majority of people, on whose labor the élite lived. Nihilism, in these circumstances, was not entirely without point. According to Bazarov's disciple, the student Arkady, "a nihilist is a man who does not bow down before any authority, who does not take any principle on faith, whatever the reverence in which it may be enshrined." Such nihilism stood for a frank recognition of reality, for a society based on science rather than on an obsolete idealism.

Those who affected the culture that the original nihilists opposed

78

took an optimistic view of human nature—that is, they made a polar distinction between their own noble nature, which was soulful, and the nature of the brute beasts. Man, in their view, was essentially divine, created in the image of his maker, and if he had fallen into evil he was still capable of the redemption that they, themselves, pretended to represent. The nihilists, responding to the initial impact of Darwinism, denied this distinction between men and beasts. (Turgenev began writing his great novel just as *The Origin of Species* was published.) For the piously optimistic view of human nature they substituted a new view in the name of scientific realism. Their denial that man was the divine creature he pretended to be took a particularly persuasive form, at last, in the works of Freud and the Freudians, who concluded that men are governed by the destructive forces that represent their basic animal nature, however either sublimation or hypocrisy may cover them up.

Throughout the Victorian Age ladies and gentlemen had pretended to be exempt from the bestial impulses that are, in fact, common to us all. The way new generations were produced was an unmentionable secret, not to be acknowledged—above all, to be kept from the members of the new generation until, inevitably, they at least learned about it in the shame of the wedding night.

With the revolt against Victorianism that followed World War I, Freudianism became a religion among the advanced intellectuals. The zeal with which it was adopted and preached in the 1920's can be understood only if one appreciates the release from former shame and inhibitions that it provided. Those of the new generation who had secretly entertained "wicked thoughts," believing that decent people did not have them, suddenly learned that everyone had them, including their hypocritical elders. The Freudian psychoanalyst, to whom so many of these people now turned, relieved them of the moral burden they had borne. They confessed to him and he took away the shame. The experience was that of an ineffable liberation.

There were other forms of liberation as well, stemming from the thesis that everyone should rid himself of his inhibitions, inhibitions associated with the hypocritical tradition of the Victorian generation. The extreme exponents of this thesis organized free-love camps and nudist communities. For the most part, however, what it produced was greater verbal frankness, together with a more relaxed and informal relationship between the sexes. Women got off the pedestal that had held them at such a distance from men, and by dressing and behaving so as to reduce the differences between the sexes they made possible a camaraderie with men that, a generation earlier, would have been regarded as improper. (They gave themselves a flat-chested appearance by means of the newly invented brassieres, which were simply tight bands; they cut their hair short, and they smoked cigarettes.) All this was the beginning of what we call permissiveness.

These two trends—the disposition to regard man as essentially beastly, and permissiveness—have both continued through the half century since the First World War, until they have at last reached the predominance they are manifesting today. Today, books advancing the thesis that man is a predatory aggressor by nature are welcomed and acclaimed by the intellectual community. At the same time, all censorship and most of the traditional restrictions on sexual indulgence are denounced.

There is a paradox of disastrous implications here. At the same time that man is represented as being an aggressive beast, incapable of moral responsibility, the inhibitions that society has hitherto imposed on his freedom to indulge his nature are to be removed.

Throughout the history of political philosophy, an optimistic view of human nature has been associated with the advocacy of freedom, a pessimistic view with authoritarianism. The pessimistic view that Plato took, in consequence of the disasters that popular rule had just brought upon Athens, was the basis of the authoritarianism advocated in *The Republic*. In ancient China, the optimistic view of human nature led the Mohists to advocate a society based on love rather than force, while the pessimistic view led the Legalists to advocate a police state. Russian authoritarianism, alike under the czars and their successors, is associated with the accepted view that men are destructive creatures who, if only for their own sakes, have got to be held down.

Our own Western tradition of liberalism, which goes back through Thomas Jefferson to John Locke, was justified by the optimistic view of man's nature that prevailed in the eighteenth century. This is also true of the Jacobin tradition, which goes back through Karl Marx to Rousseau. Marx was explicit in his conception of human nature as basically creative rather than destructive. Consequently, he looked forward to the day when, capitalism having been liquidated, the coercive state would wither away, after which men would enjoy in perpetuity perfect freedom for the indulgence of their natural creativity.

In the face of the logic these cases exemplify, how can one explain the present advocacy of permissiveness by those who regard man as an irremediably greedy, aggressive, and predatory beast? This stands opposed to the logic I have cited, which also takes the form of the principle that men can be free only to the extent that they make a disciplined use of their freedom. It is only where men are prepared to deal tolerantly with the diversity among them, and to abide voluntarily by "the rules of the game," that freedom is possible. Where men will not tolerate the expression of opinions different from their own, and where they refuse to accept decisions reached in accordance with "the rules of the game," the impositions of the police state become unavoidable. Anyone who has raised children knows, from direct experience, that freedom is a function of the capacity for socially responsible and considerate behavior.

It is the tradition of civility in the United States and Britain, expressed in self-restraint, that has hitherto made possible the relative freedom enjoyed by their peoples, and it is the extreme moderation of the Swiss in resolving their internal differences, which are great, that makes possible the freedom they enjoy today. Here we have demonstrations of the fact that human nature, at an advanced stage of civilization, is capable of such self-discipline as a free society requires.

If one looks at the mixed historical record of mankind, or if one consults one's own experience of the people one has known, it is quite impossible to believe that man is either all bad or all good. He may be properly described, it seems to me, as a beast with a soul. Even if I were willing to concede that the evil was predominant in him—in the sense that he was governed by his animal appetites, by a desire to destroy, by a lust for power—even so, if there is only one spark in the darkness of his nature, there is, in that spark, a basis for unlimited hope. In spite of the fashionable anthropology of our day, which identifies him as a predatory beast, it seems to me clear that man, in his evolution, has already made noticeable progress in rising above the level of his pre-human ancestors.

This is a view for which abundant evidence could be adduced, but it is not a view that can gain a hearing today because it is, for the depressing reasons I have already cited, so unwelcome to those who represent the intellectual fashions of our day. If I should write a book showing that man, like the great carnivores, is predatory by his unchangeable nature, I could be sure that it would be widely read and acclaimed; but if I wrote a book that took an optimistic and teleological view of man's evolution, regarding it as an ascent from the level of the beasts to something ethically and spiritually higher, it would hardly be well received and few would read it. The burden of living up to a high standard is something men can do without. I do not think that this situation will change in what remains of this century, for we seem to be in one of those long periods when civilization, in decline, produces the kind of thinking appropriate to such decline. But if the Phoenix ever rises again, its rise will be accompanied by the general optimism that periods of progress always produce.

Men tend to be what they think they are. If they accept a view of themselves as self-indulgent they will tend to be self-indulgent; if they accept a view of themselves as morally responsible beings they will tend to be morally responsible. I do not think that the widespread denial of social inhibitions on human behavior, which we call permissiveness, is altogether unrelated to the prevalent view of what our human nature really is. Here is a logic that does, in fact, associate the two trends of our time: the hopeless view of our human nature and the assault on social inhibitions. If we are really pigs, rather than fine ladies and gentlemen, then we should not be asked to behave like fine ladies and gentlemen. We should be free to use language regarded as obscene, and there should be no restrictions on theatrical exhibitions of sexual and sadistic practices, no matter how sickening some of them may be. (Whatever may be said in favor of freedom for obscenity, I submit that it is not on the same level of importance as the freedoms guaranteed by the first ten amendments of our Constitution.)

I do not offer this, however, as the primary explanation of how it is that those who regard man as fundamentally bestial are, nevertheless, the advocates of permissiveness. A further explanation is that they are not really interested in the maintenance or enlargement of a régime of freedom that, on the one hand, they tend to take for granted (having never experienced anything else), and that, on the other, does not in itself cure the intractable problems of our societies. The causes they nominally espouse are not necessarily causes they believe in, but mere pretexts for action that has other ends than their success. Any number of activist students admit in private that when they shout for Marx or Mao or Castro that does not mean they care anything about what these figures stand for. They do not carry intellectual responsibility that far.

Some of the student leaders have, on occasion, made it clear that what they really want is power for themselves (thereby exemplifying the fashionable anthropological view of human nature). At other times they have not bothered to deny that destruction is, for them, an end in itself—relieving them, as such, of any need to think beyond it. If they invoke causes that are genuinely idealistic and progressive, such as human equality or freedom, they do so for tactical purposes only. They invoke them as pretexts on the basis of which they can confuse men of good will and rally the forces of destruction. When German student leaders led their followers, last September, in a violent physical assault on the Leipzig Book Fair, the reason they gave was that the directors of the Fair had chosen President Senghor of Senegal as the recipient of the Fair's peace prize when they might have chosen, instead, Mr. Stokely Carmichael, the apostle of violence. Here the cynicism is patent.

No one, I gather, doubts the intelligence of these student leaders, however gullible their followers may be. In preferring violence to free speech they know, as the Nazi leaders knew, that its success would spell the end of such free speech as I am exercising in this article. When they deliberately and skillfully provoke a bewildered police force into acts of brutality, and then denounce its "fascism," they know the equivocation in which they are indulging. When they denounce the authorities of New York City as being the rulers of a "police state," and oppose them on that basis, they know that a police state is what their movement, if carried to the lengths they intend, would bring about.

It is no answer to say that there are real and important matters for grievance. Of course there are! The point is that the proponents of violence are not really acting, as they pretend, to eliminate these matters. Their leaders, at least, know that, if there are stupid professors (a grievance one student offered me as justification for violent demonstrations), destroying the universities is not the way to get intelligent ones. They know that white discrimination against blacks will not be overcome by a course of action that makes votes for Wallace and pushes the American society in the direction already taken by South Africa. The leaders who know these things are acting cynically, however idealistic what they are doing may seem to older intellectuals who think themselves back in 1848.

Violence and destruction for its own sake prepares the way for the police state, as violence and destruction in Germany prepared the way for Hitler's dictatorship. Specifically, they prepare the way for brutal and ignorant leaders to assume the power of a state that, in our case, possesses a nuclear armament with which it could destroy the world. For those who pursue destruction as an end in itself, the possibilities are now unlimited.

One thing that separates my generation from the generation of my children is the experience it has had of the great depression and of the decade during which the tyranny of the fascist police state seemed likely to engulf the world. My generation has vivid knowledge of how easily the structure of civilization can collapse, and of how terrible the consequences can be in terms of human suffering. Our children, on the other hand, have at best read about these experiences in history books. All that most of them have experienced at first hand is full employment, unlimited opportunity to make a living, and the remarkable freedom of speech and behavior that they have enjoyed in an increasingly permissive society. (On the Berkeley campus, a couple of years ago, I saw earnest-looking boys and girls, righteous indignation written on their faces, sitting behind a table marked "Committee for Sexual Libertinism," and I wondered who was preventing them from simply going ahead and engaging in it.)

I cannot imagine that many of those who say they are willing to face the eventuality of a police state, as the consequence of their actions, would not change their minds if ever they found themselves living under one. I have emphasized the element of cynicism in their conduct—but it is accompanied by an innocence of either experience or knowledge that contributes to their moral irresponsibility. (It was Irwin Cobb who said: the trouble with the younger generation is that it hasn't read the minutes of the last meeting.)

I have no doubt that, if mankind is on a long upward path over the millennia, that path will continue to be marked, in the future as in the past, by great crashes of civilization. I cannot quite believe that one of these crashes will spell a final end to the hopes of mankind; but we are now entering a period of human history when new dangers, produced by scientific progress, require us to exercise a greater self-control than ever before. It is not impossible, as a consequence of the breakdown in the discipline of civilization, that Mr. George Wallace or someone like him will become President of the United States in 1973, with responsibility for its international relations and with control over its nuclear armament.

I have talked to students who believe that the basic procedure of democracy is represented by violence in the streets, and that freedom means doing whatever one pleases. To the extent that each generation is responsible for educating the next, my generation must regard itself as a notable failure.

QUESTIONS FOR DISCUSSION AND WRITING

1. Halle argues that the current generation is caught up in two historical forces—"the disposition to regard humans as essentially beastly, and permissiveness"—and that these two forces, in conjunction, are leading the young down a road to "self-destruction." Do you agree with Halle's central thesis? Explain.
2. What is the relationship of the quote from Turgenev's novel which begins this essay to the thesis of the essay? What does the word "nihilism" mean? Explain.
3. In terms of the present age and its rebellion of the young and its social activism, comment on Halle's statement that "Men tend to be what they think they are." For example, is youth defined by itself or by its activities or by other people? Explain.
4. Halle says that "men can be free only to the extent that they make a disciplined use of their freedom." Comment.
5. There is a good deal of what might be termed "name-calling" in this essay. Find examples of it and show how they work in the context of the essay and its thesis.
6. If you have read the essay by Richard Poirier (p. 52) in this section, what do you think would be Poirier's opinion of this essay? Explain.
7. If Halle were the president of a large university, and students attempted to take over the administration building, demanding a louder voice in university decisions, how do you think Halle would react? What would be the basis of his actions? Would they be justified? Explain.
8. Is Halle a "conservative"? Or is he a "liberal"? Explain. What do you think Halle would consider himself?

Robert Zoellner

Confessions of a Middle-Aged Moralist:
Peering Across the Generation Gap

I am a college teacher, a member of that beyond-30 age-group which college-age Americans have been repeatedly advised not to trust—the implication being that they ought rather to trust themselves. I think that that is very good advice for any young person coming of age in the '60s. The core of the problem, of course, is the generation gap, which I can perhaps best illustrate with a personal anecdote.

I am one of the millions of more or less middle-aged American males who long ago discovered that one of the fringe benefits of a visit to the neighborhood drugstore was a quick, surreptitious glance at the gate-fold in *Playboy*. Timing is of the essence: one has to wait until the magazine rack is deserted and the druggist busy elsewhere, so that the awkward business of unfolding the gate, assessing the artwork (of necessity at arm's length, a difficult thing to do unobtrusively) and then refolding the gate and getting the issue back on the stand, can all be done with dispatch and discretion. If these innocent trepidations move some of my younger readers to incredulous laughter, they are invited to observe their fathers at any magazine rack. I do not, I think, exaggerate.

I was thus engaged one day in a drugstore just off campus when a young man and girl, both students, sauntered in. As the boy bought cigarettes, the girl paged idly through a copy of *Redbook*. The tobacco transaction completed, the boy moved casually to the magazine rack, picked up the copy of *Playboy* I had just the moment before put down— rather hastily, I fear—and flipped out the gatefold. "My God," I thought, "right out here in front of girl-friend and everybody." His glance was neither hasty nor covert, but rather cool, detached, judicious, appraisingly skeptical. And then the girl moved behind him, companionably resting her chin on his shoulder, while he shifted slightly to give her a better view. They remained thus for an affectionate moment, in silent, mutual communion over November's Bunny. "She's not as pretty as

last month's," the girl finally said, returning to her *Redbook*. "No," said
the boy, carefully refolding the gate, dropping the magazine back on
the stack, moving down the aisle in search of more compelling reading
matter—and leaving me in a state of cultural shock.

I do not mean *moral* shock; I have been observing college students
too long for that. I mean *cultural* shock, the sort of hard jolt that the
students of the '50s, earnestly intent upon romance, success, and split-
level living, never gave me, the sense of cultural distance and conceptual
alienation which perhaps only an anthropologist can really appreciate.

For this brief vignette suggested a way of communicating, and a
way of handling facts, which I suspect is entirely alien to most members
of my generation. Most striking was the openness, the frankness, the
total lack of pose: the boy unabashedly manifesting his male sexuality,
the girl accepting this as fundamental, so obvious and so normal as
to be beyond comment. Here, if I read it correctly, was a moment
of etched human simplicity and mutual, charitable acceptance—the sort
of acceptance, beyond words, which in my generation only married
couples ever achieved and then not often—uncluttered by moral qualms,
equivocations, subterfuges or legalisms, untainted by giggles or guffaws,
which often marked an older value system. It is dangerous to generalize,
but I suspect that only the supremely healthy of my generation experienced many such honest moments; we were and are, as we push toward
50, the inheritors of a sick, moribund morality, and it is this which
defines most sharply the distance between the under-30 and the over-30.

The generational distance can be seen in a number of ways. Where
these youngsters have seen "Bonnie and Clyde" and "The Penthouse,"
at their age I was following Mickey Rooney through the cotton-candy
world of the "Andy Hardy" movies. Where they are turned on by the
magnificently infantile sexuality of Brigitte Bardot, I thought Deanna
Durbin was lovely. College students rock to the pelvic beat of "Lady
Madonna" and the psychedelic sonorities of "Sgt. Pepper's Lonely Hearts
Club Band"; at the same age I was doing a shambling fox trot to "I'm
Gonna Buy a Paper Doll That I Can Call My Own." "Mairzy Doats"
was swinging stuff in 1942.

One might argue that my generation exhibited a charming innocence,
while this one's knowledgeability is frightening. But I think the case
is precisely the opposite. Within the saccharine culture which crooned
"Don't sit under the apple tree with anyone else but me . . ." and within
which we were able to cheer wildly at the news that 100,000 people
had been vaporized at Hiroshima, I entertained some ideas that could
hardly be called innocent.

When I was in my late teens, I was told, and believed, that pictures
of nude women inevitably aroused the libidinous appetite, and were
therefore "occasions of sin" that one must at all costs avoid. Such pictures
generated "impure thoughts," which were a matter for confession. And,

following the confessional ritual, one discussed such things in darkness and in whispers.

When with the boys, of course, one would admit to having the "right" wrong thoughts, but in general the youthful period of sexual hyperintensity was characterized by a thoroughly suppressive hypocrisy. Good boys pretended, when with their elders and good girls, that they were asexual. Good girls sometimes helped things along by following the nuns' advice to wear something blue ("the Virgin Mary's color") on dates. Today's generation hardly knows what a hang-up is: the idea of giving the Virgin Mother a squeeze, even at one remove, is not conducive to peace of mind.

Now all of this is immoral; hypocrisy always is. Moreover, it is totally uninnocent. Most of my generation, Catholic or otherwise, were stripped of innocence as quickly as possible because, as everyone knows, and as Melville pointed out in *Billy Budd*, the innocent have a tendency to get into trouble fast. There is nothing new about this. I recall a scene from Fellini's "8½": a gaggle of schoolboys pay a magnificently fat and garish old behemoth a few pennies to dance for them on the beach. But soon the scandalized Brothers appear and herd the boys back to the schoolyard, where their evil is hammered into them until it is obvious, even to the dunderheads doing the hammering, that their innocence has been entirely destroyed.

The only reason that the good Brothers were able to obliterate innocence was that the boys took them seriously, just as I took my elders seriously back in the '40s. And this is the immense, crucial advantage that the young people of the '60s have: they find it impossible to take their elders seriously, and therefore, despite our best efforts, we have been unable to destroy their innocence.

Unlike earlier generations, ours has been able to do on a national level what Jay Gatsby did personally in the '20s: give concrete, visible articulation to our invisible hopes and ideals, in electric carving knives, jazzy cars and the "house of our dreams" in suburbia. Thus, unintentionally, we have exposed our social and ethical penury, the niggardliness of our moral imagination.

And out of all of this, like honey from the lion, now comes a young generation which, having grown up with us, and having tasted in the most intimate way the emptiness of our lives, somehow has been set free, innocence intact, to find their own morality. They are, I suspect, the first innocent generation that America has produced.

What we who are over 30 do not, or will not, understand is that such innocence has as its inevitable correlate the lack of what we are accustomed to think of as a defined moral code. Because those under 30 have so obviously rejected our morality, we are resentfully inclined to call them immoral. But my experience on campus suggests that "immoral" does not fit the case. Neither does "amoral," or any other traditional term. Rather, I would call them *premoral*, which I would define as the quality of being morally concerned and morally aware, without necessarily being committed to a particular morality. We find it almost impossible to understand a generation which thinks moral concern to be much more important than morality. But it seems reasonably obvious that if one has to build a morality from scratch (and that is precisely the task which faces the under-30 generation, thanks to our failures), the essential first step is an assessment of reality as it is in itself, *before* the moral dimension is superimposed upon it, or derived from it, or both at once.

Generally speaking, the over-30 generation has never made such an assessment. A traditional version of reality was handed to us, along with a concomitant morality; the extreme case perhaps is the Catholic whose morality is based on an ontological assessment made during the eleventh century or even earlier. Most of us accept the idea of a just war; we have never doubted the validity of dividing sexual activity into licit and illicit; we have been more than comfortable with the idea of success as a central life-drive; we assume without question the superiority of the rational and discursive over the irrational, the intuitive and the instinctual.

The under-30 generation is not so bound. They are as free as we are unfree. They are in the process of taking a hard, clinical, *premoral* look at reality. To my mind one of the best expressions of this premoral ontological examination is the movie "Blow-Up," the central character of which is a photographer, significantly able to stop or freeze reality for closer examination. Developing pictures he took in a park, he discovers in the background of one print something that appears to be a corpse half-hidden in the shrubbery. Trying to understand what he is looking at, he begins a series of "blow-ups"—photographic enlargements—each one a more microscopic version of an indistinct reality, until reality finally dissolves in the random texture of the film emulsion. Correlated with this ontological blow-up is a sexual explosion, a romp for three, which shocked me, but which many of my students accepted quite casually as one-of-those-things-that-we-had-better-take-a-look-at.

This premoral assessment of reality is also apparent in the fascination many students have for lights, lighting and light shows: literally, they are interested in anything which offers to throw a new light on reality. They are particularly fascinated by the engineer's strobe light which technicians have been using for years to freeze or slow down the motion of high-speed machinery. Recent movies best express this ontological search for new light. The killing of Bonnie and Clyde takes in real time perhaps fifteen seconds, but seems to the viewer to be fifteen minutes of sustained horror. Bonnie on the car-seat jerks and dances like a slow-motion rag-doll, as hundreds of machine-gun slugs smash into her body; and Clyde takes an eternity to fall to the ground in a series of terrifyingly sustained strobe-segments. This scene finds a deep response in a generation that feels a desperate need to catch the ultimate, premoral truth of a reality immersed in a time-continuum moving so rapidly that assessment is very difficult. My generation can watch with considerable equanimity as napalm spews through a Vietnamese village. We are sure there is horror there, but the whole business takes less than a second, and then another and more comforting image appears on the TV screen. The under-30 generation would, if they could, stretch that napalm-instant into a strobe-hour—and then they would rub our noses in every micro-second of it.

Most difficult for the older generation to swallow, however, is young people's cool awareness of the usefulness of immorality, amorality and especially premorality in building the foundations for a moral vision. Again, there is nothing particularly new about this idea. Hawthorne's Hester Prynne achieved spiritual depth by committing adultery with Minister Dimmesdale; students these days get that message very quickly. The contemporary equivalent is "The Penthouse," which may turn out to be the most brilliant premoral movie of the decade; in comparison to it, "The Graduate" candy-coats the essential issues.

"The Penthouse" opens in the luxuriously furnished penthouse of an unfinished and deserted high-rise apartment building where a quiver-lipped anti-hero is shacked up with an equally quiver-lipped anti-heroine who is not his wife. For about half a reel we watch the two of them, in mawkish disregard of their real situation, saying the moral, proper things which are the natural, instinctive idiom of the over-30 generation. She especially professes great concern that they are not doing right, asking him to divorce his wife and marry her. She's a nice girl.

Into this oppressively moral love-nest come two absolutely amoral, funny scamps who tie up the man and, after feeding the girl whiskey and reefers, take her to bed serially. Between times, in Pinteresque dialogue, they strip away layer after layer of the moral pretensions of the hero, even persuading him to help them plan a raid on his own house. Having thus established the moral emptiness of two decent, law-abiding people, they abruptly disappear, their objectives achieved ("jobs" of this sort are apparently a way of life with them) without once resorting to violence, but simply by waving switchblades around and bad-mouthing their victims.

They are, in short, premoral knights-errant, Robin Badfellows going about the world doing pre-good. At the end, the nice girl knows that deep down, where it really counts, she's a lusty little bitch, and her companion knows beyond any possibility of escape or rationalization that he is a degenerate coward. Perceptive younger viewers find all of this not depressing, but elevating: the clear implication of "The Penthouse" is that having had premoral self-knowledge forced upon them by two beneficent bad guys, the anti-hero and anti-heroine are now in a position to begin to build a morality which may have some connection with reality.

This sort of premoral assessment happens not only in the movies that the young attend in droves; it also happens in college classroom discussions, often in such a way as to illuminate the generation gap. I recently had occasion to teach Hermann Hesse's *Steppenwolf* for the first time. The hero is a pompous German scholar pushing 50 who, while enjoying the comforts of middle-class life, still features himself as an outcast, an intellectual Ishmael, a wolf of the steppes, wild, free and dangerous. The novel's success depends on the reader's ability to conceive of a paunchy, bourgeois, comfort-loving wolf (an imaginative synthesis which I myself am unable to achieve).

At any rate, by an unlikely happenstance Steppenwolf falls in love with a beautiful young courtesan, Hermine, and this turns the novel, ostensibly, into a study of the tension between the life intellectual and the life sensual. The love of Steppenwolf and Hermine is not immediately consummated, however. The stodgy Steppenwolf is inept in bed, and so Hermine sends one of her professional colleagues, Maria, to teach him the arts of love: Steppenwolf is surprised to find Maria all tucked in and ready for the first lesson when he returns home late one night.

Because I am over 30 and incorrigibly moral, I gagged on all of this, and said so in class. I was willing to admit the importance of the sensual life, and to entertain the idea that the life which is sexually meager is no life at all—but Hermine's physical-education approach to the problem was too much for me. And then I went on to say some rather automatic and entirely predictable things about love and fidelity and so on.

The class was not made up of sophisticated seniors or graduate students but of freshmen and sophomores. One might have expected them to go along with my rather conventional reaction to Steppenwolf's first love-in. Instead they appeared to find my moralistic attitude irrelevant. They obviously felt that I was missing the point. After a few minutes of somewhat evasive discussion, a student in the front row put the issue squarely. "Well," he said, "what's wrong with Hermine having Maria teach Steppenwolf the fine points? *If you're going to do it, you'd better know how to do it right.*" His brief manifesto elicited shy guffaws from most of the boys, and giggles and blushes from the girls, but it was obvious that the class was with the student in the front row, and against me. He had succinctly stated their own real feelings about Steppenwolf's education.

The classroom vignette, like my experience at the drugstore magazine stand, may be taken as evidence of a moral decline among American youth. But I cannot give it that interpretation. The students' reading of *Steppenwolf* is not immoral; it is simply premoral. It is that forthright, frank assessment of reality which must be made *before* a consequent moral judgment can hope for validity. And how can you fault a young man—or a generation—who arrive at the premoral judgment that what is worth doing is worth doing well?

QUESTIONS FOR DISCUSSION AND WRITING

1. What does the title of this essay mean? What is "a middle-aged moralist"? Is Zoellner really one? Explain.
2. Zoellner refers to today's youth as "premoral." Explain what is meant by this. Is this the same as what Louis Halle, in the preceding essay, refers to as "permissiveness"? Explain. What is implied by the use of each of these words? Is one more accurate than the other to describe young people today? Explain.
3. What does youth's "premoral" quality have to do with its increasing involvement in social issues?
4. Zoellner says that young people today are "innocent," "free," and, by implication, "supremely healthy." Is he right? Explain.
5. Does Zoellner make any distinctions between different kinds of young people? That is, do his generalizations about them apply to the average college student as well as to what one writer has called "the gas-station set"? Explain.
6. Zoellner typifies the young as those who consider "moral concern to be much more important than morality." Explain what he means by this. Do you agree?
7. Does this essay offer a definition of morality? If so, state it.
8. Is it necessary for personal sexual activity to be subject to public concepts of morality? Is there a relationship between youth's attitudes toward sex and its attitudes toward society? Discuss.

For Further Reading

Bouma, Donald. *Kids and Cops.* Grand Rapids, Mich.: William B. Eerdmans Publishing Co., 1969. Paperback.

Cohen, Mitchell, and Dennis Hale, eds. *The New Student Left.* Boston: Beacon Press, 1966. Paperback, 1967.

Erikson, Erik H. *Youth: Identity and Crisis.* New York: W. W. Norton and Company, Inc., 1967. Paperback, 1968.

Feuer, Lewis. *The Conflict of Generations: The Character and Significance of Student Movements.* New York: Basic Books, Inc., Publishers, 1969.

Friedenberg, Edgar Z. *The Vanishing Adolescent.* New York: Dell Publishing Company, Inc., 1959. Paperback, 1969.

Gerzon, Mark. *The Whole World Is Watching: A Young Man Looks at Youth's Dissent.* New York: The Viking Press, Inc., 1969.

Mead, Margaret. *Culture and Commitment.* New York: Doubleday and Company, Inc., 1970. Paperback.

Roszak, Theodore. *The Making of a Counter-Culture.* New York: Doubleday and Company, Inc., 1969.

III ON THE UNIVERSITY

The modern American university occupies a unique and paradoxical position, having to satisfy two functions at once: it must serve the society of which it is a part, and it must also continue the search for knowledge. And it must do both jobs equally well. For example, the university has to provide society with well-educated and humanely oriented individuals, as well as with technicians, so that society may prosper. It must constantly search for ways to make our society viable for every citizen. Yet, on the other hand, the university must not be subservient to society; it has to be a free agent; it cannot allow the outlooks and fears and attitudes of society to dominate it in any way. Indeed, only because one of the university's functions is the open and unhampered exploration of ideas can the university be prepared for its other function: taking an active part in society's improvement.

Such are the ideals of the university: public service and the free pursuit of knowledge. Unfortunately, like most ideals, they have usually not been carried out in practice. The current revolution in American universities is the quest for these ideals. The academic revolution which began in earnest in the 1960's and which is gaining in momentum in the 1970's is manifested in student demands for more relevance and depth of curriculum and for more attention from their professors. It is manifested in the demands that the university as an open marketplace of ideas free itself from the imprisonment of military and war research undertaken by secret contracts. It is manifested in the demands that the university cease to act *in loco parentis* for its students. It is manifested in the desire that the university be the pinnacle of freedom and truth. And it is manifested in the division of opinion that such demands inevitably bring with them. Theodore Roszak, in *The Dissenting Academy,* has observed that the American academic has been reduced to being "a henchman of the military-industrial complex or a recluse in an apolitical ivory tower." The revolution in the universities is a search to avoid each of these very real extremes.

The writers in the following essays deal not only with the extremes but with alternatives. They attempt to discover how the university can adapt to the cultural and social milieu and how the cultural and social milieu can adapt to the university. The discovery may suggest a means to carry the present into the future.

Walter Lippmann

The University
and the Human Condition

I am free of the obligation to offer solutions of the problems which occupy so much of the time of the governing authorities in the academic world: how to raise money, how to appease the alumni, how to get around the trustees, the state legislatures, the foundations and the Pentagon, how to ingratiate themselves with the chamber of commerce, the board of trade, and the clergy, how to tranquilize the egos of the faculty, how to deal with the students in their academic lives, their ideological lives, and their sexual lives, how to be cheerful and good fellows with the excessively inquiring reporters. About all of these preoccupations I shall have nothing to say. This leaves open to me the broad, unrestricted field of the human condition and what the universities ought to be doing for it and about it.

The proposition with which I am starting is that as men become modern men, they are emancipated and thus deprived of the guidance and support of traditional and customary authority. Because of this, there has fallen to the universities a unique, indispensable and capital function in the intellectual and spiritual life of modern society. I do not say that the universities today are prepared to perform this spiritual and intellectual function. What I do say is that a way will have to be found to perform these functions if the pursuit of a good life, to which this country is committed, is to continue and to be successful.

For modern men are living today amidst the consequences of emancipation from established authority. The dream of Franklin and Jefferson, as Mr. James A. Perkins describes it in his recent Stafford Little Lecture, was of "an open society, free of both ecclesiastical and civil control, with little to fear from the uninhibited search for truth and for experiments in the application of truth." The preponderant majority of our people in America today have arrived at such an open society. They have found, I submit, that as they are emancipated from established authority they are not successfully equipped to deal with the problems of American society and of their private lives. They are left with the feeling that there is a vacuum within them, a vacuum where there were the signs and guide posts of an ancestral order, where there used to be ecclesiastical and civil authority, where there was certainty, custom, usage and social status, and a fixed way of life. One of the great phenomena of the human condition in the modern age is the dissolution of the ancestral order, the erosion of established authority; and, having lost the light and the leading, the guidance and the support, the discipline that the ancestral order provided, modern men are haunted by a feeling of being lost and adrift, without purpose and meaning in the conduct of their lives. The thesis which I am putting to you is that the modern void, which results from the vast and intricate process of emancipation and rationalization, must be filled, and that the universities must fill the void because they alone can fill it.

It is a high destiny. But it must be accepted and it must be realized.

Before we can proceed, we must ask ourselves why, in the quest of a good life in a good society, we now turn to the universities rather than, let us say, to the churches or the government. We do that because the behavior of man depends ultimately on what he believes to be true, to be true about the nature of man and the universe in which he lives, to be true about man's destiny in historical time, to be true about the nature of good and evil and how to know the difference, to be true about the way to ascertain and to recognize the truth and to distinguish it from error.

In other times and in other places, the possessors and guardians of true knowledge have been held to be the appointed spokesmen of a universal and indisputable tradition and of divine revelation. In the Western society to which we belong the traditional guardians and spokesmen of true knowledge have in varying degrees lost or renounced their titles to speak with complete authority. The hierarchy of priests, the dynasties of rulers, the courtiers, the civil servants and the commissars have to give way . . . and there is left as the court of last resort when the truth is at issue, "the ancient and universal company of scholars."

Having said this, I have not forgotten how often the professors have been proved to be wrong, how often the academic judgment has been confounded by some solitary thinker or artist, how often original and innovating men have been rejected by the universities only to be accepted and celebrated after they are dead. The universal company of scholars is not an infallible court of last resort. Not in the least. On the contrary, it is an axiom of modern thought that the very process of thinking evolves. In human affairs nothing is infallible, absolute and everlasting. There are no courts which can anticipate fully the course of events. There are none which can take account of the unpredictability of genius. Nevertheless, in the modern world there exists no court which is less fallible than the company of scholars, when we are in the field of truth and error.

This court, this universal company of scholars, comprises all who study and teach in all the universities and institutes of the world. The colleagues of each scholar are his peers, those who have qualified themselves in mastering and obeying the criteria by which, in a field of knowledge, truth and error are judged.

The company of scholars is all over the globe, and its members are duty-bound to hear one another.

Insofar as the communication among them is adequate, so that a physicist in California is aware of the experiments and criticisms of a physicist in Peking, there exists the best possible insurance available to mortal men against the parochialism, the stuffiness and the dogmatism which are the chronic diseases of academies.

I have said enough, I hope, to reassure anyone who might think that I am glorifying the professors and attributing to them more power and authority than they are entitled to have. I do not mean to do that. I have had my share of controversies with a good many professors. What I do say is that the community of professors is, in the modern world, the best available source of guidance and authority in the field of knowledge. There is no other court to which men can turn and find what they once found in tradition and in custom, in ecclesiastical and civil authority. Because modern man in his search for truth has turned away from kings, priests, commissars and bureaucrats, he is left, for better or worse, with the professors.

And while we must treat the verdicts of the professors with a vigilant skepticism, they do have a certain authority. It comes from the fact that they have vowed to accept the discipline of scholarship and to seek the truth by using the best intellectual methods at the time known to contemporary men.

To make sure that I am not overstating my thesis, let me repeat. The community of scholars is the court of last resort in those fields of inquiry and knowledge about which scholars, as scholars, are concerned. Thus, if a professor is charged with the murder of his colleague, the court of last resort is not the faculty of his university or the faculties of all the universities. It is the judiciary of the state in which he lives, for the scholar is a scholar only part of the time and in part of his activity. In the role of murderer he is outside the field of scholarship.

But if a professor is alleged to have murdered his colleague a hundred years ago, as in the case of Professor Webster at Harvard, the court of last resort *today* about his guilt or innocence a century ago is not the judiciary of Massachusetts. It is the historians who have studied the evidence now available and have been confronted with the findings of all the historians who have read the history of the case. After a hundred years, no one is more qualified than are the historians to judge the case.

Reflecting on this we come close, I think, to the essential principle of academic freedom. In his relations with the laws of the land, a professor is as subject as any other man to the laws against murder, robbery, cheating on the income tax, driving his automobile recklessly. The laws for him, as for all other men, are what the law-enforcing authorities say they are. The professor has no special privileges and no special immunity.

But in the field of truth and error about the nature of things, and of the history and future of the universe and of man, the state and its officials have no jurisdiction. When the scholar finds that two and two make four, no policeman, no judge, no governor, no legislator, no trustee, no rich alumnus, has any right to ordain that two and two make five. Only other scholars who have gone through a mathematical training equivalent to his, and are in one way or another qualified as his peers, can challenge his findings that two and two make four. Here, it is the community of scholars who are the court of last resort.

It follows that they are the court of last resort in determining the qualifications of admission to the community of scholars—that is to say, the criteria of appointment and the license to teach. No criterion can be recognized which starts somewhere else than in the canons of scholarship and scientific research. No criterion is valid here because it emanates from the chamber of commerce, or the trade union council, or the American Legion, or the clergy, or the newspapers, or the Americans for Democratic Action, or the John Birch Society or any political party. The selection and the tenure of the members of the community of scholars is subject to the criterion that scholars shall be free of any control except a stern duty to bear faithful allegiance to the truth they are appointed to seek.

A judgment as to whether a scholar has been faithful is one that only his peers can render. The supreme sin of a scholar, *qua* scholar, is to lie, not about where he spent the previous weekend, but about whether two and two make four.

If we say that the vocation of the scholar is to seek the truth, it follows, I submit, that he must seek the truth for the simple purpose of knowing the truth. The search for truth proceeds best if it is inspired by wonder and curiosity, if, that is to say, it is disinterested—if the scholar disregards all secondary considerations of how his knowledge may be applied, how it can be sold, whether it is useful, whether it is good or bad, respectable, fashionable, moral, popular and patriotic, whether it will work or whether it will make men happier or unhappier, whether it is agreeable or disagreeable, whether it is likely to win him a promotion or a prize or a decoration, whether it will get a good vote in the Gallup poll. Genius is most likely to expand the limits of our knowledge, on which all the applied sciences depend, when it works in a condition of total unconcern with the consequences of its own findings.

Believing this, I hold that the university must have at its core a sanctuary for excellence, where the climate is favorable to the pursuit of truth
for its own sake. In our conglomerate and swarming society, the last
best hopes of mankind lie in what is done, and in what example is
set, in these sanctuaries.

I do not think of them as monastic establishments shut off from the
struggles and strains of the human condition. I think of them as societies
of fellows within the great corporate institutions that our universities
have become, as societies where the relatively few who can pursue truth
disinterestedly will find the support and sustaining fellowship of their
peers.

Since man's whole knowledge of things is not inherited and must
be acquired anew by every generation, there is in every human society
a culture, a tradition of the true and the false, the right and the wrong,
of the good which is desirable and the bad which is to be avoided.
This culture is rooted in the accepted version of the nature of things
and of man's destiny. The accepted version evolves and the encyclopedias become outdated and have to be revised.

Since the prevailing tradition rests on the prevailing science, it follows
that modern men must look to the company of scholars in the universities
to guard and to preserve, to refine and enrich the tradition of civility.
They have to revise the curricula of studies and the encyclopedias of
knowledge.

This does not mean, of course, that the scientists and the scholars
are to be regarded, much less are to regard themselves, as a mysterious
elite of the initiated who can lay down the law of right and wrong,
of good and evil, in human affairs. It does mean that insofar as religion,
government, art and personal living assume or imply that this or that
is true or false, they are subject to the criticism and judgment of the
company of scholars. The prevailing and accepted science of the time
is the root from which grow the creations of poets and artists, of saints
and prophets and heroes. The science of an age is the material with
which inspiration and genius create.

I am more than a little concerned as I proceed, that you will think
that I am erecting a very high tower on a very small base, that I am
nominating the professors to carry too great a responsibility. All I can
say is that the human condition in the modern age brings us to what
I have been talking about. The dissolution of the ancestral order and
the dethronement of usage and authority in modern society have left
us dependent upon man's ability to understand and govern his own
fate. Necessarily, therefore, we are in high degree dependent upon the
men whose lives are committed to the pursuit of truth.

The responsibility may be too great for the professors to carry. But
somehow—since the responsibility must be met—we shall have to learn
to find men who will tell us how to find the professors who can carry
the responsibility. And if we are ever to find them, we must begin

by realizing the need to find them. If they cannot be found, modern man is indeed adrift on a trackless sea.

So, I venture to proceed. There is still something more, still another great function which the universities and their scholars cannot neglect, indeed cannot escape.

For there is more to the task of learning than to discover more and more truths than have ever been known before. That something more, which may mark the difference between mediocrity and excellence, is the practice of a kind of alchemy, the creative function of transmuting knowledge into wisdom.

Wisdom, says the Oxford English Dictionary, is "the capacity of judging rightly in matters relating to life and conduct." It is "soundness of judgment in choice of means and ends." The development of the capacity of judging rightly is something different from, and in some ways much more than, the capacity to know the truth in any particular field of knowledge, or to have mastered the art of applying this knowledge to some desired end. The capacity to judge rightly in a choice of both means and ends cuts across the specialties and the technologies, and it is, I dare to say, the hallmark of a liberal, as distinguished from a utilitarian or vocational, education.

We may say, I think, that knowledge is made into wisdom when what is true about the nature of things is reshaped to the human scale and oriented to the human understanding, to human need and to human hope. As this is done, the findings of scientists and scholars are transformed into the humanities, and the materials for a liberal education begin to appear.

The universities, therefore, are not only the depositories of wisdom. They are also laboratories where alchemists work, whose function it is to transmute knowledge into human wisdom. If the scholars do this, insofar as they do this, they transcend the sterile controversies about the two cultures, the scientific and the humanistic, and they learn to transcend the intellectual puzzle about specialism and generalism. For knowledge transmuted into wisdom places the sciences and the humanities within one universe of discourse.

Can it be done? There is no need to doubt that it can be done. The most revolutionary of all the intellectual achievements of the modern age has been man's increasing mastery of the art of discovery and invention. The reshaping and reorientation of knowledge, so that it is humanly accessible and viable, is the task of philosophers, of the master-minds in the special fields of learning, of the advanced students in the field of education, and of the great teachers themselves. It would be a feeble kind of defeatism to think that man, who is penetrating the secrets of matter and of life itself, is unable to make usable the knowledge he is able to acquire.

A liberal education is concerned with what Plato calls the "royal science," the science that needs to be possessed by the rulers of the state. The education of a prince who is destined to be the king has from time immemorial been the primary function of education. Now that we live in a time when, as Huey Long truly said, every man is a king, it is still the prime function of education to instruct and to train the future rulers of the state.

It cannot be said that there exists as yet an adequate royal science. It is the task of the scholars to invent and compile the royal science of the modern age, a science which can in some measure be absorbed by all who vote, and can educate the comparatively few who will actually govern.

The heart of this science will be a presentation of the history and the practice of judging rightly in a choice of means and ends. Such a body of wisdom must be composed and compiled and made communicable, if the supreme teaching function of the institutions of learning is to be successful. This is their necessary business if they are to be more than laboratories of research, institutes of technology and vocational centers for careers.

For they cannot neglect the highest function of education which is the education of the rulers of the state. Quite evidently, it is not easy to discover what should be taught to the future rulers of a modern state, how they are to be made to acquire that capacity of judging rightly, which is the essence of wisdom. We are only at the frontier of modern, democratic education, within sight of the promised land. Those who come after us will have to make, out of the accumulating knowledge of the specialists, a body of available and usable wisdom. The political scientists and the educators of the coming times will have to explore what is as yet a largely unknown continent—this royal science for our age. They will have to extract from the infinite complexity of knowledge what it is that the rulers of the state need to know.

Quite evidently, the ruler of a state, the President of the United States for example, cannot master all the branches of knowledge which bear on the decisions he must make. Yet he must have enough knowledge of a kind which will enable him to judge rightly whose judgment among the specialists he should decide to accept. He must learn the art, which is not described in the textbooks as yet, of listening to experts and seeing through them and around them. The educators of the future will have to extract from the whole body of nuclear science, for example, what it is that the President and the Congress and the leaders of public opinion need to know about nuclear science and the behavior of great powers when they are confronted, let us say, with a treaty prohibiting the testing of nuclear weapons. Out of these extracts from the body of knowledge, the educators must design the curriculum of our own royal science.

I have been meditating out loud about one central theme: that in the modern age, as the ancestral order of usage and authority dissolves, there exists a spiritual and intellectual vacuum of discipline and guidance which, in the last analysis, can be filled only by the universal company of scholars, supported and protected and encouraged by their universities.

QUESTIONS FOR DISCUSSION AND WRITING

1. Why does Lippmann discuss the university and its scholars in terms of "the human condition"? What is the human condition, according to Lippmann, and how does it impinge upon the functions of the university and its members?
2. What is "a liberal education," according to Lippmann? How does it differ from what he calls a "utilitarian or vocational education"?
3. Discuss Lippmann's distinction between "knowledge" and "wisdom."
4. Is Lippmann here dealing more with the university as it is or as it should be? Put another way, is the university the same in practice as it is in theory? What leads you to your conclusion? How does Lippmann deal with this question?
5. Lippmann argues that perhaps the "highest function" of education is "the education of the rulers of the state." For this position, Lippmann actually has some strong backing, for example from Plato in the *Republic*. Discuss Lippmann's statement.
6. What does Lippmann mean when he says that professors in a university must "bear faithful allegiance to the truth they are appointed to seek"?
7. If you think that Lippmann may be wrong to assert that "the universal company of scholars" is "the court of last resort" in matters of truth and error, who or what do you believe constitutes the court of last resort? Or is there no such court? Explain.

John J. Corson

Social Change
and the University

Student unrest, faculty disaffiliation, expanding enrollments, and similar phenomena are superficial irritants, not fundamental forces to which universities must adapt. Beneath these everyday events and conditions are several basic dilemmas that plague the entire society and that require fundamental changes in our major institutions.

For example, our increased population and increased wealth have produced not just more rich people, but some basic changes in attitudes among many people. The social cement that holds together a democracy—a widely accepted value system—no longer exists.

The young are demanding a reordering of national priorities. Not only is there a widely voiced discontent with the Vietnam war, there are vociferous complaints about the lack of housing, the conditions of the cities, the inadequacies of the welfare system, the high cost of medical care, and the persistence of inflation.

These concerns are not superficial issues created by the young as vehicles for a venting of their spleen. They are the expressions of new expectations for our society created by its own success. As the industrial society succeeded the agricultural society, and was in turn succeeded by what has been described as the post-industrial society, a new and advanced civilization with different characteristics has been emerging. These characteristics are being hammered out in riots in the cities, in court battles over equal employment, in education, and in housing opportunities; they are an attempt to forge a modernized concept of human dignity. The war on poverty—not just the federal programs but society's acceptance of the necessity for the fight—is gradually building the expectation of a national minimum that provides not only income, but health and higher education as well.

The smog over our cities, the Santa Barbara oil slick, the polluted rivers, the rising crime rates are all establishing other expectations of a livable environment. The frustration of consumers, who can't tell the relative merits of Fortrel versus Dacron, or the hazards in pesticides, cyclamates, or scores of other products, is substituting for the principle of "let the buyer beware" the expectation that government should protect the consumer.

The importance to the university of those new expectations is that the university has been, should be, and increasingly will be the institution in our society concerned with the shaping of values. The university's philosophers, economists, sociologists, historians, political scientists, if they do their job, are not just passing on what earlier scholars had passed on to them. They are helping a vastly greater proportion of the upcoming generation to understand, to modify, and to extend the lore of the past to the problems of the present. And that brings them right squarely into the forces of today, into the changing characteristics of the society.

The professors in our universities are stimulating youths to question the precepts of parents, the pronouncements of press, TV, politicians, and business leaders, and the preachings of the church. That is as it has always been. The university cannot avoid being the staging ground for battle over social issues. It is essential that the university find the structures and the practices within which these battles may be fought with words and ideas rather than with stones and fists.

Another fundamental factor is an increasing dependence on knowledge. New knowledge, whether it be about the irradiation of foods to insure a longer life for the sandwiches in vending machines or about miniaturization that permits the development of pneumatic tools for the most delicate cranial surgery, has become central to economic and social progress.

Several consequences follow from this fact. The university must be expected to be called upon to do much of or most of the research for other segments of the society. The university will become closer, probably uncomfortably closer, to the centers of economic, military, and political decision-making, and such a situation must be faced squarely and decisively.

Access to job opportunities now depends more than ever on the acquisition of a certain amount of this new knowledge, and this means that the university has become the gatekeeper to the workaday world. Because nearly 50 per cent of our young people are going on to college, it is rapidly taking on the status of a public utility, and, as it does, it must accept the obligations that go with that status.

Another consequence of the new knowledge is its increasing specialization. As invention and discovery have expanded knowledge at an ever increasing rate, the individual's field of comprehension has been narrowed even as it has been enlarged in power. This development confronts both the society and the university with a perplexing dichotomy, because the codification of new knowledge requires increasing specialization, while the resolution of society's problems requires an ability to interrelate bits of knowledge from each of a variety of specialties, and from each of a variety of disciplines. The truly educated citizen, the effective parent, the competent professional man, and the self-fulfilling individual must be broader than a mere specialist. Our colleges and universities are expected to breed broader values into the specialists they develop. This expectation poses problems of course content, of curriculum control, of departmental structure, and faculty selection and leadership.

Another social dilemma impelling change in the university is the loss of autonomy. As the university marches, or is pushed, into an increasingly influential position in the resolution of public problems, as it becomes increasingly the gatekeeper governing entry into the job market, and as its share of the Gross National Product grows, it will be subjected inevitably to an ever more intensive surveillance by its several constituencies: students, alumni, faculties, donors, including corporations, federal and state governments, and the public generally.

As this scrutiny increases, the mystique that has guaranteed autonomy for the college and university disappears. The logic has been inescapable: the state's scarce resources do not permit support of the duplication of public institutions or the duplicating of facilities within such institutions. This logic is being supplemented on private as well as public campuses by the reasoning that education is becoming too important and the costs too great to be left to the scholars. Regardless of whether that reasoning will be accepted, the moral of accumulating experience is that the university will not continue as an island unto itself.

The erosion of authority throughout our society is another fundamental condition that is changing the university. Student revolts must be viewed in relation to other contemporaneous revolutionary action. Black communities have rebelled in more than a score of cities, a substantial minority of younger Catholic priests have challenged the hierarchy of their church, and even some members of the armed services have organized on a score of military bases to voice criticisms. The new relationship of the student to the university must be viewed within the context of these similar rebellions against authority.

The obsolescence of much of the lore possessed by the older generation is one cause of this erosion of authority. Coleridge said that experience is like the stern light on a ship, illuminating only the past. In a period of rapid technological change this is all the more true. Moreover, differing values that flow out of this obsolescence accelerate the erosion of authority.

And the revolution in communication, not only in television, radio, and the press, but in communication between individuals at the supermarket, in the subway, and the like—the understanding generated by these experiences of urban living—has undermined the authority of the patriarch in American society, be he the teacher, dean, president, business executive, bishop, or even military commander.

This general erosion of authority strikes at the heart of the university governance. The authority of the teacher has been eroded by the increasing maturity, real or superficial, of the student, and by the technological advances that tend to make obsolete many of the Ph.D.s who got their doctorates before World War II. The logic of fixing authority for education in the faculty has been strained by the apparent fact that a university does not have a faculty. It has a score of faculties made up of individuals, many of whom are more concerned with their status in their discipline than in their attachment to the university that pays their salary.

The authority of the president in relation to the faculty, or faculties, was undermined when he became a fund-raiser and an administrator and lost his status as an educator. And the trustees have allowed the broad authority that they were endowed with by law and historical practice to atrophy by concentrating their attention on the financial, physical, and public relations problems of the university. For decades, they have not dared to make decisions as to faculty selection, curricular matters, and the very guts of the university operations.

The function of the university will be expanded still further and changed. Its instruction function will be limited by the growth of the community colleges and expanded by the growth of graduate professional training. Its research and community service functions will be broadened markedly. Hence, new forms and process of government must be capable of managing a collection of related laboratories, institutes, centers, clinics, and offices in relation to existing colleges and schools scattered over perhaps a dozen or more cities. The arrangements for governance of such a complex may be much more analogous to the structure of a holding company than to those of a body of scholars that we nostalgically look back to.

The trustees of the universities, both public and private, need to re-identify the constituencies they serve, and redefine the authority they will exercise. The problem of constituency in the private university is probably more severe, because the trustees have accepted little obligation to any constituency other than the alumni. They are increasingly being held accountable by students, by the faculty, by the government that contributes the major portion of the resources on which they depend, as well as by the alumni and by the general public.

These constituencies will likely demand a voice in the trustees' councils. And the boards of trustees may be forced to abandon self-perpetuation in whole, or in part, in favor of election or designation of representatives by one or more of these constituencies.

The trustees of both public and private universities will be called upon to accept greater responsibility for educational, research, and public service functions. They may not be able to avoid accepting authority in these realms by the assertion that they are concerned only with broad policy, and that they have delegated authority to the president for education, research, and student relations.

The president of a university must reclaim for himself and his principal administrators the authority to act. To achieve coordination within, to utilize effectively increasingly scarce resources, and to stimulate requisite change, the president and his deans need greater authority. That authority cannot be handed down by trustees, who, like the British Queen, have held it in abeyance so long in fact they no longer have the authority that is needed. It must be ceded by the faculties who possess it by virtue of their monopolistic control of the university's stock in trade—knowledge and the capacity to create and transmit knowledge. Faculties can be induced to cede it, if appropriate mechanisms for consultation are established, maintained, and nurtured.

One might still ask what kind of leadership is required in the president's office—educational, administrative? Both, of course, but what is needed above all in the president of a university, in an era of persistent and substantial change, is a man who makes it obvious that he knows where he wants to go and how to articulate and be persuasive in stating goals for his institution, and who has the rare combination of ability, skills, and energy needed to carry an administrative staff and a faculty along toward those goals.

The faculty—or faculties—must be helped to see themselves as a legislative body, not as an executive body. That means the faculty should be made to assume responsibility for recommending broad educational policy to the trustees, and for determining the curriculum, for faculty selection and promotion policies, and for student affairs, and also help to discipline itself to keep its hands off the executive of such policy. But the reclaiming of authority, long exercised by a small minority of the whole faculty over such minutiae as student social behavior as well as the approval of faculty appointments and curriculum, will be difficult.

The students are already being granted a larger voice in governance and will be granted a still larger voice. The problem is to determine what areas of governance students should be involved in, and then to devise ways of selecting students who have the time, the inclination, and the ability to cope with these matters in a responsible fashion.

There are forces at work that will change the function of the university, that will substantially expand the university, and that will establish new demands on the university. In coping with that change, some of the most venerated concepts, practices, and traditions of an old, old institution will be altered or abandoned.

QUESTIONS FOR DISCUSSION AND WRITING

1. Like Lippmann in the preceding article, Corson brings out the idea of the university as a provider of a utilitarian education as well as the idea of the university as a focal point of knowledge and discovery—that is, as both a sort of handmaiden to the state as well as "an island unto itself." Are these two functions compatible with each other? Explain.

2. Do you agree with the statement that because the university is "rapidly taking on the status of a public utility . . . it must accept the obligations that go with that status"?

3. What, in general, according to Corson, is the role of the university in a time of social change? When Corson defines this role, is he describing the university as it is or as it should be? What appears to be Corson's own point of view in these matters?

4. According to Corson, what are some of the "forces at work that will change the function of the university"? What is your own opinion of these forces?

5. It can be argued that this article and the preceding article, while discussing very well what they set out to discuss, nevertheless seem to omit one important aspect of universities—the students. Why this omission? Who is more important at a university, the administration or the students and faculty? Similarly, what is more important—the general question of the function of the university in society, or the specific question of whether or not students are learning anything? Or are these two questions connected? Explain.

Edgar Z. Friedenberg

The University Community
in an Open Society

At this stage in our history, the rapidly growing heterogeneity of the university both in function and clientele would certainly have led to trouble and confusion even if there were no inherent conflict among its functions. But there are fundamental conflicts that, though they stem from the heterogeneity of the university community, reflect far more than the ugliness of the kind of academic urban sprawl that has developed. As the size and jumble of the university community have increased, the university's functions have acquired conflicting meanings and value to its various constituencies. The question of governance, I believe, resolves itself into that of whether a morally defensible ordering among those functions can be achieved and made viable under the actual conditions of our society. If it cannot—and this is quite possible—then the passage of the university system should not be greatly mourned, nor unduly delayed by a series of organ-transplants and excisions designed to relieve immediate crises at further cost to the university's integrity.

The central function of higher education in America has always been vocational. Harvard was founded to train clergymen; and as the society has become more a mass, open society, its dependence on the university system for vocational training and placement has, of course, become far greater and more complex. It is well understood that the university serves society by selecting and training a wide range and enormous number of technicians who, granting its present mode of organization, are essential. The university is the instrument of the continuous talent search by which an industrial democracy assures itself that it is not systematically ignoring lower-status social groups as a potential talent-source, thereby denying them access to opportunity and itself the value of their contribution.

In a mass, industrial democracy, no function could be more legitimate.

111

Nor could any function be more heavily burdened by ideology. The furious controversy that has recently been aroused by Arthur Jensen's conclusion that there are significant innate differences of cognitive style between blacks and whites that, in this culture, operate to the disadvantage of blacks and especially hamper them in school is, for example, totally ideological.[1] *Any* difference between individuals or between social groups may be either an advantage or a disadvantage, depending on circumstances. Stupidity is often a virtue which must be feigned by those unfortunate enough to lack it; while if the Esquimaux had feet a yard long and a foot wide, they wouldn't need snowshoes. Jensen's findings, if valid, certainly establish that blacks are less well adapted than whites to respond successfully to the demands of the dominant institutions of industrial democracy, especially its schools. They leave entirely open the question of whether this is a sign of inferiority, superiority, or neither. But they are nevertheless threatening because the conflict to which they point may be impossible to resolve for a society ideologically committed both to equality of opportunity and to popular sovereignty. Even if Jensen is right, there are two ways in which this resolution could be achieved, but both appear to be politically impossible for a mass democracy. One is to provide equal respect and rewards to people with the kinds of cognitive styles blacks—or poets, or hippies, or mystics, or police, or sexual deviants—possess. There are such people; and they are indeed different from one another and from the norm. This requires, in short, genuine pluralism: a great many small events, some competitive, in which different kinds of excellence could be demonstrated and rewarded.

The second way is for society to respond openly and generously to need, without requiring that the needy—which at different times and in different ways includes all of us—prove anything or win any race at all. Except, perhaps, in its Malthusian aspects, this is now technologically possible through the instrumentality of an enormously high technical level of productivity distributed through a high guaranteed annual income or a universal credit card—instead of a university degree. But our society lacks the political means to make any such commitment. The anxiety and *ressentiment* such proposals arouse among the bitter coalition of the self-made, the self-condemned, and the vast number of poor whose sole satisfaction seems to come from the prospect of others more impoverished still; of industrial leaders fearful that too few people would work unless compelled to by threat of humiliation and want, and union officials who fear that a general rise in the standard of living unrelated to membership in the labor force would deprive

---

[1] Arthur R. Jensen, "How Much Can We Boost IQ and Educational Achievement?" *Harvard Educational Review*, Vol. 39, No. 1 (Winter, 1969), pp. 1–123.

them of a *raison d'être* make it impossible. Taken together for these
and other reasons, the majority of the American people seem incapable
of regarding misery as anything but failure; and loathe the most miserable of their number. The major premise of our ideology of opportunity
is that each should have an equal chance to succeed; but the minor
premise is that only those who do succeed may be rewarded, and that
refusal to compete should be punished or subjected to therapy as "dropping out."

The educational system has played a complex and delicate role in
mediating among these competitive hostilities and ideological problems.
It has, in effect, become a steeplechase in which comparatively few
people fail utterly; but the hazards are so cunningly designed that many
more fall somewhat behind and are cooled out. The more successful
students have been precisely those whose cognitive skills and ideological
positions have been most suited to the demands of middle and upper
managerial positions in existing institutions; so that the school has served
to reify these qualities as characteristics of the worthiest members of
society. But, in so doing, it has also established the educational system
as the supervisor of legitimate people-racing in our society. It provides
the anthrodrome; its staff are the judges and referees; it determines
which events shall be accepted as part of the decathlon, which styles
of competition are legitimate and which are cheating and hence grounds
for disqualification and exclusion from subsequent competition.

All this is familiar enough; but its converse side is less frequently
stressed and is more useful in understanding contemporary academic
stress. Victories won in and certified by the educational system may
be honored by the society with increments of status without arousing
much resentment among the underclass, so long as the educational system is thought to operate on universalistic principles. If, in fact, you
are admitted to fair competition, you are expected, in our society, to
be a good loser. But the educational system, consequently, must become
as nearly as possible the sole route to success and recognition; no con-
tender is to be seeded out of the earlier events. It is this, I believe,
which accounts for the absurd profusion of curricula in American schools
and colleges, and the universal insistence on diplomas of various kinds
as qualifications for posts and professions not even remotely related
to the skills those diplomas reputedly certify. They are not intended
to mean anything in themselves, but they have two useful social functions. They do attest that the bearer has been thoroughly socialized in
the educational system and knows the score and the name of the game,
which insures that life in bourgeois America will not end like a performance of *Turandot:* The name is not "love," though the score may be.
And they get society off the hook by ratifying its universalist pretensions:
Nobody got anything free, there has been no favoritism or nepotism,
the plastic little girl who won the national championship at baton-twirl-

ing is really the best. Her mother made her practice four hours a day, and the school taught her how to relate to strangers.

When a social group—ethnic or otherwise—whose characteristics have kept it at a competitive disadvantage becomes strong enough politically to demand a better life in America, it cannot simply demand a bigger reward as an elementary human right. Having previously accepted universalism in principle, it must complain not of *inhuman* treatment, but of *unjust* treatment—that is, of discrimination. The response of the liberal segment of society is not to redress its grievances directly, which would be politically disastrous, but to scurry around trying to think up ways of being sure it wins more events without actually cheating or showing favoritism. My own formal doctoral training happens to have been in that aspect of education called "evaluation"—that is, the design and construction of tests. For the past six or seven years, since whites have become more aware of the American racial crisis, I have, like most others trained in this area, often been called upon to participate in conferences at which funding agencies sought technical help in searching out the academic proficiency which they insisted must lie undiscovered among blacks so that this might be recognized and rewarded. They had already, of course, attempted to provide support for those whose superior promise could be identified by existing academic records or testing techniques.

Urgent as the need for a massive increase in support for black and other "disadvantaged" students was and is, it seems grotesque for these agencies to conceive their problem as a matter of test-bias. Indeed, the urgency of the problem makes this preoccupation with tests and contests grotesque. What is needed to respond more adequately to the needs of "disadvantaged" groups is not a more thorough and ingenious canvass among them for the qualities society rewards, but a broader and more adventurous—and more gracious—conception of what constitutes a socially valuable attribute. It is certainly desirable that a much larger proportion of blacks receive National Merit Scholarships than have done so in the past. It is even more fundamentally desirable that awards committees broaden their definition of what constitutes National Merit, to permit them to recognize a variety of individuals, and sometimes without demanding victory in any competition. But this might yet be fruitless if the only consequence of such recognition is to channel the recipient into the educational system, albeit under much more favorable circumstances than he would otherwise have had. A student admitted to the university by such pluralistic devices might still find himself cooled out rather quickly because the university itself was unable to recognize diversity of cognitive style and continued to define any effort to do so as "lowering standards."

Yet there remain only three possibilities, no matter what may be demanded. Unless the university *does* learn to respect a less rationalistic definition of cognition as an acceptable means toward academic achievement, or the society learns to respect personal, idiosyncratic ways of growing up and learning outside degree-granting institutions—those who, whether for ethnogenetic or purely personal reasons, are less adept at competitive striving and linear rationality will lose out in this society, as they have been doing so far. Because the second of these alternatives seems even less likely than the first, the present intense demand for black studies programs, controlled by black personnel, has arisen. The opposition to these as academically unsound reflects, I believe, the recognition of the more conservative faculty that they are indeed intended to provide protected enclaves in which black students with poorer conventional academic skills can survive. In view of the history of the university system, this recognition cannot be accepted as an adequate reason for resisting these programs. Virginity cannot be defended unsuccessfully more than once; and if defended successfully for too long, future development is arrested. The university system has, quite properly, recognized social demand in accepting faculties of engineering, of educational studies, and other studies that quite clearly lack the cultural breadth of the humanities. This is the device by which we achieve an increasingly open society. Those trained in these disciplines, too, have a different cognitive style—both because of differences in training and differences in background that are associated with these vocational choices. In any case, the "new men" are different. New black men are no more likely to do violence to the academic tradition than white and may be a little more human.

Once one accepts in principle, then, that the university system is to be maintained as virtually the sole channel of mobility, the university must respond to demands for variation in the definition of achievement needed to recognize the way in which different social groups develop different styles and different merits; and if, in fact, they develop none, illusory merits will doubtless have to be ascribed to them. Society must recognize the claims to dignity and opportunity of all its constituent groups. If the university is to continue to stand astride the only legitimate highway to advancement, it must quit demanding tolls in coins that only some travelers can acquire and calling this "maintaining standards." But the acceptance of more diverse modes of response nevertheless leads to conflict precisely with those groups which have forced themselves most recently and with greatest discontinuity to their earlier experience to make it on the more conventional terms already prevalent in the university system. No datum has more consistently recurred in current conflict within the university than the observation that the students who are least responsive to and most intolerant of the growing demands [of blacks] are whites whose parents never attended college; while those most sympathetic to and often so over-identified with the blacks as to court repudiation by them are higher-status white students who take college for granted, but are unable to tolerate its moral failures. To accede to the demands of blacks is not only to violate prejudices that many first-generation working-class students hold; it is also to change the rules of the game they have learned so laboriously and to discredit as irrelevant and morally fatuous or worse the instrument they have sought, at great sacrifice, for their deliverance. Those who have just been seated at the Round Table after a long and arduous journey are likely to get rather upset when informed that Camelot is no more authentic than Disneyland, and that Excalibur, according to the small print, was made in Hong Kong.

This, I believe, is the major source of friction between the "jocks" and commuters, who still try to take the university system seriously on its own terms, and the higher-status white activists and blacks who denounce it. The Vietnam war has, of course, infinitely exacerbated this conflict, both because it has discredited the university system morally and, more directly, because the immediate vocational opportunities to which university education leads are so likely to be war-connected. These opportunities are, moreover, *more* likely to be war-connected for lower-status students than for higher; because these, differentially, tend to locate themselves in the technological rather than the humanistic curricula. Concretely, to bar recruiters from war-industry and ROTC programs from campus is to destroy insolently, before their eyes and without their consent, the staircase that conservative students had come to college to climb. On the basis of this social model, I cannot but be convinced that black students, once they find themselves more at ease in what was never Zion, will join the jocks and repudiate their activist supporters, whose style they already seem to find grandiose and rather hysterical. Besieged college and university presidents on recent media presentations have seemed correspondingly less hostile to the blacks whose attacks on the university system, though often more aggressive than those of white activists, are also far more superficial. These men are trying, I believe, to convince black student leaders that the university system is still relevant to them, however strongly their more privileged white dissident colleagues may condemn it.

For these reasons, then, current academic conflict is complexly rooted in the university's function in the transmission of vocational opportunity to members of a society in which personal advancement, or making it, is the major basis for self-esteem. The university, moreover, serves as differential as well as transmitter; it keeps society from being overturned by permitting individuals to move at very different rates and still think they're wheels—which they are at least in the sense that it is they who bear the vehicle's burden. But conflict about the function of the university in contributing to economic and social opportunity, central as it is, is still, I believe, less fundamental a social problem than those which have now arisen *between* its vocational function and other functions less ideologically acceptable in our society and hence less frequently explicitly discussed.

A major function of the university has been to serve as a community in which many of its members have found intense and protracted satisfaction and have married or formed permanent friendships or taken lovers. This is why college and university life has become a pastoral legend in American folklore, and why alumni continue to attend class reunions in a nostalgic and futile effort to recapture briefly their student experience. Both the nostalgia and the futility have become clichés as aspects of such events. But nostalgia—grief for your own place, the guilt and loss of having uprooted yourself—is an emotion that a great many Americans would be better and more sensitive for having allowed themselves to feel, though it is more agonizing than any other experience that still leaves its victim with a future. Nostalgia is not recognized in America as the kind of suffering that teaches people anything of value, because a culture that sets its highest premium on mobility as a way of getting its business done discounts it in advance as romantic immaturity. But people who have learned to respect this agony are less likely than others to set fire to peasant huts with their cigarette lighters, and this is a desirable form of self-restraint.

The futility, moreover, is ironical, because the university is still, for some of its students, the source of the kind of intense community alumni recall nostalgically; but alumni cannot recognize this because it is these students whose styles they find most repellent and who seem to them to be trying to destroy the university. So some may be; those who love their home would sooner burn it than see it defiled. But it is nevertheless precisely the militants who have found within the university fellows with a common vision of its purpose who care enough about it to risk beatings and imprisonment in the service of that vision and who are currently having the experience the alumni think they remember—not the jocks, at a time when the football hero has become anachronistic, and certainly not the commuters who would just as soon be in correspondence school if you could really make it there and the mail service were better. The more conservative almuni are more likely to be nostalgic than the liberals who, being dedicated to progress, will have gone on through several further stages of their life-cycle without much thought about their college days. But as conservatives they cannot recognize their deeper kinship with the radicals and hippies who make the university their home and not just a stopover on their career-line.

It must be granted that the fact that college life—as we used to think of it—should have become a basis for community is largely an unintended, and in some ways a paradoxical, development of American life. The educational system is designed to make schooling both a transient and a highly competitive experience, which is highly inimical to the development of a sense of community. At most stages, no such sense develops. A high-school homecoming is, in Kurt Vonnegut Jr.'s word, a real *granfalloon;* though some working-class youth, having been less hung-up than their middle-class peers in academic competition and less oriented onward to college, *do* find the high school a home-from-home and may continue to return to it as a social center for a year or two after they have graduated or dropped out, until their friends have left. But schools, generally speaking, are ill-designed to foster intimacy and a sense of identity among their members. The devices that are intentionally employed to foster school spirit destroy spontaneity and intimacy in the interests of an automatic *esprit de corps* which is anything but homelike.

But the unintended consequences outweigh the intended. College life, though growing continuously more competitive through the years as the educational system grows more universalistic, is still much less competitive than life outside the sanctuary. There is not the constant press for conspicuous consumption. The definition of the student role as impecunious and economically dependent is neither desirable nor just, and fosters the exploitation of students as sweated labor in undergraduate instruction. But it also provides the only enclave in American life in which poverty is not dishonorable and makes it far easier for people to accept one another for what they are, to establish cooperative living arrangements and open expression of feeling. There is a certain *Schadenfreude* to be got from the fact that the custom of exploiting students by making them the university's serfs has backfired into what appears to be a permanent rejection of the middle-class community's more vulgar and driven patterns both of consumption and of uptight family life. The systematic age-grading is harmful in its broad social consequences; the universities are now perceived by the general public as ghettos that are becoming useless because they no longer manage to protect the community from the dangerous young aliens they contain. But this view, too, fosters a sense of identity and empathy among students as such—not strong enough to prevent them from being divided into warring factions by conflicting interests and values, but strong enough to leave them with a viable subgroup even when this happens. And, finally, the fact that our society withholds adult status till after the human sexual prime so that the peak of erotic intensity occurs during college years enhances students' impact on one another and the probability that something human and personal, if not necessarily agreeable, will develop. Sexuality in the young, though intensely competitive, resists the control of a competitive society, for the attributes that lead to erotic and economic success are different. The difference tends steadily to lessen, for in every society higher status characteristics come to be defined as erotically desirable: witness the vicissitudes of obesity. The conventional institutions of student life, as John Finley Scott has shown in his studies of the college sorority as a national marriage-brokerage system for conventional girls, function so as to rationalize students' erotic relationships and bring them into the university's total network of trans-actions.[2] But the fraternity and sorority system is declining and has largely been replaced by informal though enduring relationships; there are more liaisons and fewer conquests. This, too, adds to the confusion and hostility of the alumni who would never have claimed that a sexual relationship could be moral in itself, though marriage might make it legitimate and even obligatory.

For these sound, if accidental reasons, the campus has come to serve the middle-class young as a community and sometimes as the locus of their best real experience of personal relationships. That, despite its growing impersonality and dedication to a competitive *ethos*, our society has not only permitted this, but enshrined it in sentimental myths of college life is explicable, I suggest, largely because the process—as long as colleges were largely highly class-selective in the clientele they served—served the class interests of those who supported the colleges without their having to admit that such a thing existed. Simple and quite genuine patterns of affiliation could be counted on to provide American society not only with the ivy equivalent of an old-boy network at the top, but with lower networks that served both to support and ensnare potential aspirants from lower levels. Catholic universities helped educated Catholics to go on feeling Catholic, which helps make subse-quent discrimination unnecessary. Similarly, during the period of more than a decade that I taught at Brooklyn College, I came to feel that the college's sustaining vision of itself as the channel of opportunity for poor but bright and often radical students from excluded social groups had become a myth that was exploited rather cynically. In all that time, there were only four or five members of genuinely excluded ethnic groups—blacks or Puerto Ricans—among my students. They were not poor; they came, for the most part, from the homes of tax accoun-tants, furniture dealers, or other petty-bourgeois; and their brightness was often nullified by extreme provinciality. My colleagues continued to refer with satisfaction to the college's high academic rating nationally. But Norman Podhoretz's comment in *Making It*[3] suggests that the most alert Brooklyn youth of the kind the college was supposed to serve

---

[2] John Finley Scott, "The American College Sorority: Its Role in Class and Ethnic Endogamy," *American Sociological Review*, Vol. 30, No. 3 (June, 1965), pp. 514–27.

[3] In the view Norman Podhoretz attributes retrospectively to his high school English teacher, he soliloquizes: "*Slum child, filthy little slum child.* I was beyond saving; I deserved no better than to wind up with all the other horrible little Jewboys in the gutter (by which she meant Brooklyn College). If only I would listen to her, the whole world could be mine; I could win a scholarship to Harvard, I could get to know the best people, I could grow up into a life of elegance and refinement and taste. Why was I so stupid as not to understand?" *Making It* (Random House: New York, 1967), p. 10.

had already perceived what I came to see more slowly: that the true *national* function of the City College system was not merely to educate academically competent New York City youth and provide them with increased opportunity, but also to provide a reliable drainage system to keep them from flooding out the Ivy League and the western and midwestern state universities, which might have provided access to greater economic opportunity, but which would certainly have responded with ambivalence to the opportunity to provide this service.

There are clearly certain serious conflicts between the university's functions in providing economic opportunity in an egalitarian society and serving simultaneously as a base for community among the young. Competition itself poisons community; and young people for whom intimacy and communion are primary values deeply resent being forced to adopt standardized, competitive patterns of behavior by an impersonal grading system and examinations that are as objective and, hence, as unresponsive to their individualized qualities and feelings as they can be made. But this is what their peers who are using the university as an anthrodrome, and who are more concerned about the rewards to which academic success leads than with the quality of their college experience, need for their purposes. This, surely, is why the demand for ungraded curricula, experimental colleges, and the abolition of many forms of examination so neatly divides the activists and hippies from the more conventional and usually lower-status students who resist it.

But there are less direct but equally important reasons why the function of the university as a base of community interferes with its function as anthrodrome. As I have discussed more fully elsewhere, it is the community function of the university which most antagonizes the larger community outside.[4] Their hostility has several sources: a sense, more flattering than realistic, that student life is "privileged" and libertine compared to their own; the way in which the student-role is defined so that students—about the most sweated labor in America outside agriculture—are perceived as not working and as being supported by their parents or the welfare state. But most infuriating of all is merely the fact that a community exists. Below the level at which the corporate network can provide a sense of identity and of membership in a colleague group, most Americans today are bereft of intimacy and belong to very little that has meaning for them. Divided as it is, the university is one of the few institutions that still shelters enclaves of people with common values who can talk to one another; and there is a fine irony in the frequency and bitterness with which its critics complain that it has become irrelevant to human life. They are right; but of what other institution in our society would it even occur to anyone to make

[4] Edgar Z. Friedenberg, "The Campus Community and the Community," *New American Review* #6 (New American Library: New York, 1969), pp. 146–62.

this complaint? The Congress, the American Medical Association, the Chase Manhattan Bank? Except for their undoubted capacity to do irreparable mischief, nobody seriously *expects* them to be relevant any longer. Fly Jefferson Airplane, and hope for the best.

This sense of being part of a meaningful coalition and bound by realities of feeling and genuine goals to its other members is, I believe, more coveted, and the source of more bitter conflict—inner and outer—in our society than any other treasure it might, but seldom does, afford. It is this, rather than sexual gratification, that remains the illicit satisfaction; though attacks on satisfying communities are usually directed against their putative licentiousness, which is often the only language in which their detractors can identify what they think they're missing. But the jealousy and sense of deprivation, and correspondingly the hostility, engendered are intense. So far as I know, no hippy commune has been allowed to survive in America; it is either busted by outraged neighbors or destroyed by ogling tourists who move in on it looking for thrills, or both. On campus, such communities enjoy some, though declining, protection. In any case, the presence of a viable community on campus is embarrassing to the students in the anthrodrome. It generates norms of conduct by which they find themselves put down, reminds them that there are satisfactions their commitments to the future forbid them to share, and, more directly, reduces the value of their credential in the community they hope will honor it. It antagonizes and drives away the officials with whom they hoped to negotiate for preferment. The conflict between the university as community and as anthrodrome is an absolutely real one, a conflict of interests as well as tastes; and it seems either fatuous or disingenuous, therefore, to deny that what advances the interests of one is likely to be costly to those of the other.

Meanwhile, constituencies of the university other than students are, of course, involved in the conflict. Generally speaking, the interests of the faculty and administration coincide with those of the anthrodrome and are opposed to those who would find community in the university. The university is indeed fundamentally involved in the industrial and governmental activities that its critics find most reprehensible and that even its supporters no longer defend. But these activities are not merely the stuff of which academic careers are made and the source of needed financial support. They also provide the upper stages of the anthrodrome itself. The more conventionally ambitious students need them as the next step in *their* careers. And an even more fundamental commitment to the anthrodrome has been made on what may be irreversible epistemological grounds. The very conception of what constitutes knowledge in every discipline; the prevailing empiricism that reduces research even in the humanities to objective and often quantitative terms; the official dominance of "value-free" social science that willingly sells itself to the highest bidder, though now with the hope that the arrangement may be handled with discretion—all these serve the needs of the anthrodrome and have a chilling effect on the community. The self-definition of the college administrator as the broker among the various interests that affect the university, whose professional responsibility actually *precludes* his attempting to exert any moral leadership among the university's various *liaisons dangereuses,* also serves the anthrodrome; as does the university's peculiar orientation to public relations, which leads it to court public support and hence public approval even under circumstances that would clearly favor instead a policy of coolly reminding the public that it, too, is dependent on the university as a major source of revenue and employment and that it might be well advised to avoid excessive harassment even of those it does not particularly like.

So far, I have made no reference to the official functions of the university on which it bases its formal claims to esteem and support: the creation and propagation of knowledge, or, as we now more frequently say, research and teaching. This omission is the more striking since these functions might be expected to support the community within the university and require its support in turn, rather than the anthrodrome. Both teaching and research are in essence, at their best, particularistic activities. No commitment to equality of opportunity can make a teacher as useful to the students he does not turn on as he is to those he does; no amount of ambition can help a student learn much of value from a teacher who has no interest in either students or what he is teaching. But the university has evolved a highly effective device to protect universalism under these conditions: rigid control of instruction through scheduling, credits, and the definition of the process as one involving abstract, symbolic communication rather than feeling, touch, or spontaneity. The effect of this is to keep instruction almost entirely in what the great psychoanalytic theorist Harry Stack Sullivan called "the syntactic mode" and so remote from the reality of sense-data and personal experience as to seem quite unreal. This makes academic freedom, defined as the freedom to teach whatever content one wishes provided the content remains turned-off, quite innocuous, especially in a mass democracy on which concepts, as such, have no influence until they have been legitimated by the mass media as what beautiful, or powerful, people believe. It also makes teaching both puerile and detached. An effective college teacher must be more interesting, provocative, and profound than daytime TV, or lose the attention of his students. Many do.

It is true that college faculty neglect teaching in favor of research as leading to more rapid professional advancement. But it is also true that teaching in the mass university of today has become a rather degrading experience; like trying to put on an authentic display of Berber folk-dances in a Casablanca dive into which a group of sailors have been lured on the pretext that other more urgent interests would be satisfied. Neither party to this shady transaction is innocent, and the more authentic the folkloric spectacle is, the more hostile the clientele becomes, since the quality of the performance is in itself a rebuke to its genuine, if base, desires.

The Selective Service Act, with the 2-S deferment, is of itself enough to make a whore of any professor. But for this the anthrodrome might in any case suffice. If freedom of opportunity requires that instruction take place in mixed groups in which those to whom what is being considered can only be an instrument of no intrinsic interest outnumber and swamp those with whose culture it already connects, teaching must remain an unrewarding and inauthentic activity. Liberalism's answer to this is familiar and compelling: Make it connect, find new ways to reach the disadvantaged and the merely uninterested and stimulate their interests. But education can only be planned and organized experience and must build on experience already had; it cannot be grafted onto a lifeless trunk or one which rejects it as incompatible with its development. Techniques for "reaching" or "motivating" students to learn something they do not care about initially seem to me most often devices for inducing them to abandon their own past for the sake of a deal with society that will pay off in the future. The anthrodrome is willing enough to do that—that is why it came to the university—but the process of helping it does not feel much like teaching. Nor would curriculum revision intended to adapt to its interests help very much, for students who come to higher education primarily to advance their careers quite often have no interests in either ideas or experience as such—and, indeed, sense that such interests would hamper their advancement in this society. What they want is a degree and the tricks of their trade.[5]

Under these conditions, then, both the significance of teaching as a university function and its potential contribution to the university community diminish, and too massive a claim for support should not be based on it. In the case of research, a quite different set of difficulties arises. There can be no question that our society, unless revolutionized, will continue to support and conduct the kind of research now done in our universities. Whether this is useful or leads to fundamental knowledge is irrelevant. Complex, literate societies usually maintain some costly and prestigious institution in which the kind of knowledge useful to their elites is codified, recorded, and interpreted. Such institutions take on a sacred character, and a threat to them is interpreted by the elite as a threat to the integrity of the society (which, from their point

[5] By far the most vivid and insightful treatment of what such purveying to an aspiring urban proletariat does to the joy of teaching is to be found in Herbert Gold's sadly neglected essay on a crisis in his career as an instructor at Wayne State University a few years ago—a crisis whose illustrative significance has been greatly enhanced by subsequent events in Detroit: "A Dog in Brooklyn, A Girl in Detroit: A Life Among the Humanities," *The Age of Happy Problems* (Dial Press: New York, 1962).

of view, it is). The Alexandrian priesthood must have been at least as outraged and dismayed by the burning of their library as the leading citizens of Canada were by the destruction of the computer at Sir George Williams University last year. When barbarians burn centers of learning, the end of an era may indeed be at hand; and the following era will possibly define knowledge differently and rebuild the library as a tourist attraction, if it recognizes such a social role as "tourist."

Since history is written by and from the point of view of ruling elites, especially before there is mass literacy, the destruction, physical or functional, of centers of learning is automatically recorded as a tragedy—though whether the quality of life in Alexandria was on the whole improved and liberated or impoverished by the burning of the library I do not know; it certainly delayed the birth of Lawrence Durell by nearly two millennia and marked, if it did not cause, the end of Alexandria as a major power.

If the United States is to continue its present course as a major power, it will continue to maintain knowledge factories whose product resembles that of the current multiversity. Such an institution will do what we call research, because in an open, technically advanced society empirical knowledge, which is the only kind useful for manipulating persons and objects in the environment, is the kind that becomes sacred. When an American speaks of "the advancement of knowledge" or "expanding the frontiers of learning," he almost always means the kind of learning that will enable him or his kind of people to control something or do something effective to somebody else: that is, science.

Scientific knowledge, in our society, is usually defined as morally neutral in itself; moral judgments may be made only about the uses to which knowledge is put, not about knowledge itself. This seems to me absurd. A moral judgment, though not a simple one, may be made about the *kind* of knowledge that makes it possible for me to think of a child as an object to be napalmed or of the manufacture of napalm as productive. It is not just our values nor our place in history that makes us not even wince at the idea that the *value* of our most gruesome armaments is included as part—and a very large part—of our gross national *product*. It is our epistemology as well—the character of what we regard as knowledge and respect as such—that has become an expression of our national character. This conception of knowledge also makes it possible for us to insist that people die later and in a somewhat different way than they would have otherwise, though so far no less frequently; and this, which we call modern science, is usually considered good. A complex moral judgment, then; but a moral judgment on the nature of science all the same.

It is clear that Western and especially American culture is locked into this empirical conception of knowledge, and equally clear that this favors the anthrodrome—those who enjoy doing and pushing more than feeling and being and reflecting on the process. The research function, then, is one more function of the university that favors them over the community-seekers. It is less clear, however, that the research function must be carried out within the same institution as the other functions of the university. This function, and this function alone, can dispense with the presence of young persons assigned the transitory and subordinate status of students. In many societies this separation is usual: The research institute has no teaching functions; the teaching institutions do not expect their staffs to make what we call contributions to knowledge—that is, to do research and publish it.

This separation, if it were real, would have a great deal to recommend it. Much research done in American universities is done there simply because this is cheaper and keeps it decentralized and out of sight. It is harder for a snoopy reporter to put the pieces together if the answer to what happened to all those sheep lies concealed under the scanty ivy of the University of Utah rather than in the Dugway laboratory itself. Now that such functions have become an awkward source of controversy for the universities, a reverse process has set in, one in which universities divest themselves of formal institutional connection with the research institutes and laboratories to which they now assign their more macabre military contracts—a device which seems hardly sufficient to protect them from complicity and will probably not even save them embarrassment. For this separation is quite unreal and within the context of American life and values probably cannot be made real.

The problem is again epistemological; empirical research is the only knowledge-function that has enough prestige, or is considered useful enough, to command genuine support in America. It is assumed, for example, that in a college devoted to teaching rather than research course-loads should be two or three times greater than in a university where the staff is expected to do research. But this assumption misses the whole point, which is that university teaching has come to be accepted as the kind of half-assed process it is because of the primacy of research; and to do it better means to do it entirely differently and probably in a much more leisurely, intimate, and unstructured way. The gain to be sought is in the quality of the relationship rather than in the number of units to be serviced. But no support for collegiate education on this scale is likely. Even if it were, the results would not be likely to be very promising for reasons Christopher Jencks and David Riesman make clear in *The Academic Revolution:* The highest prestige *colleges* in the country ought to be free to do the best teaching, being relatively less impoverished and having better trained faculty than the more marginal institutions.[6] But, in fact, they function as what Jencks

[6] Christopher Jencks and David Riesman, *The Academic Revolution* (Doubleday: Garden City, New York, 1968), pp. 20–27.

and Riesman call university colleges: that is, they orient their teaching, their grading, and their curricula to the demands of graduate schools and pride themselves on the number of people they send on successfully to the doctorate, which ties them securely to present departmental organization and precludes serious curricular experimentation which, again, would jeopardize the career interests of their faculty, the ambitions of their more striving students, and the college's prestige.

All the major functions of the university which the society endorses and supports are opposed to its function of providing a home and a place of their own for young men and women in which they can develop a sense of personal commitment and a basis for moral judgment. These, indeed, infuriate our society, which prefers decorum to morality and success to either. They distress and frighten the universities' officials because they threaten the universities' sources of support. These officials avoid the moral issue when they can; those few who have attempted to respond to it with a measure of understanding and respect for their students have often been driven from their posts by outraged and punitive governing boards—sometimes, as in the cases of the excellent Kerr-Meyerson administration at Berkeley and that of John Summerskill at San Francisco State under which the first real experimental college program of the decade was developed, at the point at which these administrations seemed clearly on the verge of a triumphant reconciliation among discordant factions, though on terms more generous than the governing board could stomach. Leadership of this quality is too rare, however, to have been much of a challenge to regents and trustees. Much more often, university officials have redefined attacks on the ethical position of their institutions as empirical problems of governance. This, I suppose, is why the present volume of papers has been commissioned.

Most efforts to solve this problem have taken the form of structural alterations: changes in the composition of policy-making bodies within the university and sometimes token representation of students on the governing board. These measures are desirable as ways of providing more status and dignity for students and more respect for them; indeed, there are few campuses beyond the most parochial in which student sentiment and values are ignored today as they were even at schools like Columbia or Swarthmore until two years ago. But such measures do not touch the heart of the difficulty, because the difficulty is not structural but moral.

The American university system, like Dr. Frankenstein and Dr. Faustus, is in trouble not because it has failed, but because it has succeeded; and succeeded in undertakings to which it would not have committed itself had it not relinquished moral responsibility in favor of empirical mastery in the first place. If this is too harsh an indictment, it is so for one reason only: that it attributes too much autonomy to the university. University faculty, especially, are inclined to be taken in by their own traditional, but increasingly deceptive pretense that they run the place. In fact, universities are run as America is run: indirectly, by a power structure that depends on the ambitions of the faculty and the lust of its individual members to be close to sources of power to induce it to organize itself so as to do what is expected of it. Power within the university aligns itself to power outside it.

QUESTIONS FOR DISCUSSION AND WRITING

1. In general, what is the function of the university in "an open society," according to Friedenberg? What is the relationship of the university as a "community" to what Friedenberg calls the university as an "anthrodrome"?
2. At the heart of Friedenberg's difficult essay would seem to be the "vocational function" of higher education. How does this function relate to the general theses of the essay and how does it relate to the university as you know it?
3. What generally seems to be Friedenberg's conclusion about "teaching" in our universities? About "research"? Do you agree with his conclusions? Explain.
4. Friedenberg observes that many of the repressive aspects of university life—for example, "the custom of exploiting students"—have "backfired" by making the students into "a viable subgroup." Do you agree? How is this related to Friedenberg's references to the university as a "community"?
5. Friedenberg offers the perhaps shocking suggestion (to some whites) that "black students, once they find themselves more at ease in what was never Zion, will join the jocks and repudiate their activist supporters." Is Friedenberg correct? Discuss.
6. What is Friedenberg's general position on the role of the university vis-à-vis black and other "disadvantaged" students?
7. Friedenberg raises the important point that "our society withholds adult status till after the human sexual prime so that the peak of erotic intensity occurs during college years." Comment on this phenomenon.
8. Friedenberg says that "scientific knowledge, in our society, is usually defined as morally neutral in itself; moral judgments may be made only about the uses to which knowledge is put, not about knowledge itself." What does this mean? Can you think of some examples to put this idea into perspective? Should the university develop a greater moral concern for the uses to which the knowledge it discovers is put? Explain.
9. Comment on the statement that "all the major functions of the university which society endorses and supports are opposed to its function of providing a home and a place for young men and women in which they can

develop a sense of personal commitment and a basis for moral judgment. These, indeed, infuriate our society, which prefers decorum to morality and success to either." Does this mean, for example, that society at large should not have a hand in the functions of the university? Explain.

10. Explain the significance of the observation that "the American university system, like Dr. Frankenstein and Dr. Faustus, is in trouble not because it has failed, but because it has succeeded."

11. Comment on Friedenberg's style in this essay—which might be described as a combination of very complex long sentences and academic words with an occasional switch into the vernacular, such as the phrase "the kind of half-assed process." Does this style complement the content of the essay? Explain.

John and Jean Kekes

Relevance and the Involvement of Intellectuals

Be relevant! Get involved! These commands are being issued today by some students and faculty in American academic and intellectual life with such fervor and intensity that they are becoming unquestioned imperatives. It has almost reached the stature of dogma that the intellectuals be relevant to the society in which they live and that intellectuals be compelled because of special talents and training to bring their authority to bear on the political state of contemporary society.

Indeed, the exhortation to the intellectual to become politically active derives from a tacit acceptance of the longstanding anti-intellectual tradition in America. The timidity and reluctance of American intellectuals to declare openly that they are doing something unique and worthwhile results in a readiness to give up their pursuits when the going gets tough. It is on such occasions that intellectual egalitarianism reaps its sad harvest.

There are, moreover, excellent arguments for maintaining not only that the intellectual has *no* special obligation to become involved, but that he has *less* of an obligation to do so than most of his fellow citizens.

Most intellectuals are academics, but few academics are intellectuals. The two differ in the range and scope of the ideas they handle. The academic specializes, whereas the intellectual attempts to relate important ideas of different fields in ways so that a comprehensive view of these pursuits emerges. This requires great knowledge of many fields, the time for entertaining the fundamental questions underlying them, and rare personality and training. It is one thing to be this sort of theorizer, but it is quite another to be an activist—to have the interest and ability to translate theory into practice. The two are only rarely and very exceptionally united. And so the intellectual, by his very nature, is likely to be a poor activist. (Although there are exceptions: e.g., Bacon, Lenin, and Trotsky.)

If the overwhelming majority of intellectuals cannot be activists, then to insist that they ought to be is senseless. Consider the inanity of wanting to undermine Marx's stature by pointing out that he spent too much time in the British Museum and too little on nudging into consciousness the dormant sentiments of the proletariat. Such ascription of moral obligation to be an activist completely misses the mark if it is ascribed to a person who, by his very nature, cannot be an activist and still make his unique contribution to society. The majority of intellectuals cannot be activists because by personality, talent, and training they are prepared for theorizing, not for translating theories into practice.

But might it not be said, that any person, intellectual or not, may be morally reprehensible for not being involved—for not being engaged in his capacity as a civilized human being? Perhaps a person's most important obligation to society is to act in such a way as to attempt to be a useful, contributing member of it. Whereas one of his primary obligations to himself is to act in such a way as to attempt to realize his own potentialities. Most people do not discharge their obligation to themselves by discharging their obligation to society. The intellectual, however, does. And herein lies the difference between the moral obligations of the intellectual and of most other citizens.

The intellectual's value for society lies in what he is and in what he does. In this respect, the intellectual is like the artist—and being either is a way of life. Neither of these is a job that one does so many hours a day, so many days a week. Intellectuals and artists thus differ from other people in respect to the all-pervasiveness and exclusiveness of their pursuits. While other people can discharge their obligation to society by becoming engaged and involved, without thereby jeopardizing the fulfillment of their obligation to themselves, intellectuals and artists cannot. What stands in the way of their meeting their obligation to themselves necessarily stands in the way of their meeting their obligation to society. If intellectuals were to obey the "moral imperative" to be activists, they would fail in their moral obligation to society and to themselves. What this imperative suggests is that intellectuals should cease doing what they ought to do, what needs doing, what only they do well, and engage instead in an activity for which they are incompetent. The imperative, thus, is not only ridiculous, it is also morally reprehensible. Nor is the imperative any more palatable because it is urged by intellectuals themselves; they at least should know better.

What happens, however, if the very conditions that allow the intellectual to function are threatened? Is there not some point—when there are threats to his environment, country, and culture—at which he must abandon his unique role and take to the barricades?

What, for example, are the obligations of the intellectual academic in a situation in which social and political pressures upon a university result in an attempt to curtail academic freedom—the freedom to create, to theorize, to engage in intellectual pursuits? Should he defend academic freedom actively by recalling publicly the past benefits derived from it, by calling attention to the implications that curtailment may have, and by reminding the critics of the principles upon which academic freedom rests? Or, should he produce those results that are the *raison d'être* of academic freedom? The appropriate defense of the intellectual when academic freedom is being threatened is to engage in the *use* of academic freedom. The intellectual is not the guardian of academic freedom; he is a justification for it. The responsibility for active defense in the face of social or political pressures rests with the person who is an academic and who is *also* politically and socially oriented in his motives and purposes.

Another kind of threat endangering the conditions necessary for an intellectual to function is that directed against his country from either external or internal forces. The outstanding example of a country internally threatened was that of Germany in the 1930's. What was the moral obligation of the German intellectual against the Nazis? Ought he to have remained as a hostile political activist or ought he to have left to function as an intellectual elsewhere? The choice was not between being an effective political activist in Germany and an effective intellectual elsewhere. The choice was rather between being an ineffective political activist and an effective intellectual. The reasonable decision is obvious, and many German intellectuals arrived at just that decision. Moreover, the values that Hitler was determined to destroy survived partly through the many German intellectuals in exile. The point that is being made here is not that the intellectual is morally reprehensible if he becomes a political activist when his country is threatened internally, but that he is *not* morally reprehensible if he seeks freedom to continue intellectual activity elsewhere.

But what if the threat against the country of the intellectual is external? What, for example, was the moral obligation of an English intellectual in the face of the impending Battle of Britain? He could have tried to ignore the external threat; he could have left the country; or he could have stayed to help in any way he could. The first alternative is impractical and hardly possible. The dilemma comes down to this: either he should have left the country or he should have stayed and given up his intellectual pursuits for whatever task was assigned to him. England's war effort would not have been appreciably undermined if a few hundred intellectuals had left, and the gain would have been incommensurate with what the loss might have been had England been defeated. But World War II was not just a conflict of martial forces, it was a conflict of ideologies. By leaving the country, intellectuals would have ensured that the war of ideologies continued even if the physical aspect of the war had been lost. To remove such assets from England as gold deposit and works of art was not thought to be reprehensible.

Intellectuals too are assets of a country, and no less valuable. Those intellectuals who chose to leave England were thus morally blameless.

If we look at a third kind of threat, one that is directed internally or externally against the culture as a whole, the intellectual at last nears the situation in which abandoning intellectual pursuits for the sake of involvement may be a matter of moral imperative. With regard to internal threats (such as a Graecophil Roman intellectual may have felt in contemplating the onslaught of Christianity), the intellectual clearly has a duty to continue to function as an intellectual and to restate, exemplify, and contribute to those values that are being assailed. If the threat to the culture is external and it is being levelled by the use of physical force, then, and only then, the intellectual may be obliged to become actively involved in the physical defense of the culture. The difference between this predicament and the previous one is that if the culture as a whole is threatened, there is no place of refuge to which the intellectual might retire to safeguard and propagate the values upon which the culture rests. Thus, only in this extreme situation is the intellectual morally obliged to be involved.

In the light of these reasons, one can easily see upon how shallow a ground rests the assumption that an intellectual is morally obliged to become a political activist as a result of the war in Vietnam. What sort of threat is represented by the Vietnam situation? The only reasonable interpretation is to argue that it is an internal threat against the United States. The way in which the war is handled, one might argue, undermines those very principles upon which this country is based, and upon which the possibility of functioning as an intellectual rests. But even if this were true, does it oblige the intellectual to become politically involved? On the contrary, it obliges him to continue his unique function, so that those values which are being undermined by the war continue to exist.

There should be protest against the war in Vietnam. But the intellectual can be far more effective in safeguarding the values that the protesters aim at protecting if, instead of marching, attending meetings, composing petitions, and organizing resistance, he continues to contribute to these values.

QUESTIONS FOR DISCUSSION AND WRITING

1. According to the Kekes, what basically should be the position of intellectuals in a university and in a time of social change? Under what very narrowly defined conditions might an intellectual be forced to become "involved"?
2. The authors make an important distinction between "academics" and "intellectuals." What is this distinction and how does it function in terms of the thesis of the whole essay? Is it a valid distinction? Explain.

3. The authors of this essay attribute the demand for intellectuals to "get involved" to "the long-standing anti-intellectual tradition in America." Discuss this argument.

4. What is meant by the statement that "the intellectual is not the guardian of academic freedom; he is a justification for it"? What is the relationship of this statement to the rest of the essay?

5. What is "academic freedom," according to the authors? How is it related to social involvement and social improvement?

6. What is your interpretation of the word "relevance"? How do the authors of this essay define the word?

7. In your opinion, what is or should be the relationship of the university to society? What is or should be the relationship of the intellectual to society and to the university?

Leslie Fiedler

Academic Irresponsibility

To argue in favor of freedom for the teacher seems at first the most pointless sort of preaching to the converted, since everybody—as everybody hastens to assure you—is already convinced. Difficult enough under the best of conditions, everybody explains, teaching would be virtually impossible without a large degree of liberty. But everybody then adds, at the point where piety ends and candor begins, that the teacher obviously must be "responsible" as well as free; the clear implication is that freedom is *limited* by responsibility—to which everybody else assents, with the sole exception, it sometimes seems, of me.

In my objections to responsibility, I find myself not only lonelier and lonelier but more and more distant from those I had long thought my natural allies. From my earliest reading years, I had understood that Babbitt was the enemy of freedom, and responsibility his hypocritical watchword. Of this I had been assured not only by Sinclair Lewis, who baptized him, but by John Dos Passos in *U.S.A.*, by James Thurber in *The Male Animal*, by the whole consort of writers who had sentimentalized and mythicized the early academic victims of Rotarians, chambers of commerce and boards of trustees—from Thorstein Veblen to Scott Nearing and innumerable other half-forgotten half heroes fired from university posts for defending Tom Mooney and Sacco and Vanzetti or for criticizing monopoly capitalism and the war.

The campaign of vilification and harassment directed against certain leftish academics in the time of Joe McCarthy seemed the climax and confirmation of the whole thing. After the total discrediting of McCarthy, when political liberty for professors was pretty generally won and Babbitts everywhere had gone into retreat, an occasional rear-guard action on their part seemed more comic and pathetic than sinister or threatening. Picking up, for instance, a Kiwanis Club pamphlet labeled "Freedom," I am tickled rather than dismayed to discover no reference to anything that I mean by freedom, only an appeal to teachers to transmit to the young "an understanding of responsible citizenship, principles of free enterprise and values of our spiritual heritage. . . ." "Free" as in enterprise, but "responsible" in everything; it is quite what the literature I grew up on taught me to expect—something comfortably unchanged in our disconcertingly changeable world.

There is, however, one area at least where the Babbitts, even in retreat, continue to pose a real threat to freedom—a threat because the academic community is on their side. When social behavior rather than politics is involved—especially in matters of sex or the use of banned drugs (associated inevitably with sex in the fantasies of the repressors) and especially when faculty members seem to advocate, or condone, or encourage or simply permit unconventional student practices in these matters—then the faculties of universities tend to speak the same language as the Kiwanis Club. And here I am eternally shocked and disheartened.

For almost a decade now, there has been instance after instance, from the notorious firing of Timothy Leary at Harvard, through the dismissal of certain young "homosexual" instructors at Smith, to the recent failure to rehire the poet Robert Mezey at Fresno State College. Often the real issues are camouflaged, as in Leary's case; the charge pressed was not that Leary had become a published advocate of LSD but that he failed to meet his classes regularly. Or they tend to be blurred, as in Mezey's case; the fact that he opposed the war in Vietnam and defended black power might suggest the recurrence of simple old-fashioned McCarthyism, were it not that thousands of academic opponents of the most unjust of American wars continue to be reappointed or promoted so long as they do not also happen to advocate changes in the existing marijuana laws.

Sometimes the underlying issues are totally hushed up, out of ostensible regard for the reputation of the victims, who, accepting dismissal in order to avoid scandal, provide their colleagues with the possibility of copping out; so that no advocate of academic freedom is called upon to take a principled stand on freedom for potheads or queers; no libertarian is forced to confront the limits of his own tolerance. I am aware of only a single case of this kind fought hard enough and far enough to compel the American Association of University Professors to rethink its own position, defining—from a teacher's presumable point of view—the competing claims of freedom and responsibility: the now nearly forgotten Koch case.

On March 18, 1960, Leo Koch, an assistant professor of biology at the University of Illinois, wrote a letter to the campus paper in which, after some reflections—more banal and less witty than he obviously thought them—on "a Christian code of ethics already decrepit in the days of Queen Victoria," he concluded:

> With modern contraceptives and medical advice readily available at the nearest drugstore, or at least a family physician, there is no valid reason why sexual intercourse should not be condoned among those sufficiently mature to engage in it without social consequences and without violating their own codes of morality and ethics.
>
> A mutually satisfactory sexual experience would eliminate the need for many hours of frustrating petting and lead to much happier and longer-lasting marriages among our younger men and women.

Whether the course of action that Professor Koch advocated would, indeed, have led to the happiness and marital stability he promised remains yet to be proved, since he inspired no general movement to lead openly the sort of sexual life that many students, whether "sufficiently mature" or not, have been leading covertly, anyhow. If Koch was espousing anything new in his manifesto, it was presumably the abandonment of concealment and that unconfessed pact by which students make it possible for their teachers to pretend they do not know what their students pretend they do not know those teachers know.

Yet his letter had results, all the same, for it brought about a chain of events that ended in his being fired. And his firing, in turn, produced a series of statements and counterstatements about morality and freedom from the president of the university, its board of trustees, the faculty senate and many individual members of the teaching staff. This intramural debate was followed by a prolonged investigation under the auspices of the American Association of University Professors of what had become by that time "the Koch case," an investigation not finally reported on in full until three years later. The report, which appeared in the *AAUP Bulletin* of March 1963, reveals a division of opinion among college professors themselves, symptomatic of a confusion on the issues involved, that not only divides one academic colleague from another but splits the individual minds of many Americans inside the universities and out.

More interesting to me, however, and more dismaying than any of the disagreements, was a substantial area of agreement between the president and the board of trustees of the University of Illinois (who thought Koch should be fired), the faculty senate of that institution (who thought he should only be reprimanded) and Committee A of the A.A.U.P., the professed guardians of academic freedom (who thought the whole case should have been thrown out of court because of lack of due process). All four agreed that Koch was guilty of a "breach of academic responsibility" and that, regardless of his guilt or innocence, his academic freedom, like everyone else's, was and should have been limited by the academic responsibility that he was accused of having flouted. What academic responsibility means was nowhere very clearly defined in the dispute but was apparently understood by everyone involved to signify an obligation on the part of any professor to keep his mouth shut or only moderately open in cases where there is a clear danger of offending accepted morality; i.e., public opinion.

But how odd it was to find in the conservative and anti-intellectual camp a committee specifically charged with the protection of professors' rights—rights which the committee has often unyieldingly defended. What, then, moved it this time to grant that ". . . we can hardly expect academic freedom to endure unless it is matched by academic responsibility"? Surely, the topic of Koch's letter had something to do with it, and not merely the fact that his thoughts were neither well reasoned nor cogently expressed. If all cases of academic freedom involved the justification of documents as dignified and compelling as, say, Milton's *Areopagitica*, to defend liberty would be as easy as to attack it; but this, as the A.A.U.P. must have learned in its long career, is far from the truth. No, it was the subject of Koch's expostulation that made the difference; for when sex and students are simultaneously evoked, even the hardiest campus civil libertarian seems willing to cry "responsibility" with all the rest.

And the larger community has sensed this, moving in to attack—even when political motives play a considerable role—only when sex and drugs are involved. The young instructors at Michigan State University who helped edit a radical magazine called *Zeitgeist* may have offended their colleagues and administrators in many ways; but when their contracts were not renewed, a year or so ago, it was only the dirty words they had printed that were marshaled as evidence against them. And when, some years before that, Mulford Sibley, a well-known pacifist and political dissident, was brought under attack at the University of Minnesota, what was quoted against him was a speech in which he suggested that the university might be healthier if it could boast "a student Communist club, a chapter of the American Association for the Advancement of Atheism, a Society for the Promotion of Free Love . . . and perhaps a nudist club."

Predictably enough, communism and atheism tended to be soft-pedaled in the accusations brought against him, which lingered most lovingly over the fact that he was "agitating for nudist clubs" and added, apparently as the final proof of his perfidy, that "Dr. Sibley assigned books to his students resembling 'Lady Chatterley and Her Love Affairs.'" I know how disabling such a charge can be in academic circles, since, in an early encounter of my own with a really concerted effort to silence me in the classroom (the only time I ever really ran into trouble before the recent attempt to manufacture a case against me on the grounds of "maintaining a premise where marijuana is used"), I was accused not only of contempt for my then-fellow Montanans but also of having written a "dirty" poem called *Dumb Dick* and a "dirty"

story called *Nude Croquet,* which was "subsequently banned in Knox-
ville, Tennessee." Alas, some of my former colleagues, willing enough
to stand with me on political grounds, were shaken by being informed
that I was a "dirty writer."

Pornography and nudity, along with trafficking in drugs and indulging
in homosexuality, as well as refusing to condemn any or all of these
to students, are the stock charges in latter-day assaults against the freedom of the teacher by elements in the business community sophisticated
enough to know that in our time, old-fashioned accusations of being
Red or "soft on Reds" are likely to be laughed out of the court of
public opinion and have no status at all in courts of law. But there
are statutes that can be invoked against offenses of the former sort,
as in the recent police harassment of Leonard Wolf, a member of the
English department of San Francisco State College, charged with "contributing to the delinquency of minors."

Wolf is the founder of Happening House, an institution set up to
maintain a dialog between the kind of kids who inhabit the Haight-
Ashbury district of San Francisco and the local academic community.
During a conference on the problem of runaways, some of those kids,
members of a performing dance group, took off all their clothes on
stage. Wolf, who was the most convenient adult on the premises, was
arrested. He was subsequently tried and acquitted because the prosecution could not prove him responsible for the students' disrobing, but
from the start, the intent of the police seems to have been quite clearly
to impugn Wolf both as the founder of Happening House and as a
teacher. Why else charge him with acting in a way that "causes, tends to
cause or encourages unknown juveniles to lead immoral or idle lives"?
Whatever college officials thought of his classroom performance or his
outside activities, a court conviction would make him a criminal in their
eyes—and, as such, his position in the college, as well as his status
in the community, would be endangered. And just as clearly, it wasn't
only Wolf who was being put on trial, but all teachers who, insofar
as they are true to their profession, seek to release their students from
parochialism and fear, thus laying themselves open to charges of "corrupting the young" or "contributing to the delinquency of minors." A
printed statement from the Leonard Wolf defense recognizes this
fact—though it states the dilemma ineptly and misleadingly by insisting
that in his case, "The limits of any teacher's responsibility are at stake"
and that "If the attack on Professor Wolf proves successful . . . the
limits of responsibility will have been unfairly extended in the service
of repressive interests."

One cannot effectively fight an opponent whose language, along with
its assumptions, has been uncritically accepted. And to grant—even im-
plicitly—that there are just and proper limits somewhere, sometimes,
to the teacher's freedom is to give the game away to those ready and

eager to seize any show of weakness on the teacher's part. This is especially dangerous these days, when we are threatened on two sides, not
just on one, as we have long been accustomed. On the one hand, there
are the traditional "repressive interests," plus the courts and cops whom
they largely control, to whom a free faculty seems always on the verge
of going over to the enemy; i.e., the young, whom they think of as
swinging back and forth between an unwholesome flight from reality
and untidy demonstrations in the streets. And, on the other hand, there
are the young themselves, or at least the revolutionaries among them,
to whom the much-vaunted "academic freedom" of their teachers seems
only a subterfuge, a cover-up for their subservience to the *real* enemy;
i.e., the old, who, if they do not actually wage imperialist war and exploit
labor, apologize for both.

I sit at the moment looking mournfully at an "Open Letter" directed
to the faculty at the University of Sussex, an English university in which
I spent last year as a visiting professor. The document is signed by
"The February 21 Committee," a group whose chief political activity
was throwing a can of red paint over a speaker from the American
Embassy who had attempted to defend United States intervention in
Vietnam. An early paragraph reads, in part: "Students say 'free inquiry'
or 'free speech' mean that academics must permit their institution to
be used for any purpose, this freedom ends logically in irresponsibility. . . ." Syntax and punctuation have broken down a little, but the
meaning is clear—and disheartening. Whether Kiwanis Clubber,
A.A.U.P. member or Maoist student, one touch of responsibility makes
them all kin to one another, and alien to me.

Yet there is a difference, of course, between the Babbitts and the
enragés, those who boast themselves sane and those who like to think
of themselves as mad. Both demand restrictions on political freedom,
one from the right and one from the left; but the students, at least,
are on the side of erotic and imaginative freedom, in favor of love
and dreams—and when such issues are involved or can be evoked, the
free professor will find them on his side. In that area, indeed, they
are more dependable allies than his own colleagues, since even the most
liberal professors have tended to be equivocal on the subject of social,
as opposed to intellectual, freedom, for both students and themselves.
To the young, more important than the freedom to read what books
or take what courses they please is the freedom to make love as they
please; and it was therefore quite proper that the recent student revolt
in France was touched off at the University of Nanterre by protest
over restricted visiting privileges between boys' and girls' dormitories.

This fundamental inconsistency of viewpoint toward social rather than
academic freedom has tended to sap the integrity of certain faculty,
and sowed a deepening distrust in the minds of students, who, in response, have been on occasion as cavalier about the political rights of

their teachers as their teachers have been about their personal liberties. But there is an even more fundamental source of confusion in the definition of responsibility that the academic community—professors first of all, and now the students—has accepted, without sufficient wariness, from the larger community that surrounds and often resents it.

Once the teacher has granted the theory that responsibility equals restriction, restraint, censorship, taboo, he has lost in advance all those "cases" to which he must in due course come. At best, he commits himself to endless wrangles about exactly where freedom (understood as the right to express what he believes without hindrance) yields to responsibility (understood as the obligation to curtail his expression), lest he offend the taste, the conventions or the religious, political and moral codes of the community that sustains him.

There is no way out of such wrangles and not much point in going on to further debates about who (the teacher, the community or some impartial referee) is to draw the line between freedom and responsibility, once these have been postulated as opposites. And surely there is even less point in debating after the fact how harshly the "irresponsibles" are to be treated, whether by a lopping of heads or a mere slapping of wrists; i.e., whether they are to be dismissed or reprimanded. I propose, therefore, to define responsibility in quite a different way—as a matter of fact, in two quite different ways—in order to put the problem in a new light and deliver everyone from the frustration and ennui of having endlessly to rehash the old arguments.

Let me begin with a positive definition of "academic responsibility" as the teacher's obligation to *do* something, rather than not to. The teacher—not exclusively, perhaps, but, without doubt, especially—has a single overwhelming responsibility: the responsibility to be *free,* which is to say, to be what most men would call *irresponsible.* For him, freedom and responsibility are not obligations that cancel each other out but one and the same thing; and this unity of academic freedom and academic responsibility arises from the teacher's double function in our society: first of all, to extend the boundaries of knowledge by questioning *everything,* including the truths that most men at any given point consider sacred and timeless; and, finally, to free the minds of the young, so that they can continue the same task beyond what he himself can imagine.

I shall not linger over the traditional "research" function of the teacher, since its necessity is granted, with whatever secret reservations, by almost everyone except certain backward students, much given to complaining that their teachers spend more time on research than on them—not understanding that there would be nothing for those teachers to give them if independent investigation and lonely meditation were ever suspended or drastically curtailed. Thorstein Veblen, prototype of the free teacher, thought it was a mistake to attempt to combine in a single person the schoolmaster and the scholar; but American universities have long since made the decision to try, and it is incumbent on the scholar-schoolmaster to be clear in his own mind, and to make clear to everyone else concerned, the priorities of his commitments. Few of them have been as candid about it as was Robert Frost, himself a schoolmaster for some 50 years, who always insisted from the platform that the teacher's first duty was to himself, his second to his subject matter and only his third to the student. And no one who begins with an understanding of the free teacher's peculiar obligation to the free student could possibly challenge this order.

The problem to begin with is: What can, and what should be, taught? From that start, it was clear to me that teaching was a passion, not a science, and that methods, therefore, are meaningless in the classroom, that lesson plans and pedagogical strategy are vanity and illusion. But it has taken me nearly three decades of teaching to realize that even the subject matter one teaches is quickly—and, in most cases, quite correctly—forgotten, gone, certainly, with the last exam. It should no longer be considered a scandalous secret that the students believe they are hiding from teachers—or vice versa—that course subject matter is at best optional, at worst totally irrelevant.

What is required of the teacher is not that he impart knowledge but that he open up minds, revealing to his students possibilities in themselves that they had perhaps not even suspected, and confirming in them a faith in their own sensibilities and intelligence; not suffering their foolishness or indulging their errors, but all the time revealing to them the double truth that, though the student can often be wrong, he has, like his teacher, the *right* to be wrong; and that, if he is willing to live a life of intellectual risk, he may someday know more, see further and feel more acutely than any of the elders of the community, including his teachers. It is the credo of the free and truly "irresponsible" teacher that no truth except this (not even the ones he most dearly believes in) is final, since the advance of human thought is potentially unlimited.

Such a teacher addresses his students, confronts them, engages with them, in the hope that they will someday go beyond the limitations of vision built into him by the limitations of his training and his time; and that they will even escape the trap of believing that their new vision is a final one, to be imposed forever after on the generations who succeed them. My ideal teacher must teach his students, in short, to be free—which is something quite different from persuading them to write in their notebooks, "Be free!," since freedom cannot be acquired by rote any more than it can be established by law. Freedom cannot be taught by preaching it—as, by writing this, I have betrayed myself into doing—but by acting it out, living it in full view. Once we have realized that the teacher is not just a guide, much less a substitute parent or a charming entertainer (though he can be all of these things, too, if he is so moved), but a model; and that what is learned in the classroom is *him*, the teacher, we will understand that the teacher must become a model of the free man.

And yet how many of our own teachers do we remember as having been even in aspiration, much less in fact, anything like free? How many do we recall with love for having freed us from those fears and doubts about ourselves and our world that we brought with us into school, inextricably intertwined with our ignorance and bravado? There have been only a handful among the scores I encountered in my own school career: one or two in high school, none at all in college, and one in graduate school, whom I cannot forbear naming. Author of once-admired but now-forgotten poems and a splendid book about the shape of his own life, *The Locomotive God*, William Ellery Leonard once gave me, by his splendid example, certain illusions about what teaching and teachers were like that brought me into the university in the first place; and then left me, with even more splendid tact, to find out the truth for myself.

But why have so many, so large a majority not merely of my teachers but of everybody's teachers, failed in their obligation to choose to be free? It is tempting, but finally unsatisfactory to say, in easy cynicism: Well, everyone fails at everything, so why not they? Certainly there are pressures on them from all sides to be of "service" to the community as a whole, or to the past, to the present, to God, to the revolution, etc. Wherever the free teacher turns, he confronts men, sometimes his own colleagues, convinced that the function of the university is not to free the mind but to inculcate a set of values, to indoctrinate or—as we say when somebody else's values are concerned—to brainwash the student.

But the wielders of such pressures are, in a sense, not hard to resist, especially when they speak from the conservative tradition; since there are habits of response built into most professors from earliest youth that stir a reflex of resistance against movements to ban books by, say, Allen Ginsberg and William Burroughs on the one hand, or by Che Guevara and Mao Tse-tung on the other, or to fire those who ask students to read them. Whatever our disagreements with the lovers of such literature, we tend to feel them on our side. No, the most conspicuous failure of professors in this regard has been their refusal to protect the dissident right-wingers among them under attack from antilibertarians on our side. Surely one of the most scandalous events of recent academic history has been the quiet dismissal of a distinguished rightist teacher of political science from an equally distinguished Ivy League college, whose own silence was bought by buying up his contract and whose colleagues' silence apparently did not have to be bought at all.

Obviously, those who advocate reticence or "responsibility" from our side are more insidious—and sometimes, it would appear, impossible to resist. For it is our loyalty, rather than our timidity, on which such academic enemies of "irresponsibility" insist: asking us to limit ourselves (lest we give aid and comfort to a common opponent) in the free investigation, say, of the interconnections between the homosexual revolution and the first stages of the civil rights movement, or the importance of anti-Semitism and racism in the later black-power movement. Similarly, they urge us not to take away from the progressive forces certain symbolic heroes of the historical left—not, for instance, to follow up the evidence that at least Sacco, and possibly Vanzetti as well, was guilty as charged in the famous case that mobilized most decent men on their side; and that many of the organizers of the protests against their condemnation already knew the fact and strategically concealed it.

And when the voices that plead with us to lie a little about the importance of Negroes in our history, or to mitigate a little the harsh truth about the last country to betray some revolution in which we once thought we believed, are the voices of our own students, the voices of the young—how even harder it is to resist. We know that their cause, too, will be betrayed, as all causes are ultimately betrayed, but it seems churlish and unstrategic to tell them so; their strength and weakness is precisely not to know this, as our strength and weakness is to know it. And these strengths and weaknesses are complementary, make social life and intercourse between the generations not merely possible but necessary. Why, then, should we not lie to them a little when they come to us, as they do between periods of absolute rejection?

In a way, we are better off, safer, from our own point of view and theirs, when they turn their backs on us, muttering, "Old men, all we want you to do for us is *die!*" But a moment later, they return (being in need of uncles and grandfathers if not fathers: Marcuses and McLuhans and Norman O. Browns), crying, "Underwrite, sanction our revolt, tell us we are righter than you!" Indeed, how could they fail to be righter than we are still, wrong as we were at their age? But it is not our function as free teachers to tell them only how they are right; it is also imperative that we say (at the risk of being loved less, even of finally losing their ear altogether) how they are wrong—what in their movement, for instance, threatens the very freedom that makes it possible, and what threatens to freeze into self-righteousness.

Spokesmen for the "future" forget that, even as they fight for it, the "future" quickly becomes the present, then the past; and that soon they are only fighting for yesterday against the proponents of the day before yesterday. This is why the teacher dedicated to freedom must tell them *right now* the same thing he tells the Babbitts when they howl down or propose to ban some speaker, some uncongenial idea: If any kind of truth or pursuit of truth—however misguided, however wrong—seems threatening to a cause we espouse, it is time to re-examine that cause, no matter how impressive its credentials. It is also to ourselves, of course, that we're speaking, since without constantly reminding ourselves of this simple principle we will yield to some pressure group, right, left or center. But even taken together, such groups are not our deepest and most dangerous enemy.

What gets us, as teachers, into final trouble is the enemy of our freedom that ordinarily we do not perceive at all: inhibiting forces that are as impersonal and omnipresent and invisible as our total environment or our very selves. Indeed, they are a large and growing part of that total environment, especially in the United States, where more and more education for more and more people remains an avowed goal of society. There are, however, inhibitory and restrictive tendencies built into the very school system to which almost everyone born in America is condemned by the fact of his birth—condemned beyond the possibility of appeal, since what he may feel as a prison was dreamed for him by his forebears as utopia.

For better or worse, in any event, young Americans these days find themselves sentenced by law to a term lasting from their fourth or fifth birthday to their sixteenth or seventeenth—and, by custom and social pressure, to a good deal more: time added, as it were, for good behavior. But though students in large numbers are dimly aware of all this, they have tended to resist it as outlaws rather than as revolutionaries; i.e., to drop out rather than to raise as a slogan, an immediate demand, the right not to go to school. Students have been primarily—and quite properly, as far as it goes—concerned with failures of the school system to provide them with the kinds of freedom to which that system itself is theoretically pledged: the right to demonstrate or petition, to participate and advise, to control in part, at least, their own destinies *in* the schools; but the existence of those schools, and even their traditional function, they have largely taken for granted.

To me, however, the root problem, the essential restriction of freedom, seems compulsory education itself—on both the primary and the secondary levels, where it is enforced by statute and truant officers; and on the higher levels, where it is, more and more broadly, customary and enforced by the peer group plus parents and teachers. Everything begins with the assumption by the community (or some auxiliary private enterprise) of the role traditionally played in the lives of the young by their families, aided and abetted by medicine men, prophets or kindly passing strangers; and is confirmed beyond hope of reform when that community sets up ever more rigid and bureaucratized institutions to do that job for it.

From this initial requirement follows most of what is dangerously restrictive throughout the school system: the regulation of every moment of a student's day (especially in high schools) and a good part of a student's nights (especially for female students, all the way to the university level). This involves, first of all, required attendance, tardiness reports, classes artificially divided into periods and rung off and on

by a centrally controlled bell system, proctored examinations and blackmail by grades. And it implies, in the second place, a host of "disciplinary
regulations" beginning with the banning of cigarettes on school grounds,
or alcohol at school dances, or pot and the pill in dormitories, and
ending with petty decrees—totally unconnected to the laws of the larger
community—about the length of skirts and pants and hair. Hair, especially, seems the concern of school authorities, whether on the head
or on the face—as if somewhere in the collective mind of those authorities, the image persisted of youth as a sort of Samson who to be enslaved
must be shorn.

Students have, of course, protested against this; and a good deal of
what moves them, plus more that might or should move them, has been
beautifully formulated by Edgar Z. Friedenberg, beginning with a book
titled *The Vanishing Adolescent*. But their cry of "No more *in loco
parentis*" is undercut by their clearly contradictory wishes on this score.
In general, they seem to want the schools to maintain a certain parental
role in warding off police prosecution, yet to surrender that role in
maintaining internal discipline. In any case, the protesters do not begin
far enough back; for the American school system is essentially—by
definition and tradition—*in loco parentis*. And nothing fundamental is
solved by persuading it to become a permissive rather than an authoritarian parent—that is, to make itself more like students' actual parents
and less like their actual grandparents.

It is, alas, precisely those "permissive" parents who have made the
whole school system, from kindergarten to university, what it is, insisting
that it act out for them the dark side of their own ambivalence toward
their children—be the bad parent they feel guilty for not being—and
for wanting to be. If our schools are, in fact, totalitarian under their
liberal disguises, more like what the sociologists call "total institutions"
(jails, mental hospitals, detention camps) than small democratic communities or enlarged families, this is because the parents of the students
in them *want* them to be what they are. Certainly any parent, any
full adult in our society, is at least dimly aware of the tendency in
himself and his neighbors to project upon children and adolescents sexual
and anarchic impulses denied in himself. These impulses he asks his
children both to act out and to be blamed for, relieving him of his
own double guilt—and providing in its place the double pleasure of
vicarious self-indulgence and the condemnation of sin.

In addition, there is the sexual jealousy that inevitably troubles those
home-tied by jobs or children, or oppressed by the menopause and the
imminence of death when they confront others just emerging into puberty, as well as the desperation of those unable to persuade their children of the value of moral codes in which they only theoretically believe—a desperation that ends in calling out the law to enforce what
love could not achieve. And, finally, there is the strange uncertainty
of our society about just when a child becomes an adult (whatever

that elusive term may mean)—at puberty, at 16, 18, 21; when he votes, drinks legally, goes into the Army or simply becomes capable of reproducing himself. Out of this uncertainty emerge those absurd social regulations that turn the girls' dormitory into a police state, the rules whose goal is to keep those we claim we have to regulate (because they are still "children") from getting pregnant; i.e., from proving to us that biologically, at least, they are fully mature.

Small wonder, then, that our schools and universities have become, like our jails and hospitals and asylums, institutions whose structure works against their own avowed ends—leading not to the free development of free men but to the depersonalization of the student, to his conversion into a code number and an IBM card punched full of data, a fact that he may forget in the midst of the small pleasures that punctuate his boredom but of which he is reminded once, twice, even three times a year by the degrading rituals of examination and registration. The damage done the student by this system we have all begun to notice, as the resentment of his indignity has driven him to construct barricades and hurl fire bombs; but the similar damage done to his teachers we tend to ignore, since they typically respond with silence or statements read only to one another at annual meetings.

It is not merely that the teacher, too, is regulated, right down to such trivial matters as wearing a tie or smoking in class, but that also—and, finally, more critically—he, like the prison guard or the asylum attendant, becomes the prisoner of the closed world he presumably guards, a world in which he begins talking at the ping of one bell and stops at the clang of another, meanwhile checking attendance, making sure no one cheats or lights a cigarette under a NO SMOKING sign or consumes hard liquor or drugs or, God forbid, takes off his clothes in public. All of this, however, makes him a jailer or a cop, who notoriously resembles his charges; and insofar as he resists, turns him into a hypocrite, acknowledging only the infractions that someone else—the press, a planted police spy, an indignant parent—has noticed first.

How can the teacher who accepts such a system talk freedom to the students before him? Or how can he demand it for himself—academically, politically, personally—at the very moment he is denying it—socially, erotically—to those he asks to emulate his model? The historical struggle of teachers for what has been called "academic freedom"—that is, their own freedom—has been impugned throughout by their hypocrisy. No community, not even a school, can exist one tenth absolutely free and nine tenths half slave. It is an unendurable fraud, of which most of us manage to remain absurdly unaware, until some notorious "case"—the Leary case, the Koch case, the Mezey case—forces us to confront it, to confront the contradiction in ourselves. By then, however, it is too late.

Inevitably, at that point we tend to compromise or totally betray for one of us the principles we have already learned to compromise and betray for the students to whom we are, after ourselves, chiefly responsible. And here we have come, at long last, to responsibility. To avoid the word at this juncture would be as abject as having taken refuge in it earlier, since to be responsible means, in the new context, not to be restricted, which is to say, less free—but to be *answerable,* which is to say, more free.

Until a man has learned to be truly free, he cannot begin to be responsible in this deep etymological sense of the word, since the only thing for which a teacher is properly answerable is his own freedom, his necessary prior *ir*responsibility. A slave or a man under restraint, an indoctrinated indoctrinator, a civil servant brainwashed to brainwash others, is answerable for nothing. No matter what charges are brought against him, he can plead innocent; for he is the agent of another, a despicable tool, just another Eichmann, dignified beyond his worth by being brought to the dock.

The free teacher, on the other hand, must not merely suffer but welcome, even invite, criticism of what he espouses and teaches, for his job is to change the minds of the young—which those in established positions seem to view as a kind of "corruption." For him, freedom does not mean freedom from consequences; he takes, as the old Spanish proverb has it, what he wants but he pays his dues. Wanting nothing free of charge, he denies to no one the right to disagree with what he says, to criticize, to try to rebut, even to threaten sanctions. He must always be willing to argue against all comers the basic case for his freedom, which is never, and can never be, won finally and forever. But he must also be prepared to defend—one by one and each on its own merits—all of the tenets, views, opinions and analyses he finds himself free to offer.

Above all, when his ideas are proved wrong, to his own satisfaction, in the debate with those who challenge him, he must feel free to confess his error without in any way diminishing his right to have held those ideas; for he has never had any real freedom at all unless he has been free from the start to be wrong and unless he remains free to the end to change his mind. If, in the debate he has occasioned, however, he continues to believe in his position, he must—with all the assurance that comes of knowing his fallibility as well as that of his opponents—continue to maintain that position. It does not matter at all if a majority is against him, or even everybody; for even everybody has, on occasion, turned out to be wrong, and he is, in any case, not answerable to a popular vote.

He dares not betray the facts as he has learned from his teachers and his colleagues to determine them, but he must always be aware that those "facts" exist finally in his own head. And he is equally answerable to posterity—which means, for a teacher, his students—not those before him at any moment but those yet to come; best of all, those not yet born; and these, too, he must remember live only inside his skull. It is to the unborn, then, that the free man, the true teacher, is finally answerable; but it is the living students, their parents and the community that he inhabits rather than the one he dreams, that judge him and can make him suffer. If that community—parents or students, or both—desires to visit sanctions on him, he must not pretend surprise or feel dismay.

Yet they are not hard to please, really, the spokesmen of the past or those of the present; all they ask is a show of subservience either to long-established conventions or to the very latest life style. Only an allegiance to the ever-receding future dismays both; for, driven to imagine a time to come, the responsibles, both old and young, feel their authority slipping from them as they realize that someday they will be dead. But it is precisely this realization that exhilarates some men, making them feel free enough to be irresponsible, irresponsible enough to be free.

QUESTIONS FOR DISCUSSION AND WRITING

1. Does Fiedler's concept of "academic freedom" differ from that suggested in the preceding essay by the Kekes? Explain.
2. What relationship does Fiedler draw between "freedom" and "responsibility"? Between "freedom" and "irresponsibility"? What, in general, is Fiedler's conception of a "free teacher"?
3. Fiedler says that a teacher should "open up minds, revealing to his students possibilities in themselves that they had perhaps not even suspected, and confirming in them a faith in their own sensibilities and intelligence." Discuss Fiedler's opinion. What effect might such an approach to teaching have upon "the status quo"?
4. What are your own feelings about "the Koch case," as Fiedler describes it? Was Koch guilty of "a breach of academic responsibility"?
5. Do you agree with Fiedler that the cry for "responsibility" is frequently synonymous with "restriction, restraint, censorship, taboo"? Explain your answer.
6. What, according to Fiedler, is "freedom," and why does he argue that it cannot be acquired by rote memorization?
7. Why are sexual and social matters so frequently stressed when people condemn a man for his political views? And what makes "sex and drugs," in particular, such volatile issues, on campus and elsewhere? What is the relationship of this concern to the "sexual jealousy" which Fiedler says many adults feel toward the young?
8. In your opinion, is the critical examination of ideas and the exploration of knowledge more or less important than responsibility to the governing powers of society and/or the university? Explain.

Milton Mayer

ROTC: The Lower Learning

It was quiz night in Sophomore English. My moppets had their little beaks in the *Iliad,* and the classroom was quiet. I sat there scratching my sores and tutelarily wondering if college students still wondered what they were supposed to "get" out of five hundred pages of barbarous battle-cries, hideous war-whoops, and rebel yells. The silence was suddenly rent (as Homer would say) by barbarous battle-cries, hideous war-whoops, and rebel yells from somewhere inside the building; and just as suddenly restored. It was as if we had touched down on the plain of Troy and then taken off again.

The next morning I received a call from Major Veepings of the Reserve Officers' Training Corps, who asked if he might speak with me. I told him that I was at his armed service, and he said: "Professor Mayer, I want to apologize on behalf of the ROTC for the disturbance in the building last night, and to ask if it would be possible for you to find another building for your evening class. You see, sir, we have a Counterinsurgency course on Tuesday evenings, and Colonel Murgatroyd is afraid that some of your students might misunderstand what is going on." ("You mean," I said to myself, "understand.")

I told the Major that I would withdraw my forces, thanked him for the use of the barracks, and decided to do something I had not done for going on fifty years, namely, think about ROTC (or Rot-cee, as the kids call it).

What I had thought about Rot-cee going on fifty years ago wasn't flattering. Unpossessed of the martial virtues, I reprehended them. Besides, the country I grew up in was not a martial country. In those days, the statutory quota of 100,000 was the large standing army which President Washington had opposed as "dangerous to our liberties." But the recruiters on Skid Row could not find anything like 100,000 end-of-the-line derelicts to fill the quota. In the Preparedness campaign of 1916 the Secretary of what was then called War had to appeal to restaurants to remove their No Soldiers Admitted signs.

After the defeat of Kaiser Bill the citizen army (average schooling:

four years) was demobilized. But the dying echoes persisted into the early 1920s. When I reached high school in 1921 the ROTC was attracting the filling-station set of the future; a few years later, not even them. When I entered the University of Chicago in 1925 everybody who was anybody was kicking it. (Chicago had never let it in.) The immigrant hatred of "European" militarism seemed to have survived the raptures of the Great War.

World War II was strictly business. By 1943 the colleges and universities were wholly converted to war training, war research, and war production. Kill-or-die for real put the kibosh on Rot-cee. But in 1948 the United States of America adopted peacetime conscription (which Woodrow Wilson had called "the root evil of Prussianism"). ROTC immediately revived, with an instant correlation between enrollment and the Berlin airlift, Korea, and the Cuban missile crisis. Vietnam sent it soaring. "Increasing draft calls motivate additional men to apply to ROTC," says the commandant at Berkeley, where enrollment leapt from 253 to 795 during the great escalation of 1965–66. Last spring, with graduate students callable under the new draft regulations, many units reported a 100 per cent increase in applications.

If, in the 1950s, you did not especially want to canoe the Yalu River or, in the 1960s, explore the Mekong Delta, and you could not pass a science course, you enrolled in Military Science and got a guaranteed deferment. It was axiomatic (as it still is) that you could not flunk Military Science; an axiom supported by the Army's own advertisement that its six-week summer training camp "takes the place of the two-year ROTC Basic Course." If you hup-hup for two years, and then sign on for two years more of five fifty-minute periods a week, you can hardly miss an ROTC Scholarship which pays your tuition, books, and laboratory expenses, and $50 a month besides.

This doesn't mean that your mother raised her boy to be a soldier; on the contrary, it means a fighting chance of not fighting. In 1962, the compulsory ROTC programs (which forty per cent of the students always found one way or another of ducking) had a seventy per cent dropout after the required two years. Not now; four years of being fired at with blanks by college chums has a certain contemporary charm. Draft-age patriots would rather be red, white, or blue than dead.

The once high hope of getting rid of Rot-cee has gone glimmering. As a better 'ole than Vietnam it is cemented into the campuses of 250 colleges and universities across the country. It has, of course, no more to do with the higher learning than it ever had. It has to do with marching up the hill, and, if you haven't had your head shot off at the top, down again.

It does not produce good officers, because virtue is not absorbed through the soles of the feet. The only way the Army—any Army—can get good men to be trained as officers is to dragoon them. And this it can't do on the campus. Beginning in 1923 (when the University of Wisconsin threw it out) compulsory ROTC faded from all of the better (and most of the worse) institutions at the rate of twelve units a year. It faded fighting, though, until, the attrition unabating, the Army finally "approved of" voluntary programs in spite of the fact that the changeover means an instantaneous drop of never less than eighty per cent of the enrollment. Two years before the compulsory program was dropped by the University of Massachusetts in 1962, it was opposed in a student survey by seventy-five per cent of the males *and by ninety per cent of the conscript cadets.* In wartime 1942, eighty per cent of the draftees selected for Officer Candidate School were college graduates; less than six per cent of them were Rot-cee products.

Sixty-one of the ROTC units—the big ones—are in the land-grant colleges, established by the Morrill Act with Federal funds derived from the sale of the Western lands. The wholesome purpose was instruction in the agricultural and mechanical arts. But there was a war on at the time—the time was 1862—and the new cow colleges were required to offer a course in "military science and tactics." It was under this requirement that Rot-cee was born in 1916.

In time many of the land-grant schools became state universities. Most of them (and all of the best of them) no longer require ROTC. But there is no getting rid of it altogether; under the land-grant act they have to offer it. And such anguish as they may harbor is assuaged by the money that's in it. The ROTC Vitalization Act of 1964 *doubled* the scholarship funds of one state university. The money would seem to be wasted, at least in peacetime; of 2,000 lieutenants commissioned at the University of California in Los Angeles, only 200 have chosen a military career. Only in total war, when the Army Reserve is sent into combat, is there a possible payoff; but the total wars have to be no more than ten years apart or the boys who won their spurs in Rot-cee will be as archaic as the spurs.

For the students, the come-on, aside from postponement of that trip to the no longer Mysterious East, is the counting of ROTC credits toward graduation. Faculties generally despise the program, except for the A.&M.-phys-ed-campus-police amalgam and an occasional Army man in the natural sciences. Where academic bodies have the opportunity (as they did at Boston University this spring), they strip it of its credits, reducing its positive student appeal to the money they get if they stick it out. Occasional professors of engineering, looking for scholarships for their fledglings, fancy the Army's magnanimous grants for advanced training, but the Engineering Council for Professional Development strenuously opposes Rot-cee credits toward an engineering degree.

What's money, when the safety of the nation is at stake and sound bodies in a sound skin are wanted? There is no stopping the American

Army these days—at least not by Americans. And Rot-cee's piddling eighty-one million dollars a year is bargain-basement public relations. (President Johnson recently upped that figure by at least one hundred million by extending the program to 12,000 high schools.) Land-grant school administrators, necessarily preoccupied with "image," for which read "money," do what they can to appease the faculty opposition, which invariably includes the most articulate men on the campus. Many administrators have resisted such Washington "suggestions" as sending freshmen a canned letter plugging the program. But Chancellor Roger W. Heyns of the University of California, with Reagan & Co. breathing down his neck, recommends that "every entering male student, who has not made other arrangements to serve his military obligation, seriously consider joining one of the Reserve Officer Training Programs offered at Berkeley. . . . All of the programs are an integral part of the university curriculum, provide for Selective Service deferment, and include attractive pay provisions." If you suppose that it is a scandal for a university chancellor to urge one part of the curriculum rather than another, and to use its non-educational merits as an enticement, you have another supposition coming.

President Asa S. Knowles of Northeastern University, a private institution in Massachusetts, is ROTC's academic showpiece. Addressing a recent meeting of newly appointed Rot-cee instructors, he said, "You must be prepared to face intellectual hostility. The war in Vietnam is not a popular war. There are many Americans who oppose our involvement in it. Many of these people may be found on the college campus. Whether they speak out of ignorance, sincere disagreement, or are merely parroting the ideas of others, the fact remains that they have a right to speak. The college campus is no military reservation. . . . You must expect to have to defend your beliefs in the face of learned opponents. . . . The recitation of pat answers will fall on deaf ears. Appeals to patriotism are virtually meaningless. I do not mean to suggest that I condone this situation. I merely wish to inform you that it exists. . . ."

What President Knowles failed to account for was the intellectual hostility of these unpatriotic parrots *before* Vietnam—an hostility greatly exacerbated, but only exacerbated, by the war. Rot-cee may not be the only non-intellectual program on the campus, but it is the only one that is, by universal and traditional definition, anti-intellectual. Last year a subcommittee appointed to investigate ROTC reported to the Faculty Senate of one land-grant institution that "the law and political realities preclude a decision that ROTC has no place on the campus." Members of the Senate's Academic Matters Committee "generally sensed that somehow the military was different, not a part of the academic family," and the subcommittee expressed its "doubts concerning the quality of the program, quality of instruction, and quality of educational material."

War, though it may not be a liberal art, is an art, and like all arts is acquired on the job. The place to learn soldiering is the Army. Rot-cee is a pale imitation of the Army, and a still paler imitation of the job on the battlefield. If, however, the essence of soldiering is drill, drill, and more drill, Rot-cee has its use, all the way from about-face to "Operation of Telephones and Switchboards." In Military Science I, the Leadership Laboratory Program includes Squad Drill, Platoon Drill, Company Drill, Mass Drill, Review of Drill, Manual of Arms, Practice for Fall and Spring Review, and Fall and Spring Review; all told, fourteen hours out of thirty. In MS II, Leadership Laboratory includes all the drill all over again, plus Saber Manual and Command Voice. (Obey Voice does not appear in the curriculum.)

The Counterinsurgency course, given in MS II and again in MS III, was the one that broke up my sophomore English class by providing a sound track for the *Iliad*. Its objectives include "[the familiarization] of the student with the nature and causes of insurgency." No small objective, this, it is attained in five hours with the help of one of many manuals that serve as Rot-cee textbooks. (They are all prepared by the Department of the Army.) *Selected Readings in Guerrilla and Counterguerrilla Operations*, published in August, 1966, and still in use in 1967–68, informs the rising military scientist that "in South Vietnam today we have over 10,000 Army officers and men advising the Vietnamese forces. The nature of their duties is such that soldiers in Vietnam are being shot at by the Vietcong and are sustaining some casualties." (There are other minor anachronisms, e.g., "[It is] the opinion of many ARVN commanders and their U.S. advisers that indiscriminate, saturation-type aerial or artillery bombardments are detrimental to the winning of the counterinsurgency war. One does not influence people to 'join the cause' when his [sic] family, home, and friends are subjected to bombs in the front yard. [It is] better to use 'friendly persuasion' and secure a citizen, than to drive people into the Vietcong camp. When in doubt of [sic] whether a group [village] is 'friendly' or 'enemy' use 'psywar.'")

In the unlikely event that psywar is not 100 per cent effective, there has to be an antiguerrilla force, "a hunter-killer outfit capable of beating the guerrillas at their own game. . . . The problem of creating the ideal soldier for the hunter-killer units is the most difficult part. . . ." He must engage in friendly persuasion and (among other things) Armed Propaganda. Armed Propaganda "is the tactic of intimidating, kidnapping, or assassinating carefully selected members of the opposition in a manner that will reap the maximum possible psychological benefit." I have not been able to find out exactly how the five-hour course in counterinsurgency teaches the American college boy to intimidate, kidnap, or assassinate carefully selected members of the opposition. The syllabus of the Special Forces course, though it includes Escape and Evasion, Jungle and Arctic Survival, and St. Patrick's Day Parade, does not list kidnapping or assassination as such.

Rot-cee is not content to teach young men how to crack other young men's heads. They have to crack their own in the program's "academic" courses—those for which the Army is most insistent that the college or university give credit toward graduation. These courses are preeminently three in number, *American Military History, The United States Army and National Security,* and *The Role of the United States in World Affairs.* (The last in particular drives historians and political scientists up the wall.)

The competence of the men who teach these "academic" subjects is determined by the Army, not by the college or the university (which may reject an Army appointee, but almost never does in practice; and in any case finally has to accept one). If he is the commandant of the unit, the Army contract requires the institution to give him a full professorship.

His fellow professors have him cornered on the campus, and he can't get at them. What he can get at is the cadet who doesn't have the Rot-cee spirit. A major at Berkeley is telling his charges about SLAM, a Mach 3 missile with a cruising altitude of 50–100 feet. "Even if it misses its target," he says, "the sonic boom it creates will kill enough people to make it worth while." Some of his students are looking at him hard-eyed—or he thinks they are. "The Air Force," he goes on, "has broken the sound barrier and the heat barrier and is tackling the speed of light." More gas-light glares. "In spite of Einstein and his theories our boys are working out ways to fly twice, three times the speed of sound." Audible snickers now. "Go ahead and laugh, but those that do will some day be marching to the goose-step and tune of the hammer and sickle."

But the student who really wants to take Rot-cee is not generally of the snickering sort. "We don't have radicals in the ROTC," says a major on one of the country's more radical campuses, Wisconsin. "There are obnoxious elements here."—For the past ten years the Anti-Military Ball at Madison has been outdrawing the Military Ball on the same night.—"They laugh at the flag-wavers, but what we need is more flag-waving." The future flag-wavers (with, in the event, at least one obnoxious element in their midst) enter a classroom and are told not to take notes and not to tell anyone what they are about to see. What they are about to see—this at the University of Washington—is a series of three slide pictures. The first is a map of the U.S. West Coast with red dots marking the major cities and towns; the second an identification of the red dots as chapter headquarters of the Student Non-violent Coordinating Committee (SNCC), Students for a Democratic Society (SDS), the Dubois Clubs, and other "Communist dominated, Communist influenced, and Communist oriented" student groups; the third a procession of three ducks with this legend below it: "If it walks like a duck, talks like a duck, and lays eggs like a duck, then it's a duck."

After the showing the commandant requests that the cadets prepare files on fellow-students involved in these organizations. Three trusted Rot-cees are assigned to correlate the information. When the story of this educational operation broke last year, Washington's president sent an outraged letter to the Commanding General of the U.S. Sixth Army. The Army confirmed the report that it was furnishing this "guidance program" material to the ROTC and volunteered the information that the program was being offered in ROTC units at twenty-six colleges in eight Western states.

Three-fourths of the Berkeley student body had voted against compulsory ROTC in 1940; the California regents, pushed by Chancellor Clark Kerr, abolished it in 1962, twenty-two years later. Down the years the Berkeley anti-Rot-cee campaign mounted, and in 1960 a student group announced that it was going to picket. "If I or any of my staff find anyone picketing in uniform," said the campus commandant, "that student may find it very difficult to pass the course." An honor student who had got an A in Rot-cee at mid-term found it not difficult, but impossible. When the National Student Association and other organizations protested the F that followed, the Commandant said that the offender ought to have been expelled and arrested, and the NSA was informed by the Executive Office of the Army Reserve and ROTC Affairs that the action was appropriate reprisal for advocacy of a voluntary program.

Such modest restraint as the "academic" manuals display is not likely to weigh heavily against the officers' lectures, orders, warnings, "guidance kits," and slide shows. The restraint of the ROTC manuals themselves is minimal. Their assumptions are neither arcane nor exotic. The first is that the blessings of life and liberty are won and preserved by war and preparation for war; and the history of the United States is adduced to prove the point. The second is that "world Communism" is the implacable and insatiable enemy of mankind represented by the United States ("and our allies," presently unspecified); that there might be any other enemy or, indeed, any other evil abroad or at home is excluded. The third is that human wickedness (from which the Free World is happily exempt) is the cause of Communism; and the best that can be said for those who think otherwise is that they are "a motley of blind idealists, political opportunists, regenerate [sic] criminals, and misled individuals."

Given the military status of the cadet, the military status of the teacher, and the authority of the U.S. Government as the publisher of the "academic" texts, these two to four years of incessant thunder on the right ought to have a fair chance of transforming (or forming) the susceptible young man into a reflexive defender of a world that never was.

Unless he is a history major, he will never know why, or what, Nazism and Fascism were or, indeed, that there ever were such things; much less, that soldiers were hanged at Nuremberg *because* they obeyed their superior officers' orders. None of these things will he know after reading *The Role of the United States in World Affairs;* or why the free election in Vietnam required by the Geneva Agreement was never held, or how the government of Guatemala was overthrown, or what put an end to the U-2 flights over Russia. What he will know, reading *American Military History*, is that President Truman "relieved General MacArthur of command in the Far East in one of the most controversial episodes of the [Korean] conflict," but he will never know why (or even why it was controversial). But he will have read the sixty-eight-page over-sized brochure in technicolor, *Your Career as an Army Officer*, with the following words of General MacArthur centered in headline type on Page 1: "Yours is the profession of arms . . . the will to win . . . the sure knowledge that in war there is no substitute for victory, that if you lose the nation will be destroyed, that the very obsession of your public service must be duty, honor, country." No one will ever tell him (not even, come to think of it, if he is a history major) about faith, hope, love.

But he is not likely to be a history major if he's in Rot-cee.

His heroes will all be American generals like General MacArthur, whether they won, lost, or drew. And he will learn that when they lost or drew it was still a great day for the Americans: "Although Pershing failed to capture Villa, the activities of American troops in Mexico and along the border were not wasted effort. . . . Many defects in the Military Establishment, especially in the National Guard, were uncovered in time to correct them before the Army was thrown into the cauldron of war in Europe. One other result that can be attributed to the experiences of the Army on the border, in part at least, was the passage of much-needed legislation affecting national defense."

His heroes will not include civilians *or* admirals—not in *Army* ROTC: "Few Americans at the outset [of the war with Spain] had any notion that the limited campaign envisioned in Cuba and Caribbean waters would almost immediately be expanded by an aggressive Navy to include operations on the other side of the world"; but fortunately "the American soldier and his immediate superiors took the bungling in high places in stride and demonstrated an aptitude for improvisation equal to the highest traditions of the Army. . . ."

When it comes to developing *leaders*, the Army does not concede that anything surpasses Rot-cee, and "in the process it also develops the kind of junior executive or manager needed in every field of civilian endeavor." Another of its star-spangled plugs, this one entitled, *Where the Leaders Are*, addresses itself to "the young man who wants to be 'where the leaders are' on his college campus and in a military or civilian career after college," and it warns him that "many college men, if they do not take ROTC, miss this instruction in developing self-discipline, physical stamina, and bearing because comparable leadership training and experience are not normally provided in the academic courses required for a college degree. . . . No course outside of the ROTC offers this kind of leadership training."

I recently called on the commandant of a large land-grant college unit. "May I make a suggestion, sir?" said the commandant, a chicken colonel. "You may, sir," I said. "We have," said the colonel, "just received a copy of a new documentary for use in the high schools. Propaganda, you know. In color." "I know," I said (omitting the "sir" because he did). "I haven't seen it myself yet, and I have a man ready to run it. Would you like to see it?" "Yes," I said, adding the "sir" this time on my own initiative. "The man" was a sergeant-major, who leapt to attention as we entered the projection room. "Run it when ready, sergeant-major," said the colonel to the sergeant-major (whose name, sewn on his jacket, was not Gridley).

The title of the documentary was, *Those Who Lead*, the subtitle, "Follow the Leaders to ROTC." The next frame said, *A Report by Chet Huntley*. "I'll bet they didn't get *him* cheap," said the colonel. "No, *sir*," I said, wondering who the devil the colonel thought "they" were. "There are two kinds of people," Chet Huntley began, "those who lead and those who follow. Those who take ROTC are those who want to lead." I thought of the ninety-seven per cent of the male students who do not take ROTC, and I shuddered for my country.

It went on like that, for twenty-six minutes, complete with brilliant young officer-scientists in the laboratory ("I am not at liberty to reveal the exact nature of my research") and gala young officer-husbands leaping into their sports cars after kissing their lovely young wives good-bye at the door of their new suburban homes ("Social life centers around the Officers' Club"). "These young Americans know where they're going. —The Army pays the bill.—The Army pays all the bills.—'When my tour of duty is over I plan to go to law school on the G.I. Bill.'—Balancing the officer's responsibilities are higher pay and the privileges of rank.—'I'll be able to go with him, as an officer's wife, to many interesting places in this country and abroad. My husband and I both think it's a good deal.'—An officer's pay and allowances look pretty good after less than two years out of college.—'We hire reserve officers whenever we can.'—There always will be those who lead and those who follow." Good night, Chet.

The raw sell for the high school kids, without any disquieting reference to doing and dying in one of those interesting places abroad. But in the unlikely case that any of the kids are unpersuaded by the carrot, Chet lets them have a quick glimpse of the stick: "When you go on active duty, as you have to in any case. . . ." You're darned right that these young Americans know where they're going, and if they don't go quietly with Chet they'll be turned over to the secular arm for trial by fire in one of those interesting places abroad.

"Let's look closer now at today's Army officer. Who is he . . . what are his duties? His primary duty is leadership." *Well, sir, if you say so, sir, if it's my DUTY. . . . But do you think I'm cut out for it, sir?* We'll cut you out for it: "There is no such thing as a born leader. The ability to lead and to inspire others to follow is learned." *Where, sir?* "The Army Reserve Officers' Training Corps exists to develop these abilities." *In ME, sir?* Yes, even in you; you belong to "an elite group of young men, who have qualified for college." *But I qualified for college by being white and making it through high school, sir. But I wouldn't mind getting to the top, if it isn't too hard. Is it hard, sir?* "While it is not always easy to become a leader, it is well worth the effort. It is one sure way of getting to the top."

Now it's great to be a leader, whether you get there via the Marlboro, Mustang, or Military Science route. But what Rot-cee does is make followers of men who are already disposed to be followers. The second lieutenant follows the first lieutenant (who follows the captain), and the five-star general follows Harry Truman or loses the Far Eastern command. None of them leads anybody. All of them command or obey.

However handsomely the cadet has done in that branch of Leadership Laboratory described as Command Voice, the Voice will never be heard in the presence of a statutory superior. The self-discipline that Rot-cee advertises consists of his doing whatever a statutory superior orders him to do. The first thing the prospective dough-face is told is that he salutes the uniform, not the man. But leadership is the leadership of men and of statutory equals.

The reason why "no course outside of the ROTC offers this kind of leadership training" is that a college or a university that is any good at all does not offer what neither it nor anyone else can deliver. To the extent that a college tells its students that this course or that (or all of them together) "will contribute to success in any career you may follow after graduation," it is a bad college; and to the extent that a university does it, it is not a university at all.

The college or university that maintained that leadership can be taught—much less trained—would be running a confidence game. But at one point in the game, Rot-cee makes a much less pretentious claim. One of the objects of Leadership Laboratory is "to convince the individual that it is both desirable and possible for him to be an effective leader." *That* the con man can do, given the convincible individual. No fewer than fourteen courses in the Berkeley ROTC program are intended "to give the student a sense of mission." But education does not try to convince or give a sense of mission; it tries to teach. ROTC has no resemblance to education. What it is may be a great thing in itself and a great asset to the national life. *Where* it is is wrong.

It may be able to liberate nations. It can not liberate men, because men are liberated by reason, and it is not the soldier's (including the five-star soldier) to reason why. It can not liberate men, because reasonable men are free to choose for themselves. The Army's characteristic treatment of choice is found in another four-color flier called, *Your Son and the ROTC*. Your son's alternatives "in the barest terms" are two, and two only—ROTC or induction into "active service." The alternatives are alternative ways of going into the Army. The alternative of not going into the Army (an alternative provided by Congress and specified by the Selective Service Act) is not mentioned anywhere in the "literature" of the ROTC, and young men who have heard of conscientious objection have heard of it from sources other than the institution which claims to be "a process of education which trains a man's attitudes and teaches him to respond to the correct and ethical way of doing his duty. It teaches honesty. . . ."

If Rot-cee were to turn honest, it might teach honesty by its example. Even then it would not be an educational process. For the end of education is an informed and insistent intellect, and the end of intellection is choice. No free choice—no free men. No free men—no free world.

QUESTIONS FOR DISCUSSION AND WRITING

1. What advantages are there in approaching a controversial subject in a humorous vein, as this article does? Is it an effective method? How can you tell that Mayer is actually quite serious?
2. Comment on Mayer's frequent use of quotations from military officers and ROTC handbooks to convey his own attitudes. What connotations do these comments assume when they are quoted?
3. What does Mayer mean when he says that "If Rot-cee were to turn honest, it might teach honesty by its example. Even then it would not be an educational process." What is the difference between education and training, between learning and education?
4. Do you think that the military and its goals are incompatible with the university and its goals? Can you conceive of a way in which military science might be taught and be valuable? Explain.
5. Do you feel that ROTC should be allowed in the university or should it be abolished? Does ROTC on the campus suggest more serious and far-reaching problems concerning military involvement with the functions of the university? Explain.

For Further Reading

Buchanan, James M., and Nicos E. Devletoglou. *Academia in Anarchy: An Economic Diagnosis.* New York: Basic Books, Inc., Publishers, 1970.

Foley, James A., and Robert K. Foley. *The College Scene: Students Tell It Like It Is.* New York: Cowles Book Co., Inc., 1969.

Jencks, Christopher, and David Riesman. *The Academic Revolution.* New York: Doubleday and Company, Inc., 1969. Paperback.

Levi, Edward H. *Point of View: Talks on Education.* Chicago: University of Chicago Press, 1970. Paperback.

Ridgeway, James. *The Closed Corporation: American Universities in Crisis.* New York: Random House, Inc., 1968. Paperback, 1969.

Roszak, Theodore, ed. *The Dissenting Academy.* New York: Vintage Books, 1968. Paperback.

Schwab, Joseph J. *College Curriculum and Student Protest.* Chicago: University of Chicago Press, 1969.

Taylor, Harold. *Students Without Teachers: The Crisis in the Universities.* New York: McGraw-Hill Book Company, 1969.

IV ON COMMUNICATION AND EXPRESSION

A society is frequently judged by its forms of communication and expression, whether artistically or in daily intercourse. Today, America is experiencing a revolution in these forms.

Although it is not revolution in the sense of being rapid and radical, it is nevertheless change. Scientific discoveries and technology have drastically altered our ways of viewing not only the universe and reality but also our ways of regarding traditional art forms. Mass media and instantaneous communication have considerably altered our attitudes toward obscenity, for example, and our ways of communicating with each other. The social and political concerns of the young have initiated new trends in music and are reflected in the immense popularity of the cinema. There is change taking place in all these forms of communication and expression, as well as in many others.

The essays in this section explore a variety of changes in expression and communication, and are themselves representative of these changes—from clothing as a form of expression to the film as a reflection of social reality, from the concept of the environment as an art form to the aesthetic of social activism.

Marshall McLuhan
Harley Parker

The Emperor's New Clothes

In his poem "Esthétique du Mal" Wallace Stevens writes:

> This is the thesis scrivened in delight,
> The reverberating psalm, the right chorale.
>
> One might have thought of sight, but who could think
> Of what it sees, for all the ill it sees?
> Speech found the ear, for all the evil sound,
> But the dark italics it could not propound.
> And out of what one sees and hears and out
> Of what one feels, who could have thought to make
> So many selves, so many sensuous worlds,
> As if the air, the mid-day air, was swarming
> With the metaphysical changes that occur,
> Merely in living as and where we live.

He indicates that the slightest shift in the level of visual intensity produces a subtle modulation in our sense of ourselves, both private and corporate. Since technologies are extensions of our own physiology, they result in new programs of an environmental kind. Such pervasive experiences as those deriving from the encounter with environments almost inevitably escape perception. When two or more environments encounter one another by direct interface, they tend to manifest their distinctive qualities. Comparison and contrast have always been a means of sharpening perception in the arts as well as in general experience. Indeed, it is upon this pattern that all the structures of art have been reared. Any artistic endeavor includes the preparing of an environment for human attention. A poem or a painting is in every sense a teaching machine for the training of perception and judgment. The artist is a person who is especially aware of the challenge and dangers of new environ-

164

ments presented to human sensibility. Whereas the ordinary person seeks security by numbing his perceptions against the impact of new experience, the artist delights in this novelty and instinctively creates situations that both reveal it and compensate for it. The artist studies the distortion of sensory life produced by new environmental programing and tends to create artistic situations that correct the sensory bias and derangement brought about by the new form. In social terms the artist can be regarded as a navigator who gives adequate compass bearings in spite of magnetic deflection of the needle by the changing play of forces. So understood, the artist is not a peddler of ideals or lofty experiences. He is rather the indispensable aid to action and reflection alike.

Therefore the question of whether art should be taught in our schools can easily be answered: of course it should be taught, but not as a subject. To teach art as a subject is to insure that it will exist in a state of classification serving only to separate art off from the other activities of man. As Adolf Hildebrand points out in *The Problem of Form,* "Deflected thus from his natural course, the child develops his artificial rather than his natural resources and it is only when he reaches full maturity that the artist learns to think again in terms of the natural forces and ideas which in his childhood were his happiest possession." In the space age of information environments, art necessarily takes on new meaning and new functions. All previous classifications of these matters lose their interest and relevance.

In his *Approach to Art* E. H. Gombrich notes the extraordinary shift from making to matching that began for Western art in fifth-century Athens. In discovering the joys of matching or of realistic representation, the Greeks were not behaving like free men, but like robots. In the representation of reality stress is laid upon the visual sense usually at the expense of all the other senses. Such representation began with the rise of phonetic literacy and cannot occur at any time or at any place without the presence of a technology that favors the visual sense at the expense of all the other senses. For many people it is one of the horrors of our present age that we must live amidst the effects of technologies that do not favor the visual sense in anything like the degree that phonetic literacy does. The phonetic alphabet, as explained in *The Gutenberg Galaxy,* is the only form of writing that abstracts sight and sound from meaning. This fact is stressed by David Diringer in *The Alphabet.* By contrast, pictographic writing tends to unite the senses and semantics in a kind of gestalt. When the visual sense is played up above the other senses, it creates a new kind of space and order that we often call "rational" or pictorial space and form. Only the visual sense has the properties of continuity, uniformity and connectedness that are assumed in Euclidean space. Only the visual sense can create the impression of a continuum. Alex Leighton has said, "To the blind all things are sudden." To touch and hearing each moment is unique, but to the sense of sight the world is uniform and continuous and connected. These are the properties of pictorial space which we often confuse with rationality itself.

Perhaps the most precious possession of man is his abiding awareness of the analogy of proper proportionality, the key to all metaphysical insight and perhaps the very condition of consciousness itself. This analogical awareness is constituted of a perpetual play of ratios among ratios: A is to B what C is to D, which is to say that the ratio between A and B is proportioned to the ratio between C and D, there being a ratio between these ratios as well. This lively awareness of the most exquisite delicacy depends upon there being no connection whatever between the components. If A were linked to B, or C to D, mere logic would take the place of analogical perception. Thus one of the penalties paid for literacy and a high visual culture is a strong tendency to encounter all things through a rigorous story line, as it were. Paradoxically, connected spaces and situations exclude participation whereas discontinuity affords room for involvement. Visual space is connected and creates detachment or noninvolvement. It also tends to exclude the participation of the other senses. Thus the New York World's Fair defeated itself by imposing a visual order and story line that offered little opportunity for participation by the viewer. In contrast, Expo Canada presented not a story line but a mosaic of many cultures and environments. Mosaic form is almost like an X-ray compared to pictorial form with its connections. The Canadian mosaic aroused extraordinary enthusiasm and participation, mystifying many people.

The same difference exists between movie and TV. The movie is highly pictorial, but kinematically it is discontinuous and nonvisual, and thus demands participation. This discontinuous quality has been very much played up in such movies as *The Seventh Seal* and *Blow-Up*, to name only two in a rapidly developing métier. A movie is a succession of discrete images which are separated by extremely small spans of time. Because of their rapid succession, the images are fused in the conscious mind and appear connected. Our relatively recent insights into the power of the preconscious in both the creation and the apprehension of works of art indicate that the subliminal is in fact a strong force in psychic reorganization. It is in this sense that the movie form can be described as a medium which deals in disconnected spaces.

TV, on the other hand, is a kind of X-ray. Any new technology, any extension or amplification of human faculties, when given material embodiment, tends to create a new environment. This is as true of clothing as of speech, or script, or wheel. This process is more easily observed in our own time when several new environments have been created. In the latest one, TV, we find a handful of engineers and technicians in the 10 per cent area, as it were, creating a set of radical changes in the 90 per cent area of daily life. The new TV environment is an electric circuit that takes as its content the earlier environment, the photograph and the movie in particular. The interplay between the old and the new environments generates an innumerable series of problems and confusions which extend all the way from how to allocate the viewing time of children and adults to pay-TV and TV in the classroom. The new medium of TV as an environment creates new occupations. As an environment, it is imperceptible except in terms of its content. That is, all that is seen or noticed is the old environment, the movie. But even the effects of TV on the movie go unnoticed, and the effects of the TV environment in altering the entire character of human sensibility and sensory ratio are completely ignored. The viewer is in the situation of being X-rayed by the image. Typically, therefore, the young viewer acquires a habit of depth involvement which alienates him from the existing arrangements of space and organized knowledge, whether at home or in the classroom. However, this condition of alienation extends to the entire situation of Western man today.

The function of the artist in correcting the unconscious bias of perception in any given culture can be betrayed if he merely repeats the bias of the culture instead of readjusting it. In fact, it can be said that any culture which feeds merely on its direct antecedents is dying. In this sense the role of art is to create the means of perception by creating counterenvironments that open the door of perception to people otherwise numbed in a nonperceivable situation. In Françoise Gilot's book *Life with Picasso* the painter notes that: "When I paint, I always try to give an image people are not expecting and, beyond that, one they reject. That's what interests me. It's in this sense that I mean I always try to be subversive. That is, I give a man an image of himself whose elements are collected from among the usual way of seeing things in traditional painting and then reassembled in a fashion that is unexpected and disturbing enough to make it impossible for him to escape the questions it raises."

Under the heading "What exists is likely to be misallocated" Peter Drucker in *Managing for Results* discusses the structure of social situations: "Business enterprise is not a phenomenon of nature but one of society. In a social situation, however, events are not distributed according to the 'normal distribution' of a natural universe (that is, they are not distributed according to the bell-shaped Gaussian curve). In a social situation a very small number of events *at one extreme*—the first 10 per cent to 20 per cent at most—account for 90 per cent of all results." What Drucker is presenting here is the environment as it presents itself for human attention and action. He is confronting the phenomenon of the imperceptibility of the environment as such. Edward T. Hall tackles this same factor in *The Silent Language*. The ground rules, the pervasive structure, the over-all pattern elude perception except insofar as an antienvironment or a countersituation is constructed to provide a means of direct attention. Paradoxically, the 10 per cent of the typical situation that Drucker designates as the area of effective cause and as the area of opportunity, this small factor, is the environment. The other 90 per cent is the area of problems generated by the active power of the 10 per cent environment. For the environment is an active process pervading and impinging upon all the components of the situation. It is easy to illustrate this.

The content of any system or organization naturally consists of the preceding system or organization, and in that degree the old environment acts as a control on the new. It is useful to notice that the arts and sciences serve as antienvironments that enable us to perceive the environment. In a business civilization we have long considered liberal study as providing necessary means of orientation and perception. When the arts and sciences themselves become environments under conditions of electric circuitry, conventional liberal studies, whether in the arts or sciences, will no longer serve as an antienvironment. When we live in a museum without walls, or have music as a structural part of our sensory environment, new strategies of attention and perception have to be created. When the highest scientific knowledge creates the environment of the atom bomb, new controls for the scientific environment have to be discovered, if only in the interest of survival.

The structural examples of the relation of environment to antienvironment need to be multiplied in order to understand the principles of perception and activity involved. The Balinese, who have no word for art, say, "We do everything as well as possible." This is not an ironic but a factual remark. In a preliterate society art serves as a means of merging the individual and the environment, not as a means of training perception of the environment. Archaic or primitive art looks to us like a magical control built into the environment. Thus to put the artifacts from such a culture into a museum or antienvironment is an act of nullification rather than of revelation. Today what is called "Pop Art" is the use of some object from our own daily environment as if it were antienvironmental. Pop Art serves to remind us, however, that we have fashioned for ourselves a world of artifacts and images that are intended not to train perception or awareness but to insist that we merge with them as the primitive man merges with his environment. Therefore, under the terms of our definition of art as antienvironmental, this is nonart except insofar as the illumination of the interior environment of the human mind can be regarded as an artistic stance.

The world of modern advertising is a magical environment constructed to maintain the economy, not to increase human awareness. We have designed schools as antienvironments to develop the perception and judgment of the printed word, but we have provided no training to develop similar perception and judgment of any of the new environments created by electric circuitry. This is not accidental. From the development of phonetic script until the invention of the electric telegraph, human technology had tended strongly toward the furtherance of detachment and objectivity, detribalization and individuality. Electric circuitry has quite the contrary effect. It involves in depth. It merges the individual and the mass environment. To create an antienvironment for such electric technology would seem to require a technological extension of both private and corporate consciousness. The awareness and opposition of the individual are in these circumstances as irrelevant as they are futile.

The structural features of environment and antienvironment appear in the age-old clash between professionalism and amateurism, whether in sport or in studies. Professional sport fosters the merging of the individual in the mass and in the patterns of the total environment. Amateur sport seeks rather the development of critical awareness of the individual and, most of all, critical awareness of the ground rules of the society as such. The same contrast exists for studies. The professional tends to specialize and to merge his being uncritically in the mass. The ground rules provided by the mass response of his colleagues serve as a pervasive environment of which he is uncritical and unaware.

The party system of government affords a familiar image of the relations of environment and antienvironment. The government as environment needs the opposition as antienvironment in order to be aware of itself. The role of the opposition seems to be, as in the arts and sciences, that of creating perception. As the government environment becomes more cohesively involved in a world of instant information, opposition would seem to become increasingly necessary but also intolerable. It begins to assume the rancorous and hostile character of a Dew Line, or a Distant Early Warning System. It is important, however, to consider the role of the arts and sciences as Early Warning Systems in the social environment. The models of perception they provide can give indispensable orientation to future problems well before they become troublesome.

The legend of Humpty-Dumpty suggests a parallel to the 10–90 per cent distribution of causes and effects. His fall brought into play a massive response from the social bureaucracy. But all the King's horses and all the King's men could not put Humpty-Dumpty back together again. They could not re-create the old environment; they could only create a new one. Our typical response to a disrupting new technology is to re-create the old environment instead of heeding the new opportunities of the new environment. Failure to notice the new opportunities is also failure to understand the new powers. This means that we fail to develop the necessary controls or antienvironments for the new environment. This failure leaves us in the role of mere automata.

W. T. Easterbrook has done extensive exploration of the relations of bureaucracy and enterprise, discovering that as soon as one becomes the environment, the other becomes an antienvironment. They seem to bicycle along through history alternating their roles with all the dash and vigor of Tweedledum and Tweedledee. In the eighteenth century when *realism* became a new method in literature, what happened was that the external environment was put in the place of antienvironment. The ordinary world was given the role of art object by Daniel Defoe and others. The environment began to be used as a perceptual probe. It became self-conscious. It became an "anxious object" instead of being an unperceived and pervasive pattern. Environment used as probe or art object is satirical because it draws attention to itself. The Romantic poets extended this technique to external nature, transforming nature into an art object. Beginning with Baudelaire and Rimbaud and continuing in Hopkins and Eliot and James Joyce, the poets turned their attention to language as a probe. Long used as an environment, language became an instrument of exploration and research. It became an antienvironment. It became Pop Art along with the graphic probes of Larry Rivers, Rauschenberg and many others.

The artist as a maker of antienvironments permits us to perceive that much is newly environmental and therefore most active in transforming situations. This would seem to be why the artist has in many circles in the past century been called the enemy, the criminal.

Pablo shook his head. "Kahnweiler's right," he said. "The point is, art is something subversive. It's something that should *not* be free. Art and liberty, like the fire of Prometheus, are things one must steal, to be used against the established order. Once art becomes official and open to everyone, then it becomes the new academicism." He tossed the cablegram down onto the table. "How can I support an idea like that? If art is ever given the keys to the city, it will be because it's been so watered down, rendered so impotent, that it's not worth fighting for."

I reminded him that Malherbe had said a poet is of no more use to the state than a man who spends his time playing ninepins. "Of course," Pablo said. "And why did Plato say poets should be chased out of the republic? Precisely because every poet and every artist is an antisocial being. He's not that way because he wants to be; he can't be any other way. Of *course* the state has the right to chase him away—from *its* point of view—and if he is really an artist it is in his nature not to want to be admitted, because if he is admitted it can only mean he is doing something which is understood, approved, and therefore old hat—worthless. Anything new, anything worth doing, can't be recognized. People just don't have that much vision." (Françoise Gilot and Carlton Lake, *Life with Picasso*)

It helps to explain why news has a natural bias toward crime and bad news. It is this kind of news that enables us to perceive our world. The detective since Poe's Dupin has tended to be a probe, an artist of the big town, an artist-enemy, as it were. Conventionally, society is always one phase back, is never environmental. Paradoxically, it is the antecedent environment that is always being upgraded for our attention. The new environment always uses the old environment as its material.

In the Spring, 1965, issue of the *Varsity Graduate* of the University of Toronto, Glenn Gould discussed the effects of recorded music on performance and composition. This is a reversal or chiasmus of form that occurs in any situation where an environment is pushed up into high intensity or high definition by technological change. A reversal of characteristics occurs, as in the case of bureaucracy and enterprise. An environment is naturally of low intensity or low definition. That is why it escapes observation. Anything that raises the environment to high intensity, whether it be a storm in nature or violent change resulting from a new technology, turns the environment into an object of attention. When it becomes an object of attention, it assumes the character of an antienvironment or an art object. When the social environment is stirred up to exceptional intensity by technological change and becomes a focus of much attention, we apply the terms "war" and "revolution." All the components of "war" are present in any environment whatsoever. The recognition of war depends upon their being stepped up to high definition.

Under electric conditions of instant information movement, both the concept and the reality of war become manifest in many situations of daily life. We have long been accustomed to war as that which goes on between publics or nations. Publics and nations were the creation of print technology. With electric circuitry publics and nations became the content of the new technology: "The mass audience is not a public as environment but a public as content of a new electric environment." And whereas "the public" as an environment created by print technology consisted of separate individuals with varying points of view, the mass audience consists of the same individuals involved in depth in one another and involved in the creative process of the art or educational situation that is presented to them. Art and education were presented to the *public* as consumer packages for their instruction and edification. The members of the mass audience are immediately involved in art and education as participants and co-creators rather than as consumers. Art and education become new forms of experience, new environments, rather than new antienvironments. Pre-electric art and education were antienvironments in the sense that they were the content of various environments. Under electric conditions the content tends, however, toward becoming environmental itself. This was the paradox that Malraux found in *The Museum Without Walls,* and that Glenn Gould finds in recorded music. Music in the concert hall had been an antienvironment. The same music when recorded is *music without halls,* as it were.

Another paradoxical aspect of this change is that when music becomes environmental by electric means, it becomes more and more the concern of the private individual. By the same token and complementary to the same paradox, the pre-electric music of the concert hall (the music made for a public rather than a mass audience) was a corporate ritual for the group rather than the individual. This paradox extends to all electric technology. The same means which permit a universal and centralized thermostat in effect encourage a private thermostat for individual manipulation. The age of the mass audience is thus far more individualistic than the preceding age of the *public.* It is this paradoxical dynamic that confuses every issue about "conformity," "separatism" and "integration" today. Profoundly contradictory actions and directions prevail in all these situations. This is not surprising in an age of circuitry succeeding the age of the wheel. The feedback loop plays all sorts of tricks to confound the single-plane and one-way direction of thought and action as they had been constituted in the pre-electric age of the machine.

Applying the foregoing to the Negro question, one could say that the agrarian South has long tended to regard the Negro as environment. As such, the Negro is a challenge, a threat, a burden. The very phrase "white supremacy," quite as much as the phrase "white trash," registers this environmental attitude. The environment is the enemy that must be subdued. To the rural man, the conquest of nature is an unceasing challenge. It is the Southerner who contributed the cowboy to the frontier. The Virginian, the archetypal cowboy, as it were, confronts the environment as a hostile, natural force. To man on the frontier, other men are environmental and hostile. By contrast, to the townsmen, men appear not as environmental but as content of the urban environment.

Parallel to the Negro question is the problem of French Canada. The English Canadians have been the environment of French Canada since the railway and Confederation. However, since the telegraph and radio and television, French Canada and English Canada alike have become the content of this new technology. Electric technology is totally environmental for all human communities today. Hence the great confusion arising from the transformation of environments into antienvironments, as it were. All the earlier groupings that had constituted separate environments before electricity have now become antienvironments or the content of the new technology. Awareness of the old unconscious environments therefore becomes increasingly acute. The content of any new environment is just as unperceived as that of the old one had been initially. As a merely automatic sequence, the succession of environments and the dramatics accompanying them tend to be rather tiresome, if only because the audience is very prone to participate in the dramatics with an enthusiasm proportionate to its lack of awareness. In the electric age all former environments whatever become antienvironments. As such the old environments are transformed into areas of self-awareness and self-assertion, guaranteeing a very lively interplay of forces.

The visual sense, alone of our senses, creates the forms of space and time that are uniform, continuous and connected. Euclidean space is the prerogative of visual and literate man. With the advent of electric circuitry and the instant movement of information, Euclidean space recedes and the non-Euclidean geometries emerge. Lewis Carroll, the Oxford mathematician, was perfectly aware of this change in our world when he took Alice through the looking glass into the world where each object creates its own space and conditions. To the visual or Euclidean man, objects do not create time and space. They are merely fitted into time and space. The idea of the world as an environment that is more or less fixed is very much the product of literacy and visual assumptions. In his book *The Philosophical Impact of Contemporary Physics* Milic Capek explains some of the strange confusions in the scientific mind that result from the encounter of the old non-Euclidean spaces of preliterate man with the Euclidean and Newtonian spaces of literate man. The scientists of our time are just as confused as the philosophers, or the teachers, and it is for the reason that Whitehead assigned: they still have the illusion that the new developments are to be fitted into the old space or environment.

One of the most obvious changes in the arts of our time has been the dropping not only of representation, but also of the story line. In poetry, in the novel, in the movie, narrative continuity has yielded to thematic variation. Such variation in place of story line or melodic line has always been the norm in native societies. It is now becoming the norm in our own society and for the same reason, namely, that we are becoming a nonvisual society.

In the age of circuitry, or feedback, fragmentation and specialism tend to yield to integral forms of organization. Humpty-Dumpty tends to go back together again. The bureaucratic efforts of all the King's horses and all the King's men were naturally calculated to keep Humpty-Dumpty from ever getting together again. The Neolithic age, the age of the planter after the age of the hunter, was an age of specialism and division of labor. It has reached a somewhat startling terminus with the advent of electric circuitry. Circuitry is a profoundly decentralizing process. Paradoxically, it was the wheel and mechanical innovation that created centralism. The circuit reverses the characteristics of the wheel, just as Xerography reverses the characteristics of the printing press. Before printing, the scribe, the author and the reader tended to merge. With printing, author and publisher became highly specialized and centralized forms of action. With Xerography, author and publisher and reader tend to merge once more. Whereas the printed book had been the first mass-produced product, creating uniform prices and markets, Xerography tends to restore the custom-made book. Writing and publishing tend to become services of a corporate and inclusive kind. The printed word created the Public. The Public consists of separate individuals, each with his own point of view. Electric circuitry does not create a Public. It creates the Mass. The Mass does not consist of separate individuals, but of individuals profoundly involved in one another. This involvement is a function not of numbers but of speed.

The daily newspaper is an interesting example of this fact. The items in the daily press are totally discontinuous and totally unconnected. The only unifying feature of the press is the date line. Through that date line the reader must go, as Alice went, "through the looking glass." If it is not today's date line, he cannot get in. Once he goes through the date line, he is involved in a world of items for which he, the reader, must write a story line. He makes the news, as the reader of a detective story makes the plot. In the same way the relatively open-ended movie at the Czech pavilion in Expo allowed for intense audience participation through the easy availability of the consensus.

Just as the printing press created the Public as a new environment, so does each new technology or extension of our physical powers tend to create new environments. In the age of information, it is information itself that becomes environmental. The satellites and antennae projected from our planet, for example, have transformed the planet from being an environment into being a probe. This is a transformation which the artists of the past century have been explaining to us in their endless experimental models. Modern art, whether in painting or poetry or music, began as a probe and not as a package. The Symbolists literally broke up the old packages and put them into our hands as probes. And whereas the package belongs to a consumer age, the probe belongs to an age of experimenters.

One of the peculiarities of art is to serve as an antienvironment, a probe that makes the environment visible. It is a form of symbolic, or parabolic, action. Parable comes from a word that means literally "to throw against," just as symbol comes from one meaning "to throw together." As we equip the planet with satellites and antennae, we tend to create new environments of which the planet is itself the content. It is peculiar to environments that they are complex processes which transform their content into archetypal forms. As the planet becomes the content of a new information environment, it also tends to become a work of art. Where railway and machine created a new environment for agrarian man, the old agrarian world became an art form. Nature became a work of art. The Romantic movement was born. When the electric circuit enveloped the mechanical environment, the machine itself became a work of art. Abstract art was born.

As information becomes our environment, it becomes mandatory to program the environment itself as a work of art. The parallel to this appears in Jacques Ellul's *Propaganda*, where he sees propaganda not as an ideology or content of any medium, but as the operation of all the media at once. The mother tongue is propaganda because it exercises an effect on all the senses at once. It shapes our entire outlook and all our ways of feeling. Like any other environment, its operation is imperceptible. When an environment is new, we perceive the old one for the first time. What we see on the Late Show is not TV, but old movies. When the Emperor appeared in his new clothes, his courtiers did not see his nudity, they saw his old clothes. Only the small child and the artist have the immediacy of approach that permits perception of the environmental. The artist provides us with antienvironments that enable us to see the environment. Such antienvironmental means of perception must constantly be renewed in order to be efficacious. That basic aspect of the human condition by which we are rendered incapable of perceiving the environment is one to which psychologists have not even referred. In an age of accelerated change, the need to perceive the environment becomes urgent. Acceleration also makes such perception of the environment more possible. Was it not Bertrand Russell who said that if the bath water got only half a degree warmer every hour, we would never know when to scream? New environments reset our sensory thresholds. These, in turn, alter our outlook and expectations.

The need of our time is for a means of measuring sensory thresholds and a means of discovering exactly what changes occur in these thresholds as a result of the advent of any particular technology. With such knowledge in hand, it would be possible to program a reasonable and orderly future for any human community. Such knowledge would be the equivalent of a thermostatic control for room temperatures. It would seem only reasonable to extend such controls to all the sensory thresholds of our being. We have no reason to be grateful to those who haphazardly juggle the thresholds in the name of innovation.

Redesign of the so-called "light shows" so that they cease to be merely bombardment and become probes into the environment would be most beneficial in an educational sense.

The Two Cultures by C. P. Snow is a handy instance of our contemporary dilemma between visual and nonvisual methods of codifying and processing reality (C. P. Snow seems to be blowing both horns of the dilemma). The dilemma is the same as that which confronted Alice in *Through the Looking Glass*. Before she went through the looking glass, she was in a visual world of continuity and connected space where the appearance of things matched the reality. When she went through the looking glass, she found herself in a nonvisual world where nothing matched and everything seemed to have been made on a unique pattern. (As a matter of fact, because of electric technology we do have two cultures. They are the culture of our children and that of ourselves;

we don't dialogue.) The work of Robert Ardrey in *The Territorial Imperative* is a kind of report from Alice after she had gone through the looking glass. Territoriality is the power of things to impose their own assumptions of time and space by means of our sensory involvement in them. Again, it is a world of making rather than of matching. Modern physics in general carries us into an unvisualizable territory. The speeds as well as the submicroscopic character of its particles are beyond visual representation. John R. Platt in *The Step to Man* explains how it would be possible to incorporate the twenty million books in the world today into an electronic library no larger than the head of a pin.

The present concern with "the death of God" is very much related to the decline in visual culture. The theologian Altizer tells us that the death of God happened roughly two hundred years ago "when the understanding of history grew to supplant an old God-concept. The Christ preserved by the Church has been so progressively dissolved and the God it preached so far decomposed that it is not possible to begin to see Jesus as the core of faith and as incarnate in humanity wherever there is life, and to see God as the opposite of humanity, life, progress—that is, as death." (James Heisig, *The Wake of God*, Divine Seminary, 1967.) In a visual sense God is no longer "up there" and "out there" any more than twenty million books in a pinhead could be said to be "in there." Visual orientation has simply become irrelevant. Some feel that Christianity's existence must always stand in the tension between being in the world and standing outside it. Kierkegaard was keenly aware of this, as were St. Paul and, later, Martin Luther. But the tension between inner and outer is a merely visual guideline, and in the age of the X-ray inner and outer are simultaneous events.

As the Western world goes Oriental on its inner trip with electric circuitry, it is not only the conventional image of God that is deposed; the whole nature of self-identity enters a state of crisis. God the clock-maker and engineer of the universe is no more an essential visual image to the West than is the identity card or the visual classification as an image of private personal status. The problem of personal identity first arose in the West with King Oedipus, who went through the crisis of detribalization, the loss of corporate involvement in the tribal group. To an ancient Greek the discovery of private identity was a terrifying and horrible thing that came about with the discovery of visual space and fragmentary classification. Twentieth-century man is traveling the reverse course, from an extreme individual fragmentary state back into a condition of corporate involvement with all mankind. Paradoxically, this new involvement is experienced as alienation and loss of private selfhood. It began with Ibsen and the Russian writers like Dostoyevsky, for whom there remained a much larger degree of awareness of the old tribal and corporate life than anything available to other European writers in the nineteenth century. The novelists and dramatists who began the quest to discover "Who am I?" have been succeeded by the existentialist philosophers, who meditate upon the meaninglessness of private lives in the contemporary world:

> One can say, in short, that meaninglessness is spreading before our eyes. A strange inner mutation is thereby produced which takes on the aspect of a genuine uprooting. Entirely new questions are being asked, they insist upon being asked, where one hitherto seemed to be in an order which contained its own justification; it is the very order to which the barracks man belonged in the days when he was still a living being, when he was in the present.
>
> He for whom reflection has become a need, a primordial necessity, becomes aware of the precarious and contingent character of the conditions which constitute the very framework of his existence. The word "normal," which he once made use of in a way which now seems to him so imprudent, is emptied of its significance—let us say at least that it is suddenly, as it were, marked by a sign which makes it appear in a new and disturbing light. (Gabriel Marcel, *Problematic Man*, Herder and Herder, 1967)

Marcel is quite aware that there are no concepts or categories that can resolve this crisis:

> Let us now go back to the questions which the barracks man was asking himself: *Who am I? What sense does my life have?* It is obvious that one does not resolve these questions by saying to this man (or to myself if I ask them of myself): You are a rational animal. An answer of this kind is beside the point. I said earlier that meaninglessness was spreading: that is to say that I, who have a profession, a country, means of existence, etc., cannot help but turn these questions somehow towards myself. Why is this so? Let us reason *a contrario*, and suppose that I shut myself up prudently, jealously, in that favored category where these questions do not arise. But if I have really managed, by an effort of imagination, to put myself in the place of the barracks man, it is through his eyes that I will be brought to consider the step by which I placed myself once and for all in the category of the privileged, who know who they are, and what they are living for. In other words, by the combined action of imagination and reflection, I have been able to bring about a change which bears not only upon the object, but upon the subject himself, the subject who questions.

However, he seems to favor the illusion that these dilemmas are ideological in origin rather than a consequence of a reprograming of the human environment in its sensory modes. The rear-view mirror is the favorite instrument of the philosophical historian:

> In particular, one can hardly contest the fact that nationalism in its modern, post-revolutionary form is the product of an ideology that developed in the eighteenth century and combined, under conditions very difficult to state precisely, with a pre-romanticism whose origins seem to be found in Rousseau. Abandoned to its own inclination, this ideology led to a kind of cosmopolitanism of reason. The nationalism which issued from the French Revolution built itself to a large extent upon the ruins of the basic communities which had persisted until the end of the *ancien régime*, but which the individualism of the philosophy of the Enlightenment inevitably helped to dissolve. One cannot deny, on the other hand, that there was a close connection between this fact and the devitalization of religion which occurred in the same period. But the industrial revolution, at least during the first part of the nineteenth century, was destined to play a part in considerably aggravating this tendency—to a large extent, moreover, under the influence of a liberalism which on the economic plane (as we know all too well) was destined to engender the most inhuman consequences, the individual being reduced to a more and more fragmentary condition, under the cover of an optimism which seems to us today to have been the height of hypocrisy.

Marcel occasionally entertains the possibility of considering existence not as a classification or category, but as a total environment:

> The profound justification of the philosophies of existence has perhaps consisted above all in the fact that they have brought out the impossibility of considering an existent being without taking into consideration his existence, his mode of existence. But regarding this very existence, the words *rational animal* furnish us no genuine enlightenment.

But in general he is aware of the futility of history. In the electric age, however, history no longer presents itself as a perspective of continuous visual space, but as an all-at-once and simultaneous presence of all facets of the past. This is what T. S. Eliot calls "tradition" in his celebrated essay "Tradition and the Individual Talent." Eliot's concept seemed quite revolutionary in 1917, but it was in fact a report of an immediate and present reality. Awareness of all-at-once history or tradition goes with a correlative awareness of the present as modifying the entire past. It is this vision that is characteristic of the artistic perception which is necessarily concerned with making and change rather than with any point of view or static position.

The bourgeois nineteenth century referred only to those faces and features which were most strikingly visual in their tidiness and order. That world now persists in some degree in suburbia with the Educational Establishment as its sustaining bulwark. Antithetic to suburbia is the beatnik world, which in the nineteenth century was Bohemia. This is a world in which visual values play a very minor role. One hippie was heard to say, "I have no use for this Cromwell character. I'm a Cavalier!" Cromwell was a sort of *avant-garde* program of visual values. His "Ironsides" were an advance image of industrial production and weaponry. Their "Roundheads" are now the "square" citizens of the upper executive world. "Square," of course, simply means visual and uninvolved.

The transition between worlds may have occurred at the moment of the hula hoop. Mysteriously, people were fascinated by hula hoops as an invitation to involvement and gyration, but nobody was ever seen rolling one in the approved style of the hoop and stick of yesteryear. When exhorted by their elders to roll these hoops down a walk, children simply ignored the request. An equivalent situation today is the disappearance of the word "escapism" in favor of the word "involvement." In the twenties all popular art, whether written or photographed for the movies, was branded as pure escapism. It has not occurred to anybody to call TV viewing escapist any more than it had occurred to anybody to roll the hula hoop as though it were a wheel. Today popular art is intensely involving, and it contains none of the visual values that characterized respectable art a century ago. Popular art has indeed swamped Bohemia and enlarged its territories many times. The aesthete, 1967 model, does not affect any nineteenth-century elegance, but in the interest of involvement presents a shaggy and multisensuous image. Upon meeting him we may well be inclined to say, "You're putting me on!" This is indeed the case. The image to which both beatnik and Beatle aspire is that of "putting on" the corporate audience. It is not a private need of expression that motivates them, but a corporate need of involvement in the total audience. This is humanism in reverse, instead of the corporate image of an integral society.

The revolt against the exclusively humanistic conception of art has been long in gestation, but it first comes into visible existence in the painting of Cézanne, and Cézanne's fundamental importance in the history of this revolution is due precisely to the fact that he was the first who dared assert that the purpose of art is not to express an ideal, whether religious or moral or humanistic, but simply to be humble before nature, and to render the forms which close observation could disentangle from vague visual impressions. The consequences of this peculiar kind of honesty were hardly such as Cézanne himself would have expected. First came cubism, and then a gradual purification of form which reached its logical conclusion in the abstract or nonfigurative art of Piet Mondrian or Ben Nicholson. This formalist type of art is now widespread among artists in every medium, and whether you like it or not, like technology it has come to stay. (Herbert Read, *The Redemption of the Robot*, Trident Press, 1966)

A somewhat different approach to the problem of the transforming action of new environments upon older ones can be taken by the study of cliché and archetype. The world of the cliché is itself environmental since nothing can become a cliché until it has pervaded some world or other. It is at the moment of pervasiveness that the cliché becomes invisible. In their study of *The Popular Arts* Stuart Hall and Paddy Whannel have provided many illustrations of the principle by which a world of cliché, by the art of enveloping an older cliché, seems to turn the older cliché into an archetype or art form. They point to the world of Mickey Spillane, in which the free-lance avenger saves the law by working outside it. Raymond Chandler is much more sophisticated:

> As Chandler's work develops, his themes emerge with greater clarity. When he died he was still at work on *The Poodle Springs Story*. This was to be only incidentally a thriller. Marlowe, married to a wealthy girl, is in danger of becoming her "poodle," confined to the empty round of California cocktail parties. "The contest between what she wants Marlowe to do and what he will insist on doing will make a good sub-plot. I don't know how it will turn out, but she'll never tame him. Perhaps the marriage won't last, or she might even learn to respect his integrity," Chandler wrote, ". . . a struggle of personalities and ideas of life": the thriller becoming the novel of manners.

It is not only that a new medium creates a new environment, which acts upon the sensory life of its inhabitants. The same new environment acts upon the older literary and artistic forms as well:

> As these various satirical modes are more fully employed we begin to understand Chandler's real achievement. Like the true satirist, his gift lies in a disenchanted view of life, and depends upon a highly artificial style. Like the mock-heroic writers and poets, who made play with "heroism," Chandler makes play with the notion of "toughness." He inverts the thriller conventions, draws attention to their artificiality. A hard, polished prose surface permits his wit to play freely. Where the lesser practitioners in the field break their

necks to build up the arch-hero, the superman, at the centre of their work, Chandler sets out to portray the most practised of anti-heroes. Apart from Marlowe, who is keeper of both conscience and consciousness in the novel, and through whose elliptical eye every detail is observed and placed, few of the other characters have true "depth." They are consciously two-dimensional, like the characters in a Ben Jonson play or in Restoration comedy. Perhaps, like the latter, a Chandler novel is a decadent work of art, and there are signs of this in the language (for one thing the similes tend to be over-elaborate and ornate or bizarre). But his use of the witticism or the wisecrack has the same pointed "surface" effect as the rhymed couplet or the epigram in Restoration comedy. There are countless effects of a literary kind which lesser novelists, prac-tising in the more major literary genres, are able to achieve, but which escaped Chandler. But there are many compensating plea-sures which are not to be found in their work. Few writers have used so compromised and over-worked a popular literary form with such skill, craftsmanship and tact.

The hero of the modern thriller puts on the audience, as it were, in a typical gesture of total involvement, whereas the hero of the older adventure story was an aristocratic individual. The new hero is a corpo-rate rather than a private individual figure:

> As Orwell showed in his comparison between *Raffles* and *Miss Blandish,* the modern thriller-hero can no longer afford to stand as:de from the action in his story with that aristocratic detachment which was possible in his immediate predecessors. Unlike Sherlock Holmes or Lord Peter Wimsey or that meticulous *deus ex machina* Hercule Poirot, the thriller-hero must finally enter the action as the main protagonist. The omniscience of the earlier detective-heroes provided some distance between them and the mere mortals caught up in the drama and confusion of the crime. But now this hero, of all the figures in the novel, must be the *most* exposed to the play of passion and violence, the one most intimately caught up with the actual experience of punishment. And if we ask why this change has come about we are forced to give a complex set of reasons, all of which suggest how deeply rooted the literature is in the social imagination. Perhaps it is because we can no longer accept the figure who stands outside the action and yet knows all the answers: we demand greater verisimilitude today. Perhaps it is because these impersonal figures seem now too superhumanly remote: since the revolution in our thinking effected by Freud and psychoanalysis, we take a different view of crime, punishment and violence which the thriller reflects. We cannot believe in the hero

who is himself wholly free from the inner compulsions of violence and lawlessness—we demand that he should stand closer to the villain, exposed to the very evils he is dedicated to remove: "there, but for the grace of God . . ." Certainly, the philosopher would argue that the thriller also shows a collapse in the belief in an abstract and incorruptible justice.

What Hall and Whannel are saying is that the new hero is constituted differently by virtue of being representative of the entire reading public.

The Mike Hammer and James Bond stories are, of course, fantasies—but fantasies which communicate a graphic and heightened realism. Characters may be overdrawn, situations stereo-typed, resolutions predictable. But the fictional life of these stories is convincing at the very level at which the modern reader, especially the young reader, is likely to find himself most under pressure: at the level of the sensations. In a quite precise sense, the thriller novel is a novel of the sensations. Its power lies in its experiential quality, in the absence of relieving factors and the starkness of the action, and in the image of human behaviour which it offers.

In exactly the same way the modern painting does not allow for the single point of view or the dispassionate survey. The modern painter offers an opportunity for dialogue within the parameters inherent in an art form which is moving away from the rational-visual and into the total world of man's sensory involvement.

QUESTIONS FOR DISCUSSION AND WRITING

1. Early in his essay, McLuhan says that "Since technologies are extensions of our own physiology, they result in new programs of an environmental kind." What is the importance of this statement to the essay as a whole? What is its relationship to the oft-quoted statement by McLuhan that "the medium is the message"?

2. The following terms are crucial to an understanding of this essay: "environment" and "antienvironment." In general, what does McLuhan mean by these terms and how are they related to each other? What is the relationship of McLuhan's concept of "environment" and "antienvironment" to his thoughts about art? What is or should be the function of the artist in our society, according to McLuhan?

3. According to McLuhan, what is the relationship between "the new environment" and "the old environment," in most cases? How do these terms relate to the title of this essay?

4. McLuhan says that "One of the most obvious changes in the arts of our

time has been the dropping not only of representation, but also of the story line." Discuss this, particularly taking note of McLuhan's comments about the Canadian World's Fair (Expo 67).

5. What is the chief thing which McLuhan considers significant about the Balinese remark, "We do everything as well as possible"?

6. McLuhan cites at least one profound "paradox" which "extends to all electric technology . . . The age of the mass audience is . . . far more individualistic than the preceding age of the *public*." Do you agree? Explain.

7. Discuss the effects which "electric circuity," according to McLuhan, has had upon religion.

8. Compare and contrast the ideas presented in this essay to the ideas expressed in the essay by Margaret Mead on p. 44.

9. In general, what, if anything, does this essay by McLuhan contribute to your understanding of the world you live in? Explain.

Amy Goldin

Deep Art and Shallow Art

Most people think that new ideas travel in a single direction, like water. We suppose that the fountainhead of thought is high culture which flows downwards, picking up reality as it goes. Popular culture supposedly represents what is left of high culture after it has been brought down to earth, popularized, and debased. High culture is the good stuff, the crystal stream of theoretical knowledge and truth, while low culture is full of colorful over-simplifications. Middlebrow culture is supposed to be in the middle, closer to pure, clear thought in essence, but less precise and more concrete in expression. I doubt if this was ever wholly true; it is certainly not true today. Middlebrow theorizing is unlikely to borrow much from specialized investigations aside from rhetorical details. Their popularity depends on the delight of finding that what everybody knows can be used to explain what they don't know.

In a very dynamic society, however, what everybody knows is not uncommonly wrong. By the time everybody has learned something, new questions and new answers have superseded. Theoreticians are probably formulating the most pressing questions in other terms or in relation to other matters. By updating and extending popular assumptions, middlebrow culture often reinforces old-fashioned and false ideas. We cannot simply assume that new theories represent intellectual growth or refinement. They may be flatly reactionary, inhibiting the spread of genuinely new ideas and making their acceptance more difficult. Popular theories, like politicians, win power by being fundamentally banal, and they gain plausibility by being vague. McLuhan is a notable case in point. Although he uses the rhetoric of information theory, in which meaning *is* system-bound, he does not take into account the problem of noise—that is, the possibility of meaninglessness. So he is free to identify media with messages, and the forms of communication become "contents." McLuhan's is not the only recent cultural theory that struggles with the old form-and-content problem and ends by embracing it. Negritude

184

or Negro culture is characterized by "soul," a formless content, and theories of modern art try to account for the significance of abstract, "contentless" form.

The difficulties of the form-and-content structure are notorious. Why does it persist? Form-and-content is a beguiling explanatory device because it allows us to interpret appearances any way we like, attributing importance to them or withdrawing it as we please. We can assure ourselves of the permanence of something desired, like love or creativity, by saying that the form has changed but the content remains the same. Conversely, we can claim that something unwanted, such as anti-Semitism, is changing despite appearances, and that new attitudes are concealed by the persistence of rigid forms. The important thing to notice is that "content" in these theories cannot be inferred from material evidence and must always be intuited. Form-and-content acknowledges a theoretical complexity but allows us to act simplistically. If we divide a complex situation into an important aspect and a trivial one, we can neglect its complexity with perfect righteousness. And either form or content can be considered beside the point, according to taste.

Form-and-content is so shoddy a framework for thought that it is most often found in off-the-cuff, informal theorizing. In the arts, however, the form-and-content scheme is entrenched. Art theory has steadily stumped along on these twin pillars, holding beauty in the appropriate place, between them. Style is considered to be roughly equivalent to form, and subject matter to be the ultimate source of content. The meaning of a landscape, for example, might be summed up as "the artist's interpretation of nature." This is not a very satisfactory explanation, but the problem of accounting for pictorial meaning did not become acute until the advent of art without subject matter. In the past the confusions of traditional aesthetics were eased by the satisfactoriness of art. Today art itself looks meaningless. My fundamental argument is that what is difficult and problematic about modern art has little to do with style. It depends on the complex nature of artistic meaning itself.

I

Explanations of modern art usually proceed historically. Beginning with the Impressionists, art history is read as a series of revolutions, a quasi-Hegelian sequence of styles and theories that followed each other so rapidly that meaning got lost in the shuffle. There is a suggestion that each "historical factor" walks onstage, plays its part, and disappears into the wings. We get a narrative in which the decline of the French Academy is linked to social change, the Dada movement to moral protest, and the appearance of Cubism to abstraction. The present state of art is explained away as the outcome of social and cultural forces.

Indeed, it no longer exists as an opaque situation at all. It is hardly more than the accumulation of cultural debris left behind by the march of time.

Because many people continue to find contemporary art opaque, I propose to deal only with the present. Neither historical explanations nor persistent exposure to art is likely to reduce the frustration aroused by modern art. Some of its meaninglessness is built in. Unfamiliar kinds of meaning go unrecognized. However, regardless of the reasons for the experience of meaninglessness, the attendant cultural malaise is not trivial. Primitive societies define the human condition by locating themselves within and over against nature; we define ourselves historically. To be old-fashioned is to be lost, a stranger in one's own time. Bombarded by the culture explosion, it is easy to be seized by a metaphysical nostalgia for feeling at home in one's own culture. Such nostalgia leaves one especially vulnerable to traditionalist theories that rationalize and harden alienation.

Beginning with the artistic situation at present, I shall begin, too, with a description of what I take to be common assumptions about that situation. Although popular culture has grown more respectable, most people still believe that art can be divided into its nearer and farther reaches: into deep art and shallow art, or high art and low. This division does not simply correspond to good art and bad, but represents different levels of artistic aspiration. We acknowledge that commercial posters or carpets can be judged artistically, as good or bad examples of their kind. It is in high art, "serious" painting and sculpture, that we expect meaning.

Low art, we feel, tends to be easy to take, decorative, and at times old-fashioned or conservative. We don't expect low art to mean much; it's shallow. High art, on the other hand, is supposed to mean a great deal. That's how it got so high, by having all those layers of meaning piled up on each other. It may be difficult to untangle the layers of meaning, but we imagine that its ultimate decipherability can be intuitively felt. The presence of meaning seems almost tangible, even though we can't say what it is.

The difficulty of modern art, whatever experimental complexities of form the artist has chosen to get involved in, is stubbornly approached as a problem in locating meaning. We "intuitively" set up a list that locks like this:

Deep Art	Shallow Art
meaningful	decorative
hard	easy
abstract	representational
radical	conservative

Having assumed that high art is meaningful, we expect certain personal and social consequences to follow. We expect to have to struggle to grasp that meaning. We expect to find ideas in art, we expect the art to have cultural importance, we expect high prices, critical attention—the whole bit falls into line. And, in fact, the social trappings and the theoretical claims of high art have remained stable and recognizable. It seems as if the only thing that's changed is the art. Or, if the art is still high art and the artists are playing their "traditional" roles as cultural innovators, the elite audience has somehow become stuck, somewhere around Picasso's *Guernica*.

The trouble is that high art, nowadays, is not deep at all. It's shallow. To equip yourself with aqualungs and flippers to penetrate its depths of meaning becomes ludicrous. Yet people will not tell you that meaning has been displaced.

Why not? Because nobody is quite sure what's happened to it. Moreover, now that it seems to be gone, nobody remembers what it looked like. Cultural conservatives say it looked like subject matter and was consequently incompatible with abstract art. People who are culturally with-it say that meaning looked like artistic quality and it's still there, only you have to be terribly sensitive to recognize it because styles have changed so. The question of meaning in art has become a matter of faith, a dogma separating the believers from the unbelievers. The hostiles say that contemporary art is meaningless and empty; the defenders claim that art is still meaningful, and that nothing has changed but style.

What is meaning? For most people, most of the time, meaning is something moral. It has to do with behavior. In daily life, meaning in the lexical, definitional sense of the term rarely becomes an issue. When it does, the "problem" of meaning can usually be cleared up quickly, and the issue is felt to be trivial. But when the verbal meaning is clear and we ask someone, "What do you mean by that?" we are asking him to clarify his intentions or his attitude, so that we can know if he is well- or ill-disposed toward something. If we ask of a theatrical performance or a piece of writing, "What does it really *mean?*"—we initially try to find whether the author wants us to respect the thesis or situation presented or whether we are supposed to laugh and deplore it. It is the author's attitude toward his subject matter that we are trying to locate, so that we have a norm with which we can agree or disagree.

Whatever it may have experienced or felt, an audience deprived of moral orientation feels deprived of meaning. Uncertain of its own role in the artistic situation, the audience is likely to deny that it has felt anything, for lack of a position from which shades of feeling can be identified. Regardless of the grounds offered for admiration or disapproval, people want to know what moral attitudes are aesthetically appropriate. An audience, uncertain about whether it is supposed to be amused or respectful, is an unhappy audience. Deprived of moral clues, it is deprived of meaning.

Abstract Expressionism was given an aura of nobility when it was baptized "Action Painting." "Action," with its connotations of personal heroism and social significance, is clearly a Good Thing, so Abstract Expressionism became the latest member of a series of icons celebrating the identity of the Good, the True, and the Beautiful. Abstract art was saved for moral idealism. Almost as soon as the style was thoroughly accepted by the artistic establishment, however, it was abandoned by a new artistic generation.

The artists of Pop, Op, and Happenings, and the sculptors grouped around Minimal art *all* made gestures and verbal statements repudiating the idea of cultural heroism. Whatever their work looked like, the artists talked as if they had something against art. Anti-art statements from artists and writers, however, only make sense as a notice to the audience that the artists are shifting their artistic intentions. What intention could be expressed in such a range of styles?

The one element common to all recent art is the insistence that the audience's approval is irrelevant to the meaning of the work. This art wishes to disengage itself from appeals to strong, morally unconflicted emotion. It makes no appeal to feelings of human tenderness and admiration. Our habitual attempt to interpret art as a pleasant form of moral propaganda while enjoying and approving of our own feelings is deliberately flouted or evaded.

Those artists appear most up-to-date who, with greater or lesser steadfastness, refuse to participate in things that encourage the public's love. Stylistic developments allied to Pop—Funk art and various forms of theater—actively reject it by incorporating repulsive and scatological materials. Abstract sculpture and modernist painting withdraw from being lovable by insisting on an impersonal *look*, which is reinforced by a critical theory that makes it appropriate to react to those works as purely aesthetic, amoral objects.

Although Pop is presently not a widely used style, I wish to discuss it briefly because it uses subject matter, and uses it in a manner that neutralizes and complicates our emotional reactions to it. As soon as the element of emotional uncommittedness or complexity is lost and affectionate nostalgia is allowed to dominate, Pop shades off into Camp. Pop is most ambitious when it manages to preserve its bite. How does it do this?

By treating advertising, pornography, and news photos as artistic subject matter, Pop began as an in-joke at the expense of art's pretensions to spiritual elevation. Largely as a result of the genius of Claes Olden-

burg and the intelligence of Rosenquist and Lichtenstein, Pop was able
to extend its range of reference while maintaining a precarious suspen-
sion of moral commitment. Using the materials of the commercial world,
it presents the businessman's Garden of Eden. The conventional Good
Life is deep feeling, fun, and gracious living without either affirming
or denying the value of these things. Unharmonized color, weightless-
ness, and relatively broad scale help to keep the viewer at a public,
nonintimate aesthetic distance. The style functions to separate the picture's meaning from that of its subject matter, the way quotation marks
do in isolating the tone of jargon or colloquial expressions from the
tone of the surrounding sentence. "Task Force Oregon announced that
it had killed . . . 3300 enemy soldiers and 'detained' five thousand people." The inner quotation marks report a specific situation and call attention to the reporter's withdrawal from full acceptance of the official
point of view—"They said it, I didn't"—while refraining from taking
any direct issue with it. It's a neat trick, but difficult. Pop can sustain
its ironical good humor and its consequent emotional complexity only
by being extremely careful about keeping its subjects of reference highly
charged while emphasizing its own formal cool. When this tension is
lost, it can easily fall into Campy chic (Lichtenstein is particularly liable
to this) or dramatic gesture (Oldenburg's midnight "burial" in Central
Park).

Contemporary abstract art is so thorough about repudiating human
involvement that it looks like the result of industrial processes even
when it's handmade. Canvases seem stained rather than painted, sculptural forms are bland and regular, and variations of surface and form
are everywhere limited or suppressed.

Work in monumental size avoids "aggressiveness" or strong movement,
suggesting the simultaneous assertion of the presence of power and the
fact of its being sealed off, so that the viewer is left unthreatened.
Other sculptural styles present the audience with unfocused sequences
of industrially defined spaces or forms as "environments," "fields," or
"progressions" which make a point of leaving the spectator disengaged
from anything but a vaguely architectural situation. This work presents
itself as pure artifact, unusable and inhuman, a sort of simplified maze
in which you cannot lose yourself or a circular supply room with an
entrance but no exit.

None of this stuff means anything. The artist's message to the viewer
is: "I have no intention of charming you or frightening you. I don't
intend to do anything to you. I just make things. What you see is what
you see." Feelings of density, awareness of stasis or unfocused movement, the experience of unwilled, inorganic, but rational repetition—these are complexes of sensation that are not easily available to
ordinary consciousness. Nor are they feelings that are likely to strike
us as being noteworthy or interesting, lacking as they do any special

moral orientation. That is, they seem neither particularly desirable nor undesirable, dangerous or comforting. Yet it cannot be denied that these feelings, now made available for the first time in art, seem to be particularly insistent in a mass industrial society. Our art forces us to acknowledge them and refuses to judge them. It also refuses us the commonplace humanistic reassurances, leaving us uncertain whether their absence is to be taken as warning, prophecy, or mere observation. Our art only says, "Notice it. Maybe it means something."

The artistic problem involved in making the repudiation of meaning and emotion explicit in Minimal art lies in the quasi-involuntary beauty of simple orderliness and smooth industrial finishes. In terms of artistic form, this work, which effaces itself as anything beyond a physical presence, cannot easily avoid being assimilated to architectural or interior decoration. The artists' denial of any extra-aesthetic intention does not succeed in creating a moral Switzerland for them to work in. They are still pitifully vulnerable to being loved *anyway*. As artists, they are accepted as purveyors of the usual depth and beauty.

It is curious to see how hard it is to develop a style that will evade implications of moral commitment. It seems as if the audience is determined to find art uplifting, no matter how strenuously artists try to discourage them. Be that as it may, the point remains that the evasion of emotional approval is sought, and that this evasion constitutes the deliberate "meaninglessness" of modern art.

II

I have insisted on the primacy of treating artistic meaning as a moral concept although the idea that the plastic arts carry moral connotations was generally banished from criticism a long time ago. It was revived only for special styles: the social protest art of the thirties and for the Existentialist message of Abstract Expressionism. In general, art criticism has tended to proceed as if the content or meaning of modern art were intellectual rather than moral.

I assure you that this idea is ludicrous. Intelligence is common, among artists as elsewhere, but original ideas of any sort are very rare indeed. There are few artists with original ideas, and those they have are likely to be bad. In this they resemble chemists, engineers, teachers, doctors, and lawyers.

I suggest that ideas in art are, like beauty, to be found chiefly in the eye of the beholder. No matter how thoroughly abstract a picture is, critics can always be found to tell you what it's about. Pictures that are smudged or airy-looking are often supposed to be about moods, feelings related to nature, or images of one or another state of the inner man. (Since nobody knows what the inner man looks like, who can deny it?) Abstract paintings with fewer and more decisive marks have recently been interpreted as being "about" art. Sometimes it's art materials or elements—what critics call the pure *fact* of paint, or of color, or of space. But more often it's style. The implication is that art history or aesthetics is somehow the work's implicit subject matter, and that if you don't know anything about those subjects you can't expect to understand the work. Assertions that abstract art is *about* anything, and particularly about abstractions like time, science, or Cubism, are nonsense—desperate attempts to preserve the old form-and-content structure of artistic meaning. Artistic meaning cannot be created by fiat. Even if the artist says that he wants his work to be interpreted in some particular way, his expressed intentions do not constitute a rule that establishes meaning.

The Formalist thesis that artistic meaning corresponds, at any particular moment, to the essential formal conventions of a given style is simply obscurantism. Formal conventions may be the focus of interest for a hard-working art critic, but he has no reason to suppose that the entire world of art is a gigantic conspiracy to provide him with professional puzzles. The suggestion that extensive study of aesthetics and art history is necessary in order to understand contemporary art is utterly false. Our art is so far from being a privileged message, a game intelligible only to highly trained players, that it is truer to say that the less you know about art the better. Irrelevant expectations of meaning will not distract you from the essentially simple-minded, sensuous pleasure to be derived from it. It even seems as if a high degree of literary culture can be positively inhibiting. Certainly some very refined and artistically well-educated people—Bernard Berenson, for one—have found themselves unable to tolerate modern art at all.

Before the end of the nineteenth century, it was possible to understand art without particularly concerning yourself with artistic ideas. On the other hand, in order to grasp an artist's meaning you usually did have to know what vices and virtues were considered important. Consequently you needed a rather firm grasp of Christian and pagan myths and symbols, but you knew where to look for artistic meaning. The same habits don't work for modern art. Today the range of experience relevant to art has shifted, and it is narrower, not wider than it used to be.

But if art today is so simple, and requires neither enthusiasm nor high intelligence, what is it that *seems* so difficult? The answer is that the general location of artistic meaning has shifted. Art no longer aims at being inspiring. We need new emotional habits for it, and it is very hard to get new attitudes together.

We are commonly liable to feel that anything unfamiliar and large is intellectually challenging. The most complex structures and phenomena, as long as they are familiar, seem easy. Nobody thinks of his monetary or kinship system as presenting intellectual difficulty; they seem natural. In fact, they *are* natural, in the same way that art is. They isolate and structure the pervasive social values, and we can scarcely conceive of "money" or "relatives" or "art" apart from the structures with which we are familiar. Ideas about art, however simple, are characteristically hard to grasp, abrasive, and indigestible.

The shift in art away from the traditional moral location of meaning is a major idea, one of the sort I described as very rare. Although it is an old idea by now, it has become commonplace without being thoroughly grasped. Nor have the appropriate revisions of art criticism or aesthetic theory been made. Meanwhile, most (not all) of the developments in painting and sculpture of the last eighty years or so have been statements, variations, and investigations of nonmoral artistic ideas.

Most artistic ideas are not the sort of things we usually call ideas at all. They are fragments or clots of feeling-about-something, intrinsically complex, like ordinary experience. It is because new artistic ideas *are* in part new feelings that we don't know what to do with them. They can interrupt old patterns of feeling and demand a place for themselves while we are still uncertain about whether we want them. A novelty or a commercial gimmick is always welcome, because it brings an air of freshness without disturbing anything. We are offered something that we can react to in a familiar way, with only the slightest shift of nuances. But new feelings, like new ideas, can disrupt the psychic economy.

A "new" feeling, of course, is not a heretofore unexperienced emotion. It is a new complex, a new feeling-about-something. If we are suddenly presented with the fact that we are reacting to A in a way that we had always supposed was appropriate only to B, we seem to get something we can call either a new feeling or a new idea. Suppose you suddenly found yourself feeling about a boy in a way you had always supposed you could feel only in relation to girls. You can see that a new feeling in this sense could require at least as much psychic reorganization as a new idea of what the relationship between the sexes should be. Because new artistic ideas are feelings-about-something, they can be presented either with or without familiar subject matter. Pop art offers an example of the first; Cubism an example of the second.

Artistic ideas are the particles of artistic meaning, and it is as difficult to define them outside the context of art as it is to define a word outside the context of language. Understanding—grasping meaning—is something people *do*, whether meaning is verbal or pictorial. Meaning is not a physical characteristic like weight, though the old form-and-content division makes it easiest to think of meaning as something tangible or "graspable." Similarly, art objects are not a special class of things. Our museums are full of things that became art after respectable careers as pots or illustrations or ornaments. But we no longer use them as pots, illustrations, etc. When we reclassify them as art objects we deal with them in a special way, and that "dealing" is the process of understanding rather than using.

Art is also cheap, exactly as life itself is cheap. Art always means something, but it needn't mean much. Creativity is absurdly overrated nowadays—it's what is created that counts. In folk art, for example, meaning is usually so banal that we hardly notice it. Advertising is the folk art of industrial societies, and it is usually pretty dull, too. Because so many kinds of artistic meaning are repetitive and trivial, the pleasure we get from art, as opposed to any knowledge or profit, becomes very important. And because modern communication techniques make the repetition of sounds, images, and ideas ubiquitous, we are frenziedly grateful for variation and novelty.

At the same time, artistic meanings are extremely varied; the feelings and ideas art carries range from the picayune to the exalted. Therefore it is possible to conceive of art as a melting pot of the sacred and the profane, an alembic for the clarification and redefinition of what men consider important. Both rejection and celebration are necessary to this process: Pop art can be read as raising the fallen world. That is, the squalid, fragmented world of contemporary entertainment or advertising becomes a part of the iconic, highly ordered structure of fine art, thus creating the possibility of a jollier, more unified existence.

The importance of art lies in its effect on extra-artistic meaning, for it inevitably *has* effects, quite independently of whether it is high art or low, good art or bad. A work of art that satisfies us binds us to the world and, by doing so, reinforces some of society's established values. A work of art that repels us exacerbates our sense of social and personal incoherence and facilitates the dissolution of social conventions into new attitudes and new ways of appraising experience.

I would like to suggest that artistic meaning can best be understood as arising from three interacting levels of experience, *none of which ever occurs in isolation*. At any point in time we *are* physical, social, and moral beings, and although most of our experience calls on us to make a highly discriminated response, art stops us. It characteristically blots out extra-artistic discriminations and unifies experience into a closed, focused system.

For instance, a sudden loud noise is primarily a physical experience; our response is to jump and look around to see if we are in physical danger. An ordinary question addressed to us ("What time is it, please?") requires a social response: an answer offered in an appropriate language and manner. A problem or a confrontation can call for an act or a moral decision. If the question addressed to us is an indecent proposal, we have to decide whether to accept it, ignore it, walk away, or maybe call a cop.

The important thing to notice is the way these classes of experience nest into each other. The social implies the physical, the moral implies the social. The formal level of experience—the range of choices and behavior appropriate to a class of experience—can shift swiftly and easily, even though the physical components remain stable.

A work of art always addresses us in terms of sensuous, physical experience. This is the primary level of artistic form, the formal level of art, and it corresponds to the physical level of experience. All art sustains formal analysis, although confused or undeveloped methods of analysis can make such procedures trivial. Abstract art tends to stress this level of response.

A work of art also engages us on the level of conventional social communication: the level of genre. A genre defines the social function of art, and generic distinctions allow us to discriminate advertising art, political cartoons, or religious art as providing special, highly specific kinds of meaning. Religious, literary, and other sorts of social symbolism are established on this level. Sometimes a stable iconography developed in one genre spreads to others.

Any response more lively than flat indifference engages us morally. If we find a work attractive, we want to keep on looking; if we are repelled, we want to escape or attack it. The fact that art can spark behavior, sometimes in very direct ways, is probably the reason most people get interested in it. We first learn to respect art on the basis of its brute power to move us, to make us cry with pity, burn with indignation, squirm with concupiscence. Pornography, propaganda, and advertising are kinds of art that set out to affect behavior without stopping at "Go" to pay its respects to aesthetic values. They have repeatedly been disowned as not belonging to the category of art at all. This is silly. It is merely a sign of the authoritarian temperament that would like to bind all power to the service of a selected slate of attitudes. The fact that art stimulates such sanctions and judgments is merely further evidence of its ability to engage us on this level of behavior.

The moral level of response includes all behavior including more innocuous reactions: seeing a still life can make us decide to buy it or resolve to go home and bake a cherry pie. Art can affect us as demanding an urgent, active response, yet it is a mistake, I believe, to equate this vividness with the apogee of artistic power. Ultimately more far-reaching is the tendency of works of art to bind and coagulate feelings, values, and meanings, the tendency to become iconic, stabilizing our sense of what is true, important, and beautiful. Most people assume that all artists want to move them morally above all, for this is the way in which they most want to be moved: vividly, emotionally, and in familiar directions.

Modern art rarely aims at this response. It focuses on the first level of experience, emphasizing body feelings of openness or closure, and avoiding, as far as possible, suggestions that any state is ideal or deplorable. This is likely to strike most people as surprising, indeed, barely intelligible as an artistic intention. (I think that the artists themselves have found it difficult to keep from idealizing and embellishing their work, turning boxes into icons of the private, inner-directed man. The unprofessional public is not alone in its habit of interpreting works of high art as microcosmic or macrocosmic emblems.) Perhaps we should see the will to make art that inhibits easy moral responses and tries to engage directly with "reality" as itself embodying a moral intention. It looks like one to me, a proto-ethic of a highly rationalistic sort that places great importance on not lying or overstating anything. The emotional austerity of Pop and Minimal styles tends to create a low-pressure experience for the audience at the opposite pole from appetite-oriented advertising. The moral suggestion lies in the implication that dispassion is valuable.

Probably the most serious question posed by the withdrawal of our best artists from a willingness to mean anything in the traditional sense of artistic meaning is the problem of accounting for the prestige of high art, the respect it receives and demands. It is reverence for art that seems to be called into question when we have serious art that insists on fooling around and making jokes, the way some Pop does, or when, like Minimal sculpture, it solemnly renounces the status of art in favor of object-hood. Perhaps the fine arts are still "high" because they still imply the artist's impersonal seriousness, his attention to the implications and moral consequences of attending to artistic meaning. Of course, this sort of seriousness doesn't necessarily produce great art. It can encourage an owlish solemnity that is hilarious to an unsympathetic audience—Neo-Classicism provides many examples. Moreover, we should not forget that the connection between moral or religious intentions and art of high formal coherence may simply be a sometimes thing, a matter of historical fact.

What does it mean to say that a picture is intelligible, or that we understand a work of art? We have been so sentimentally eager to "appreciate" art that the question has barely been raised. We have tried to settle for love, without regard to the complex transactions of meaning that actually take place in all experiences of art. If critics were less eager to see themselves as defenders of the cultural faith, they might have something useful to tell us. In this age of mass communication we are an audience longer and more thoroughly than we are citizens. The arts are charged with social power, and the Victorian assumption that culture is intrinsically elevating is a twentieth-century joke.

QUESTIONS FOR DISCUSSION AND WRITING

1. According to Goldin, what are the chief characteristics of "deep art" and "shallow art," as most people consider them? Does Goldin agree with the usual distinctions between these two types of art? Do you? Explain.

2. "For most people, most of the time, meaning is something moral," Goldin says. Discuss this concept of meaning-as-morality and explain how it works.
3. What is the author's complaint against "form-and-content" as "a framework for thought"? How does it lead people to the conclusion that modern art is "meaningless," according to Goldin?
4. Goldin works very hard to clarify the notion of "meaning" in modern art. What, generally, are her conclusions? Do you agree with them? Explain.
5. Goldin says that art affects us on three levels—the physical, social, and moral. Take any work of art that comes to mind as an example and explain how this process works.
6. If Goldin is correct that modern artists are intent on producing a style "that will evade implications of moral commitment," what is the significance of this fact and how did it come about? For example, does Goldin mean to imply that artists are insensitive to moral questions or that we, their audience, are? Explain.
7. Does this essay seem to you to adequately characterize and explain modern art? Has Goldin left anything out? Discuss.

Ernest Callenbach

The Movie Industry
and the Film Culture

When I first found out about films, it was through a kind of secret society known as the Documentary Film Group: a student film society at the University of Chicago. Unlike too many "student organizations" of today's multi-versities, which use student fees for their operations but are controlled by the administration, Docfilm was an independent affair, full of internecine disputes, struggles for succession, and the glories of self-propelled activity: it put on a taxing program of two double-features per week and focused serious interest in films (by no means only documentaries) on a campus not exactly surrounded by culture.

In those days, being interested in films was distinctly strange. Our president for a while, besides being the dedicated kind of old red who lectured in a monotone about Film & Reality, was also a member of the campus Rocket Society, which was then considered a half-baked gang of visionaries. Although it was Chaplin who lured me into my first business meeting of Docfilm (and, to be perfectly candid, the mistaken belief that a girl named Marjorie was a member) I soon discovered what my rural and filmless childhood had given me no chance to know—that films were a marvelous and mixed medium, combining chance and patterns, passion and precision, life and craft, in mystifying and sometimes overwhelming ways. At Docfilm we had a scholarly bent; we went systematically through the arcane catalogues of the Museum of Modern Art Film Library, Brandon, Cinema 16. We showed *everything*, as a good film society should, trying to be stringently catholic, even to the point of booking films that only one member really fought for. And we had a profound sense of being on the unknown, growing edge of something: the new understanding of a beleaguered art, precious, endangered on every hand by commercialism, censorship, and

197

the manifold sins that sound had made film heir to. We were disciples, and we spread the word as we could, with the devotion of disciples. We read and studied, we schemed to stay alive financially, we prepared long program notes, we worked many unpaid hours to carry out the actual arduous labor of publicizing and showing our films. It was lonely work, but serious, and in a way exhilarating.

Twenty years later, active film societies exist on literally hundreds of campuses. The distribution of 16mm films is becoming big business: Contemporary Films has merged with McGraw-Hill, Audio Films with Macmillan; even Brandon is reported negotiating a merger. Progress, surely? Or will the major corporations which have snatched up the formerly independent distributors play it safe, releasing only conventional, acceptable pictures? If another McCarthyism arises out of the frustrations of a continuing Vietnam war, will these corporate giants keep on supplying "subversive" films, as Brandon did? Or will the standards that apply to television and textbooks—precooked controversy, conventional wisdom—also be applied to film?

The old-established film schools (USC, UCLA, NYU) have been joined by others with full film programs; many other universities are gingerly offering film courses of one kind or another; colleges and secondary schools are incorporating film study into their curricula from one end of the country to the other. Film books need no longer be hunted up in secondhand bookstores; Rudolf Arnheim's *Film as Art,* which our Docfilm library possessed in its rare British edition, may be found in any paperback store and sells thousands of copies every year. *Film Quarterly,* which uses many long words and makes no attempt to be popular, may be seen on newsstands next to *Popular Mechanics* or *Hot Rod.*

And where young people during my Docfilm years thought of film as outside the pale of the established arts (drama, poetry, fiction, painting, and music were still the *real* arts, with histories, duly certified basic works, and accepted canons of taste) nowadays professors of literature bemoan their students' faint interest in literary art, and find them willing to talk seriously only about movies. Hairy young men who would have once said they were poets now declare themselves film-makers, and invite girls over to see a few reels of their latest 8mm footage.

Is this satisfying spread of film enlightenment and activity perhaps only another manifestation of Callenbach's Second Law, viz., "Success Is Failure"—though the principle itself was derived from a study of Hollywood career lines? Is the real frontier now elsewhere, in computer art, or portrait painting, or the home fabrication of Molotov cocktails? I have no answer, except to propose a lightning tour of the film scene as it seems to me to have evolved during the ten years *Film Quarterly* has existed; and that will lead us to still more questions.

THE STATE OF THE ART

Are the movies "falling apart," as Pauline Kael has charged, because the plot structures of many current (and popular) films are not the neatly built structures of earlier American movies? This is not merely a trivial debate over changing tastes; it raises the larger cultural question of what is happening to form in contemporary art generally. "Perhaps," writes Miss Kael, "people prefer incoherent, meaningless movies because they are not required to remember or connect" and she goes on to discuss the misfortune that is "the acceptance of art as technique." After some experience with teaching them, I do not share her worry that young audiences will be bulldozed into reacting to movies in the safe, anxious ways they have been taught to react to Shakespeare; but it seems to me that narrative form *has* certainly been taking a beating, and we critics have not been actively enough exploring the implications of this. I do not find the fracturing of old narrative standards a menace in itself. Jiggling a time sequence to no purpose seems to me exactly as tiresome as keeping a time sequence chronological to no purpose—no more and no less. An episodic structure, like that of Godard's *La Chinoise,* may seem intriguing to some viewers and irritating to others; but this phenomenon is at least partly explainable by differing expectations about the "allowable" forms of film. People who are reasonably willing to let poets write lyrics which are non-narrative do not always extend the privilege to film makers, whose control of the viewer's time is absolute and literal (unless he closes his eyes). Yet of course our reactions even to a strictly orthodox narrative film, like *The Thomas Crown Affair* or *The Graduate,* depend on many substantial non-narrative questions: whether we find the characters credible and interesting, whether the atmosphere created by the film seems in good faith, whether the imagery is rich or dull, whether the ideas conveyed in the style and in the dialogue have any relevance to our concerns, and so on. *Une Femme est Une Femme* and *Pierrot le Fou,* two Godard films I do not greatly prize, could have been made with conventional plot structures; but that would not have made them any more interesting. It is doubtful whether *La Chinoise,* or 8½, or *This Sporting Life* could be given any other treatment than they have. The real question, then, is whether contemporary structural innovations have not been essential for artistic reasons—whether, that is, the sacrifice of the kind of action "suspense" associated with the old narrative structures has not been obligatory for certain kinds of films. Films like *Persona* or *L'Avventura* do not goad us to keep wondering "What's going to happen next?" The implicit motto of most modern films is rather "What the hell is going on here?"

Miss Kael is very impatient with the idea that time is important as a "theme" in films. She hates *Marienbad;* and indeed *Marienbad* is a crucial case. For it is at least arguable that a film about obsession could literally not be made convincingly with the old linear causal structure—which is precisely what obsessions negate. Hence Robbe-Grillet and Resnais had to construct a style where the regular flow of time and causation did not obtain, or only haltingly. The result may be, as I think, a lasting work, or it may be, as some believe, an empty bore; but it is a singular achievement, a peculiarly French display of rigor and precision. Nobody is required to like it, or to like Descartes, or Citroën cars. But there is surely room for it in the canon of what cinema can do—unless we wish to close off certain areas of human experience as out of bounds to film makers.

Percy Lubbock's *Craft of Fiction* is a book for which we badly need a cinematic counterpart, because most major stylistic developments of the past decade have been matters of what we might call point-of-view. The narrative structure of the old Hollywood film in the thirties through fifties was that of the omniscient narrator, who could know everything and see everything at all times. The camera, like God, had "the whole world in his hands." Films were structured by universally accepted rules: unless a dissolve or a fade intervened, geographical and temporal continuity was assumed, reinforced by the aural continuity of the sound track. A film made on these stolid assumptions seems cloddish to us now. Even *Petulia,* with its arbitrary contrivances of structure, seems nearer to an honest artistic stance than the regular Hollywood article: we can take it seriously because its camerawork and editing *are not literal.* It is not made in the routine artistic bad faith that underlies the ordinary narrative film, say *The Heart Is a Lonely Hunter,* or *The Fox,* where no difficult questions of point of view have been allowed to arise out of the bland camera's presence.

Why do we now think it immoral of film makers to pretend to omniscience, when earlier viewers were perfectly willing to accord that as the artist's privilege or indeed his duty? One thing that has happened is that the visual image has lost its magic quality because of TV and *cinéma-vérité.* It has been borne in upon us by the casual sloppiness of TV camerawork that the existence of a visual image requires the presence of a taking lens, which some poor slob is operating. Traditional documentaries never lost the luster of artfulness; Flaherty's skies were filtered, and Grierson's workers were posed. But we now know, from the direct cinema films, what life looks like when it is captured with very little interference. We know instinctively, by the feel and movement of the image, that the theatrical film is built upon interference, control, preparation. We accept the presence of the camera there too, but we demand that the artist acknowledge its presence. In return we accord the artist certain new freedoms. His performers may now look at the lens—formerly a sacred taboo. His film may bear visible marks of having been worked upon: obtrusive editing, special titles. Most precious of all, he is no longer obliged to pretend that his film came into existence automatically or magically. The modern film is visibly constructed by the hand of man, and not by the eye of God. It has become, for sensitive viewers, slightly embarrassing to watch a film built on other assumptions—like watching a man who doesn't realize that he has a hole in his pants. The modern artist whom we find comfortable has sewed on a bright-colored patch, or is busy exploring the hole with his finger. With him, we know where we are.

THE STATE OF FILM CULTURE

Every television viewer—which means just about everybody—has some grasp of the changes outlined above. But understanding of film developments in the sense of following the appearance of new artists, making an effort to grasp the significance of new trends, has been spreading to a larger group of informed and curious students, film-society people, film makers, and so on. Clearly, the chosen people have multiplied. More Americans now know far more about films than they did in 1958. They have seen more films, and more varied kinds of films. They read more film books and magazines. They support film festivals in San Francisco and New York. It is no longer necessary for us to lecture on why film is an art; *Life* magazine takes care of that. We may not have a Cinémathèque such as they boast in Paris, but we have admirable repertory theaters in several major metropolitan areas. Censorship restraints on film have been chiseled away through the decade, thanks to legal actions by exhibitors and distributors, until only a few local ordinances remain; the screen has been accorded the same constitutional protections as other forms of expression. The feared Hollywood Code, by which a narrow Catholic moralism was forced upon a compliant industry, resulting in the hypocrisy and perverted puritanism of earlier decades, has been revised and reinterpreted, like some awkward early encyclical, to accommodate the big companies' need to compete in sexual candor as well as sadism and violence.

Before World War II, it would not have been far wrong to say that the only people who knew anything substantial about movies were the people in the studios. The situation has now changed so drastically that cynics ask whether anybody *in* the industry knows anything about movies—and that this is not an idle jest may be learned from those who have, for instance, gone through the experience of having their film publicized by a big movie company, or talked to a Hollywood movie-maker about his reactions to "foreign films." Perhaps it would be more accurate to say that people in the business care about the business; people outside care about films. There are now literally thousands of Americans outside the industry who have watched films carefully enough, or made enough films of their own, that they can tell when camerawork is incompetent or editing is sloppy; they can spot phony lighting; they laugh at idiotic dialogue; they can tell when a film maker is making it, and when he is just wasting their time. It is often startling for Hollywood film makers to come into contact with young people, even those outside film circles; one gathers that they had not expected to be found out, or subjected to such embarrassing questions. Intelligent film columns appear in most mass-circulation magazines, and in many smaller periodicals; they are read by millions of people.

Surveys of the general mass audience, nationwide, urban and rural, tells us it is younger and better educated than before. Even old-timers in the industry do not seem to talk any more about "the twelve-year-old mind." Theaters are not being called Bijou or Embassy any more, but Cinema II or New-Metro. Mass audiences have no difficulty in following *Tom Jones* or *Help!*, perhaps because the visual acuity they presuppose is no greater than that of the better television commercials. Camp films—the would-be-serious middlebrow films of the thirties and forties—are popular not only in homosexual circles but because self-consciousness has come to seem inescapable anyway; so why not enjoy it in Bogey or Bette? The audiences are growing hippier, warier, less easy to fool. Yet they keep coming into the theaters; and money is going into the construction of new walk-in theaters, while drive-ins become more and more the exclusive preserve of the family trade and the young who need a place to make out.

THE STATE OF THE INDUSTRY

Hollywood, like Italy, may be "only a geographical expression"; its sound stages are filled nowadays with TV quickies, while many movies are shot elsewhere. Yet even after the dissolution of the old studio system and the rise of the "independent" method of film financing, the industry has hardly become the welter of small competing firms a naive economist might have expected. Some power has indeed been diffused, from the former studios toward their former employees: the high-priced stars, a diminishing band who have now incorporated themselves and operate on percentages not salaries. And the initiative has moved from studio executive offices to the offices of packagers—independent producers and agencies—who juggle tested properties from fiction and the stage with tested performers, and come up with satisfactory combinations. But there is still somebody the packages must be satisfactory to; and as it happens these are the major distributing firms—the remnants of the old film trust—which, like the body of a beheaded chicken, go on running around and flapping their wings.

The name of their game is desperation, for the old rules have failed, and the risks are rising. There is no such thing as a safe picture any more; audiences have grown unaccountably fickle and unpredictable. Things are obviously changing when *The Graduate* challenges *The Sound of Music* at the box office. But what are they changing to? Nobody knows, and everybody knows that nobody knows.

A healthy situation, ripe for important organizational innovations, one might imagine; yet the one thing that seems certain is that the industrial process of manufacturing films will *not* change. An occasional picture like *The Graduate* may succeed because vast numbers of young people think it is expressing their attitudes (with a terrible irony, they may be right). Such flukes can keep the game going for a long time. Over the next decade the budgets and crews of Hollywood (read "Hollywood-financed and -distributed") pictures will certainly grow still more extravagant. A business is measured by the dollar volume thereof; and the personal interests of its participants are served by monetary expansion, so long as the risks do not get out of hand, because there are bigger pies for everybody to get a slice of.

Going by most lists I know of, not one of the ten or twenty best films since the invention of the art has cost more than one million dollars to produce. Yet a picture with that small a budget is almost impossible to finance in the American film industry today. Americans think big. It is only the results whose size is questionable. And this is not merely an aberration of one small industry. The American method of making films is like the American method of waging war in Vietnam: it involves immense expenditures but it is indiscriminate in its objectives; it provides many lucrative jobs, utilizes ingenious technology, yet the operation is conducted out of touch with significant human reality. Both the war game and the film game have their own reality, of course: they are conducted with real guns, real cameras, and real people, some of whom mean well, at least when they begin to play. But the rules forbid taking into account certain discomfiting facts: that art is produced by artists, that people love their countries and defend them bitterly. Film makers who work like artists (who insist on doing their own work and controlling its finished form) are like Vietnamese who insist on running their own country. They refuse to play the game. They are a threat. Hence Godard's slogan: Create many Vietnams in the film industries of the world.

It is little realized that the American method of film manufacture has been spreading rapidly, in the past several years, on a wave of American finance that has at last penetrated European production to a significant extent. American control of the patterns of film distribution in Europe (and the rest of the capitalist world) was established by the twenties. American companies now control much production not only in England, where this is abetted by government subsidies intended to protect the home industry, but also in France and Italy. Budgets have been rising in Europe too; only the Swedes, with the thrifty example of Bergman always before them, seem to have escaped so far.

Moreover, through communication-satellite agreements and related developments, we must anticipate that in the next decade American interests will come to have an important degree of control over communication media throughout the capitalist world, and the international homogenization of films and television will make a Mustang commercial like *A Man and a Woman* look like virgin Gallic culture.

I do not argue that the emergence of individual talents, of the kind *Film Quarterly* has always watched for, has become impossible in the American film industry; but only a fatuous optimist would think it has been getting easier. We are currently witnessing a small boom in the stock of writers, largely on the strength of the unexpected success of *Bonnie and Clyde;* and greater influence for the writers of original scripts could hardly hurt an industry so parasitic on ideas formed and tested in other media. But the proving of new talents is rigorously commercial; if *Bonnie and Clyde* had failed like *Mickey One*, it would be cited as another case of insufficient caution in trusting untried materials. There are no modest successes in today's Hollywood, and the writer-producers or writer-directors will, like everybody else, have to make it big or not make it at all.

Once upon a time, we are told, the giant studios with their picture-a-week schedules year in and year out maintained a relatively rational apprenticeship system, with promising young men on low salaries making shorts, to show what they could do and learn their profession. Moreover, an astounding percentage of the men in their sixties and seventies who have until very recently been the workhorses of Hollywood (men like Ford, Hawks, Wellman, Vidor, Stevens, Cukor) got into the industry in its early days, before the studios had entered their full-blown factory phase. It was possible, in those days, for a young man with some talent and moderate gifts as a con man to persuade a small producer to let him try something with a couple of thousand dollars. No neophyte can be trusted with a couple of million. The result is that there is practically only one route of entry into film directing at present, and that is from television directing. Yet, since the early-fifties advent of Frankenheimer, Ritt, Lumet, and Mann, this route has not been traveled by any significant talents; evidently the experience of TV direction does something to people. They come through like Elliott Silverstein or Stuart Rosenberg: competent craftsmen in a small way, but with no original vision. Mike Nichols, with a string of Broadway staging successes as credentials, directed an excellent version of *Virginia Woolf;* but after *The Graduate* we realize that much of *Virginia Woolf's* stylistic vitality depended on Haskell Wexler's camerawork, and we look forward uncertainly to *Catch-22.* Francis Ford Coppola parlayed stage connections into a fashionable bit of kookery in *You're a Big Boy Now;* after *Finian's Rainbow* he is attempting a very personal project in *The Rain People,* which he is shooting with a workable-sized crew although with industry money.

Coppola's method of work—which is the method used by the great American pioneers, of course, as well as contemporary European directors—was only possible after lengthy and difficult union negotiations, and it is important to understand this aspect of industrial film-making. The industry has got the unions it deserves. The union position is simple: if movies are multimillion-dollar operations where stars, producers, and directors are paid fantastic sums, then the wealth should be spread around to the working men who push and haul, string the cables, run the machines. Heretofore, the unions have not been willing to recognize that other kinds of movies also exist, with modest budgets and where the film makers and actors are paid modest salaries, and which cannot sustain the costs of huge studio-type crews. Some movies are being made in the world, and even in the United States, by crews of a dozen men. Serious movies not only *can* be made by small crews, they *need* to be made by small crews. Sooner or later, union regulations must take account of the basic quantum-jump in film budgeting; rules that are fitting and proper for monster-budget pictures need to be complemented by rules that are sensible for small-budget pictures. In the long run, a film industry that has no place for small-budget films will find itself without new talents. Indeed it is the panicky realization that its old hands are retiring, and few youngsters are around to take their place, that has led the industry to support the American Film Institute and the film schools, with their schemes for the training of new directors.

It has not been lost upon industry figures that notions of cinematic style and interest have greatly widened since World War II; the commercial successes of *La Dolce Vita, The 400 Blows, Tom Jones, A Hard Day's Night* each pushed back a little the previously accepted ideas of what theatrical films should be. Not only the commercial confidence of the industry but its moral confidence seem to have suffered; the malaise of intelligent and talented Hollywood film-makers confronted by the free and original achievements of *8½* or *The Silence* or *Blow-Up* has been considerable. Nobody likes to feel he is being left behind, and one senses the bitterness when American directors defensively quote their box-office take as opposed to the Europeans'. They cry all the way to the bank, no doubt, but that's better than not crying at all.

OUTSIDE THE INDUSTRY

In any enterprise, distribution is the key. Faced with the massive caution of the established industry, film people in the past decade have pushed in other directions. Interest in foreign and short films has been fostered and served by the 16mm distributing firms and the 35mm importing firms; the result has been a kind of shadow industry, by-passing the regular theatrical system. Persistently, although against great obstacles, independent producers have made feature films for this market; and countless short-film makers have made films, sometimes for no market at all. Even the experimental film makers, who are not very interested in the business side of things, have organized cooperative distribution centers to book their films. The Film-Makers Co-op in New York led the way; now there is also the Canyon Cinema Co-op in San Francisco. Though undercapitalized and understaffed, they serve a growing number of people, and send back a high proportion of revenue to the film makers. (Thus, like co-ops in the grocery business, they give a competitive check against the profit-making firms.)

The volume of work being done in 16mm has become very large in recent years—that is, films made by experimentalists, students, documentary people, outside the special world of the 16mm sponsored film. Much of this work is not very good, but then neither is much industry work. What counts is that, compared to the days when Maya Deren and a few others championed the cause of the personal, "avant-garde" film, dozens of people with talent are busy, and their films are being seen. The center of creative gravity, that mysterious theoretical point, has moved in the United States to a point hovering over the boundaries between the industry and outside film-makers. When historians get around to adding up influences, the names of Bruce Conner, Ron Rice, and Jordan Belson are likely to loom larger than those of Richard Lester and Stanley Kubrick; for they are the men who invented the new forms that *Help!* and *The Trip* and *2001* later cannibalized.

In a curious way, film history is beginning to repeat itself. For new developments in 16mm technology (the light, portable camera, and the portable synchronized tape-recorder) have restored film to something like the simplicity it had in the earliest days of 35mm. We are approaching, in fact, a curious and critical point in our definition of what "a film" is. During the era of Hollywood's dominance, culminating in the elephantine budgets of today, a film has been something requiring the services of several hundred employees to manufacture, the investment of several million dollars, and the commitment of a giant organizational mechanism to distribute. But what if a film is, as it was once thought, only a band of images which can be made by anybody with talent and a couple of thousand dollars? What if both synchronous sound and image can be recorded by two men, operating without wires, cables, lights, reflectors, motor-generators, portable dressing rooms, refreshment trucks? What if it can be distributed through film societies, colleges, museums, 16mm-equipped art theaters? Above all, what happens if ambitious beginning film makers with the most talent begin to make films for this audience rather than to beat at the iron gates of Hollywood?

We face still other puzzling prospects in 8mm. A British device will shortly be available in this country which synchronizes any 8mm battery-driven camera to any tape recorder, at a cost of less than $100. Inexpensive editing and mixing devices will presumably follow. When this happens, any talented person will be able to make films with the flexibility of 35mm, though naturally without the photographic definition. And videotape recorders are now becoming cheap enough to be widely available. Does this matter? Judging from what has been happening with student films, if you give several hundred aspiring film-makers the equipment and stock to work with, at least a couple of them will turn out to be highly talented; one in five hundred may be a really interesting and original artist. Such ratios are not pejorative; they apply also to people who get the chance to make studio films. But what happens to this statistical game if ten thousand or a hundred thousand people begin to put themselves forward as film-makers?

Such a remarkable development, which is more than a gleam in the eye of Eastman Kodak, does not mean that we are about to enter a period when film art takes some kind of qualitative leap to higher levels. But it *does* mean that film at last can operate on the same basis as writing or painting: the means of production are within the grasp of any dedicated person, and the testing of talents can proceed in a more natural fashion. Jean Renoir, whose family had gained a modest fortune from his father's paintings, once remarked that it was a big help to a beginning film-maker if he was rich. What we can expect of the new technology is to diminish the extra obstacle to artistic achievement that the heavy costs of film-making have posed since film became heavy industry. This is not to say that it was easy to become Méliès or Porter or Griffith, any more than it has been easy to become Bruce Baillie or Yoji Kuri or Chris Marker. Nor is it to say that it will be easy, even given work of the highest caliber, to secure public circulation and recognition for it—just as it is not easy to get novels or poetry published. Great notoriety and financial success may now be coming more readily to certain artists, including film-makers, who touch a nerve of the mass society and have a talent for publicity, such as Andy Warhol. But for most serious film-makers, the practicalities of their situation will not be easy. Serious film-makers, however, know that only a fool expects the artist's situation or his work to be easy. Like science and politics, art is worth doing because it is *not* easy.

THE STATE OF OUR AUXILIARY INSTITUTIONS

The Museum of Modern Art in New York, together with the Cinémathèque in Paris, first led the way; today archives exist in many countries, industriously conserving both films and early machinery, film literature, and so on. General museums have begun to regard film as one of their proper concerns. The San Francisco Museum of Art struck out boldly with the Art in Cinema series in the fifties, followed by the early mixed-media shows called Vortex. Today museums across the country are sponsoring miniature "film festivals." Recently a novel and promising archive for experimental, personal films has been set up in the new Art Museum at the University of California, Berkeley; it will conserve the 16mm work of artists whose films have heretofore often been at the mercy of household fires and other hazards. The national collection of films in the Library of Congress has been reviewed and rationalized under a new film-trained curator; and recently, through grants from the American Film Institute, the remaining problem of transferring decomposing early films onto more lasting acetate stock has at last been solved. The history of the art, with certain painful exceptions in the form of apparently lost films (among them Stroheim's complete *Greed*), has been secured. And works of film history, though still rare, are being written; slowly but surely, historical scholarship in film is developing a tradition.

When Colin Young described a plan for an American Film Institute in these pages in 1961, it seemed a lovely idea but unlikely to happen. Today, a nongovernmental, part-industry, part-foundation organization exists, and is going ahead with ambitious plans to bolster our archives, provide grants for young independent film makers, perform scholarly and reference services, and improve American film education at all levels. Plans also exist—though fraught with various uncertainties—for feature films to be produced by new film makers under joint Institute-industry auspices, on "moderate" budgets (about twice Godard's or Bergman's).

Publishers, whose products were after all the first mass medium, no longer routinely reject manuscripts on film. Indeed books about film are sold in numbers that would have been unbelievable a decade ago: books that appeal to dedicated movie goers and also books of a specialized research nature. Many university libraries are building up respectable film collections that would have been hooted off the shelves by academicians earlier.

And the foundations? Their record is not a bright one, if we take seriously their press releases about providing "risk capital for culture." Ford's admirable $120,000 grant program to a dozen experimental film makers in 1964 reaped astonishing fruit: Belson's *Re-Entry*, Conner's *Report*, Emschwiller's *Relativity*—three films that will last. Yet a muddled and ignorant attack in *Time* led Ford timidly to draw back from a projected second round. (Nobody bothers to attack the ballet and music projects which consume enormously greater sums.) Recently the Rockefeller foundation began a modest and intelligent set of small grants to experimental film makers; and even the Guggenheim foundation, whose grants chiefly go to established academicians who don't need them, has given a couple of grants to film makers. A few ingenious souls have been able to pry money out of local or smaller foundations. But in general foundations wish to back respectable, already successful people; as one foundation mogul wrote to me, "We leave poverty programs to the federal government." In plain English, this means that they do not care about artists as much as about their own prestige, and that in particular they do not care about new artists, who are not yet widely known and do not yet have powerful friends and clients. It is well to keep in mind that, press releases aside, a foundation is basically an entity set up for tax and public-relations purposes. Foundation grants are erratic tidbits, useful but irrelevant to the long-range problem, which is how beginning artists can manage to eat while they are discovering if their talent is significant. That problem will only be solved when we have some kind of guaranteed minimum income, so that those strange and gifted individuals who wish to pursue unremunerative activities like writing or painting or film making can at least be sure they won't starve while they try it. Work, in the old sense of labor performed for another man's profit, in return for wages, is indeed going out of style. Millions of members of the expense-account middle class have learned this since the war, and it is at last getting through to ordinary working people and labor organizations. "Work" in the advanced technological society is becoming a formal and party fictional phenomenon; one watches the dials and buttons, but it isn't necessary to actually *do* much. And so increasing numbers of people are able to contemplate what it would be like to work for something, or on something, that genuinely interests them. (As we students, members of a leisured class, used to do in Docfilm.) A great race is on, in American society, between the massive forces of conflict and disintegration set in motion in Vietnam and the decay of the cities, and forces for new and freer ways of living which are being generated. Film is a weapon in that struggle, for only film can literally show it like it is. But film is also a prize: to the winners will go the images of the future.

QUESTIONS FOR DISCUSSION AND WRITING

1. According to Callenbach, what is the relationship between "the movie industry" and "the film culture"? What are their similarities and differences? Is one a part of the other? Explain.
2. In speaking of the seeming disjointedness and incoherence of many modern films, Callenbach quotes Pauline Kael as saying that "people prefer incoherent, meaningless movies because they are not required to remember or connect." Callenbach, on the other hand, says that "I do not find the fracturing of old narrative standards a menace in itself." Do you agree with Kael or with Callenbach? And, menace or not, what do you think is the significance of such films being made and appreciated?
3. Callenbach has a good deal to say about the economics of film-making,

citing for example the extreme importance of "distribution" in this matter. Do you agree with most of his conclusions? Explain.

4. What significance do you see, if any, in the fact that films such as *Easy Rider* and *The Graduate* (at the time this is written) are replacing in popularity films such as *The Sound of Music* or *Camelot*? Does it suggest only that film audiences are growing younger, or that film audiences in general have a greater sense of social awareness? Discuss.

5. If you have seen any or all of the films mentioned by Callenbach in this essay, comment on his attitudes toward them. For example, do you feel that *Last Year at Marienbad* is "a lasting work" or "an empty bore"? Might it be both at the same time? Explain.

6. In speaking of the era of social turmoil in which we live, Callenbach says that "Film is a weapon in that struggle, for only film can literally show it like it is." Do you agree with Callenbach on this—is film part of the "struggle," and can film "show it like it is"?

7. It certainly seems arguable, from reading Callenbach's essay and from a glance at the world around us, that the film is gradually replacing many of the other art forms—particularly fiction—as a source of interest, communication, and aesthetic pleasure. In general, what would you say accounts for this shift and what are its implications?

Peter Michelson

An Apology for Pornography

Trickster, the archetypal fool of Winnebago Indian mythology, was possessed of a phallus so large that he had to carry it over his shoulder. He did not, according to the legend, know either what it was or how it was to be used. But its very bulk reassured him against those who ridiculed his subjection to the huge burden and claimed he could not rid himself of it. For to carry it required, after all, a substantial and unique strength. This mockery, however, eventually took its toll, and Trickster wearied of the weight and mystery; he determined therefore to remove them. Whereupon he discovered, of course, that the joke was on him. Great as it was, his strength could not equably bear the burden, nor his wit devise a release from it.

This is a sobering myth. Rather than celebrating power and potency, like most phallic legends, it documents man's sexual anxiety and ignorance. But it is honest, more honest than men customarily are about their sexuality. There are, for instance, primitive Australian tribes whose traditional teaching does not recognize that copulation causes pregnancy. And the traditions are honored; pregnancy is explained by the woman having slept under a certain tree or having been graced by the light of the moon. In their hearts—and presumably their loins—they may know what's what, but they must speak with a forked tongue.

Nor is this paralyzing duality peculiar to primitive cultures. The stable civilized culture is even more afraid of its own beastly libido (this neurosis is the subject of Weyland Young's *Eros Denied*). Whether rational (as in Plato's *Republic*) or hysterical (as in the Salem witch trials) such a fear attacks the culture's particular libido image. The literature of sexuality has been every bit as victimized by hysteria as were Sacco and Vanzetti. Pornography, it is supposed, constitutes both a social and psychic threat. Society will be terrorized by the rampant lewdness induced by pornographic books—our wives and daughters raped, law and order dissolved. And our sons (somebody has to do the raping) will either be driven to mad carnality or will become idiots driveling in the wake of luxurious onanism. *We—i.e.* the patriarchal we—of course remain impervious.

The legal starting point is the social threat. And here the machinations of the courts at all levels to find evidence of social value in "pornographic" books have resulted in monumental irrelevance. While there are responsible decisions, such as Judge Woolsey's judgment in favor of *Ulysses,* their irony is that, however good they are in particular, they are based on the wrongheaded obscenity laws. Judge Woolsey was critically right to find that *Ulysses* is a complex work, the end of which is not obscenity. But he felt compelled to explain away the pornography and obscenity that are in the novel in order to grant its freedom. The real issue is articulated by Judge Frank's dissenting opinion about the Roth case in 1956. He defined the issue as whether or not pornography, quite distinctly from its social or artistic merit, constitutes a "clear and present danger" to society. He argues that there is no evidence that it does and that such research as has been done is either inconclusive or negates the idea that crimes or neuroses are caused by pornography. Until such time as there is evidence of this, Judge Frank's seems to me the only reasonable standard. There is nevertheless the kind of decision reached through the Supreme Court's recent caprice in the Ginzberg case. In that decision, incisively criticized by Justice Douglas, the character of the book is determined by the kind of advertising with which it is merchandised! An observation of censorship in *Rights and Writers* suggests the sort of patriarchal hysteria which seems to prompt such decisions: "We know of no case where any juror or judge has admitted that *he* found material erotically stimulating or a stimulus to irregular conduct; on the contrary, the expression of concern is always that someone else or some other class of people will be corrupted."

We don't prosecute books or television for misrepresenting marriage, or politics, or religion, or war. But we do prosecute where we think sex has been misrepresented. Plato, for all the dangers of his moral metaphysics, would have at least prosecuted all supposed stupidities equally. It would be neither more nor less criminal in his republic to represent man as pure sexuality than it would be to represent marriage as pure idyll or God as pure saccharine.

As usual in the event of emergency, it's women and children first. But such data as we have (*e.g.* the Kinsey reports, and the Glueck studies for the Harvard Law School) indicate that pornography has little or no effect on women or children. There probably is a psychic threat, but a threat no greater than that posed by any popular fantasy literature. Emma Bovary shows that a mind deluded by romance will make a bad job of reality. That is the danger of romance or fantasy whenever and in whatever way it dominates the mind. And pornography is a kind of romance but no more socially or psychically pernicious than the romance of passion that dominates the lives of Emma Bovary or Heathcliff or the mundane romance of *Please Don't Eat the Daisies*. The representation of life as all passion or all idyll or all sexuality is a delusion but not one that will determine the behavior of any but an already pathological personality. A *preoccupation* with pornography or any other kind of romance may be an index of mental imbalance or even potential criminality, but it is certainly not a cause.

LIMITLESS POTENCY, LIMITLESS LIBIDO

To understand the contemporary working of pornography we must conceive the term in its widest context. Originally it signified writings about prostitutes. But as amateur promiscuity has increasingly supplied erotic fantasy material, pornography has created a new and larger being, *homo sexualis*. This has two images, the erect phallus and the carnal woman. The phallic symbol has become not only a psychological and literary commonplace, but also a cultural joke, and we are long since accustomed to finding one in everything from a new Buick to the Empire State Building. But the female image of *homo sexualis*—the essential pornographic image—is never funny, even in parody. Al Capp's cartoon women, for example, parody this image, enormously breasted and buttocked. But even the parody rides the edge of lust, and these images are much more desirable than ridiculous. For the pornographic world is peopled with men of limitless potency and women of limitless libido. O, the protagonist in *Story of O*, is a good contemporary example. No concerns in the narrative are allowed to obscure the translation of her total existence into terms of sexuality.

In what is perhaps the best critical study of pornography, *Pornography and the Law*, Eberhard and Phyllis Kronhausen observe that, "Both erotic realism and pornography, each in their own way, fulfill certain functions and answer basic needs in the human psyche which have been recognized by many societies and periods; for instance, in ancient Greece and Rome, in the Near East, as well as in China, Japan and India, where erotic art and literature have always been integral parts of the total culture." In whatever art form, pornography documents both man's neurotic and his archetypal concern with sexuality. The neurotic (not to be confused with the pathological) engagement with pornography is the private confrontation of the individual psyche with its sexual needs. The larger cultural engagement with pornography is the public confrontation with archetypal—and usually subliminal—sexual impulses. Pornography then, for better or worse, is the imaginative record of man's sexual will. Let's look briefly at some of the implications of this.

Steven Marcus (*The Other Victorians*) suggests that there is an inverse correspondence between a rising concentration on the dominating and sadistic image of masculine sexuality in pornography and the diminishing actuality of these qualities in real life. He finds evidence for this in the extravagant sense of phallic power so characteristic of pornography, where, as he puts it, "the penis becomes the man: it does the thrusting and not the man; it is its own agent." And in the world of pornography, where sexuality is the prime mover, the penis takes on a kind of omnipotence. Marcus tends to regard this extravagant phallic metaphor as another sign of pornography's juvenility. But its psychological dimensions signify something well beyond the rhetorical crudeness of its masculine vanity.

In her book *Psychic Energy* M. Esther Harding, a colleague and student of Jung, analyzes what might be called the sexual ages of man. The earliest stages are phallic, in which man is synecdochically conceived as penis. There are intermediate stages, where sexuality is stylized and idealized. The graphic representations of the early stages are of course the graffiti of the ages—phallic imagery and symbology. The intermediate stages are represented in the expansion of man's image from penis alone to the whole body—*e.g.* in stylized nude statuary. The advanced stages, dealing in emotional as well as physical sexuality, are more difficult of representation. The dynamics of psychic sexuality are beyond the static restrictions of painting and sculpture, but perhaps the film can overcome this. Yukio Mishima's recent film *Rites of Love and Death* or the Swedish film *Dear John* may be examples. But the point is that we do experience these archetypal sexual ages, perhaps all of them simultaneously, and in both a personal and cultural context. And it is a natural impulse to express them. Pornography, in the sense that I am defining it, is the primal manner of this expression. As our knowledge of sexuality increases and is assimilated into the culture, as psychological studies (we are still explicating Freud, Jung, *et al.*), sociological studies (such as the Kinsey reports), and physiological studies (such as Masters' and Johnson's recent *Human Sexual Response*) give us greater understanding of human sexuality, so will pornography, the literature of that sexuality, exhibit a greater artistic sophistication.

A comparison of the contemporary *Story of O* with the eighteenth century *Memoirs of a Woman of Pleasure* (*Fanny Hill*) will authenticate this evolutionary progress. *Fanny Hill* describes a prostitute's life, with the end of exploiting the obvious orgasmic stimuli in the subject. Fantasy is central to this end, and to induce it a kind of realism is affected through description of an occupation where rampant sexuality is made believable so that the reader can identify with it. Thus the action adopts the epistolary narrative device, the trappings of a specific sociological setting (eighteenth century London), and is resolved with a gratuitous moral apostrophe on virtue and honor. In these respects it parodies the techniques of the eighteenth century novel. Fanny's first letter puts it thus: "Truth! stark, naked truth, is the word; and I will not so much as take the pains to bestow the strip of a gauze wrapper on it, but paint situations such as they actually rose to me in nature, careless of violating those laws of decency that were never made for such unreserved intimacies as ours; and you have too much sense, too much knowledge of the ORIGINALS themselves, to sniff prudishly and out of character at the PICTURES of them. The greatest men, those of the first and most leading taste, will not scruple adorning their private closets with nudities, though, in compliance with vulgar prejudices, they may not think them decent decorations of the staircase, or salon."

This is a good and true argument. But it is rather a rhetorical gambit persuading the reader to believe in the descriptions and not feel guilt, which would of course ruin their effect. From this point the novel turns a standard eighteenth century plot into a paradise of erotic fantasy. Fanny, a poor, provincial innocent, goes to London where she is de-flowered and debauched by urban decadence and aristocratic profligacy. In a nice touch, the story is resolved when Fanny is reunited with her first despoiler and true love; they marry and live ever after in virtue, honor and penitence. The key here is that the story is essentially description of sexual acts to the end of inducing some kind of orgasmic fantasy. Although the standard situations of the early English novel are employed—Fanny's world is shot through with the vicissitudes of poverty and innocence in the clutches of City and Aristocracy—the story is altogether focused on fantastic sexuality. There is a suggestion of moral causality, but it is so slight and so overshadowed by sex that it signifies nothing. There is no attempt to *explore* any of the implicit moral or psychic problems.

THE STORY OF O

The essence of *Fanny Hill* is simplicity, simplicity of theme and simplicity of description. *Story of O*, on the other hand, adopts the complexity of abstraction and metaphor so characteristic of the modern novel. It is a metaphor of love as libido. If that figure contains all the paraphernalia of pornography—whips, chains, tortures, sadism, masochism, masculine power, feminine submission, sexual anonymity (At one point O is blindfolded and brought into a room where "A hand seized one of her breasts, *a* mouth fastened on the tip of the other." Sex without superego.), and so on—it also contains the complex apparatus of the psyche. O submits herself to a brotherhood of sexuality which exploits and punishes her body, exorcises her will, dominates her total being, and finally is the cause of her self-destruction. She gives herself again to her surrogate lover, proving and taking refuge in her capacity of love; he abandons her also and she kills herself, but only after securing her master's permission.

The story provides, thus, two erotic points of view. From the masculine perspective it describes a complete liberation of the sexual libido. Men possess and enjoy O anonymously, without consequence or emotional responsibility. Her need for love brings her to them, which is a nice male power fantasy. And once they are through with her she is simply discarded; they have in fact the power of life and death, another nice male power fantasy. But from the female viewpoint the story arouses intense anxiety, a sure antidote to pornographic fantasy. O's captivity may be ended whenever she wishes, but to wish it is to forfeit the love she so desperately needs. Thus she is confronted constantly by the fear of loss. And of course she does lose that love, twice. And the consequence is suicide. Here is another classic female anxiety, that love for a man will subsume self identity, and the loss of the love will leave her without reason to be.

What is important here is that O becomes the ur-woman in quest of love. She is thus exposed to its complete domination and consequent agony. Is she, then, an allegorical figure, perhaps the first *Everywoman?* Certainly everything about her is feminine stereotype—her love, her submissiveness, her sexuality, her annihilation of self, her anxieties, everything. At one point in *Peyton Place* (also written, remember, by a woman) a young girl says to her paramour, "Come on Honey. Love me a little. . . . Come on Honey. . . . Hard. . . . Do it hard, Honey. Bite me a little. Hurt me a little." This is O's position; except she says, "Hurt me a *lot.*" On the one hand, she is the answer to every man's secret dream. On the other hand, she is an object awful in her implications. It is the former quality that makes her story pornographic. And it is the latter quality that takes her story beyond simplistic exploitation of sexual fantasy and lets it metaphorically explore a fundamental human condition.

Admittedly, these examples have higher artistic claims than most pornography. But I am interested here in its nature and artistic potential, and must consider therefore its highest stages of development. The hard core or commercial pornography is static and its ends are served by the simplest of descriptive techniques and rhetorical gambits (see Eberhard and Phyllis Kronhausen's *Pornography and the Law* and Steven Marcus' *The Other Victorians* for analyses of pornographic structure). But there is another and higher form of pornography which might be called *literary;* it is an exploration of human sexuality. This is real pornography (not what the Kronhausens call erotic realism). It does more than exploit its subject. We are, as Freud observed, *all* of us more or less neurotic. One aspect of human neurosis is the rhythm of expectations and frustrations which marks our sexual lives. Pornography on its lowest level exploits this rhythm by providing easy fantasy gratifications. On its highest level it *explores* this rhythm, its moral and psychic implications, and to the degree that it does this it is poetic. This is the pornography being absorbed into what we call Literature, and it is represented by such works as *O*. The fact of pornography's evolution out of its own genre and into the larger literature means that pornography must also be considered as a rhetorical device for that literature. Faulkner, for example, although no mere pornographer, is certainly one of the most pornographic of modern writers. He often uses pornographic scenes and situations (the cockpit copulation in *Pylon*, the romance of Mink Snopes in *The Hamlet*, etc.) to articulate his total scheme. It is perhaps in this latter rhetorical role that pornography will assume its final form and have its greatest significance.

DENYING HUMAN SEXUALITY

What I have been arguing is that pornography, like any literature, is a way of knowing. The irony of its subject, sex, is the irony of another social pariah, the whore. We either deny its literary existence or privately acknowledge our private intimacies with it; and we are correspondingly either astonished or embarrassed to meet it on the street. Critically, if we don't ignore pornography altogether, we condescend to it like reformed sugar-daddies. Legally we invoke "contemporary community standards" against it, as if they were not a fantasy morality derived from vestigial Puritanism rather than human experience. And thus we insure our ignorance of what it can tell us about the interaction of moral imagination and sexual being. Meanwhile science, having escaped community standards and academic condescension in the guise of a white coat, goes on documenting a reality we deny our imagination.

For Plato the true was necessarily the beautiful. For us the true is much more likely to be the ugly or grotesque. A whole tradition argues this. Stanley Kowalski calls on his "colored lights," but it is finally the bright white light of revelation that brings the play's moment of truth and beauty—Blanche, Stanley and Mitch all exposed, ugly and helpless. And Martha and George in *Who's Afraid of Virginia Woolf* expend their full energies to show their young guests the true, the blushful Hippocrene—their monumental ugliness. Our literature adopts an aesthetic that aims to reveal the ugly as the true, and it often uses the sexual libido, which our culture has turned into a species of the ugly, as part of its rhetoric.

For the eighteenth and nineteenth centuries ugliness was artistically tolerable only when used as a dialectical agent (*e.g.* satire) to enforce the idea of a beautiful and harmonious nature. It was an aesthetic that dismissed all aberrations as irrelevant. Contemporary aesthetic practice uses this process but reverses the values. Like Satan, it says, "Evil, be thou my good," and plays the role of devil's advocate, using the ugly to penetrate a cosmos no longer thought to be either benevolent or harmonious. It is at best indifferent, at worst malign. The ugly, then, becomes an ironic figure of revelation, exposing an implacable universe unrelieved by moral or spiritual design. Sartre's concepts of *slime* and *nausea* are eloquent statements of an aesthetic of the ugly. And the Theater of the Absurd is its most prominent practitioner. Pornography, the kind represented by *Story of O*, is a manifestation of the ugly. It does not romanticize sexuality; sex, unlike John's other wife, is not beautiful. It is simply there, at the center of man's life, dominating love, aspiration, happiness, all human experience.

Perhaps, as Freud suggests, our sexual impulses cannot be gratified without being cultural outlaws. Perhaps sexuality requires being worked out through cultural taboos. If so, this argues a fearful human necessity. We take LSD trips in an effort to find (or escape from) the true and maybe the beautiful. The danger is that our vision (perhaps of ourselves) will be destructive and make us flip altogether. But our ignorance is desperate enough so that we take the risk. Although the dangers are much smaller, pornography is part of this contemporaneous urgency to pursue the true. It too explores the unknown and therefore fearful in us. Our glimpses into that world refute our private and public lies. We can keep going—into the psyche as into space—and risk the dislocations that new knowledge brings, or we can collapse at the naked sight of ourselves. Not to explore the impulse to pornography is a form of denying human sexuality. We are, willy-nilly, brought to the overriding question of the modern imagination: how much deceit can we afford?

QUESTIONS FOR DISCUSSION AND WRITING

1. Michelson begins his essay by recounting the myth of Trickster, the archetypal fool with a huge phallus. What is the importance of this myth to the rest of the essay?
2. Michelson points out that we "don't prosecute books or television misrepresenting marriage, or politics, or religion, or war. But we do prosecute where we think sex has been misrepresented." What does he mean by this?
3. In his discussion of *Story of O*, Michelson suggests that O may represent "the first *Everywoman* . . . the answer to every man's secret dream . . . an object awful in her implications." Discuss.
4. What is the difference between "pornography" and "obscenity"? Between "pornographic" and "erotic"? Is a pornographic photograph, for example, the same as an erotic or obscene novel? Explain.
5. Michelson quotes the Kronhausens as saying that "Both erotic realism and pornography, each in their own way, fulfill certain functions and answer certain needs in the human psyche. . . ." And Michelson himself says

that "Not to explore the impulse to pornography is a form of denying human sexuality." Do you agree with this general view? Explain.

6. In general, does Michelson seem to be arguing for allowing or encouraging pornography in our society, or is he arguing for a greater degree of self-awareness? Explain.

7. Can pornography be regarded as a form of cultural expression? For example, America is considered by many Europeans to be the pornography capital of the world. Do you feel that pornography is especially suited as a mode of expression to American society? Discuss.

8. Michelson says that "For Plato the true was necessarily the beautiful. For us the true is much more likely to be the ugly or grotesque . . . the ugly, then, becomes an ironic figure of revelation." If Michelson's statement is true, what are its implications? If you think it is false, explain why.

Tom Wolfe

The Put-Together Girl

In San Francisco, Broadway is "the strip," a combination of Macdougal Street in Greenwich Village and strip row on "East Bal'more" in Baltimore. It is about four blocks long, an agreeably goofy row of skin-show nightclubs, boho caves, saturated in black paint, with names like "Mother's," featuring light-projection shows, monologuists, *intime* jazz shows with brooding Negroes on the bass, and "colorful" bars with names like Burp Hollow. There is one tree on Broadway. It is about three inches in diameter, about 12 feet tall, and has 342 minute leaves on it and a tin anti-urine sleeve around the bottom. Carol Doda was standing under this tree as if it could hide her. A colored fellow from the parking lot up the street was standing out in the street trying to get her a cab. It is hard for Carol Doda herself to stand out in the street on Broadway and start waving for cabs. There is no telling what would happen or how many flaming nutballs would stop or—who the hell knows what?—because of "them," *them* being her breasts.

Old Italian women walk by her on the street and say to each other, "*Strega! Strega!*"—not knowing that Carol is a nice Italian girl herself from Napa Valley, and understands that they are saying, "Witch! Witch!" because of *them*.

Middle-aged women, the kind of Hard Lips who wear bib-chains on their eyeglasses and work behind hotel cigar counters, walk by at lunchtime and say, "Aw, go back to jail"—because of *them*.

About 3:30 p.m. grown men wearing rep ties and just emerging from long—tuh-*unh!*—liquid lunches walk by her and grin and aim their fingers at her like needles or guns or something and say, "Pop! Pop!"— because of *them*.

Even Carol Doda has started thinking of them as *them*. There they are secured to her pectoralis major like *acquisitions*.

"When a man asks me out, I never know if he is interested in me or *them*." That is the way she thinks about it.

Them! Carol Doda has had injections of a silicone emulsion put into her breasts in regular installments over the past three years. They have grown, grown, grown, enlarging like . . . dirigibles, almost as if right in front of the eyes of the crowds—they line up out there—who come every night of the week to see Carol Doda's "topless" act. Every night, seven nights a week, Carol Doda descends through a hole in the ceiling of the Condor Club. She comes down doing a dance called the Swim by herself on top of a piano that has been pulled up to the ceiling on pulley wires. The Condor modestly advertises her on the marquee outside as "Miss Carol Doda, the Girl on the Piano." But the crowds line up out there every night, where the sidewalk curves down the hill on Grant Street, it comes right into Broadway right there, and all those people are out there practically panting. Topless, topless, the girl who blew up her breasts, Wonder Breasts, Wonder Breasts, Gimme a mih . . .

Then all the spotlights shine up to the ceiling, and Sam the Man and everybody go into a rock 'n' roll song called "Memphis, Tennessee." The lights shine on a nutty-looking thing, the bottom of a cocktail-grand piano, the top of which is flat up against the ceiling. Carol Doda! The piano starts coming down slowly on its pulley wires, and the first thing everyone sees is a hole in the ceiling with a heavy red ruffling inside of it, sort of like a gigantic Louis XIV version of a heart valve. Two legs are sticking out of it and down on the piano. Carol Doda! Carol Doda is descending, dancing the Swim. First, her legs, perfectly white legs, churning about, then her thighs, her hips—she is wearing a rather remarkable bikini cache-sex of some sort that starts up around her waist but has no side at all, just stretched down through her loins. She is also . . . *bottomless,* as they say in the trade, but this room full of craning heads, tilted back in a silent glom barely even notice that. They are all waiting . . . for *them.*

The piano settles down, Carol Doda is on top of it dancing the Swim, the Jerk, the Frug, the Jump, the Spasm, the—her face is up above there like a pure white mask, an Easter Egg yellow explosion of hair on top, a pair of eyes with lashes like two sets of military shoe brushes, ice-white lips, two arms writhing around, her whole ilial complex writhing around, but all just a sort of pinwheel rosette for *them.* Carol Doda's breasts are up there the way one imagines Electra's should have been, two incredible mammiform protrusions, no mere pliable mass of feminine tissues and fats there but living arterial sculpture—viscera spigot—great blown-up aureate morning-glories.

The whole performance is—it is not a strip tease, it is no kind of *tease,* it is an animated cartoon, like the old Tom & Jerry cartoons where Tom, the cat, sees the bulldog coming and about forty-four sets of round white eyes—*boing*—go springing out of his eye sockets. Carol Doda is not teasing anybody. Her prize is up there as if on a platter,

She never smiles; she just draws her big ice-white lips into an O from time to time. She doesn't even have the old pig-bladder choreography of the burlesque houses; she just jerks, spasms, and writhes in the standard American twist-frug genre dances like any little high school bud from the garden apartment next door at the Saturday-night dance bumping away doing the Monkey under a strawberry Feather Duster coiffure while her mother looks on from the side with a pleasant smile on her face as if to say, Well, yes, Carmen is very social.

Sam the Man goes into an elaborate parody of ecstasy. He swings the saxophone down between his legs and then over his shoulders, he rolls his eyes, *Pretty woman walking down the street,* he flaps his brown jowls, he breaks into a sweat, he lolls his tongue out. Carol Doda does the Puppet. Oldie but goldie! "O" go her lips. They all break into *I Left My Heart in San Francisco*—Sam the Man starts moaning in front of the microphone as if in utter ecstatic depletion. "Oh-h-h-h-h-h, I can't s-t-a-n-d it! It's too mu-u-u-u-u-uch! Ah-h-h-h-h-h! O-o-o-o-o-o-o-o-o-o-o! Eee! Eee! U-u-u-u-u-um! Wheeeeedeeeeeeeeeee! Eeeeh! Yuh! Yuh! Oink! Blooogeeee! Snerk! Wiffle! Pooooom—poompoom! Gush! Mips! Eeeeeeeh-yah! Eeeeeeerrrrrrrrgggggh! Make her stah-ah-ah-ah-ahp it! Lock me up! I'm going crazy! I'm flipping! I'm wigged out! I'm zonked! I'm erk-erk-erk blooooooooooooogeeeeeeeeeeeeeeeeee! It's unbelieva-bobba-beeva-bova-bavvy-bipblap-blupbloop-poobog-mih-mih-scoony-scaggy-mimsy-poppy! Too mu-u-u-u-u-ch! Bad ma-a-a-a-a-a-a-n! Th ol' wild bird is gra-a-a-a-a-abbin' me! I caint tuh-*unh* tuh-*unh!!*"—and so on and so forth. But all the Hard Worsted set just sits there refusing to take the comic cues—I'll be damned, so that's what they look like, yes, I'll be damned, look at that, you get that, there it is right up there in front of me. And even the women—they want to *study* this phenomenon. All right, it's *freakish*—see, they don't . . . *give,* they hold *forth,* they're substan—but what does it feel like? it must weigh— and then look at them all fastened on her, heads craned back, *goggling*— until the piano starts ascending toward the hole in the ceiling with Carol Doda still twisting and jerking about with the lights lighting *them* from below as she goes up. *I lost my heart, in San Fran-cis-co.* The silent anointed heads of all the worsted lovelies in here start craning back, back, back again while Tony Cassara and Sam the Man play the anthem of San Francisco, *I left my heart—*

The anthem indeed. The Topless, Carol Doda and *them* are suddenly one of San Francisco's great resources, along with the cable cars, the hills, the Bay, the View, and the Golden Gate. There are at least fifteen "topless clubs" in San Francisco. They are nightclubs, chiefly, like the Condor, offering bare-breasted girls in bikini versions of the G-string, like Carol Doda's, just standing up there and doing ordinary American dances, the Twist, the Frug, the Swim, and so forth. Yet there is no greater tourist and convention attraction in America, with the possible exception of Manhattan.

The most curious of all are two clubs, the Off Broadway and the Cellar, which have "topless waitresses," as they are called, serving lunch wearing nothing but flesh-colored bikini underpants and high-heeled shoes. The new business lunch for—

—the 6 a.m. specters of Russian Hill. At six o'clock in the morning one can look up Russian Hill, San Francisco's best apartment area, from the foot of Broadway, where it suddenly turns steep up the hill, above the tunnel, and down the hill, silhouetted against the first pink-ash light of dawn, come good straight cleaned-and-pressed figures in hard worsted, carrying attaché cases, the leather lunch pails of Wall Street, walking down the slope, one here, one there, the 6 a.m. specters of Russian Hill, well-to-do, anointed with after-shave and Stephan's hair oil which his regular barber lets him have—San Francisco brokers going to work on Montgomery Street, the financial district, at 6 a.m., since by then it is 9 a.m. in New York, and the Exchange is opening and won't wait, and down they come down the hill as if in some Fellini scene.

A group of "underground" moviemakers who live in quonset huts beside the Berkeley railroad tracks are still up with their hand-held camera filming some sequence in which three music students wrapped in Reynolds Wrap leap like Raji-Putra, the Indian dancer, against the first rays of the rising sun. They just stare stupidly at the anointed specters and miss the real movie. Leap, Raji-Putra! Anyway, by twelve noon, these same stock-broker specters of Russian Hill, along with more, sometimes hundreds of San Francisco businessmen, are filing up toward the Off Broadway, the Cellar, along with favored clients, for a "topless lunch." It's a *lark*, a novelty, I mean, one's clients really get a kick out of this screwy spectacle—but the same faces keep coming back, over and over.

The Off Broadway has a deep black-light Soho gloom in it. All the topless places in California set themselves in this gloom, presumably so the customers can feel that nobody can watch them watching the club's amateur galaxy of bare breasts.

The Style Show starts. Girls start parading up on the bandstand. Sandra has on a transparent lace bed jacket or whatever it is, just hanging down from the shoulders, and she parades about in her bikini underwear and high heels in the fashion-show manner. A girl at the microphone says in the boulevard manner of the fashion-show announcer, ". . . using heavy lace, of course, for *added support*."

The Off Broadway's *them*—the Off Broadway has a girl named "Yvonne D'Anger." She comes out from an illuminated theatrical gauze dressing room at one end of the bandstand—the star!—a round-faced girl, almost petite, but with great tumescent dirigible breasts sitting out.

She walks about the stage, then winds her way through the tables, then back to the stage, where she strikes a cheesecake pose, lying down with her legs curled up and her breasts pointing straight up, like vanilla sundaes, not mushing off to the side the way most girls' would, but sitting straight up, and then another topless girl comes out and takes a picture of her with a Polaroid camera—*flash!*—the flash catches all the craning Hard Worsted faces in an instant, the 6 a.m. Russian Hill specters sitting here, anointed, goggled.

They have missed the Off Broadway's most extraordinary show, however, which is in the kitchen. There is something unforgettable about half a dozen girls wearing nothing but high heels and cache-sexes straining at awkward angles over serving tables in the rising Veg Soup steam trying to balance salads on their arms while their breasts dangle hopelessly in the smeary Roquefort, French, Green Goddess and Thousand Island thickets and a battery of spade chefs yell at them like they were nothing but a bunch of unusually clumsy waitresses in the lunchtime rush . . .

Carol Doda's doctor on Ocean Avenue in San Francisco has an on-going waiting list of women of all sorts, not showgirls, who want the series of injections. Well, why should any woman *wait*—wait for what?—when the difference between dreariness and *appeal* is just a few centimeters of solid tissue here, a line stretched out there, a little body packing in the old thigh, under the wattles there—or perfect breasts? The philosophy of "You have only one life to live, why not live it as a blonde?"— that is merely the *given*. Even in old-fashioned New York there is hardly a single gray-haired woman left in town. And why stop short of the perfect bosom? Why do people talk about "the natural order"? Such an old European idea—one means, well, the *wheel* violated the natural order, for God's sake; hot and cold running water violated it; wall ovens, spice bars, Reddi-Tap keg beer and Diz-Poz-Alls fracture the natural order—what are a few cubic centimeters of silicone?

The silicone is injected in the form of an emulsion into the muscles and tissues all around the breasts where they join the chest. Exactly what happens to the emulsion after it is injected is not known. But some of it *moves around*. The shots bring the breasts up taut, at first, but then they begin to sag; continued booster shots are necessary. Sometimes a ring of shots seem to slip into a lake or puddle down in there somewhere. Sometimes the emulsion disappears; it goes off somewhere in the body. Whether or not it can cause cancer is simply not known.

But there are plenty of women in California who are willing to take the chances, whatever they are. There are about seventy-five doctors in Los Angeles giving the treatments, and one of them does twenty-five women in a week. There are two hundred women taking the course in Las Vegas alone. More than half of all these patients are housewives, and some women bring their teenage daughters in there because they aren't developing fast enough to . . . compete; well, Carmen *is* social.

And actually it's such a simple thing in a man's world where men have such simple ideas. After all, Carol Doda *developed*, from a bust measurement of about 35, up, up, month by month, to 44, through twelve months, eight sets of shots, $800. And why not? After all, one, anyone has fillings in the teeth, plates in the skull, a pin in the hip—what is the purpose of living, anyway? just to keep on living or to enjoy, be adored, favored, eyed—or—

Carol Doda turns around under the tree. A man in a white suit comes along. He just met her the other day. He invites her into Enrico's, the café. The colored guy isn't having any luck hailing a cab anyway. Enrico's is a kind of Via Veneto café for San Francisco. It has an outdoor part, under an awning by the sidewalk, and then a plate-glass front and more café tables inside. All sorts hang out there, actors, advertising men from the Jackson Square section nearby, women from Pacific Heights down at North Beach shopping. They head inside, but Carol Doda looks a little apprehensive. Carol is wearing a thin white turtleneck sweater, and *them* form a rather formidable shelf, but the leather Eton jacket covers her up pretty well. Everybody around Enrico's recognizes her; Burgess Meredith is in there in a great sport jacket. Herb Caen the columnist is in there. Larry Hankin and a lot of other people from "The Committee" are in there. But there is always this possibility, this business of, well, frankly, getting thrown out. Enrico's wife or somebody threw her out of there once, and just the other day Mrs. Pacini over at Amilio's threw her out. Carol is looking around a little in Enrico's.

"What do they say to you?"

"I don't know— She kept saying, 'We don't allow Topless here. Put your coat on, we don't allow Topless here.' I wasn't *topless*. I mean I had a regular dress on, what I wear all the time."

Carol Doda's mouth keeps changing from a smile to some kind of bewilderment when she talks about all this. She has a slightly husky voice but not a low voice. She has model-goggle sunglasses up over her face like two huge shields, and she keeps looking around.

"What did your friends think?"

"A lot of them . . . they don't have the same *air* about them anymore. They used to treat you palsy-walsy. I mean when I was a cocktail waitress. And then suddenly people begin to change. They act like *I've* changed, like they think I'm a snob or something now. It really used to bug me, I couldn't figure it out; I mean, I hadn't changed, *they* had changed. It used to break my heart. Then I realized the public will not let you stay the same. I'm never snobbish. It's them, they refuse to accept you because you're well known. I don't know, maybe you have to change, because the public insists that you change."

She is sincere about all this; *changing*. She has a lot of the old

North Beach I'm-searching, self-analysis syndrome. What is going on? She's a celebrity, and she likes that, but people have funny attitudes.

She *has* changed. Look at *them;* maybe that is what is on people's minds. But *she* hasn't changed, says Carol Doda. The silicone treatments were just a cosmetic; it wasn't all that drastic a thing. She was working as a cocktail waitress, and actually she had built up a big following in the Condor. Of course, people knew her. She used to wisecrack with them. She looked great. She had a great trim figure. Then she started dancing on the piano. It began almost like a gag. One night—this whole topless bathing suit thing had been going on, in the papers and everything, and the guys there said go ahead, go *topless,* Carol. So she did, right there, and Topless was born. There was Carol Doda, dancing in a topless bathing suit.

Carol Doda—Topless!—was great stuff from the start. Customers were piling in. But Carol—Carol had a nice figure, a trim figure, a real dancer's figure, but she wasn't . . . spectacular. It was one thing to have a nice overall figure, but if you were Topless, the thing was to be showing something spectacular; otherwise why take the top off? So guys around there started saying, Why didn't she get *the shots?*

"I was really scared when I went to the doctor," Carol is saying to her pal in the white suit. Then she brings her hands up. "The needle—well, it's about *this* long, it's like a horse needle or something. It really looks awful. Some of the shots he puts in all around here, near the surface. But some of them are really deep. When the needle goes in—it really scared me at first, these pains shoot all up through here and down your arms. You can feel it all the way down in your arms."

"Are you worried about the long-range effect, what the silicone might do to you?" says White Suit.

"No," Carol says, "the tissue grows around the silicone. It's just a short process."

"Does the whole thing make you—your breasts—feel any different?"

"Yes." She laughs but not very uproariously. "I'm conscious . . . of them . . . all the time. They weigh a lot more, a couple of pounds. I have to wear a special heavy brassiere. I have to wear it to bed at night, and I can't sleep on my stomach, it's too uncomfortable. In fact, I can't sleep on my side, either, that's kind of uncomfortable, too. I have to sleep on my back.

"That's one reason I work out all the time. I work out with weights at a gymnasium to build up . . . my pectorals. It helps me support them better."

Self-improvement! But of course! She is a great self-improver. It goes along with the self-analysis. She doesn't smoke; she eats health foods; in fact, on her diet she builds up such tremendous energy, she has to find some outlet for it; the dancing isn't enough; that isn't even tiring; she goes to a gymnasium every day and works out; she lifts weights; she works seven days a week at the Condor, every night, coming down on that piano doing the Swim and the Watusi; it takes a lot of self-discipline, it really does; a side of it nobody knows about—

"Some days when I wake up, I just don't feel like getting up at all and going through the whole thing again," she says. The smile is kind of swimming off her face and then back on and then back off. "But I make myself get up, because if I don't, I'm not really hurting anybody else, I'm letting myself down."

"What are you aiming for, eventually?"

"Well, I'd like to have a big show. I want to be first-class, in New York or Chicago or Miami, some place like that. I've had a chance to go to Nevada, to Las Vegas, but I'm waiting for something big."

"You probably make a lot of money here now."

"Well, not really. Actually, I used to make more money as a cocktail waitress . . . the *tips* and everything . . ."

"You made more money *then?*"

"Yes—but, well. A lot of places here offer me more money and all that to move to their place, but I don't see any point in a lot of moving around like that. That doesn't really get you anything. I'm waiting for something first-class. How do you think the act would go in New York?"

A tall man with great rake features, long Barrymore hair, comes over all of a sudden, some guy she knows, and starts talking and says to Carol, "Hey, Carol, take off those glasses, I can't *see* you."

She looks up with her smile going on and off. "I can't," she says. "I don't have any eye makeup on, I'll feel undressed. I mean it!"

"Aw, come on, Carol—" This goes on for a while, and finally she pulls the glasses off, the great model-goggle shields, and—*strega*, honest *strega*—she is right. Her eyes blink there in the middle of her perfectly white face like something surprised in a nest.

"I always wear eyelashes, top and bottom."

But of course! A heroine of her times! Carol Doda wears false eyelashes, but only to go with her Easter Egg yellow hair, dyed from brown, which goes with her soapstone skin, so perfectly white from remaining forever, every night, within the hot meat spigot casbah of Broadway —Electra of the Main Stem!—in order to show the new world a pair of—at last!—perfected twentieth-century American breasts. You have only one life to live. Why not live it as a put-together girl?

QUESTIONS FOR DISCUSSION AND WRITING

1. What is the tone of this essay? That is, what is Wolfe's attitude toward Carol Doda? How can you tell?

2. How does the style of this essay complement Wolfe's subject matter? In what respects are the style and content of the essay the same? Explain.
3. Does this essay make any statement about the culture which produces a Carol Doda? Does it suggest any trends toward cultural or self-expression? Explain.
4. What do you think of Carol Doda's ambition to go to New York or Miami, or someplace where she can be "first-class"?
5. Wolfe says that "Carol Doda's breasts are up there the way one imagines Electra's should have been . . . great blown up aureate morning-glories." Can you explain the allusion? What is its function?
6. By injecting silicone into her breasts, is Carol Doda practicing deceit, living a lie? Who strikes you as being more "honest," Carol or the people who come to see her?
7. Explain the irony of the final statement of the essay: "You have only one life to live. Why not live it as a put-together girl"?
8. Have you ever known "a put-together person"? Describe her. For instance, would you describe such a person as being a conformist or a non-conformist? Why?
9. In what respects is Carol Doda "a symbol for our times"?
10. Is Wolfe's essay obscene? Pornographic? Erotic? Dirty? Explain.

John M. Johansen

An Architecture
for the Electronic Age

Most of us for some time have been aware of the field of cybernetics and the vast effects of the current electronic revolution. Norbert Wiener, in his book *The Human Use of Human Beings* (1954), presented these matters most vividly. Since that time electronics has made possible accelerated development of computers for data processing, worldwide communication systems by Telstar, and guidance of weapons and space craft. Already several newspapers have installed computer typesetting; soon we will have three-dimensional TV, and at the Massachusetts Institute of Technology a team is developing a nationwide computer network that will make all knowledge, whether stored or presently recorded, instantly available anywhere. Publishing will almost surely undergo a radical transformation; the book will be replaced by research packages assembled to suit specific needs. The takeover by datamation of traditional methods is borne out by the recent news that the Radio Corporation of America has bought out Random House: a very significant event. In addition, cybernetics has already had its influence on teaching, psychology, language and mathematics.

In each period of well-established cultural achievement, there is apt to be a consistency in the thinking and experience of the arts, science and philosophy. In his book, *Music, History and Ideas*, Hugo Leichtentritt points out that in the seventeenth century, for example, as the concept of infinity became widely accepted for the first time in scientific thinking, it was also expressed in the endless vistas of the Baroque painters and sculptors, and in music by the elaborate and boundless developments by composers of the fugue and concerto. Although it may be disputed whether such consistencies in any time were conscious or unconscious, the fact remains that consistencies are indeed found and that for us today there are likely to be similar consistencies. It is with this background in mind that I am prompted, after reading Marshall McLuhan's *Understanding Media*, to examine the new aspects of experience predicated by the electronic revolution, and find their effects, established or predictable, upon our architecture. While certain of our architects who seem not to be aware of the present need reorientation, other architects, who sense the current change, deserve encouragement, reassurance, and a cause around which to rally their valuable talents.

The effects of the electronic age upon architecture may be felt in the following ways:

First, the overwhelming presence of electronic devices will lead to a degree of imitation in the design of our buildings. We witnessed this happening in the 1920's and 1930's when Le Corbusier romanticized and imitated the machine and industrial products. Mies Van der Rohe expresses the industrial processes of rolled steel in the application of standard sections to the facades of his buildings; and Walter Gropius made his great contribution by bringing design talent to manufacturing and building methods. But with the passing of the industrial age, we may now expect an architecture conceived more as a computer, of components rigged on armatures or chassis connected by circulation harnesses. The use itself of electronic terms conjures up new mental pictures of architecture. There should be a new kinetic quality in this manner of assemblage that will be more convincing than buildings that imitated moving mechanical parts yet did not themselves move. Interchangeability of parts with different circuit patterns for various performances may suggest that very different building types, the house, the high-rise office building and the theater, will be assembled of different combinations of the same components or sub-assemblies.

Habitable chambers may be arranged not for closest physical connection, but according to most practical circuiting. Circuit patterns, whether for public use or mechanical equipment, will be shown vividly coursing through, overlaid or circumventing one another as one now sees them in the rear view of a TV cabinet. Intercommunication systems themselves, although less conspicuous, will be given expression. *Plug-in City*, the science-fiction proposal by Peter Cook in 1964 in England, is certainly a bold effort to state our environment in new terms. In this design, buildings old and new were to be plugged into, or removed, at will from a vast raceway of service conduits providing power, water, sewage and transportation. Here, however, the value of this liberating idea derives from a sense of city organization rather than from imitation. So although this influence through direct imitation may be the most readily apparent visually, it is probably the least significant or valuable.

The second influence will be felt through the use of the computer. Already scaled drawings are made from architectural data. Even perspectives are constructed when a computer is given plan and elevation. However, more influential in the design process will be the instantaneous assembly, organization analysis and conclusion of controlling conditions or determining design factors which can relieve us of endless calculation, research and comparative study. The effect will be to make the building in process of design as malleable as clay, which can be manipulated and recomposed or reorganized before our eyes. The aid then is more in planning; the architect will see alternate solutions of building types, configurations and functional organizations simultaneously and instantaneously, by programming different design data into the computer. This will also free the architect's mind, we hope, for greater aesthetic evaluation and judgment, or intuitive flow of creative ability.

Third, architecture must constantly be thought of in new terms that have force and meaning for us today. Such a term is "Cyborg," which may be defined as the entity resulting from the application of attachments to the human body of any mechanical or electronic device, to extend and enlarge the perfomance of its physical or mental faculties. The computer as an extension of the brain is of course the most revolutionary. But why cannot the buildings we live in be considered "extensions of man"—of their inhabitants? The control of natural or artificial light relieves diaphragm adjustment for the eye. The floor platforms and the elevator assist the legs in setting our position in space. The protective walls and roof supplement the limited and inadequate protection provided by our epidermis. Air conditioning is an addition in extension of the nasal functions of constant air temperature control and of the cilia hairs which filter out dust. The concept of "building and man as Cyborg" may well free our thinking architecturally; the extension of man as grafted or as portable equipment and the more fully equipped building may soon be indistinguishable. Then again, as we can already see in terms of self-opening doors and fully programmed temperature control, the building itself will eventually develop into a sensory organism with feedback and consciousness of its own performance.

A fourth influence will be electronic communication itself used within or between buildings. The telephone obviously has already decentralized cities, administrative and government agencies, and much of light industry. In a similar way, the parts of buildings will be decentralized. As McLuhan says, the implosion due to electronic communication will cause an explosion of population and physical plant. Within the building, rooms and departments will be more loosely assembled, as is already true of one college in the West. It is fully equipped for communications, and can provide one hundred and thirty-six lectures simultaneously at any time at any student study on the campus. This arrangement replaces the lecture halls with dormitory rooms or individual student study cubicles possessing total reception. The library will be metamorphosed into a single computer room with limited staff space, which will receive data from its own tape library or from any other library or fact-storage center; it will select, edit, xerox and transmit written and pictorial material.

Generally then, with proximity of building elements no longer necessary for reasons of communication, the building design will be more loosely conceived. The long conduit will replace the short corridor. The new functional configuration will be found to be consistent to or sympathetic with the aesthetic configuration, which for satisfaction of our reconditioned psyche will follow its own process.

However, aside from the planning and organizational aspects of our buildings, the architectural expression is of particular interest and concern. The fifth influence will be the most subtle but the most inevitable of all: that of our reconditioned minds and senses. The architect will undergo—has already partially undergone—a retraining of his perceptive habits, his psyche, his methods of thinking, his language, the relative acuteness of his senses and his aesthetic values. The influence upon him will be partially subliminal, the change in his design partially unconscious. He will produce sooner or later, inevitably, a new architecture.

The sixth and last influence, as I see it, will also be upon aesthetic content, but will be governed by conscious awareness of our changing technology and environment. From what has already been said, it is rather unlikely that a number of the fanciful tacks of current architectural expression will find a place. Historic revival—neoclassic and neobaroque opera houses and museums, neomedieval castles to house factories, neo-Gothic dormitories, and the "mono-pitch school"—is out-of-date. The air terminal that looks like a bird: the "architecture of imagery" is out-of-date. And since the mechanical age has been replaced by the electronic age, buildings styled after machines are out-of-date. Those who do not derive their forms from the experience of our present environment upon our changing habits of perception are out-of-date. Those who approach architecture from an academic or fine arts or "master work" point of view, the "beauty seekers" and the formalists, have no place. As Wiener observed, a rigid deterministic world has given over to one of contingency and organic incompleteness and probability. We can therefore assume that perfectionism and rationalism are irrelevant. For architects oriented in these directions offer society no interpretation or reconciliation with our technological environment—instead, merely an escape. For, as Mr. McLuhan says, we must first understand our environment if we are to control it.

In the mechanical age, action and reaction were not closely connected in time, response was slow, involvement limited, consequences of our actions unreal. In the electronic age, action and reaction are almost simultaneous. "We have extended the central nervous system itself in a global embrace, abolishing time and space," writes McLuhan. This separation of action and reaction or consequence formerly meant noninvolvement. Now, with the technological extension of the self including all mankind, we necessarily participate, and in depth, in the consequences of every action. The theater of the absurd dramatizes the dilemma of Western man who appears not to be involved with the consequences of his actions. The electric speed of bringing all social and political functions together in sudden implosion has heightened human awareness to an intense degree; and the partial, specialized or detached point of view will not serve in the electronic age. The "all-inclusive image" prevails. Wholeness, empathy and depth of awareness is of our time.

The images of the electronic world are continuous, simultaneous, non-classified or noncodified. They run counter to the traditional Platonic compartmentation of ideas and things, and counter to the analytic and rational processes of thought. Images are abstracted and require the viewer's involvement and participation for their complete transference. They represent a continual flow of data, not measured or measurable. This process has been described as a "mosaic" effect of composite impressions producing a total comprehension. Many effects and impressions are absorbed by the viewer instantaneously, involving a fusion of all the senses. The spectator becomes part of the system or process and must supply the connections. He is the screen upon which images are projected. Images as on TV are low definition, therefore requiring high participation. In this sense, the new experience is anti-"square," since "squares" don't get involved. It is "cool," in that the message is implicit. The new media deal in slang rather than in eloquence, since slang is the outgrowth of firsthand experience and the immediate scene; not restated, refined, edited, but real. No detached point of view, whether of physical position or state of mind, is longer possible.

Now we may attempt to restate these experiences and attitudes in architectural terms. If we have been reconditioned to an intensely heightened awareness of places and events, the viewer will expect all parts and aspects of buildings to be made known, to be immediately comprehensible, not as a composite impression but as an all-inclusive image. Buildings will reveal themselves totally. They will clearly express their elements, functions and processes. The viewer will identify with them, feel an empathy with them. "Package design" is out-of-date, and there will be a conscious attempt to force an expression of elements and processes to the exterior, or by pulling apart the elements to allow the viewer to see in depth within, possibly to inner buildings. We are not interested in the epidermis or skin, only, but insist on knowing the mesoderm and the endoderm; that is, the bones and internal organs.

Intercommunication systems within the building will further allow the pulling apart of elements, relieving the current prosaic and boring compactness and density in favor of a vastly more interesting form—space composition effected by the multiple impact of many parts.

The "facade" in the traditional sense, no matter how richly sculpted or how irregular or bold, will disappear in favor of separate habitable enclosures posed freely in space. If it can be said at all that there will still be a facade, it will be a composite of all facets of all enclosures, their four walls, roof and soffit. To use Mr. McLuhan's words, it will become a "mosaic" of facades, a bombardment of the eye by many images. Already I find among the drawings of my current designs, not only the four exterior elevations, but many more sheets devoted to the interior elevations; the inward and side-facing facets.

In this heightened human awareness which the viewer will be trained to feel, occupants will not be lost from view when in the building, but their infusion through space will be seen from outside as well as in. Or, if occupants themselves are not in view, the loci of their coursing will be felt by the shaping of the habitable spaces and passages; we will feel in the enclosed forms the loci of their movements.

The rational, analytic aspects of architecture will give over to a non-classified accretion of elements in continuous uninterrupted flow without any particular sequence. As modern physics no longer sees a universe in which everything happens precisely according to law, which is compact, tightly organized and in which everything is governed by strict causality, so too, our impressions will not be ordered, controlled or in sequence. Impact will derive from group effects, and on every view, the mosaic of staccato images will present themselves. Views will not be selected or limited, but will include unplanned peripheral sensations; adjacent, oblique, marginal experiences; adjunct images of other functions, structures or mechanics. Perhaps the view of a stairway, for example, will be inseparable in a composite view of other elements, or may itself be purposely broken into multiple images.

As buildings become looser assemblages, less finite and static, they will become volatile, will reach out and fuse with adjoining buildings and lose their identity in a continual froth of space-form. It would appear that the current concept of the city as one continuous building is borne out. The individual building appears to be many; the campus, neighborhood or city may in fact be one. The total architectural environment, as McLuhan has said, will be a mythological world in which all things are connected in the human mind and experience, as opposed to the Aristotelian classified world of knowledge and exact definition. We are now closer to the flux, continuous currents, coalescence and change of the earlier philosopher Heraclitus. If architectural elements are not defined or codified, recognizable symbols will not be used, and there will be no fixed architectural language.

The experience we derive from our buildings will be drawn from a fusion of the senses: the impact swift, instant, condensed, total; the message immediate, direct, possibly crude, unedited, unrehearsed, but real. Textures of exposed finishes, for example, allow us to feel with our eyes from a distance; or we see with our sense of touch.

Our designs will use architectural slang. Eloquence in architecture, now so much in vogue, will be out. Slang will be used because as in speech, it is direct, vivid, brash, effective, sometimes ingeniously poetic, and has always to do with immediacy in time and situation; with firsthand experience. This is indeed typical of modern communications. Architects will make known through their design the fact that they have had immediate participation in "pre-living" their buildings, while occupants will in actual "re-living" read back the firsthand experience. Like the computer, the building has "memory," by which previous conditions can be recalled. The architect will reveal his processes of design, and the contractor's processes of construction—may in fact show the building in stages, even incomplete or unresolved in order to allow the viewer to participate in the processes. This is "cool architecture," that is, low definition, high participation, as in electronic communications today. The viewer is required or encouraged to extend his powers to "make the connection," as McLuhan says; to fill in that additional content which is only implied. Low definition will mean that the architectural expression is implicit, not explicit, understated, not overstated, suggested, not hammered home.

Akin to this characteristic is the coming insistence that the architect and occupants will not be detached from the realities of architecture, in the sense that they will not take a detached or contrived point of view, be it academic, preciously professional, or one of personal isolation. Since we cannot detach ourselves from conditions and events as they really are anywhere on the world—or off—we are in fact there. We no longer will have patience with the hypothetical, the make-believe, the isolated event out of natural context, with sophistries, stunts or mannered poses. Architecturally this would condemn historic revival, literary reference, moralizing, academic or fine arts attitudes.

As electronic communications have made it possible to assume a station point anywhere in time and space, our way of viewing our buildings will change for all time. Not only is the fixed axial reference point of the Renaissance out-of-date, but so also is the "Space Time," or moving, station point conceived by Siegfried Giedion, which might be said to represent the mechanical age of the wheel. Now I would make the observation that we will have a new station point of the electronic age: one that is multiple and simultaneous, a "simul-station." Obviously we don't change our physical position within a building as instantaneously as we follow an intercontinental discussion by Telstar. However, we may now be trained to project ourselves into positions, to identify ourselves with many other stations and circumstances. Buildings then will be designed by architects who can project themselves in this way, and for occupants who will easily respond with this same developed faculty of identification in space. Applied literally, any or all station points, fixed positions or loci of moving occupants will be identified and expressed. Rooms or other spaces can be designed to suggest by scale and form, their use; passages, tunnels, bridges, tubes, troughs, arches, platforms can be so vividly expressed as to make us extend ourselves in space, as it were.

Finally, Mr. McLuhan's observation that "the medium is the message" has its parallel in architecture. This simply means that the influence of the vehicle by which the message is sent is greater than that of the message itself. Correspondingly, the building as an instrument of service has greater effect upon our lives than the functional service itself. To any serious architect this is hardly new. We should expect today, however, that this will be recognized more than ever. Further, we can fulfill our social purpose by designing buildings not as "consumer commodities," or as "diet for the privileged," as McLuhan says, but as instruments for explaining and helping all to understand and adjust to our often bewildering environment of rapid technical change. Great and responsible artists and thinkers in all times both have been affected by their technology, and have helped to find a meaning in it for their society. It should certainly be expected of the architect today that he be aware of the vast growth and influence of the electronic revolution, that his perceptive habits be retrained, and that his architecture in turn be a consistent and valid expression of his times.

QUESTIONS FOR DISCUSSION AND WRITING

1. Briefly summarize the changes Johansen suggests may come about in architecture as a result of our electronic technology. Are you pleased with the prospect of each of these changes? Explain.
2. Is this essay purely speculative, or is it optimistic that the changes it suggests will eventually be realized? How can you tell?
3. Johansen says, as one of his main premises, that "In each period of well-established cultural achievement, there is apt to be a consistency in the thinking and experience of the arts, science, and philosophy." Is Johansen correct? Suggest some examples from our time that either prove or disprove Johansen's contention.
4. Precisely what connections does Johansen draw between "media" and architecture? Between the theories of McLuhan and architecture? Explain whether or not you find Johansen's arguments convincing on these points.
5. How can architectural design employ "slang"? How can a building be "eloquent"? What do these terms mean and what is the relationship between them? Are there any similarities, do you think, between "slang" and "eloquence" in architecture and what Amy Goldin (p. 184) terms "deep art" and "shallow art"? Explain.
6. According to Johansen, what is the difference, architecturally, between "the mechanical age" and "the electronic age"? What would be some examples of architecture or other art forms of each type?
7. Can you somehow picture in your mind the types of buildings that Johansen predicts? Will they be tall? Transparent? Curved? Colorful? Attempt to draw a word-picture of such a building. Do buildings of this sort already exist? Describe them.
8. Johansen concludes his article by saying that "It should certainly be ex-

pected of the architect today . . . that his architecture . . . be a consistent and valid expression of his times." Do you agree? What might be some good reasons for an architect *not* to express or represent his times?

9. Some people have accused those who have become involved with improving the human environment of "copping out." In regard to Johansen's article, they might say that what we need is not a revolution in architecture, in our buildings and homes, but a revolution in racial matters and against social oppression. Do you agree? What should have the highest priority, an improved environment or improved social conditions? Or are the two inseparable? Explain.

Louis Kampf

Notes Toward a Radical Culture

These notes are mainly for the eyes of my brothers and sisters in the movement.* For to discuss radical culture is, at the present time, to discuss the culture of the movement. And what is the movement? Those who know are already a part of this culture: they know its private—and rapidly shifting—language; they understand its physical mannerisms; they are wise to its tensions, loves, divisions, and hatreds. But there are not enough who know; and too many who know are merely voyeurs—celibates of the movement. This is one way of saying that this culture is not deep enough; it is not quite real. Our task is to make its secret language public by realizing words in acts, images in institutions, analyses in practice. If the movement does not become embedded in the general culture, the concept of a radical culture will remain a ghost visible only to the elect.

Material need—hunger, lack of shelter, disease—is an oppressive reality for many Americans. In much of the rest of the world people are starving to death. Why, then, the concern over something so seemingly trivial as culture? There are times when I find it difficult not to gag on the word. Yet those who have attained the material comforts which accompany a middle class income know that relative economic security can go hand in hand with profound feelings of social inferiority and an abandonment of will. Such wrenchings of individual sensibilities have a social source; they are an index of cultural failure. Only devotees of the Gross National Product need be surprised, since periods of economic growth have always engendered new individual needs. If the struggle for economic betterment fails to develop a culture which helps individuals to define both themselves and their relation to society, these new needs are inevitably shaped by the pressures of the economic sys-

* When I use the word "movement," I mean *white* radicals in America. The cultural problems of blacks are obviously different.

238

tem—that is, of economic growth. Manipulative instruments such as advertising consequently define the individual's new yearnings; the desire for greater—or different—material satisfactions becomes his culture. How to break through this circle of economic motivation? Not much less than a restructuring of our culture seems to be in order. A cultural revolution? Perhaps.

Amongst radicals one hears much talk of a crisis for capitalist institutions. The very notion of a high Western culture has begun to take a beating. But the doubts about traditional concepts have also created a crisis for the movement. Change hardly ever comes about in the expected ways, and concepts which have been the radicals' bread and butter become as stale and rancid as any capitalist ideology. Thus institutions which have begun to shake disturb our own norms, and force us to reconsider the nature and locus of our activities. How are we to take advantage of loosened foundations? How do we initiate fundamental social change? Often enough our reactions to events are wildly inappropriate because they are given direction by concepts which have turned to stone. We have yet to develop a set of reflexes which would constitute a radical culture. Such reflexes should sustain us, and give our thought and actions continuity; they should be at the center of our lives.

A radical culture is a necessary component of the movement's program, yet we cannot create it by force of will. However, the present historical moment seems favorable. Western culture is in disrepute, some of its central ideas having become masks for the drive toward universal destruction. The pursuit of knowledge, we have assumed, is a good in itself and an agent of progress: it has led to the hydrogen bomb; the concept of rationality is at the foundation not only of scholarship, but of activities relating to work and political and social institutions: it has been used to justify the bureaucratic rationalization typical of industrial states. Intellectuals—the producers of such knowledge and instruments of rationalization—are under serious attack. They have manufactured the ideologies of the Cold War while hiding under the skirts of Western Civilization. The Hudson Institute, we are given to understand, is the natural offspring of Plato's academy. The rootlessness of intellectuals, which in the past has been a sign of independence, has led many to sell themselves to the highest bidder. Such whoring was bound to elicit strong reactions from the young. In the nineteenth century, the most common reaction of young intellectuals and students to rootlessness was a passionate commitment to the culture of nationalism. This commitment to a national culture made revolutionaries of many; unfortunately, it also turned some into the first ideologues of fascism. But today nationalism is not a live option for young movement intellectuals; the rediscovery of a natural culture cannot provide a cure for the individual's sense of separation from society. However, given the movement's stress on

community, intellectuals may be able to plant their roots in the movement itself. This implies that the movement must become a culture—that
is, a way of life. The very forces which have brought about the alienation
of intellectuals and the young have propelled us toward that historical
moment appropriate for creating a radical culture.

These notes are written toward that uncertain end.

Uncertain and puzzling, because the very concept of culture is rooted
in social elitism. In the English speaking world it has been given its
most typical formulation in Arnold's definition of culture as the study
of perfection—that is, of the best that has been thought or said. It
is an admirable notion. Who would quarrel with a program which asks
us to study both classic and modern masterpieces so that we may become
better men? But looked at within a social context, the program turns
out to be the property of a privileged class. The best that has been
thought or said? Whose best, one is tempted to ask. And what people
is this best available to? Whose property are the great masterpieces?
What, in fact, do they teach? What interests do they serve?

Some British scholars have begun to look at the notion of culture
from a different social perspective. Richard Hoggart and E. P. Thomp-
son, amongst others, have tried to see what the study of perfection
might look like from the bottom. The view is quite different; the very
concept of culture is transformed into something else. There are important lessons to be learned from these scholars, but their work does not
help us to formulate a radical culture for a movement which is primarily
composed of middle-class whites. We are the inheritors, alas, of Arnold's
sweetness and light; we are bearers of the tradition which is the property
of an elite.

Some have tried to circumvent this traditionalism by inventing new
styles. But decoration (of the body, of the mind) is the luxury either
of those who can afford it, or of those alienated enough to divest themselves of the past. By itself, the enrichment of surfaces will not create
a political culture. Yet who would want a political culture without style?

Radical theorists have insisted often enough that a political revolution
must be accompanied by a cultural one. But there is no general theory—or even a set of strategies—to guide us toward that end. We discuss
the transformations of culture in terms set by the nineteenth century.

We must find the terms which are our own.

Let me begin once more—this time at the beginning. What is the meaning of the term "culture"? Perhaps one should ask a different question
first: What is the task of a radical culture? Answer: to bring about
a social revolution; to make institutions democratic; to make us free;
to make life more beautiful and humane.

Such objectives demand that the roots of the state's powers be torn out. These roots ultimately reach down to the *social* division of labor. The division into classes is the foundation—perhaps the substance—of our culture, and therefore must be resisted continually. The partial ruptures we thus effect in the class system will, in turn, become one element in the creation of a different culture.

These tasks, we have ordinarily assumed, are to be performed by the intelligentsia—the technocrats of revolution. But to reach to the roots means to renovate ways of thinking, feeling, looking and, ultimately, acting. This is not quite the same as a vanguard fixing on a particular issue through which it hopes to heighten political consciousness.

Radical culture must be instrumental in obliterating class divisions. Therefore it must lead to a general participation in that culture. The existence of an intelligentsia (of technocrats) has provided some of us with the luxury of privacy. The special skills of the intelligentsia—including those of the revolutionary vanguard—make general participation in the affairs of society unnecessary. But the price we pay for this modern luxury is the domination of our culture by technocrats. Now their existence as a social class is necessarily tied to the existence of industrial society. We cannot wish the intelligentsia away. The real alternative for radical culture is to develop new social functions and contexts for intellectual work. This is not likely to be accomplished by enlightening technocrats about their social responsibility. Considering their involvement with those who hold power, they will have to be fought. One task of a radical culture is to clear our minds of elitist prejudices, so we can see the intelligentsia for what it is.

Why do I—a cultured man, my students and friends might say—choke on the word "culture"? There is the matter of cost. What price has humanity paid for our cultural monuments? For a long time I have been obsessed with the emotional possibilities of baroque architecture. I have traveled, gotten grants, studied, looked and looked—and I have been deeply moved. But at whose expense were my sensibilities deepened by the experience of Rome? And why is the joy of a refined esthetic emotionally available to me—a middle-class academic, an intellectual—but not to others? When I last stood in the Piazza Navona, watching my fellow tourists more than Bernini's fountains, I hardly dared think of the crimes, the human suffering, which made both the scene and my being there possible. I stood surrounded by priceless objects—and I valued them. Yet I hate the economic system which has invested finely chiseled stone with a price. Our esthetics are rooted in surplus value.

Had the advocates of black power who damaged a Rembrandt at the New York Metropolitan Museum been caught, they would have been read a lesson on the values of culture by a philistine judge. More than likely they would have been jailed: a piece of canvas is obviously more valuable than a man's freedom. How could these savages do damage to the Metropolitan? It was built, after all, to bring art to the masses. A million dollars is spent on a painting to improve the lot of the poor. Don't they remember the privilege of museum field trips during grammar school? Oddly enough, some blacks see the culture of the Metropolitan as an instrument of oppression. Culture for the masses! Whose culture?

America's cultural institutions have no more than an incidental relationship to culture—high or low. The most recent version of Roman magnificence, Lincoln Center, was built upon the ruins of a low-cost residential area in midtown Manhattan.

And why not? Magnificence should preside at the center of things. What better place than a depopulated area for the confluence of diverse cultural streams? Besides, entertainment for the rich is at least as important as housing for the poor. But according to a recent story in *The New York Times*, there are difficulties facing this grand attempt at cultural enrichment. I quote Howard Taubman, *The Times'* official keeper of the cultural heritage:

> The trouble is that Lincoln Center is running out of operating funds. Working capital as of Jan. 1 was down to $900,000 and a good deal of that was tied up. . . . The financial report for fiscal 1968 . . . shows that expenditures were $8.06 million and income amounted to $4.93 million. The deficit . . . was cut . . . by contributions and the use of substantial sums from the Lincoln Center Fund.

An income of $4.93 million! Clearly nothing is too much for the sake of the national esthetic. However, there appear to be extra-esthetic reasons for some of the expenditures. Mr. Taubman continues:

> "Consider our security costs," Mr. Ames went on. "We spend $300,000 a year for exterior guarding alone. The spaces—plazas, walks and passageways—at Lincoln Center are so large that we must have many guards, not only when performances are on but also at other times when thousands of visitors come streaming through the center."

But who is Lincoln Center being protected from? The performers? The visitors? The dissatisfied customers? Perhaps it is from the people who were thrown out of their homes so that their esthetic needs might be fulfilled. Alas, the horde does not seem to understand that performances it cannot afford to attend add luster to the national—that is, the horde's very own—culture. How, one wonders, could these misguided souls do damage to something they own, to a national monument? A bit more of Mr. Taubman's story might help to explain.

> Mr. Ames stressed that Lincoln Center was a significant economic as well as cultural asset for the city. In an area of 37 blocks radiating from the center there have been improvements in land use and new buildings that have brought the city more than $20 million in new taxes, he pointed out, and by 1972 the taxes in this area will probably be more than $30 million.

So much for the national esthetic. Culture for the masses? It will no doubt be provided for out of that $30 million in taxes.

The movement should have harrassed Lincoln Center from the beginning. Not a performance should go by without disruption. The fountains should be dried with calcium chloride, the statuary pissed on, the walls smeared with shit.

General Maxwell Taylor was the first president of Lincoln Center, Inc. He left his post—reluctantly, of course—when President Kennedy issued the call for even higher duty, and eventually became well-known for his strategic thinking about Vietnam. The general's career suggests an appropriate designation for Lincoln Center: a cultural enclave whose freedom is being protected by $300,000 worth of cops. Counter-insurgency against undesirable elements in surrounding districts is no doubt next on the cultural agenda.

The Great Tradition is dead. Does one really need to repeat Baudelaire's words? It is surely dead for those committed to radical social change. Each component of the Tradition may be alive for me as an individual: Pope's late poetry moves me profoundly. Yet *An Epistle to Dr. Arbuthnot* does not exist for me as part of a humanistic continuum. Indeed, there is an anomaly—even preciousness—in my reaction to Pope; I have taken an unnatural leap in time, and embraced someone whose historical location makes him my enemy. Pope, the last major voice of Renaissance Humanism! How is that textbook category a part of my culture?

The Great Tradition is dead because it assumes that cultural continuity lies solely in books. And so it does—for some. For the educated middle class *The Communist Manifesto* is a cultural object, an anthology piece which appears at some point after the selection from Hegel, very near that of Darwin's, and before the one from Ruskin. The cultural tradition embalmed in this anthology is the property of a privileged class. Worse, it is an instrument of oppression. The anthology, we are told, is the repository of our spiritual values. But as Jan Myrdal has observed, spiritual values are the ideology of the ruling class.

The sense of tragedy, it is most commonly agreed, is the most profound of our spiritual values. The experience of classical tragedy ennobles us because it teaches us to accept our fate. Those who reap the benefits of a society can readily afford to accept their fates; they can even afford to elevate suffering to a peerage, and endow it with hereditary nobility. The meek poor, we all know, are rich in spirit; the unmeek ones are brutes without culture.

Brutes, we all know, should be humanized. And what better instruments of humanization, what better repositories of the great tradition, than our colleges? We deposit the uncultured in one for four years so they may become imbued with the tragic sense before venturing into the arena to discover their inevitable fate. They sit and study their grammar and their Homer, swallowing their bad medicine, but only half believing that the mastery of a culture alien to their lives will lift them from their own class, assuring them of membership in a ruling elite. The poor trapped instructor becomes the convenient object of hatred, for he is the most visible symbol of their oppression. However, there is little to fear. Culture, Freud has assured us, is civilization's chief instrument of conflict resolution. It conveniently transforms anger into self-hatred and belligerence into feelings of guilt.

But does the imposition of the great tradition really resolve conflicts? Does it not merely suppress them? Radicals must find ways of allowing such conflicts to be expressed. These conflicts are embedded in a cultural tradition which is not necessarily expressed in our official masterpieces or in our spiritual values. But they do represent a spiritual actuality. The task of radical culture is both to divest tragedy of its nobility, and to direct cultural conflict toward a deeper understanding of the individual's social role—an understanding which leads beyond the limiting hatred of the instructor to the ultimate sources of oppression.

Let me repeat an earlier question: What do I mean by the term "culture"?

First, there is Culture (I shall capitalize it) in the larger sense. A partial list of its components includes the way we live, our manners and rituals, our habits of work and play, what we do with our leisure time. A significant feature of our own Culture, for example, is the relation leisure bears to the notion of efficiency. I might ask, while investigating the relationship, why industrial workers tend to give up their leisure and work overtime. I would learn that in our Culture people need to escalate their consumption of goods if they are to maintain a sense of their own value and uphold their self-respect. Investigating further, I would discover that the leisure activities most common to our Culture are, in fact, attempts to escape from society, to get away. Such attempts lead, of course, to the purchase of consumer goods necessary for the escape. And the purchase leads to further production, and that leads to capital investment, and that to long-range financing and research, and so on and so forth. Underlying the whole process is the feeling of alienation from work; the feeling that work deprives human beings of control—over the means of production and over their own lives.

To understand, then, the relationship of leisure to efficiency—that is, a single element in a definition of the larger Culture—one should study the history of industrialism. Most important for the state of the Culture is industrialism's increasing need for ever more subtle forms of rationalization, and the consequent formation of a large bureaucratic force, headed by a technocratic elite, to implement that rationality.

Though not always practiced, devotion to the principles of efficiency and rationality has been fervent for over a century. These principles demand that the productive process be totally separated from all other aspects of life. Work is performed during a designated part of the day, at a designated place, and in a predetermined manner. The time not used for sleeping or for performing household tasks is called leisure. Leisure is—just time; it is time divorced from all the ordinary activities, just as work is divorced from the rest of life. Leisure creates the necessity for culture (lower case) in the smaller sense: the autonomous arts, pure scholarship, and the various forms of entertainment—all of them unproductive activities. Historically (and quite logically) the smaller culture has become increasingly dissociated from the larger. Indeed, the former has become an independent entity with its own history and its own internal logic. Most of us seek to fulfill ourselves through culture: it is what we live for. Not unexpectedly, there are some forms of culture which are more prestigious—and desirable—than others.

Culture in the smaller sense seems to stand in opposition to the rationalization of the productive process—indeed, to the very nature of our work. It is at war with the larger Culture. Since culture in the smaller sense is the primary source of human fulfillment, our very beings become split. This separation, both in society and in our minds, leads to the arts having the life squeezed out of them for they have lost their connection to the larger Culture: they become a self-indulgent irrelevance, a search for more refined sensations or more exquisite techniques. As for the larger Culture, being deprived of the arts, it survives (perhaps perishes) by the inhuman spirit of rationalization.

Like any warrior resorting to diplomacy, the larger Culture attempts to neutralize—indeed, use—the smaller by rationalizing it. The social task of culture is not to make us more noble, though it may do so incidentally, but to facilitate the wider reproduction of labor. André Gorz, in his *Strategy for Labor,* has put the matter well:

> It is impossible in a modern production unit, even of medium size, to be on top of one's job without becoming familiar with world history in the process. And it is impossible to be ignorant of political, scientific, technical, socio-economic, and cultural evolution in the largest sense, or else one will lose the ability to enter into relation-

ships with others, however close, or of suffering that absolute oppression which consists of knowing that one does not know what
others know.

That is why cultural activity is an integral part of the necessarily
broad reproduction of labor power, that is, of the ability of individuals to cooperate in a given common task. That also is why cultural
activity is a *need*.

But this need of the industrial system may be exploited by radicals.
The condescending imposition of an official high culture must be discredited. We should demand that various constituencies be allowed to
control their own cultural activities, developing those forms and styles
which emerge from or relate to their own lives and their own traditions.
Thus culture might once again become an instrument for defining class
interests, rather than one for their obliteration.

I shall briefly sketch the fate of one performing art, "serious" music,
in industrial society, in the hope of locating the source of some of our
cultural difficulties.

The development of large cities and their appropriation by the middle
class clearly had an enormous influence on the conditions of musical
performance. From the Renaissance through much of the eighteenth
century, most "serious" music developed as an integral expression of
the aristocratic milieu within which it was performed. Concerts were
court occasions, primarily concerned with performance of new composi-
tions. Since the music was always new, and since it was generally performed by some members of the court along with the composer and
the hired musicians, it had a most immediate relationship to the cultural
assumptions of the audience. In the eighteenth century large cities began
to develop cultural institutions for the middle class. Concert halls were
built. They became the homes of large orchestras and opera companies
which developed historical repertoires that are repeated over the course
of generations to the present time. What relationship does this repertoire
have to the living culture of the audience? The hall, the orchestra, the
opera, the conductor and the singer all become exhibition pieces in
a museum. And museums are commodities. People buy their tickets,
they sit down and listen passively, because attending a musical performance is one mode of consumption, one way of filling one's leisure time.

Such conditions of musical performance necessarily affect the possibilities of composition. Composers begin to write for the repertoire; they
relate not to the cultural suppositions of a specific audience, but to
a musical tradition or to the market. The most honest stance becomes
the composition of repeated variations on one's musical autobiography:
sincere, often moving and brilliant, but almost inevitably self-indulgent.

There is a way out, however, in twentieth century America. The academy has become a new haven for musical genius, and produced the

professor-composer-computer expert. The implications of this development for our culture are immense. The recent Lincoln Center performance of Professor Milton Babbitt's *Relata II* prompted the composer to make some crucial remarks on the subject. I quote a few of them from *The New York Times:*

> Finally there's the question: who will hear this piece? No one is concerned about my interested musical colleagues, those for whom I really offer it. . . . My associates across the country will not have any opportunity to hear it. . . .
>
> On the other hand, the regular Philharmonic audience does not want to hear this piece. And why should they have to? How can it be coherent for them? It's as though a colleague of mine in the field of philosophy were to read his paper on the Johnny Carson show. . . .
>
> The university, the composer's last hope, turns with delight to the electronic field because it is self-contained, requiring neither performance nor publication. The medium provides a kind of full satisfaction for the composer, too. I love going to the studio with my work in my head, realizing it while I am there, and walking out with the tape under my arm. I can then send it anywhere in the world, knowing exactly how it will sound. My last electronic work . . . has been played hundreds of times in universities. These are the people—the university people—whom we regard as our appropriate colleagues. I feel closer to members of my Philosophy department than to many who regard themselves as musicians.

Composition as a self-contained entity! The artist pushing the stops on his synthesizer and going home with his cultural goods on tape: could there be a more appropriate emblem of the social role of the arts in the industrial state?

Babbitt and his "appropriate colleagues" assume that their fun and games, their stockpiling and incessant refining of "knowledge," in laboratories, libraries, conferences and seminars—most of it, of course, at the expense of the taxpayers—are necessary for the advancement of civilization. But whose advancement? And whose civilization? The leisure of a divinely appointed elite, critics have told us for centuries, is a prerequisite for the birth and continued good health of culture. But is such a notion anything more than a self-serving ideology for that elite? Culture which is owned and administered by the chosen, the rest watching their mysteries with adoration, can be little else but an instrument of class oppression.

Cultural elitism reveals itself most clearly in the division between high and low culture. Since John Gay's *The Beggar's Opera* became a hit on the London stage in the eighteenth century, artists have consistently used—more accurately, exploited—popular materials for the purposes of high art. One could hardly call this a marriage entered into on equal terms; it is rather like the nobleman condescending to marry the servant girl so she might bear him healthy children; the latter will, in due course, take up their appropriate places in the ranks of the nobility. In America, despite endless protestations, jazz is still thought of and treated like a low art—except when it is raped by the nobles of Lincoln Center. If Archie Shepp and Leonard Bernstein were to get together, it would be a grand occasion for the public relations industry; however, their union would not give birth to an equal partnership in America's cultural enterprise.

Can there really be a culture which transcends all classes? Matthew Arnold taught us that culture, being available to those individuals from all classes willing to express their "best selves," is independent of class origin. But this only means that people from the lower classes are invited to reject their own culture, and exchange it for the more valuable goods of the elite. There can be no culture transcending classes as long as we live in a class society. Consequently, radical culture must for the present be a culture of communities or constituencies.

The cult of the great artist is the cultural myth most natural to a competitive society. The artist's dream is to rise to the heights, to be above mortality, to be more than human. At the least, he strives to be better than all other artists. But in a society where art is a commodity, such dreams get translated into a desire for personal advancement. So the artist allows himself to be packaged along with his art, and to be put on the market. Better yet, he markets himself, thus becoming a manipulator, while being unconsciously manipulated himself. Industrial society is expert at putting individualism to the system's use.

The existence of great figures in the arts is a reflection of social disease. Their disappearance will help to erase the line between the larger and the smaller culture: as art stops being the special province of the great, as it stops being the expression of a competitive individualism, it will have the opportunity to develop as a living part of the larger Culture, rather than continuing to be rationalized by the system as a commodity. But such goals cannot be fully realized until class and property relations have dissolved. Meanwhile, we must stop looking to experts to perform the tasks of culture for us. We should try to engage people in those cultural activities which will allow them to express their "best selves"—their beings—as an integral component of the life of their communities. Art should not be a source of intimidation for the uninitiated; it should not be a cause of social shame; least of all should artists stand in the way of the arts playing a democratizing role in the life of the larger Culture.

Art as the only possible fulfillment of life: the notion is perhaps our most important cultural expression of middle-class individualism. It dominated discussions of culture in the nineteenth century and has since then served as the ideological foundation for those typically modern masterpieces, most notably Proust's, whose subject is the relation of art to the life of the artist. But the possibility of fulfilling oneself through high art, as Ruskin and Morris recognized, is generally available to only a very few members of a privileged class. That we have to look to high art as the devout once looked to their gods points to the failures of the larger Culture: to its failure to develop new communal relationships where the old have disintegrated; to its incapacity for meeting collective needs; to its hardening of the distinction between private and external desires. Such failures impel us to force art into playing a false role. Art cannot be the end of most people's lives. Museums—those monuments to the religion of art—illustrate the point: they afford fulfillment for no-one except the curators; for most a visit to one provides, at best, an occasion for passive absorption. Art may have the power to elevate, but not to fulfill; at its best, it has the capacity to uncover the limitations of our Culture.

A short note on criticism.

We take Tolstoy's *What Is Art?* much too lightly. The standard reaction to his magisterial anger is a guilt-ridden giggle or a pedantic quibble about the logic of his esthetics. Tolstoy's simple—and overwhelming—message is that we must consider, to the exclusion of almost everything else, what art does for the quality of life now, this moment. It is difficult for critics to deal with such a dogmatic insistence on the relation of art to life. The critic is ideally concerned with eternal truths, not with the present conditions of life; his task is to transcend his own time, not to let his judgment be engaged by the needs of the moment. Eternal truths, we all know, are noble. Furthermore, literary criticism is concerned with "human nature," not with the feelings of real men, living at a specific time, and belonging to a specific class.

The humanists of the eighteenth century—Pope, Johnson, Voltaire, Goethe—were the last great upholders of the concept of general nature. They used the notion, quite consciously, in an attempt to keep alive an aristocratic culture which was beginning to take its last gasps. Critics today are not so conscious of their own motives. They cannot deal with Tolstoy, because to even admit the possibility of Tolstoy's moral validity would threaten the self-serving mystifications—eternal truths, human nature, timeless judgments—which uphold the class interests of professional criticism.

America's serious journals have been instrumental in creating an intellectual culture which is founded on the false consciousness of intellectuals. Instead of describing the real conflicts in American life, analyzing the specific attempts to deal with them, and proposing new courses of action, our journals have specialized in creating conflicts between intellectuals. The world is the journal. America's intellectual life is autonomous and divorced from political realities. When shall we produce a theoretical work like Gorz's *Strategy for Labor?* That is, a serious work which directs its proposals for revolutionary change to political activists, not to readers of journals and not to fellow intellectuals. Those young academics who have tried to address themselves to activist constituencies, rather than to their peers, have generally paid the price of professional ostracism.

In conclusion, I must admit to not knowing what a radical culture will really look, sound, smell, or feel like—although I have a clear sense of the contours of the larger Culture in a socialist society. The movement's street theaters, radical newsreels, and musical groups perform an important service. But they are internal to the movement, and beyond having a superficial effect on commercial entertainment, they have little impact on the general culture. New institutions like community galleries and worker-artist alliances do effect structural changes and therefore lay the foundation for radical culture. We are beginning to shoot Niagara, and the social transformations we envision imply something more deep—and hopefully less elitist—than experimentation with new art-forms. What is at stake is a new conception of the relationship of art and knowledge to the larger Culture.

QUESTIONS FOR DISCUSSION AND WRITING

1. Kampf begins by saying that this essay is mainly for members of the white radical movement, but that others should read it as well. Does Kampf succeed in making his thoughts clear to these others, to those who are not radicals? Discuss the nature of Kampf's problem with his audience.
2. What does Kampf mean by referring generally to culture as "elitist"?
3. Kampf says that "Western culture is in disrepute, some of its central ideas having become masks for the drive toward universal destruction." Comment on this idea.
4. What is the significance of the statement that "Our aesthetics are rooted in surplus value"? How does the example of the Lincoln Center relate to this idea? Can you think of other examples which reflect the idea of culture as a leisure activity for the economically privileged? Explain.
5. What is a "radical culture"? Does Kampf use the term with regard to culture as a pattern of shared beliefs and customs or with regard to culture as a form of artistic expression? Explain.
6. Explain the distinction that Kampf draws between "culture" and "Culture." He says that the two are "at war." Why?

7. Kampf's article often moves back and forth between the concepts of a "radical culture" and a "social revolution." How are these two concepts related, according to Kampf? Can one be had without the other? Explain.
8. Explain Kampf's statement that "The cultural tradition . . . is an instrument of oppression."
9. What does Kampf suggest as an alternative to aesthetics which are based on economic motivations? For example, would it be possible to have an aesthetic of the social, an aesthetic based on the beauty and dignity of human beings rather than on the beauty of inanimate objects? Explain.
10. In addition to "community galleries and worker-artist alliances," what else could be instituted to effect a radical culture? Can you make any suggestions?
11. Do you agree with Kampf's restatement of Tolstoy, that "we must consider, to the exclusion of almost everything else, what art does for the quality of life now, this moment"? Would Amy Goldin (p. 184) agree with this view? Explain.

For Further Reading

Berger, John. *The Moment of Cubism and Other Essays.* New York: Pantheon Books, Inc., 1969.

Brown, Norman O. *Love's Body.* New York: Vintage Books, 1966. Paperback.

Freeman, Gillian. *The Undergrowth of Literature: A Study of Pornography.* New York: Delta Books, 1967. Paperback.

Kael, Pauline. *Kiss Kiss Bang Bang.* New York: Little, Brown and Company, 1968. Paperback, 1969.

Kostelanetz, Richard, ed. *The New American Arts.* New York: Horizon Press, 1965. Paperback, 1967.

McLuhan, Marshall. *Understanding Media: The Extensions of Man.* New York: McGraw-Hill Book Company, 1964. Paperback, 1965.

Nuttall, Jeff. *Bomb Culture.* New York: The Delacorte Press, 1969.

Renan, Sheldon. *An Introduction to the American Underground Film.* New York: E. P. Dutton and Company, Inc., 1967. Paperback.

Sontag, Susan. *Against Interpretation.* New York: Delta Books, 1966. Paperback.

Wolfe, Tom. *The Pump House Gang.* New York: Farrar, Straus and Giroux, Inc., 1968. Paperback, 1969.

V ON THE DEMOCRACY

The 1960's forced many American citizens into a critical reappraisal of the very system under which they lived. Large segments of the nation asked themselves whether democracy remained or would remain a workable and meaningful system of government and society.

This agonizing question, though ignored by many for reasons of narrow patriotism, blind pride, or ignorant fear, centered on the conflicting meanings of civil liberties and civil rights. America was, of course, founded on the principle of civil liberties, the concept of the freedom of the individual to pursue happiness in his own way—to "do his own thing," in the jargon of our time. But as the nation matured, it was discovered that there were many other forces in addition to the government from which the individual needed protection. Through such things as the institution of slavery and what de Tocqueville called "the tyranny of the majority," the problem became one of guaranteeing all members of the society not only liberty of action but the right to liberty itself.

As we have noted, the revolution of the 1970's is an attempt to reconcile the ideals and practices of democracy. It is a search also for the solution of the difference which exists between individual liberties and social rights. The individual must be protected from the society and the society must be protected from the individual.

The essays in this final section deal with the problem of democracy itself, exploring the ways in which democracy can be made meaningful to the entire society rather than to just some portion of it. These final essays consider the state of the democracy in the American present in the hope that there will be a democracy in the American future.

William O. Douglas

Civil Liberties:
The Crucial Issue

Most modern constitutions contain promises of things that government must do for people. Our Constitution, an 18th Century product, guarantees no one such benefits as an education, social security or the right to work. It is not a welfare-state document. To the contrary, it specifies in some detail what government may *not* do to the individual. In other words, it was designed to take government off the backs of people and majorities off the backs of minorities.

It stakes out boundaries that no executive, no legislature, no judiciary may violate. The "law and order" advocates never seem to understand that simple constitutional principle. An example will illustrate what I mean. The First Amendment says that government may not abridge the free exercise of religion. Suppose a city enacts an ordinance that provides that no minister may deliver a sermon without first obtaining a permit from the Department of Safety. To exact a license before the citizen may exercise a constitutional right is to abridge that right. No minister worth his salt would knuckle under. If he defied the ordinance, he would be acting in the best American tradition. If he were prosecuted, the unconstitutionality of the ordinance would be a complete defense. The person who concludes that a law is unconstitutional and defies it runs the risk, of course, that he guessed wrong. Yet his punishment is not thereby compounded. Law and order is the guiding star of totalitarians, not of free men.

This principle of civil disobedience can be appreciated only if the antecedents of our Constitution and Bill of Rights are understood.

The ideas of freedom, liberty and sovereignty of the individual reflected in the two documents come from a long stream of history. The ideas of political freedom trace at least as far back as the Athenian model. But the political freedom of classical Greece did not guarantee private freedom, which was first emphasized by the Romans through the development of natural law. The church added the tradition of a divine order and a set of precepts based on the integrity of the individual before God; the Reformation gave the individual a choice of religio-political orders. The divine right of kings—one form of the social contract—was successfully challenged by the end of the 17th Century. Rousseau's *Social Contract* was a frontal assault.

But the single thinker who had the most direct impact on the framers of the Constitution was John Locke. Locke taught that morality, religion and politics should conform to God's will as revealed in the essential nature of man. God gave man reason and conscience as natural guides to distinguish between good and bad; and they were not to be restrained by an established church or by a king or a dynasty. Isaac Newton, who in 1687 published *Principia*, his great work, seemed to abolish mystery from the world and enable a rational mind to uncover the secrets of nature and nature's God. This parallel thought gave wings to Locke, who wrote:

> Men being . . . all free, equal and independent, no one can be put out of his estate, and subjected to the political power of another, without his consent. The only way whereby any one divests himself of his liberty and puts on the bonds of civil society is by agreeing with other men to join and unite into a community, for their comfortable, safe and peaceable living one amongst another, in a secure enjoyment of their properties and a greater security against any that are not of it. . . . When any number of men have so consented to make one community or government, they are thereby presently incorporated and make one body politic, wherein the majority have a right to act and conclude the rest.

These ideas were well known to our Colonists through the church as well as through Locke, Newton and many other writers. God, nature and reason were the foundations of politics and government; they were extolled in the Declaration of Independence and further distilled in constitutional precepts.

The foregoing is but an outline of the history of ideas behind the Constitution. They were translated into the body of Anglo-American law in a series of crucial test cases over a period of at least 400 years.

The political counterpart of heresy in the 16th Century was treason. The law of England allowed a man to be tried for treason if he "doth compass or imagine the death" of the king. This was called "constructive treason," for the accused did not have to lift his hand against the king to be guilty; all he need do was wish the king were dead. As a result, treason is narrowly defined in our Constitution: "Treason against the United States shall consist only in levying war against them, or in adhering to their enemies . . ." and the proof required is very strict. That clause is the product of the philosophy of Madison and Jefferson. Madison wanted treason narrowly defined, because history showed that "new-fangled and artificial treasons" were the "great engines" by which partisan factions "wreaked their alternate malignity on each other." Jefferson had the like view, pointing out that the definitions of treason often failed to distinguish between "acts against government" and "acts against the oppressions of the government." Madison and Jefferson are strangers to our law-and-order school, whose spokesmen go so far these days as to call dissent to our Vietnam policy "treason."

In the 17th Century, it was the practice to force citizens to make loans to the British crown, failing which the citizen would be jailed and languish there without bail. Thomas Darnel met that fate in 1627. From his prison, he applied for a writ of habeas corpus, the conventional way in those days of testing the legality of a confinement. The case was argued before judges who were appointees of the king, serving at his pleasure. They ruled that they were required to "walk in the steps of our forefathers," that the word of the king was sufficient to hold a man, saying, "We trust him in great matters." This case resulted in the Petition of Right of 1628, which led to vesting in Parliament, rather than in the king, the authority to levy taxes; and it also established the prisoner's *right to bail.*

The legislative branch was also a source of oppression. A bill of attainder is an act of the legislature punishing individuals or members of a group without a *judicial trial.* Its vice is that it condemns a person by legislative fiat without the benefit of a trial having all the safeguards of due process of law. English history, as well as our own history between 1776 and 1787, is replete with instances where the legislature, by its own fiat, subjected men to penalties and punishments. The Constitution abolishes bills of attainder outright, both at the state and at the Federal level.

The foregoing are merely examples of how the sovereignty of the individual was, historically speaking, jeopardized by acts of all branches of Government—the Executive, the Legislative and the Judicial.

The fear of our forefathers was also a fear of the majority of the people who from time to time might crush a minority that did not conform to the dominant religious creed or who in other ways were ideological strays.

One episode that occurred in this nation just before the 1787 Philadelphia Convention is illustrative. Times were hard in 1786. A post-War depression had hit the country. The state legislatures were swept by agrarian influences. Debtors wanted relief. There was no strong central government. Only Congress, under the feeble Articles of Confederation, had national authority, and it was not in a position to act decisively.

Up at Northampton, Massachusetts, in August 1786, Daniel Shays moved into action. His armed group seized the courthouse in order to put an end to legal proceedings for the collection of debts. The example at Northampton was followed in other parts of the state, about 2000 armed men joining Shays. Courts were paralyzed. In September, Shays' men moved on Springfield and overawed the court with their claims that their leaders should not be indicted and that there should be a moratorium on the collection of debts. They also insisted that the militia be disbanded. The stakes were high, because at Springfield there was a Federal arsenal filled with artillery, guns and ammunition, which Shays planned to take. The decisive engagement took place on January 25, 1787, the Shays group being routed by militia equipped with Federal cannon.

Shays' Rebellion gave impetus not only to a strong central Government but also to checks and restraints on populism. The mercantile, financial and large landed interests were getting tired of talk of the rights of man; they were becoming concerned with the protection of their property. Too much democracy in the state governments, it was argued, was bringing bad times on the country. Massachusetts, New Hampshire and Rhode Island were said to be disintegrating. General Henry Knox, in the mood of our modern law-and-order men, wrote Washington from Massachusetts in the fall of 1786: "This dreadful situation, for which our Government has made no adequate provision, has alarmed every man of principle and property in New England."

Though Shays' Rebellion was shortly put down, the populist or agrarian forces remained in control of some state legislatures and repudiation of debts remained a threat. Majorities in state legislatures ruled without restraint. The commercial, financial and landed interests moved to Philadelphia for the Constitutional Convention in an antidemocratic mood. A republican form of government emerged that, to use the words of Madison, was designed "to protect the minority of the opulent against the majority." This majority, Madison said on another occasion, might well be the landless proletariat.

Numerous barriers were written into the Constitution designed to thwart the will of majorities. As Charles A. Beard said in his monumental work *An Economic Interpretation of the Constitution of the United States*, those who campaigned for ratification of the Constitution made "their most cogent arguments" to the owners of property "anxious to find a foil against the attacks of leveling democracy."

While the House was to be elected for a short term by the people, Senators (until the 17th Amendment) were selected by the state legislatures; and the President was picked for a fixed term by electors chosen by the people. Thus, a measure of assurance was granted that *majority* groups would not be able to unite against the *minority* propertied interests. Moreover, amendment of the Constitution was made laborious: Two thirds of both the Senate and the House were to propose amendments; three fourths of the states were to ratify them. A final check or balance was an independent judiciary named by the President, approved by the Senate and serving for life.

The "minority of the opulent" were also protected when it came to the Bill of Rights, as in the provisions in the Fifth Amendment that "private property" could not be taken for a "public purpose" without payment of "just compensation."

But the Bill of Rights went much, much further. It was concerned with all minorities, not only the minority of the opulent. Government was taken off the backs of all people and the individual was made *sovereign* when it came to making speeches and publishing papers, tracts and books. Those domains had "no trespassing" signs that government must heed.

Great battles have raged over those guarantees. Peaceful and orderly opposition to the Government—even by Communists—is, of course, constitutionally protected. Chief Justice Charles Evans Hughes said: "The maintenance of the opportunity for free political discussion to the end that government may be responsive to the will of the people and that changes may be obtained by lawful means, an opportunity essential to the security of the republic, is a fundamental principle of our constitutional system."

American law also honors protests, whether they are in the form of letters to the editor, picketing, marches on the statehouse or rallies to whip up action. As already noted, police historically have arrested dissenters for "disorderly conduct" and "breach of the peace," often using these devices to suppress an unpopular minority. But such charges are no longer permissible at either the state or Federal level, though the law-and-order men often try to use "vagrancy" or other misdemeanors to suppress dissent or to promote racism.

Government is also constrained against interfering with one's free exercise of religion. A man can worship how and where he pleases. Government at times has preferred one religion over another, giving it privileges as respects marriages, baptisms and the like, and even putting some prelates on the public payroll. The Bill of Rights bans this practice by prohibiting the "establishment" of any religion by the Government.

It was the pride of British tradition that a man's home was his castle. Even the king could not enter without legal process. On this side of the Atlantic, British officers had ransacked homes (and offices as well) under search warrants that were good for all time and for all kinds of evidence. This led to the Fourth Amendment, which, in general, requires an officer making a search to have a warrant issued by a judge on a showing of probable cause that a crime has been committed. And the warrant must describe with particularity the scope of the search and the articles or person to be seized. Modern technology has developed electronic devices that can record what goes on in the sanctuary of a home without entering the home in any conventional sense. They, too, have now been included within the Fourth Amendment. Yet the law-and-order propagandists would brush aside the Fourth Amendment and use any short cut to convict any unpopular person.

The much misunderstood self-incrimination clause of the Fifth Amendment had a similar history: "No person . . . shall be compelled in any criminal case to be a witness against himself." At one time in England, the oath that one takes to tell the truth was used against the accused with devastating effect. If he refused to take the oath, he was held in contempt and punished. If he took the oath and then refused to answer a question, the refusal was taken as a confession of the thing charged in the question. Thus were men compelled to testify against themselves.

A widely heralded defiance of this practice was that of John Lilburne, who was charged with sending scandalous books into England. He refused to be examined under oath, saying that the oath was "both against the law of God and the law of the land." He announced that he would never take it, "though I be pulled to pieces by wild horses." Lilburne was held in contempt, publicly whipped, fined and placed in solitary confinement. That was in 1638. On February 13, 1645, the House of Lords set aside that judgment as "against the liberty of the subject and law of the land and Magna Charta." And in 1648, Lilburne was granted damages for his imprisonment.

The idea spread to this country. The Puritans who came here knew of the detested oath that Lilburne refused to take. They, too, had been its victims. *The Body of Liberties,* adopted in 1641 by Massachusetts, afforded protection against self-incrimination either through torture or through the oath. The high-handed practices of the royal governors who believed in law and order and who sought to compel citizens to accuse themselves of crimes also whipped up sentiment for the immunity. A majority of the colonists, therefore, as part of their programs for independence, adopted bills of rights that included the immunity against self-incrimination. Later, it was written into the Fifth Amendment and into most state constitutions.

The immunity has been broadly interpreted. It extends to all manner of proceedings in which testimony is taken, including legislative committees. It was early held by the Supreme Court to give immunity from testifying not only to acts or events that themselves constitute a crime or that are elements of a crime but also to things that "will tend to criminate him" or subject him to fines, penalties or forfeitures. As Chief Justice John Marshall put it at the beginning, immunity protects the witness from supplying any "link" in a chain of testimony that would convict him. Yet in spite of this long history, the law-and-order propagandists denounce the decisions that forbid the police from using coercion to obtain confessions from people in custody.

The protection against double jeopardy, the right to counsel, the right to confront the person who accuses one, the guarantee against cruel and unusual punishment—these all have a similar specific and detailed history of abuse by government. Each reflects a clear and calculated design to prevent government from meddling with individual lives.

The law-and-order people say that "criminals" and "Communists" deserve no such protection. But the Constitution draws no line between the good and the bad, the popular and the unpopular. The word is "person," which, of course, includes "aliens." *Every* person is under the umbrella of the Constitution and the Bill of Rights. The Bill of Rights purposely makes it difficult for police, prosecutors, investigating committees, judges and even juries to convict anyone. We know that the net that often closes around an accused man is a flimsy one. Circumstantial evidence often implicates the innocent as well as the guilty. Some countries have the inquisitorial system, in which the criminal case is normally made out from the lips of the accused. But our system is different; it is accusatorial. Those who make the charge must prove it. They carry the burden. The sovereignty of the individual is honored by a presumption of innocence.

The principle of *equality* entered our constitutional system with the Civil War amendments, which banned discrimination based on race, creed, color or poverty. So today we stand for both *liberty* and *equality*. The Russians who protested the 1966 Ukrainian trials came out strong for *liberty*: "The highest saturation of material goods, without free thought and will," creates "a great prison in which the food rations of prisoners are increased." Whatever continent one visits, he finds man asserting his sovereignty—and usually receiving punishment for doing so. There are few places in the world where man can think and speak as he chooses and walk with his chin held high. Yet in spite of our commitment to both, we are confronted with tremendous internal discontent. Some are in rebellion only to obtain control over existing institutions so that they may use them for their own special or selfish ends. But most of the discontent, I think, comes from individuals who clamor for sovereign rights—not rights expressed in laws but rights expressed in jobs and in other dignified positions in our society. We face civil disobedience on a massive scale.

Civil disobedience, though at times abused, has an honored place in our traditions. Some people refuse to pay taxes because the money raised is for a purpose they disapprove. That is *not* a permissible course of conduct; for, by and large, the legislative branch has carte blanche to prepare budgets and levy taxes. It would paralyze government to let each taxpayer exercise the sovereign right to pay or not to pay, depending on whether he approves of the social, economic or political program of those in power. The same is true, in general, of most other laws imposed on the citizen, whether it be observing a speed law or obeying a zoning ordinance or a littering regulation.

Gandhi's much-publicized civil disobedience was quite different. It expressed a universal principle. Gandhi had no political remedy to right a wrong. Disobedience of the law embodying the wrong was his only recourse. Colonial India, like Colonial America, was under a foreign yoke. Regulations were often imposed from overseas or taxes exacted by the fiat of the colonial ruler. The subject had to submit *or else.* "Taxation without representation" was one of the complaints of both Sam Adams and Mahatma Gandhi. Our Declaration of Independence stated the philosophy—all men are created equal; they are endowed by their Creator with certain "inalienable rights." Governments derive their just powers from "the consent of the governed"; and whenever a form of government becomes "destructive to those ends, it is the right of the people to alter or abolish it." Thus, the right of revolution is deep in our heritage. Nat Turner did not get the benefit of our Declaration of Independence. But he moved to the measure of its philosophy. These days, some people are caught in a pot of glue and have no chance to escape through use of a political remedy. Civil disobedience, therefore, evolves into revolution and is used as a means of escape.

Revolution is therefore basic in the rights of man. Where problems and oppression pile high and citizens are denied all recourse to political remedies, only revolution is left. Sometimes revolution with violence is the only remedy. Violence often erupts these days in Latin America and Southeast Asia, where feudal and military regimes hold people in a vise, making it impossible for them to be freed from oppression by the political processes. In some nations, a trade-union organizer is considered an enemy and is shot. So is a person who tries to organize the peasants into cooperatives. In those extreme situations, there is no machinery for change except violence.

We have had civil disobedience accompanied by violence, the bloodiest one being the Civil War. Prior to that, there was the widespread rebellion under John Adams against the Alien and Sedition Acts, which made it a crime to utter any false or malicious statement about the nation, the President or Congress. The Virginia and Kentucky Resolutions called them a "nullity," because—by reason of the First Amendment—Congress may pass no law abridging freedom of speech or press. Those laws expired under Jefferson and for years the country reimbursed the victims for the wrongs done.

The Embargo Act was a self-blockade, in the sense that it forbade the departure of any ships from American ports to foreign countries. Jefferson tried in vain to enforce it, and it was repealed in 1809.

In World War One, there were about 300,000 draft dodgers, in spite of the fact that Congress passed a declaration of war.

Some of those episodes were accompanied by violence and many people were fined or imprisoned for their misdeeds. During those crises, the majority clamored for conformity. The minority, impatient at the existence of laws they deemed unjust, took matters into their own hands and did not wait until the power to correct the abuse at the polls could be exercised.

Today the dissenters, both black and white, claim that the changes needed to admit the lower fourth of our people into an honored place in our society are being thwarted. There is a growing feeling that the existing political parties are not likely instruments of change. The colleges' and universities' administrations, in general, walk more and more to the measure of traditional thought and have lost their revolutionary influence. The Cold War flourishes, diminishing our overseas potential and making the military the most potent force in our lives and in our economy. The puritan ethic—hard work and industry will guarantee success—is not valid in a system of private enterprise that is less and less dependent on labor. For many, the only recourse for employment is in the public sector; yet blueprints for an expanding public sector are hardly ever in public view. Racial discrimination takes an awful toll, as partially evidenced by the fact that the average annual income of whites who go to work at the end of the eighth grade tends to be higher than the average annual income of blacks who go on to college and enter the professions.

The crises these days are compounded because the *real* dissenters from the principle of equality in our laws and in the Constitution are often the establishment itself—sometimes a municipal, county or state government; sometimes slumlords allied with corrupt local machines; sometimes finance companies or great corporations or even labor unions. That is to say, these existing institutions often ask minorities to conform to practices and customs that are unconstitutional. People are apt to overlook the fact that those who make such a request are the offenders, not the vociferous minorities who demand their rights.

Rebellion by members of the establishment against full equality cannot be met with apathy and inaction, for that is the stuff out of which violent revolutions are made. Blacks and whites must join hands in momentous programs of political action. Those who put law and order above liberty and equality are architects of a new fascism that would muzzle all dissenters and pay the individuals in our lower strata to remain poor, obedient and subservient.

Unprecedented civic action is needed. When my friend Luis Muñoz Marin first ran for governor of Puerto Rico, he actually drafted and had printed and circulated the precise laws he would have enacted when elected. He was elected and the laws were passed. Those who march need specific proposals in their hands—proposals to put an end to a particular injustice. India, when dealing with the explosive problem of the untouchables, required about 15 per cent of all matriculating students and about 15 per cent of all government employees to be drawn from those ranks. While the maximum age for taking examinations for government service was generally 24 years, it was increased to 27 years in the case of the untouchables. And this once-abhorred group also has a certain minimum number of seats reserved for it in the national parliament and in the state legislatures.

We need to think in terms as specific as those in dealing with our own minorities, whether black or white. No one today is on the side lines. We are all caught up in a tremendous revolutionary movement. It starts with a demand for equality in educational and employment opportunities. It extends to a removal from our laws of all bias against the poor. It embraces a host of other specifics that will, if faced frankly and adopted, make a viable and decent society out of our multiracial, multireligious, multi-ideological communities—and both preserve the sovereignty and honor the dignity of each and every individual.

QUESTIONS FOR DISCUSSION AND WRITING

1. What is the importance in this essay of the lengthy historical discussion of the Declaration of Independence, the Constitution, and the Bill of Rights?
2. According to Douglas, what is the relationship between "law and order" as they are defined in the Constitution and in the Bill of Rights and as they are defined by the sloganeers for "law-and-order"? Does Douglas denigrate "law and order"? Does he denigrate the users of the slogan? Explain.
3. Is there a difference between "liberty" and "equality"? Between "liberty" and "freedom"? Is it possible to be "free" and not "equal"? "Free" but not have "liberty"? Explain.
4. Explain the difference between "civil liberty" and "civil rights." Is each necessary to the well-being of a democracy?
5. Douglas says that "the *real* dissenters from the principle of equality in our laws and in the Constitution are often the establishment itself . . . government . . . slumlords . . . finance companies . . . great corporations . . . even labor unions." Explain what Douglas means by this and whether or not you agree with him.
6. Douglas says that "Civil disobedience, though at times abused, has an honored place in our tradition." But then he says that civil disobedience in the form of refusing to pay taxes "is *not* a permissible course of conduct." Explain Douglas' reasoning. Do you agree with it? For example, was Thoreau wrong?
7. In speaking of Nat Turner, Douglas says that he "did not get the benefit of our Declaration of Independence. But he moved to the measure of its philosophy." Discuss. Are there any "Nat Turners" today of whom the same things might be said?
8. Do you agree with Douglas that civil liberties is "the crucial issue"? Or is something else more crucial? Explain.
9. As part of a statistical survey in 1969, a professor of political science

distributed copies of the opening lines of the Declaration of Independence to several hundred people and asked them to endorse it with their signatures. Nearly ninety per cent of the people did not recognize the lines (the source was not given) and of this number nearly half felt that the ideas expressed in the lines were "probably communist-inspired" or the results of "a few radical students." Some of the people even accused the professor and his research team of treason. In the light of Douglas' article, comment on this situation.

Paul Goodman

Notes of a Neolithic Conservative

1. For green grass and clean rivers, children with bright eyes and good color, and people safe from being pushed around—for a few things like these, I find I am pretty ready to think away most other political, economic, and technological advantages.

Some Conservatives seem to want to go back to the Administration of McKinley. But when people are subject to universal social engineering and the biosphere itself is in danger, we need a more neolithic conservatism. So I propose maxims like "the right purpose of elementary schooling is to delay socialization" and "innovate in order to simplify, otherwise as sparingly as possible."

Liberals want to progress, that is, to up the rate of growth by political means. But if the background conditions are tolerable, society will probably progress anyway, for people have energy, curiosity, and ingenuity. All the resources of the State cannot anyway educate a child, improve a neighborhood, give dignity to an oppressed man. Sometimes the state can provide capital for people to do for themselves; but mostly it should stop standing in the way and doing damage and wasting wealth. Political power may come out of the barrel of a gun, but, as John L. Lewis said, "You can't dig coal with bayonets."

2. Edmund Burke had a good idea of conservatism, that existing community bonds are destroyed at peril; they are not readily replaced, society becomes superficial and government illegitimate. It takes the rising of a prophet or some other irrational cataclysm to create new community bonds. It is like a love affair or a marriage—unless there is severe moral disagreement or actual physical revulsion, it is wiser to stay with it and blow on the embers, than to be happily not in love or not married at all. The hard decisions, of course, are when people imagine that they are already in love elsewhere; but nations of people are rather cautious about this.

In his American policy, Burke was a good conservative; he was willing to give up everything else to conserve the community bonds. It is just here that phony conservatives become trimmers and tokenists and talk about "virtual representation" or "maximum feasible participation of the poor," protecting their vested interests. A proof that the American Revolution was justified is that the British government did not take Burke's and Pitt's advice. Later, during the French Revolution, Burke was a sentimentalist clinging to the bygone, for after Louis tried to go over to the invaders, there were no community bonds left to conserve.

3. The problem is to avoid emergency, when dictatorship is inevitable and decent people sometimes commit enormities. There was the real emergency of Hitler, and we have not yet finished with the growth of the military-industrial that was rooted back there. But Woodrow Wilson foresaw the military-industrial in 1916 and we did get out of it. So long as ancient Rome had vitality, it was able to dismiss its dictatorships. We, however, have trumped up the at least partly paranoiac emergency of the Cold War now for more than twenty years.

But the worst is the metaphysical emergency of Modern Times: feeling powerless in immense social organizations; desperately relying on technological means to solve problems caused by previous technological means; and when urban areas are already technically and fiscally unworkable, extrapolating and planning for bigger urban areas. Then, "Nothing can be done."

I think it is first to escape feeling trapped that I improvise dumb-bunny alternatives. I can then show that the reasons men are not free are only political and psychological, not metaphysical. Unlike most other "social critics," I am rather scrupulous about not attacking unless I can think up an alternative or two, to avoid rousing metaphysical anxiety. Usually, indeed, I do not have critical feelings unless I first imagine something different and begin to improvise upon it. With much of the business of our society, my intuition is to forget it.

4. Coleridge was the most philosophical of the conservatives writing in English: "To have citizens, we must first be sure we have produced men"—or conserved them. The context of this remark, in *The Constitution of the Church and State*, was his critique of the expropriation of the monasteries by Henry VIII. The property was rightly taken away from the Whore of Babylon, to stop the drain of wealth from England to Rome; but Coleridge argued that it should then have been consigned to other moral and cultural institutions, to produce men, rather than thrown into the general economy. He made the same point vividly in another passage, in *The Friend*. A Manchester economist had said that an isolated village that took no part in the national trade was of no importance. "What, sir," said Coleridge, "are 700 Christian souls of no importance?" The English factory towns destroyed people for the economy. We increasingly do not even need people for the economy.

As a man of letters, I am finally most like Coleridge (with a dash of Matthew Arnold when the vulgarity of liberalism gets me by the throat). Maybe what we have in common is our obsessional needs, his drug addiction and my frustrated homosexuality. These keep us in touch with animal hunger, so we are not overly impressed by progress, the Gross National Product, and credentials and status. For addicts and other starving people, the world has to come across in kind. It doesn't.

My homosexual acts have made me a nigger, subject to arbitrary brutality and debased when my outgoing impulse is not taken for granted as a right. It is not that I don't get what I want; nobody (except small children) has a claim to be loved. But there is a way of rejecting someone that accords him his right to exist and be himself and is the next best thing to accepting him. I have rarely enjoyed this treatment.

Stokely Carmichael once told me and Allen Ginsberg that our homosexual need was not like being black because we could always conceal it and pass. That is, he accorded us the lack of imagination that one accords to niggers. (Incidentally, this dialogue was taking place on national TV, that haven of secrecy.)

A vital nigger can respond with various kinds of spite, depending on his character. He can be ready to destroy everything, since there is no world to lose. Or he might develop an in-group fanaticism of his own kind. In my case, being a nigger seems to inspire me to want a more elementary humanity, wilder, less structured, more variegated. The thing is to have a Liberation Front that does not end up in a Nation State, but abolishes the boundaries.

5. Usually we ought to work to diminish social anxiety, but to break down arbitrary boundaries we have to risk heightening social anxiety. Some boundaries, of course, are just the limits of our interests and people beyond them are indifferent or exotic. But as soon as we begin to notice a boundary *between* us and others, we project our own unacceptable traits on those across the boundary, and they become foreigners, heretics, untouchables, persons exploited as things. By their very existence, they threaten or tempt us, and we must squelch them, patronize them, or with missionary zeal make them shape up.

Thus, the excluded or repressed are always right in their rebellion, for they stand for our future wholeness. And their demands must always seem wrong-headed, their style uncalled for, and their actions to violate due process. But as in any psychotherapy, the problem is to tolerate anxiety and stay with it, rather than to panic and be in an emergency.

Curiously, the half-baked and noisy culture of the young is hopeful in this respect just because it is so dreadful. It is embarrassed or brazen, sometimes resigned, sometimes spiteful, but it is not up tight. It is a kind of folk art of urban confusion, and where there is a folk art there might get to be a high art. It is not advance-guard, for they don't know enough to have an edge to leap from. It is not even eclectic but a

farrago of misunderstood styles. But it *is* without some previous boundaries. There is something in its tribalism, as they call it. It is somewhat
a folk international. And it is boring, like all folk art; a litttle bit goes
a long way.

6. Lord Acton, who understood conservatism, praises the character—George Washington was a good example—that is conservative in
disposition but resolute in the disruptive action that has to be performed.
A good surgeon minimizes post-operative shock, and having cut, he
at once resumes as a physician, saying, "Nature heals, not the doctor."
The advantage of a conservative, even backtracking, disposition in a
successful revolutionary is to diminish the danger of take-over by new
bosses who invariably are rife with plans. After the American Revolution,
the conservative disposition of the chief leaders blessed us with those
twenty-five years of quasi-anarchy in national affairs, during which we
learned whatever has made the American experiment worthwhile. "It's
a free country, you can't make me"—every immigrant child learned
to say it for over a century. The same would have occurred in the
French Revolution if they had enjoyed our geographic isolation from
invasion. The first French revolutionary leaders were the reverse of
Jacobin; Danton wanted to get back to his wine and girls. But a defect
of Leninist revolutions is that, from the beginning, they are made by
Leninists. They have ideas.

7. I myself have a conservative, maybe timid, disposition; yet I trust
that the present regime in America will get a lot more roughing up
than it has, from the young who resent being processed; from the blacks
who have been left out; from housewives and others who buy real goods
with hard money at inflationary prices hiked by expense accounts and
government subsidies; from professionals demanding their autonomy,
rather than being treated as personnel of the front office; from every
live person in jeopardy because of the bombs and CBW. Our system
can stand, and profit by plenty of interruption of business as usual.
It is not such a delicate Swiss watch as all that. Our danger is not
in the loosening of the machine, but in its tightening up by panic
repression.

8. It is true that because of massive urbanization and interlocking
technologies, advanced countries are vulnerable to catastrophic disruption, and this creates a perceptible anxiety. But there is far more likeli-
hood of breakdown from the respectable ambitions of Eastern Airlines
and Consolidated Edison than from the sabotage of revolutionaries.

In a large modern complex society, it is said, any rapid global "revolutionary" or "utopian" change can be incalculably destructive. I agree;
but I wish people would remember that the Establishment itself has
continually introduced big rapid changes that have in fact produced
incalculable shock. Consider, in the past generation, the TV, mass higher
schooling, the complex of cars, roads, and suburbanization, mass air

travel, the complex of plantations, chain grocers, and forced urban-ization; not to speak of the meteoric rise of the military industries and the Vietnam War and the draft. In all these, there has been a big factor of willful decision; these have not been natural processes or inevitable catastrophes. And we have not begun to compound with the problems caused by these utopian changes. Rather, in what seems an amazingly brief time, we have come to a political, cultural, and religious crisis that must be called pre-revolutionary—and all because of a few willful fools.

9. There is also authentic confusion, however, not caused by bad will. Worldwide, we are going through a rapidly stepped-up collectiviza-tion which is, in my opinion, inevitable. I have just been watching the first lunar landing and the impression of collectivity is overwhelming. We do not know how to cope with the dilemmas of it. Surely the only prudent course is to try piecemeal to defend and extend the areas of liberty, locally, on the job, and in mores. Any violent collective "remedy" would be certainly totalitarian, whatever the ideology.

Needless to say, I myself have hankered after and pushed global institutional changes: Drastic cut-back of the military industries, of the school system, and of the penal system; giving the city streets back to the children by banning the cars, and the cities back to the citizens by neighborhood government; vigorous nourishment of decentralized mass-communications and rural reconstruction; guaranteed income and a sector of free appropriation. I look for the kind of apprentice system that would produce workers' management, and the kind of guild associa-tion that would affirm authentic professionalism. The effects of these changes are also incalculable; it is hard to think through the conse-quences in our society that would flow from any and all of them. But I believe that in the fairly short run they would be stabilizing rather than explosive.

10. A moment's reflection will show that in any advanced society there is bound to be a mixture of enterprises run collectively and those run by individuals and small companies; and either kind of management may try to be busy and growing or conservatively content to satisfy needs. Thus, there are always "socialism" and "free enterprise," "produc-tion for profit" and "production for use." The interesting political question is what is the right proportion and location of these factors in the particu-lar society in the particular circumstances. Safety from exploitation, safety from bureaucratic tyranny, flexibility and style of innovation, the possibility of countervailing power, all those political things depend on this balance. But cost efficiency also depends on it: "For any set of technological and social conditions, there is probably a rough optimum proportion of types of enterprise, or better, limits of unbalance beyond which the system gives sharply diminishing returns. A good mixed sys-tem would remain within the efficient range." (*People or Personnel*, ch. V)

But nobody wants to explore this subject any more. When I was young, it used to be a respectable liberal ideology called the Scandinavian Way. Now if I say that a mixture is inevitable and desirable, it is dismissed as "common sense," meaning a trivial platitude.

Since I am often on Canadian TV and radio, I tell it to the Canadians. If they would cut the American corporations down to size, it would cost them three or four years of high unemployment and austerity, but then Canada could become the most livable nation in the world, like Denmark but rich in resources, space, and heterogeneous population, with its own corporations, free businesses, cooperatives, a reasonable amount of socialism, a sector of communism or guaranteed income as fits modern productivity, plenty of farmers, cities not yet too big, plenty of scientists and academics, a decent traditional bureaucracy, a nonaligned foreign policy. A great modern nation not yet too far gone in modern mistakes. There would be a flood of excellent immigrants from the south.

11. In one of his later books, *The Third World War,* C. Wright Mills had a conventional proposition far below his usual strong sense. The concentration of decision-making in our interlocking institutions, he argued, makes possible big changes for the better if the decision-makers can be rightly influenced—he seemed to be thinking of John Kennedy. It is doubtful if any administrator indeed has the kind of power to make an important change of policy; by the end of 1961, the Kennedy people complained that they could not. But even if it would and could make policy, concentrated power can't produce human results anyway; it freezes what it touches. But, there is perhaps a different kind of truth in Mills's idea. The interlocking of institutions, the concentration of decision-making, and the mass communications are the things that render people powerless, including the decision-makers; yet because of these same things, if freedom-loving people, honest professionals, or any other resolute group, indeed fight it out on their own issues, the odds are against them but their action is bound to have resonance and influence. In a reckless sentence in *Growing Up Absurd* I said, "One has the persistent thought that if ten thousand people in all walks of life stand up on their two feet and talk out and insist, we shall get back our country"—and damned if I don't still think so, with more evidence than I had then.

12. The right style in planning is to eliminate the intermediary, that which is neither use, nor making for use. We ought to cut down commutation, transport, administration, overhead, communications, hanging around waiting. On the other hand, there are very similar functions that we ought to encourage; like travel and trade, brokering, amenity, conversation, and loitering, the things that make up the busy and idle city, celebrated by Jane Jacobs. The difference seems to be that in logistics, systems, and communications, the soul is on ice till the intermediary activity is over with; in traffic, brokering, and conversation people are thrown with others and something might turn up. It is the difference between urbanism that imperially imposes its pattern on city and country both, and the city of squares and shops and contrasting rural life.

It was the genius of American pragmatism, our great contribution to world Philosophy, to show that the means define and color the ends, to find value in operations and materials, to dignify workmanship and the workaday, to make consummation less isolated, more in process forward, growth as well as good. But in recent decades there has occurred an astonishing reversal: the tendency of American philosophy, e.g. analytical logic or cybernetics, has been to drain value from both making and use, from either the working and the materials or from moral and psychological goods, and to define precisely by the intermediary logistics, system, and communications, what Max Weber called rationalization. The medium is all the message there is. The pragmatists added to value, especially in everyday affairs. Systems analysis has drained value, except for a few moments of collective achievement. Its planning refines and streamlines the intermediary as if for its own sake; it adds constraints without enriching life. If the computation makes no difference to the data or the result, e.g. "garbage in, garbage out," then, to a pragmatist, the computation adds to the garbage. In fact, the computation abstracts from the data what it can handle, and limits the possibilities to the questions. Certainly, cybernetics could be enriching, as psychiatry or as ecology, but it has not yet been so—an exception is the work of Bateson.

It is interesting to notice the change in the style of scientific explanation. At the turn of the century they spoke of evolution, struggle, coping, the logic of inquiry. Now they emphasize code, homeostasis, feedback, the logic of structure.

13. A decade ago it was claimed that there was an end to ideology, for the problems of modern society have to be coped with pragmatically, functionally, piecemeal. This seems to have been a poor prediction, in view of the deafening revival of Marxist-Leninist rhetoric and Law and Order rhetoric. Yet it was true, but not in the sense in which it was offered. The ideological rhetoric is pretty irrelevant; but the pragmatic, functional, and piecemeal approach has not, as was expected, consigned our problems to the province of experts, administrators, and engineers, but has thrown them to the dissenters. Relevant new thought has not been administrative and technological, but existentialist, ethical, and tactical. Administrators and planners write books about the universities and cities, extrapolating from the trends—and asking for funds; but history does not seem to be going in their direction.

Rather, pragmatism has come to be interpreted to include the character of the agents as part of the problem to be solved; it is psychoanalytic; there is stress on engagement. (Incidentally, this is good Jamesian pragmatism.) Functionalism has come to mean criticizing the program and the function itself, asking who wants to do it and why, and is it humanly worth doing. Piecemeal issues have gotten entangled with the political action of the people affected by them. Instead of becoming more administrative as expected, affairs are becoming more political. The premises of expertise and planning are called into question. The credentials of the board of trustees are scrutinized. Professionalism is a dirty word. Terms like "commitment," "dialogue," "confrontation," "community," "do your thing" are indeed anti-ideological—and sometimes they do not connote much other thought either; but they are surely not what *The End of Ideology* had in mind. And it turns out that they are relevant to the conditions of complex modern societies.

14. An advantage I have had over many others—I don't know whether by luck or by character—is that I have never had to do, nor forced myself to do, what was utterly alien to me. I was good at school work and liked it. From age fifteen I never had a job that was altogether useless, or harmful, or mere busywork, or that did not use some of my powers, so that I could try to do a good job in my own style. This does not mean that I did what I wanted. Sometimes the work was unpleasant or boring and it was almost never what I should have been used for. I was poor, without connections, bisexual, and socially inept, so that I was always driven by need and had to take what turned up, without choices. But I could not do—I did not consider as a possibility—anything that I could not somewhat identify with. If somebody had offered me a stupid job at good pay, I could hardly have refused, but this never happened. I always worked hard in a way that made sense to myself—and sometimes got fired. I often had no job at all, and wrote stories.

It is devastating that this is not the common condition. If people go through motions that do not make sense to them and do not have their allegiance, just for wages or other extrinsic rewards, there is an end to common sense and self-respect. Character is made by behaviors we initiate; if we initiate what we do not mean, we get sick. And we see, the accumulation of such motions that are not continually checked up as meant can produce calamities.

15. The time I spend on politics—it is not much time but it is more than I have—is a fair example of how I work at what is mine but is onerous and boring. As a conservative anarchist, I believe that to seek for Power is otiose, yet I want to derange as little as possible the powers that be; I am eager to sign off as soon as conditions are tolerable, so people can go back to the things that matter, their professions, sports, and friendships. Naturally, politics is not for me. In principle I agree with the hippies. They become political when they are indignant, as at the war or racist laws, and they also have to work at power and politics in order to protect their own business and community, e.g.

against police harassment; but otherwise they rightly judge that radicals are in a bag.

But I am political because of an idiotic concept of myself as a man of letters: I am that kind of writer who must first have done his duty as a citizen, father, and so forth. Inevitably, my disastrous model is John Milton—and it's a poor state to be waiting to go blind in order to be free to write a big poem. But at least, thereby, I write with a good conscience. I do not have to be a political poet. I am immune from the stupidity of Sartre's artist *engagé*—how the devil would an artist, relying on the random spirit as we do, choose whether or not to be *engagé*?

16. In normal fiscal conditions, the way for free citizens to check the government has been to grant or refuse taxes, usually through the parliament, but if both the parliament and the government are illegitimate, by individual refusal. At present, some are refusing their Federal taxes, or 70 per cent of the amount, in protest against the armaments and, of course, the Vietnam War. (They estimate the military budget as about 70 per cent of the total.)

I agree with the principle of refusal, yet, except for the surtax and the telephone tax, I pay the taxes because of a moral scruple; for in the present fiscal set-up, the kind of money I get is not really pay for my work, is not mine, but belongs to the very System I object to. I have a comfortable income. I well deserve an adequate one and a little more; I worked hard till forty-five years of age, and brought up children, on an income in the lowest tenth of the population; nor have I found that my late-come wealth has changed my thoughts, work, or even much my standard of living. But most of my money is "soft" money, from the military economy and the wasteful superstructure, and I cannot see how I am justified to keep Caesar's share from dribbling back to him through my hands. For instance, I am paid a large sum to give a lecture—mainly because I am a "name" and they want to make their series prestigious; the lecture series is financed by a Foundation; and you do not need to scratch hard to find military-industrial corporations supporting that Foundation—perhaps as a tax dodge! I give the lecture innocently enough; I am probably not indispensable to give it, but I do my best and say my say. But it would not help to refuse the money, or most of it, since by Parkinson's law that all the soft money will be spent, the money will certainly be spent.

I wouldn't know how to estimate the pay that I get for hard work in hard money, on which I would feel justified in refusing the tax because it is mine to give or refuse, but it cannot be much of the whole. There is an hypothesis that in our society pay is inversely proportional to effort. The idea, I guess, is that big money accrues from being in the System, and the higher you are in the System, the less you move your ass. But empirically it is not quite accurate. Top managers and professionals work hard for long hours for high pay; those on a thirty-six-hour week work much less, at varying pay; farmers, hospital orderlies, dish-washers, and others work very hard for miserable pay; some students work hard and it costs them money; unemployable people do not work for inadequate pay. In my experience, there has been no relation what-ever between effort and pay. For twenty years I averaged a few hundred dollars a year for good writing that I now make good royalties on; I work hard for a possibly useful cause and lay out fare and a contribu-tion, or I do the same work at a State college for a handsome honorarium and expenses. Third class on planes is usually the most luxurious be-cause, if the plane is not full, you can remove the seat arms and stretch out. My editor takes me to costly lunches at the firm's expense and the food is poor.

The lack of correlation between effort and pay must be profoundly confusing and perhaps disgusting to the naive young. In my opinion, it is unfortunate at present but promising for the future: it creates the moral attitude, "It's only money," and politically, a soft-money affluent society can easily come to include a sector of communism, in the form of guaranteed income or free appropriation or both.

The telephone tax, however, was explicitly a war tax and my wife and I don't pay it, getting the spiteful satisfaction that it costs the gov-ernment a couple of hundred dollars (of the tax-payers', our, money) to collect $1.58. We also have refused the 10 per cent surtax, which rose directly out of the Vietnam War. This tax for the war is like the ship tax that Charles I exacted for his Irish War, that John Hamden refused. The FBI seems to be breathing down our necks about it, but if they arrest me I'll bring up that shining precedent—and they'll be sorry that they picked on me. (No, they finally simply attached my account.)

17. In otherwise friendly reviews and expostulatory fan mail from young people, I read that there are three things wrong with my social thinking: I go in for tinkering. I don't tell how to bring about what I propose. I am a "romantic" and want to go back to the past. Let me consider these criticisms in turn.

My proposed little reforms and improvements are meaningless, it is said, because I do not attack the System itself, usually monopoly capital-ism; and I am given the philological information that "radical" means "going to the root," whereas I hack at the branches. To answer this, I have tried to show that in a complex society which is a network rather than a monolith with a head, a piecemeal approach can be effec-tive; it is the safest, least likely to produce ruinous consequences of either repression or "success"; it involves people where they are compe-tent, or could become competent, and so creates citizens, which is better than "politicizing"; it more easily dissolves the metaphysical despair that nothing can be done. And since, in my opinion, the aim of politics is to produce not a good society but a tolerable one, it is best to try to cut abuses down to manageable size; the best solutions are usually not global but a little of this and a little of that.

More important, in the confusing conditions of Modern Times, so bristling with dilemmas, I don't know what is the root. I have not heard of any formula, e.g. "Socialism," that answers the root questions. If I were a citizen of a Communist country, I should no doubt be getting into (more) trouble by tinkering with "bourgeois" improvements. The problem in any society is to get a more judicious mixture of kinds of enterprise, and this *might* be most attainable by tinkering.

18. A second criticism is that I don't explain how to bring about the nice things I propose. The chief reason for this, of course, is that I don't know how or I would proclaim it. Put it this way: I have been a pacifist for forty years and rather active for thirty years, and. . . . But ignorance is rarely an excuse. What my critics really object to is that I accept my not knowing too easily, as if the actuality of change were unimportant, rather than just brooding about it, when in fact people are wretched and dying.

As I have explained, I do not have the character for politics. I cannot lead or easily be led, and I am dubious about the ability of parties and government to accomplish any positive good—and which of these is cause, which is effect?—therefore I do not put my mind to questions of manipulation and power, I do not belong to a party, and therefore I have no tactical thoughts. Belief and commitment are necessary to have relevant ideas. Nevertheless somebody has to make sense, and I am often willing to oblige, as a man of letters, as part of the division of labor, so to speak.

I do agree with my critics that there cannot be social thought without political action; and if I violate this rule, I ought to stop. Unless it is high poetry, utopian thinking is boring. "Neutral" sociology is morally repugnant and bad science. An essential part of any sociological inquiry is having a practical effect, otherwise the problem is badly defined: people are being taken as objects rather than real, and the inquirer himself is not all there.

For the humanistic problems that I mostly work at, however, the sense of powerlessness, the loss of history, vulgarity, the lack of magnanimity, alienation, the maladaption of organisms and environment—and these are political problems—maybe there are no other "strategies" than literature, dialogue, and trying to be a useful citizen oneself.

19. I am not a "romantic"; what puts my liberal and radical critics off is that I am a conservative, a conservationist. I do use the past; the question is how.

I get a kind of insight (for myself) from the genetic method, from seeing how a habit or institution has developed to its present form; but I really do understand that all positive value and meaning is in present action, coping with present conditions. Freud, for instance, was in error when he sometimes spoke as if a man had a child inside of

him, or a vertebrate had an annelid worm inside. Each specified individual behaves as the whole that it has become; and every stage of life
as Dewey used to insist has its own problems and ways of coping.

The criticism of the genetic fallacy, however, does not apply to the
negative, to the *lapses* in the present, which can often be remedied
only by taking into account some simplicities of the past. The case
is analogous to localizing an organic function, e.g. seeing. As Kurt Goldstein used to point out, we cannot localize seeing in the eye or the
brain, it is a function of the whole organism in its environment. But
a *failure* of sight may well be localized in the cornea, the optic nerve,
etc. We cannot explain speech by the psychosexual history of an infant;
it is a way of being in the world. But a speech defect, e.g. lisping,
may well come from inhibited biting because of imperfect weaning.
This is, of course, what Freud knew as a clinician rather than a
metapsychologist.

My books are full of one paragraph or two page "histories"—of the
concept of alienation, the system of welfare, suburbanization, compulsory
schooling, neutral technology, the anthropology of neurosis, university
administration, citizenly powerlessness, missed revolutions, etc., etc. In
every case my purpose is to show that a coerced or inauthentic settling
of a conflict has left an unfinished situation to the next generation, and
the difficulty becomes more complex in the new conditions. Then it
is useful to remember the simpler state before things went wrong; it
is hopelessly archaic as a present response, but it has vitality and may
suggest a new program involving a renewed conflict. This is the thera-
peutic use of history. As Ben Nelson has said, the point of history is
to keep old (defeated) causes alive. Of course, this reasoning presup-
poses that there is a nature of things, including human nature, whose
right development can be violated. There is.

An inauthentic solution complicates, and produces a monster. An
authentic solution neither simplifies nor complicates, but produces a new
configuration, a species adapted to the on-going situation. There is a
human nature, and it is characteristic of that nature to go on making itself
ever different. This is the humanistic use of history, to remind of man's
various ways of being great. So we have become mathematical, tragical,
political, loyal, romantic, civil-libertarian, universalist, experimental-
scientific, collectivist, etc., etc.—these too accumulate and become a
mighty heavy burden. There is no laying any of it down.

20. I went down to Dartmouth to lead some seminars of American
Telephone and Telegraph executives who were being groomed to be
vice-presidents. They wanted to know how to get on with young people,
since they would have to employ them, or try. (Why do I go? Ah,
why do I go? It's not for money and it's not out of vanity. I go because
they ask me. Since I used to gripe bitterly when I was left out of
the world, how can I gracefully decline when I am invited in?)

I had three suggestions. First, citing my usual evidence of the irrelevance of school grades and diplomas, I urged them to hire black and Puerto Rican dropouts, who would learn on the job as well as anybody else, whereas to require academic credentials puts them at a disadvantage. Not to my surprise, the executives were congenial to this idea. (There were twenty-five of them, no black and no woman.) It was do-good and no disadvantage to them as practical administrators. One said that he was already doing it and it had worked out very well.

Secondly, I pointed out that dialogue across the generation gap was quite impossible for them, and their present tactics of youth projects and special training would be taken as, and were, co-optation. Yet people who will not talk to one another can get together by working together on a useful job that they both care about, like fixing the car. And draft-counseling, I offered, was something that the best of the young cared strongly about; the Telephone Company could provide valuable and interesting help in this, for instance the retrieval and dissemination of information; and all this was most respectable and American, since every kid should know his rights. Not to my surprise, the executives were not enthusiastic about this proposal. But they saw the point—and had to agree—and would certainly not follow up.

My third idea, however, they did not seem to know what to do with. I told them that Ralph Nader was going around the schools urging the engineering students to come on like professionals, and stand up to the front desk when asked for unprofessional work. In my opinion, an important move for such integrity would be for the young engineers to organize for defense of the profession, and strike or boycott if necessary: a model was the American Association of University Professors in its heyday—fifty years ago. I urged the executives to encourage such organization; it would make the Telephone Company a better telephone company, more serviceable to the community; and young people would cease to regard engineers as finks. To my surprise, the prospective vice-presidents of A.T. and T. seemed to be embarrassed. (We were all pleasant people and very friendly.) I take it that *this*—somewhere here—is the issue.

I am pleased to notice how again and again I return to the freedoms, duties, and opportunities of earnest professionals. It means that I am thinking from where I breathe.

QUESTIONS FOR DISCUSSION AND WRITING

1. Why does Goodman refer to himself as "a neolithic conservative"? At another point he calls himself "a conservative anarchist." Are these two things the same? Is Goodman a "conservative" in the popular sense of the word? Explain.

2. Goodman says that "All the resources of the State cannot educate a child, improve a neighborhood, give dignity to an oppressed man." What is the importance of this statement to Goodman's definition of himself as a "conservative"? Do you agree with Goodman as to what the State can and cannot do?
3. What is the importance of "community bonds" and why is Goodman so anxious to "conserve" them?
4. Goodman says that he has been accused of "tinkering," of offering "piecemeal" solutions rather than "radical" ones. How does Goodman refute this charge? Do you agree with his reasoning? Discuss.
5. "I have just been watching the first lunar landing," Goodman remarks at one point, "and the impression of collectivity is overwhelming." What does Goodman mean by this? If Goodman's impression is a valid one, what are its implications for our society and the world we live in?
6. Would "radical students" agree with the majority of the ideas in this essay? With what ideas would they disagree? Why is Goodman such a popular author among many young people?
7. Goodman makes good use of personal experiences to make observations not only about our society but about the development of his own brand of conservatism. If you consider yourself a liberal, or a radical, or a conservative, cite some of the personal experiences you think contributed to your own political ideology. Would it be possible for two people to have identical experiences and one of them turn out a liberal and the other a conservative? Explain.
8. If Paul Goodman is in fact a "conservative," what is a "liberal"?

Ellen Willis

The Lessons of Chicago

I

The Chicago protest was one of those rare political events that is not merely attended, but lived. What was most remarkable about it was how much living was concentrated in such a short time; the week of the Democratic Convention summed up a period of Movement history as no other action has done since the historic Mississippi Summer Project. Chicago was an emotional marathon; between bouts of rage and fear, exhaustion and boredom, pessimism and euphoria, we slept little and badly. It was an experience from which, as I write this, I am still learning.

It started out badly. The Mobilization had never recovered from the confusion following President Johnson's withdrawal (was the war over? was Robert Kennedy going to lead us into the light?), while Mayor Daley's scare campaign was a triumph of reverse public relations. McCarthy and Lowenstein urged their supporters to stay home; SDS was noncommittal; hippies accused the Yippies of luring kids to a bloodbath instead of a "Festival of Life"; local radical organizers worried about repression that would make it more difficult for them to operate within their communities. Only a tiny fraction of the expected 200,000 people showed up, and some of the local organizers even left town to make sure the police couldn't blame them for anything. Poor organization resulted in potentially disastrous gaffes: centering the protest in isolated Lincoln Park rather than a downtown site; staging an illegal march in the middle of a park, with the only escape routes a few easily-blocked bridges.

Yet sometimes a political demonstration (like a play, or a love affair) just miraculously jells. Chicago jelled. All our mistakes somehow turned into assets; all Daley's mistakes got him deeper in trouble. We succeeded in disrupting the Convention—spiritually at least—and demoralizing the

279

Democratic Party. But this was secondary; like typical Americans, we got our biggest kicks from contemplating our image in the media. The publicity was graphic and slanted in our favor, and we obtained it at notably little cost: no one died demonstrating, and most injuries were painful rather than disabling. Instead of the bitterness, political infighting, and accusations of contrived martyrdom that would have followed killings there was a feeling of community that almost transcended ideological differences; added to the comradeship that came from spending so much time on the streets of a strange city was the solidarity forced on us by the authorities, who treated us all—hardcore street-fighters, McCarthy liberals, and those somewhere between (me)—with equal animus.

After Black Wednesday, we walked the streets grinning, greeting strangers "Peace, brother," and meaning it, flashing the V sign at every opportunity. Our expansiveness was accentuated by the unexpected friendliness of local people. Blacks radiated especially welcome sympathy. I had not experienced such genuine interracial good will in years; genuine, I say, because looking suspiciously for sarcasm and secret glee at white injuries, I found only respect for kids willing to put their bodies on the line. But white workers (not necessarily under thirty) also gave us the V; even a young cop, directing traffic on Michigan Avenue, spread two fingers and winked and smiled. Then there were the Chicago kids. All week they had been coming up to Lincoln Park to play dialogue with the weirdos—tensely polite high school footballers arguing solemnly with revolutionaries, teenies asking half seriously how to go about breaking away from their parents. There wasn't much overt hostility from the public. I heard that a few demonstrators got beaten up in the white working-class neighborhood near the International Amphitheater. Thursday night some white vocational students lay in wait for Dick Gregory's march up Michigan and chanted, without much enthusiasm, "Hippies go home." But that was about it.

I went to Chicago mainly for negative reasons. I thought that the Movement could not, without looking foolish, allow the Democrats to play their game in a complacent, business-as-usual atmosphere; further, to have panicked in the face of Daley's threats would have been to display weakness and invite a general crackdown on dissent. I left knowing that something very positive had happened to me. Specifically: never had I been so conscious that what I was involved in was a rebel *community*, whose emotions and sensations had a collective life of their own; although I didn't always agree with what was happening, I was always part of it. At the same time, I became more acutely sensitive than ever before to our problematic relations with the larger community. In its name we had been clubbed and gassed, yet in some ways it had been far more hospitable to us than we deserved. For we were and still are too much disposed to see ourselves as the beautiful green planet around which the vast body of the American people sluggishly revolves. What we need, if we are to understand and change this society, is a Copernican theory of politics.

II

The Yippies saw the Chicago action as theater, and they were right. The clashes between demonstrators and police—four major "confrontations," from the first skirmish in Lincoln Park on Convention eve to the Wednesday night extravaganza, and dozens of minor conflicts—were theater that bordered on religious ritual. This is not to imply that the emotions and the injuries were in any sense unreal; on the contrary, they were super-real—not only personal and concrete but collective and symbolic. On the streets and in the parks of Chicago the Movement lived two of its most potent myths: the myth of insurrection (let's stop talking about it and *do* it) and the myth of revelation (this time we're going to make everyone *see* the whole motherfucking mess once and for all).

The insurrectionary myth could be seen at its purest in Lincoln Park. Since the atmosphere of the city, as well as direct restrictions, had squelched the Yippies' counter-convention Festival before it began, and since the Mobilization had planned no activities early in the week, the focus of the protest had shifted completely away from the Convention and Vietnam to a battle over turf. What made the battle mythic was that so many of the participants believed—or at least convinced themselves they believed—that its outcome was in doubt. In fact, the main argument among the militants in the crowd was whether the 3,000 of us should concentrate on liberating the park or taking over the city. Would-be organizers who tried to give advice on how to get out of the park in a hurry, or information on free housing, were received with almost universal hostility. It was as if stagehands were to interrupt a play to tell the actors where the emergency exit was or to set up props for the next scene.

During the tense precurfew hours, against a background of garbage fires and African drumming, the militants' exhortations and responses functioned as an improvised Greek chorus:

"If one of us dies, how many pigs will die?"

"Ten!"

"Twenty!"

"They got the guns, but we got the numbers."

"We gonna stay in the park. We all gonna stay together, right?"

"Yes! Yes!"

"Let's get out on the streets. Fuck over the city. Do them in."

"The park is ours!"

"The streets are ours!"

The images on everyone's mind were Paris and Columbia; the presiding spirit was Che's. But no one seemed to realize that Paris was a defeat, leaving De Gaulle stronger than before; that Columbia was still a slumlord and still part of the war machine; that Che had died without creating a single Vietnam. Nor in all the self-congratulatory talk about the courage of "the people"—meaning us, not the seventy per cent of Chicagoans who had given Mayor Daley his last election victory—was there any recognition that revolution is a matter of life and death, not split scalps and dented police cars. The mythic impulse disdained such practical details.

The drama of insurrection developed more or less spontaneously, as a reflex response to Mayor Daley's ban on camping in the park. The drama of revelation, on the other hand, was carefully planned—produced and directed by the Movement's most inventive imagemaker, Jerry Rubin. Not only were the Festival of Life and Pig-for-President ploys more effective than any of Mobe's efforts in getting people to come to Chicago, but Rubin's nominal organization of perhaps a dozen activists impressed the media so much that "Yippie" became virtually a generic term for demonstrator. (In the aftermath of the protests, police claimed that TV officials had told Rubin where cameras would be located so that he could plan accordingly—a not implausible charge.) The Yippie conception of the demonstrations as radical theater for a mass audience was a more sophisticated, imaginative extension of the line espoused by straight radicals like Tom Hayden and Rennie Davis—that the purpose of confrontation was to prove to millions that our putative democracy is governed not by consent but by force.

This rationale has always made me uncomfortable, because I don't believe that confrontations, in themselves, prove anything of the sort. The government has never pretended not to back its laws with force; what radicals must demonstrate is that the laws do not represent the majority will, or—what is even more complicated—that the majority will is consistently manipulated to oppose its own interests. The Chicago confrontations showed only that Daley's actions were possibly unconstitutional and certainly vindictive, and that the police were unnecessarily violent. Liberals might easily argue that it was not the inherent repressiveness of the system that had been exposed, but the stubbornness of a particularly dictatorial, xenophobic politician and the general benightedness of policemen; the remedy, then, was not revolution but reform of the Democratic Party and a college education for cops. As for the mass of Americans, they could be expected to conclude that the troublemaking freaks—and after all, none of us denied that we came to make trouble, to disrupt a National Convention, no less—simply got what they asked for.

Nevertheless, the theory of revelation-through-confrontation was tenaciously defended. When it was suggested to Tom Hayden that Mayor

Lindsay would have given the demonstrators Central Park, let them march wherever they wanted and ordered the police to keep hands off, Hayden replied that since Lindsay would not have scared away potential demonstrators, a New York action would have drawn 750,000 people, too many to be peacefully contained. Besides, he said, the prevalent belief that the war was going to end because corporate liberals had decided it was a mistake was all wrong; on the contrary, the war was going to be pressed, and the reaction of the Chicago police showed that the power structure had decided to crush dissent. I thought Hayden's statistic was fanciful—after all, the highest total estimate of demonstrators in Chicago had been 15,000 ("And that," remarked one disappointed radical, "is if you count everybody twice"). His analysis of the political situation struck me as equally facile. The outcome of the war was still in doubt, but the extent and respectability of the opposition, which had split the nation's ruling party, could not help but reflect bitter conflicts of interest among the powerful—conflicts that were reflected not only in differing policies but in differing styles. Hayden underestimated the ability of the Lindsay-style politician to neutralize dissent by avoiding conspicuous abrasion. After Martin Luther King's death, the New York police had stood by while arsonists gutted several blocks of Lenox Avenue stores. Many peculiar things were possible in this peculiar moment of history.

Of course, I am oversimplifying. For one thing, most big-city mayors are more like Daley than Lindsay. For another, the security measures at the Convention and Daley's prohibition of the march on the Amphitheater were not simply whim, but were rooted in the social crisis: the danger of assassinations was real, and so was the possibility of a violent clash between demonstrators and angry residents of the Stockyards neighborhood. And in calling on the National Guard and Federal troops, Daley was merely behaving like a conscientious liberal—the Kerner Report had recommended the use of large numbers of police to intimidate rioters without bloodshed. If the Chicago convulsion was no metaphysical necessity, neither was it just a fluke. In a sense it did reveal the system—though only at its crudest, at its most rigid, inflammatory, and provincial. Radicals who took that part for the whole were making an understandable inductive leap to a not improbable future. The problem was, it was not ourselves we had to convince—it was those people Out There.

It soon became clear that favorable publicity could not be equated with favorable public opinion; poll after poll showed that a large majority supported the police action. Publicity had been sympathetic because Daley had tried to restrict television coverage, because newsmen had been manhandled by police and security guards, and most of all because the average reporter is a good liberal, with the proper aristocratic prejudices against cops and machine politicians. But people who are not good liberals—that is, most people—do not necessarily take their cues from the media any more than radicals do. More likely, they lump reporters with those pseudointellectuals George Wallace reviled. Anyway, the honeymoon between the media and the demonstrators ended almost simultaneously with the Convention. Under pressure from indignant citizens as well as Mayor Daley, his police chief, the Democratic Party and the United States government (ominously, the FCC announced it would investigate charges of bias in television coverage of the demonstrations), the newspapers and TV stations went into paroxysms of self-doubt: Did we get too involved instead of maintaining our objectivity? Were we unfair to the police? If "the other side of the story" had indeed been stinted, it soon came into its own; September was the month of the On the Other Hand press. Besides atoning for real or imagined misfeasances, the media had the burden of reporting all the evidence various police and government sources were accumulating to show that the disturbances had been engineered by "a handful of dedicated revolutionaries": an undercover cop accused Jerry Rubin of plotting to kill a policeman; a cache of vituric acid (the active ingredient in stink bombs) was discovered in a bus-station locker; and so forth and so on.

Yet the reaction that many dreaded has so far turned out to be rather mild, its tone more pro-police than anti-demonstrator. The HUAC hearings were a joke, and the President's Commission on Violence even labeled the events in Chicago a "police riot." It may be that neither the radical left nor the right benefited as much from Chicago as the Democratic doves. The one thing the demonstrations certainly accomplished was to strengthen the anti-Humphrey forces in the party and galvanize local reformers. And since the movement to the right is more one of desperation than of positive enthusiasm—in the pre-election polls a significant percentage of Wallace voters revealed that their second choice had been Robert Kennedy or even Gene McCarthy—the anti-war liberals could mop up in 1972. The way the week ended—with dissenting liberal delegates sitting in the dirt, singing "We Shall Overcome," getting arrested and otherwise adopting the style of protest politics circa 1963 (liberals have their myths, too)—seems a portent. Radicals have been accused of duping hordes of innocent McCarthy kids into risking life and limb. But suppose it's just the opposite—suppose the street-fighters were really only shock troops for the reform Democrats, stalking-horses for Teddy Kennedy? Suppose the power structure isn't preparing to crush us, only to absorb us, as usual? America—and we ought to know this by now—is not a gun but a gigantic vacuum cleaner.

No matter. We forced a national political conclave under the gun. Every such activity saps the efficiency of government, diverting energy, money, manpower. More, it forces the authorities to keep taking us into account. If they know that whenever they do A we will do B, they have to stop each time and calculate: is it worth the trouble?

And whether or not the publicity created any new radicals, if it just showed some kid in Des Moines that we exist, it served its purpose. Visibility is the difference between a movement and ten thousand people in search of one.

III

The Chicago project cannot be judged simply by its concrete political results. In the long run, its influence on the attitudes of the participants may be more important. For all of us it was, among other things, a week-long exercise in political education, in which tactical experiments succeeded or failed, in which prejudice—and myth-making—came up against experience. The street community provided a continuing forum for gut-level debate about what had been and what should be done. Spokesmen for a variety of issues—Huey Newton, the Chicago transit strike, the California grape boycott, chemical and biological warfare— came to state their cases and mobilize subsidiary demonstrations. The constant argument and exchange of information, which meshed with the action in a way that should have delighted progressive educators as well as revolutionaries, was extended and amplified by the street media: the *Ramparts*-sponsored *Wallposter,* the best source of street news and analysis;[1] SDS's polemical broadside, *Handwriting on the Wall,* which was tacked to trees in the park; the usual underground and radical press; and leaflets on every conceivable subject.

For obvious reasons, our most impassioned discussion concerned the police. Before I go on, I should say that I am a policeman's daughter. My father is atypical (Jewish, intellectual, and—for a cop—dangerously liberal) and anyway, since cops distrust all civilians, my entrée to the police subculture is limited. But from years of parental inside dopesterism and personal contact with policemen I have learned many things. One of the simplest is that cops are not by definition vicious subhumans. This is not a truth generally accepted among political activists. In Chicago, the street fighters saw the demonstrations almost exclusively in terms of "the people" versus the cops, who were, depending on one's favorite metaphor, either animals or machines. For most of the week this attitude dominated, at least on a rhetorical level. Shouted in anger, "pig" was a relatively mild epithet; used as a routine synonym in the Black Panther mode ("And then three pigs got out of their car . . .") it became monstrous. I thought it was self-deceptive—another pretense that white bohemians and radicals are as oppressed as ghetto blacks; and arrogant—a special case of that fierce bohemian contempt for all those slobs who haven't seen the light. Many

[1] For the first few days; later, *Ramparts* editor Warren Hinckle insisted on playing up convention gossip and the Chicago staff quit in protest.

cops thought it was funny; they made jokes about "bringing home the bacon" and "Lincoln Pork."

First to question the cop-hating orgy were the McCarthy kids and the few genuine hippies. With no revolutionary *machismo* to protect, they could afford to observe that most of the cops were doing their job with no special zeal, that some of them were even friendly ("We're all different—you're a nonconformist, and I'm a conformist"), and that in any case, the practice of reading whole groups of people out of the human race has a bad history. For many radicals, second thoughts began when the National Guard arrived. An important recent development on the Left has been the discovery that servicemen are people— that a soldier is not necessarily a fascist because he would rather serve than go to jail, or because he thought he would get good training in the Army, or because he believed what the government said about our mission in Vietnam. And though there were shouts of "Sieg Heil!" at the troops in Chicago, the consensus was that these boys were not our enemies; they were only being used. Although there are obvious differences between soldiers and cops—a policeman's job is permanent and always voluntary—there are also obvious analogies. The police-baiting began to cool, and the crowd to hear don't-blame-the-cops-but-the-system speeches with increasing frequency. At the Mobilization rally on Wednesday afternoon a line of cops rushed into the bewildered crowd, sending at least two people to the hospital; the cause of the disturbance, it turned out, was an attempt—which most of the demonstrators had not even seen—to lower an American flag and run up a red flag in its place. Shortly after this incident, Dick Gregory spoke: "At least after World War II, people blamed Hitler first and the troops second. The police are worse off than you—at least you can demonstrate. The police are the new niggers. They can whup your heads, but it won't get them a raise—they gotta go downtown and ask." Though anti-police feeling had been aggravated by the gratuitous violence, Gregory got an enthusiastic ovation and inspired cries of "More pay for cops!" and "Join us!"

The reaction was a good sign. The police issue is really part of the much larger problem of anti-working-class prejudice. The authoritarian character, far from being a special affliction of the policeman, is endemic to the lower socio-economic brackets. (If anything, cops are *more* tolerant of deviant behavior than the average workingman—they see so much of it they get calloused.) The policeman happens to be doing the dirty work; the others just wish they could. Liberals and radicals dislike cops not only because they have the guns and the clubs, but because they are undereducated proles who like television and think Negroes are lazy. And almost invariably, virulent cop-haters have little use for ordinary people. The guerrilla mentality that came to full flower in Chicago denies the first principle of guerrilla warfare—that the population must be sympathetic or at least not actively hostile. The street-fighters think they can and should do it all by themselves; Mark Rudd has put down organizing as a cowardly alternative to rebellion.

Before the Wallace campaign, most radicals assumed that white workers were too well integrated into the system to be an important force for change. Those leftists who did insist on the importance of working-class organizing tended to explain away workers' conservative, racist attitudes as a superficial aberration, the result of ruling-class divide-and-conquer tactics. The flaw in this analysis was its failure to observe that divide-and-conquer tactics work both ways: radicals also lashed out at the white working class because their real enemies were beyond reach. White workers, economically and psychologically ill-equipped to cope with change, were the group most affected by domestic social upheaval. They suffered most from increasing crime, paid most—percentage-wise—for welfare and poverty programs, depended most on the disintegrating public school. But the Left, preoccupied with its own oppression, could not see them as human beings with real grievances. Liberal politicians (with the concurrence of radicals) dismissed the workingman's fear of crime as racist paranoia and his resentment at having to support people who did not work as social backwardness. Liberal experts (with the silent complicity of radicals) proclaimed that poor blacks and students must be consulted on policies that affected them, but treated white workers like inert material to be socially engineered at will.

It took George Wallace to make radicals understand that white workers were in fact a vast disaffected constituency that had been fairly begging for someone to care about its problems. Then, just as this new consciousness began to make a substantial impact on the Left, Chicago happened. For anyone who wanted to look at it that way, Chicago was a case study in the indifference-cum-contempt that radicals, especially post-hippies, reserved for ordinary Americans. Many of us felt the contradiction very deeply.

Talking to local activists, I began to realize that the problem of elitism was at least partly a function of geography. Most radicals came from New York or San Francisco, where dissidents were numerous enough to develop viable subcultures and where even larger numbers of liberal sympathizers stood ready to support mass demonstrations. In such an environment, an emphasis on cultural radicalism and confrontation politics came naturally. But outside the coastal enclaves and their microcosms, the university campuses, radicals found themselves isolated. If they wanted to have any effect at all they had to go to the people. In Chicago itself there were several fairly sophisticated projects aimed at improving relations between radicals and white workers. Organizers lived in working-class city and suburban neighborhoods, worked with the people on consumer problems, taught in local schools. Cities like Cleveland had similar programs. But for the cosmopolite Left, this was unexplored territory; it was hard even to imagine a typical New York radical cutting off his hair and moving to Queens. Given these social facts, it meant something that the demonstrations took place in Chicago, without a Lindsay or 900,000 liberals to act as a buffer between us and the people—as represented by Daley's cops but also, let us not forget, by the construction workers who gave us the V sign and the high school kids who asked us why we liked the, uh, Viet Cong. We could not have learned nearly so much from a New York protest.

In recent months radicals have been increasingly critical of confrontation politics—not as one sometimes-useful tactic among others, but as an all-purpose religious rite. Discussion about working whites has become at once more sympathetic and more realistic. The next step is for radicals in significant numbers to break out of their ghettos and go live in America. It's too late to do anything about the cops—most of them, anyway. But we need their children.

QUESTIONS FOR DISCUSSION AND WRITING

1. What is the function of Part I of this essay? How is it related to the analysis which follows it?
2. Early in the essay, Miss Willis defines herself as neither "a hardcore street-fighter" nor a "McCarthy liberal," but "somewhere between." Later on she reveals that she is the daughter of a policeman. Why do you think she chose to reveal these items in this order? What is the effect upon you as the reader of these revelations? What particular vantage point do these facts about Miss Willis give to her essay?
3. According to Miss Willis, what in general are the lessons to be learned from Chicago? Do you agree with her conclusions?
4. What is meant by "The Yippies saw the Chicago action as theater"? Explain the function of "theater" in current "radical" theories of social change. Is "theater" effective? In such "theater," who are the actors and who is the audience? Does the essay by Louis Kampf in the preceding section (p. 238) help you to understand this idea?
5. What is meant by "the theory of revelation-through-confrontation"? Miss Willis doesn't seem to think it works. Do you agree with her? Explain.
6. Miss Willis says that "America . . . is not a gun but a gigantic vacuum cleaner." Comment.
7. Discuss Miss Willis' views on the police and her assertion that "police-hating" is "really part of the much larger problem of anti-working-class prejudice." How does this relate to Miss Willis' assertion that for a successful social revolution "the population must be sympathetic or at least not actively hostile"?
8. As William O. Douglas observes in his essay (p. 254), revolution may often be a justified and practical course in a democracy—indeed, it is sanctioned in our founding documents. Was what happened in Chicago "a revolution"? Was it "democratic"? Explain.
9. According to Miss Willis, who won "the battle of Chicago"? What is your opinion?

Leopold Tyrmand

Reflections:
Revolution and Related Matters

THE INDOMITABLE FLAWLESSNESS OF DAWN

Scientists are not certain when man invented the wheel—a disc or circular frame, designed to revolve on an axis, that permanently altered his notions of distance and weight. They presume that the event occurred sometime during the Neolithic period of the Holocene epoch, between six thousand and ten thousand years ago. But they generally agree that the wheel was the most difficult invention in the history of civilization, and that its technological importance overshadows anything man had done before or has done since. It took an infinitely longer time to achieve the wheel—if one counts from the species' very beginning—than it took afterward to construct a combustion engine or to split the atom or to build the lunar module. Yet this device, both conceived and applied by Stone Age thinkers, still serves superbly. For all his technological miracles, man has not yet replaced the wheel with anything better. I have always been impressed by its weird, hoary, never extinct usefulness. Which leads to the thought: Perhaps it hasn't been necessary to replace it. Perhaps the wheel's form, nature, and essence are ultimate, and only its functions can be constantly increased and perfected. The idea that an early discovery might remain timelessly applicable hasn't appeared to be much *en vogue* of late, but it's worth considering anyway.

The principle at the core of democracy is not very much younger than the principle of the wheel. A power of decision drawn from a majority, with the ever-open possibility of a minority's turning into a majority, seems not totally alien to the earliest communities of *Homo sapiens*. Century after century, new features were added to the rudimentary pattern as countless men of thought and of action commented on and enriched its sense and substance. Unlimited abuses and outrages were committed against it or in its name, but the fundamental principle remained sound and unchanging. Some of the most potent minds argued convincingly that the power of the majority equals immorality, stupidity, and callousness, that it smells foul, and that it strips the human being of both dignity and the capacity for progress. But whatever they advocated to take its place revealed itself to be worse. Others attempted to endow democracy with a new sort of excellence, but the final effects were much like the effects of improving the wheel by shaping it into an octagon. "True freedom exists only in the place where there is no ordinary freedom," a disaffected Eastern European playwright once wrote, with bitter irony. He could have said the same of democracy. I'm afraid that there exists no possibility of inventing anything better than ordinary democracy. Like the wheel, it is an organic element of our reality. What is left is the endless possibility of increasing and perfecting its functions.

CHILDREN OF THE CENTURY AND HEROES OF OUR TIME

The adolescent American revolutionary of today is a repetition. His predecessor was the Romantic rebel of the first quarter of the nineteenth century. Their ideals and ways of thought are similar. Their behavior patterns are all but identical. The textures of their lives tend to have much in common. Even their concepts of outward accessories and symbols have some striking resemblances.

The Romantic rebel turned against the insensitiveness that was, in his eyes, embodied in his contemporaries, against the post-feudal system of society, against political tyranny, and against the blight he perceived in oncoming industrialization. He derived pride from his lofty "loneliness," which was then the fashionable word for alienation. He felt contempt for conventions, for order, and for all bonds except the natural ones. He yearned for individual distinction, strove to prove himself, and valued flights of ambitions, fresh impulses of the heart, intensity of emotion and action. He had his passionate chroniclers, some of them the literary geniuses of his epoch; Goethe, Byron, Pushkin, Alfred de Vigny perpetuated his memorable traits. By the force of their art, they monumentalized both his virtues and his ridiculous aspects. They made the gap between him and his environment appear wider than it really was, and that was a great publicity hat trick—one that has also been skillfully performed by the American press of late—because nothing attracts more surely than the cumulative, much advertised partisanship of the attractive or than mythology disguised as reporting. Alfred de Musset coined for the Romantic rebel a proud and tender epithet: "L'Enfant du Siècle." Mikhail Lermontov called him, more forcefully, "Geroy Nashego Vremeni," or "A Hero of Our Time." They made of him the Style of the Era—a notion encompassing everything from Weltanschauung to hairdo. He was a paradigm to be followed by those who craved glossy prescribed and codified ideals for instant use.

The Romantic rebel was persecuted by those he combatted, but the persecution was not really severe. The feudal and monarchic structures were antique, and therefore were in transition. Those who embodied them felt old and tired, and grew skeptical about the set of values they were supposed to protect. They revelled in political machinations, malicious wisdom, and irony. A rebel had to have perpetrated a serious misdeed to be seriously chastised. The monarchs and their governments bestowed upon revolutionaries all kinds of compromises and cour-tesies—passports, with exit visas when needed, and mild punishments that made heroes out of them for a song. The monarchs flirted with the revolutionaries, praised their audacity, invited them to court, en-couraged their effronteries, bantered with them, and perversely helped to build up their publicity.

History has proved that the Romantic rebellion was reactionary rather than progressive. Its followers consistently turned against civilization and finally despaired of progress. In the more distant future, their decadent anti-rationalism strengthened the ideological premises of Fascism and Nazism. Before that, however, the crumbling monarchic orders became constitutional, were transformed into cradles of modern liberalism, positivism, and scientific advancement, developed industry and humanitarianism, and nurtured the best traditions of tolerance, re-straint, and social forbearance.

There were other heroes at the time, but they were less conspicuous, being more modest. Nevertheless, they were often accused of op-portunism. These were the men busy extracting the secrets of life from nature and contributing significantly to various branches of science, con-quering disease and extending human life. They thereby helped insure that the next edition of the Heroes of Our Time, when they appeared on the world scene, would be mass-produced and thus infinitely more numerous.

The distinction between the Romantic and the Hero of *Our* Time lies in their different sense of pride. The former wanted to fight, and welcomed all the consequences of the struggle. He considered feudalism an evil, scorned it, didn't want anything from it, and recognized its right to fight back in self-defense. Being chiefly aristocratic in origin, the Romantic rebel cared for dignity and knew that only a readiness to pay the full price would give it to him. He welcomed persecution, for it gave his fight moral legitimacy. The Hero of *Our* Time demands all possible privileges from the order he tries to shatter. He claims the right to ruin without responsibility; in fact, he asks for the right to annihilate from those he desires to annihilate. Their resistance he calls oppression. Their arguments in defense of themselves and their values he brands as conformism. What do you call it when someone who has been beaten up for some abusive attack, which he proclaims a virtue, vilifies his chastiser, forgetting to mention that he himself attacked in order to bite off the other's ear? A Romantic rebel would have called it undignified, and perhaps would have added the word "squalid."

THE VICISSITUDES OF ORDER

Whatever youth perceives makes sense. Conversely, maturity has a sensation of a messy *déjà vu*, which subverts every meaning, and this makes the young seem to have a mystical sense of order. Their particular way of perceiving things as they are is the most important reason for the young's compulsion to revolt *against* order at each step. For someone young, the world has an ordered meaning, things and ideas fit into well-classified compartments, strict evaluations contain an inward logic and are worthy of belief. The slightest abuse, suffered by imaginative inexperience, legitimatizes revolt. People of age have an overwhelming, though not always conscious, sense of life's anarchy. Largely for this reason, they yearn hopelessly for order and constantly accuse youth of creating disorder.

THE INEVITABLE AND THE UNACCEPTABLE

No social revolution has ever resulted in moral transformation. That is, no revolution has ever improved human nature or turned any of life's inherent evils into anything better. Coming from Eastern Europe, I have had painful opportunities to check up on this. Revolutions change banners, colors, and inscriptions, and they may change ways of life. or what purists call "social conditions." Even those members of a population who appreciate the new, post-revolutionary condition soon find out that only the form, not the content, of their lives has been affected. Success is the only social factor that revolutions seriously tackle; as a rule, one who is successful before a revolution is rarely supposed to be so after. As a matter of fact, this rule is usually violated, in most intricate ways, and the history of social change is interlarded with pre-revolutionary reactionaries who made resplendent careers after a turn-over. A career is largely the product of personal abilities geared to favorable circumstances—a combination that plain, simple-minded people call good luck or cleverness—and revolutionary idealism has proved too faint a force to deal with it effectively.

Some think of revolutions as epileptic seizures, inflicting horrible sufferings on the convulsed body. History, however, indicates that the process of convalescence and recuperation from their appalling consequences leads to all those feebly defined values others call progress. Healing their wounds turns into what can be described as achievement. It is, then, almost impossible to imagine today's world without its previous revolutions. For centuries, our sages have insisted, blandly but doggedly, that we are doomed to be wrong. Never are we permitted to choose between good and bad—only between better and worse. This is something that all revolutionaries (and reformers as well) should keep in mind. The sociopolitical potentialities of the human race are as narrowly restricted by gravity as one's body is. That fact doesn't absolve us from the obligation and the privilege of seeking change, but as we do so we must be aware of the simple truth that change in itself is by no means a supreme virtue. Though nothing frees us from pursuing what we consider right and fighting against what we see as wrong, the task does become boring after thirty-five.

BRIEF ENCOUNTER

On a bus heading toward a university campus, I met a girl with a folded red flag. She was black-haired and myopic.

"Hi, Dolores," my companion said to her. And he whispered to me, "Spanish names are chic among revolutionaries nowadays. Not Russian anymore."

"What a nice color," I said, indicating the flag.

"It's the color of Socialism," the girl said.

"Is that so?" I felt well instructed.

"I'm a Socialist," she added proudly.

I said, "Congratulations," which sounded rather silly, but I wanted to honor somehow her adamant devotion to the cause.

A bit vexed, apparently, she shrugged and said, "Well, what could *you* possibly know about Socialism?"

"Not much," I admitted. "I lived only twenty years in a Socialist country."

"And what of that?" she said, with open scorn. "What did you see there? What did you learn from it? For me, twenty days in Moscow was enough to recognize how beautiful it is! Beautiful, beautiful, beautiful . . ." As she repeated the word, a sort of voluptuous beatitude came over her face.

How interesting it would be, I thought, to locate that delicate membrane which separates bliss from idiocy.

ART AND POLITICS AND SOCIAL CONSCIENCE

Having acquired position and also a New York style of awareness of the sociophilosophical ills of our time, a young artist from Texas declared during a press interview, "All people are political prisoners in the sense that they are prisoners of the system into which they are born." It's hard to deny that this sentence is a curious example of thinking. It would be interesting to know, though, what the thinker thinks about the systems of specific countries where men can spend half their lives in prisons because they think that a human individual has the unquestionable right to think freely. And what our pundit thinks about the strange circumstance that in his own country—and its political system— he does not risk being imprisoned for what he thinks, even if he shapes his ideas in a blatantly preposterous way, from both a logical and a semantic point of view, and then expresses them in speech and in print.

OPTIMISM

One noticeable feature of American democracy is that young simpletons repeating the most thoroughly worn-out and discredited slogans in a loud voice amplified by devices of the modern mass media are thoughtfully listened to by the older and wiser. Some observers find this depressing. I think it is encouraging, even cheering, and certainly it is an inexhaustible source of vaudeville.

TYRMAND'S LAW

I wish to see my name, henceforth forever, connected to a law that I have discovered and formulated; namely, "The quality of a revolutionary is inversely proportionate to the quality of the system he fights against. The more oppressive and cruel the system, the more heroic and self-sacrificing the rebel. And, conversely, the better and more indulgent the system, the more flippant the revolutionary."

Of course, since it is a natural law, I didn't invent or shape it; I merely uncovered an aspect of reality that my contemporaries had stubbornly refused to see. Each social system, and each system of values, has had its revolutionaries. But in a society with a long democratic tradition of free expression the public's qualitative assessment of the revolutionaries gets hopelessly muddled by shallow, perfunctory press reports and interpretation. An occupier of a university building who resists a policeman trying to drag him out can by no means be called a hero. The young Russian intelligentsia struggle heroically for a clearly defined set of liberties which the young American intelligentsia fully enjoy. Young Russians pay for their demands with long jail terms, concentration-camp tortures, ruined health, wrecked lives. They have their heroes—Sinyavskys, Daniels, Litvinovs, Ginzburgs. It would be interesting to ask whom the Western student rebellion could cast as a counterpart. Maybe the London Maoist student who goes about armed with a stupendous gadget that covers his face with red paint the moment a policeman approaches or press photographers zero their cameras in on him. The American campus warriors love to draw a parallel between themselves and the Czech students, but the latter would hardly recognize them as fellow-rebels. The young Czech fights desperately for the basic right to protest—one that his American counterpart fully possesses but considers a minor asset, and abuses. The word "freedom" has different meanings for them: for a Czech it is a value he is willing to risk his life for; for the American rebel it's a natural condition, like breathing, and passes unnoticed unless it is put into words. A Russian or Czech student who has been marked as an opponent of the regime is expelled from his university in disgrace, and the expulsion cancels any possibility of a reasonable existence thereafter. An American student who spends his period of education in revolutionary activities is headed toward a bright future. His nonconformity is usually considered a sign of brilliance. He is hailed for stirring up parochial environments and ending mental stalemates; his rebellious spirit is seen as a source of fresh ideas that enrich the prospects of progress. As a rule, he is accorded, a priori, a *positive* role in society, and if after concluding his studies he does not commit himself to bomb-throwing, he is assured of an excellent job, his bloodthirsty past benefitting him whether he is a newly converted moderate or an intransigent firebrand who can make a posh living purveying revolution to other affluent revolutionaries. Last year, a paper published by rebellious students in New York sported a proud heading under the name of the paper: "1968—The Year of the Heroic Guerrilla." Heroic? What's heroic about a fight whose consequences can be annulled with fifty dollars' bail?

I am not trying to belittle anything. All I want to say is that it's not true, as some hypocritical reconciliators argue, that the two systems are *equally* bad and the two establishments are *equally* criminal. It doesn't require a very sharp eye to perceive that one of them is much better in every respect. A social system in which one who tries to rectify it by force can enjoy personal freedom for the price of a blazer is infinitely more valuable than a system in which one has to pay for the same attempt with his life.

REVENGE

Children often grow rebellious because they are ashamed of their parents in public. This feeling of embarrassment accompanies them long enough to impel them to join the ranks of subversion. They overcome it when they discover that they are approaching a stage at which someone may have to be ashamed of them.

PROFESSOR MARCUSE

Reading Professor Herbert Marcuse, one gets a notion of him as a distinguished intellectual who has been spared the necessity of barely surviving Hitler and Stalin—the dismal experience that so many intellectuals in Europe have not been spared—and who therefore now feels anxious. He is called the father of the modern youth revolution. This parentage might prove to be one of the causes of the revolution's miserable performance. Anger, despair, determination, and fanaticism have generated revolutions until now, but never anxiety, which might be held responsible solely for fashionable attitudes, poses, and countenances. According to Mr. Marcuse, air pollution is one of the most destructive elements of repressive American capitalism as it is organized by the inhuman incorporated monster that revolution is authorized to annihilate mercilessly. Air pollution considered as an instrument of social oppression is of dubious value when it is noticed that the oppressors are forced to inhale it as we do. The arguments that Mr. Marcuse uses in his neo-dialectical manual of upheaval and transmogrification qualify him not as a redoubtable opponent but, rather, as a symbol of the modern mind's colorful restlessness, very handy for public manifestations and press releases. Somewhat like the Beatles in the earlier era of rock and roll.

MAOISM

At a party, I met a young man with a frail Victorian face, of a sort often to be found in Massachusetts post offices, who was soon busy explaining to me his devotion to the Maoist cause. I asked him if he could produce what he considered the finest sample of the Little Red Book's wisdom. He quoted a verset of such improbable platitude and pompous, commonplace, truistic character that I was gripped by sudden fright. Are we slowly being engulfed by a monumental failure of common sense? And which is worse—to drown in an ocean of brutishness and cruelty or to be swept away by sanctified, institutionalized imbecility? There came to mind an Israeli gentleman who once said to me, "Adoni, a stupidity that is successful ends by being accepted as great wisdom."

HATE ME OR LEAVE ME

"I hate America," my hostess said while taking a bite of duckling to assure herself that it was properly crisp and tender. "America is a combination of insidiousness and churlishness." She sipped a bit of wine with careful attention, prepared for whatever nasty surprises a bottle of Pauillac (good year) may conceal. "Life is no longer possible here, under the inhuman pressure of mammoth corporate structures." She was good-looking, well groomed, and in her middle years, and had been several times married, each time to someone wealthier than his predecessor. "The heavy atmosphere of fiendishly well-organized repression here suffocates your individuality," she continued, with persuasive certitude. "Even if one seeks to be peaceful and impartial, one is gripped by a compulsion to fight against this blight, to revolt, to change it. The only hope is those poor, oppressed kids at the universities, who know so well what they want and how to want it."

I felt an influx of sympathy and compassion, much increased by her flawless complexion. "And what about leaving the United States?" I said, looking for a solution. "Maybe life somewhere else would give you a sense of meaningful existence?"

"Never," she said firmly. "This is my country. I hate it, but I also hate to hate it, which is very optimistic and good of me. I find a lot of comfort in my positive, constructive hatred."

"Of course," I said. "It may even be turned into a successful state of mind—at least from the financial point of view. There are several essayists and playwrights who make an excellent living exhibiting their hatred and contempt for America in print and by word of mouth. They call it bold, constructive criticism. The greater their hate and scorn, the larger their American readership and their theatre audiences. I wonder how they reconcile their bottomless disdain with their earnings. Spitting on America has proved to be the best way for a foreign artist in this country to acquire a substantial income. The most undeserved insults sell best."

"That goes with our tradition," she said thoughtfully. "America is ludicrously provincial, and people in the provinces are too hypocritical to admit to the faults in their institutions. Hence only people from the outside tell them the truth."

"But how do the haters see the truth from the Himalayas of their uppish pseudo-intellectual disgust and when they are blinded by hatred?" I said. "Besides, the provincial people's readiness to pay for it seems to me quite worldly."

"And what *should* we do with all the money?" she said. "There is enough of it going to all those fake anti-Communist organizations. We are smothered by our inability to counteract them—which only confirms our oppressors' hideous cleverness."

"You're admirable," I said. "I shall never grasp how it happens that modest, overworked, badly dressed underdogs adore this country and people who receive everything from it hate it."

"Very simple," she said. "We who hate it are sensitive. Radicalism— that is sensitivity."

"Too simple," I said. "Radicalism—that is a very complex, psychologically inexplicable inability to concede the justice of someone else's reasoning, to agree with him even if his argument is based on objective truth. In my opinion, you live in the United States because American democracy constitutes *a better reality in every respect* than any other sociopolitical reality in today's world, including Russian, Cuban, and Chinese Communism."

"Nonsense," she retorted.

"Oh, no." I smiled. "Being an America-hater, you are by nature incapable of admitting that America can be better than something else in any respect. It's incompatible with your innermost beliefs. But for me intellectual superstition is the worst of all prejudices. Capitalism appears to be one of the most thoroughly discredited words in the modern vocabulary; nevertheless, there is no denying that after one century of experience it has proved to be better than Socialism. I know that the statement may only provoke shrugs, yet capitalism has turned out to be more flexible and more likely to change according to life's spiritual and material needs, claims, and demands than Socialism as we know it in its various contemporary versions. Moreover—what seems to me decisive—capitalism is transformed faster in practice than Socialism is even in theory, and this circumstance may turn out to be lethal for the latter. You can hate capitalism and America—such an attitude may contain, I admit, a dash of provocative charm—but I'm afraid the facts are against you."

In spite of all my positive efforts, which were wholly detached from politics and dialectic, I have never been able to dine with this lady again.

A STATEMENT

I do not think that American society is sound, well functioning, law-abiding, and moral, offering equal opportunities to all. But it is probably the only society with galactic problems that tries hard to be so. And certainly the only one that scores some points in this game.

KREMLINOLOGISTS

American universities are full of American scientists who are devoting their lives to scrutinizing, analyzing, and evaluating Communism, its history, its exploits, its accomplishments, its failures. I was recently asked what I think of these scientists.

"They are terrific," I answered. "Their research ability and their theoretical knowledge are imposing. They seem to know everything. However, to me it seems that much of their tremendous effort will go to waste."

"What do you mean?"

"You see, they know virtually everything about hog raising, for instance. They've collected dramatic statistics, mastered, with tantalizing precision, all existing information about the quality and characteristics of pork. They have data on Communist pigs that people in Eastern Europe do not have. But the people there know one thing that the Kremlinologists remain totally ignorant of; namely, how to find and buy a slice of ham."

CREDO

I have decided to defend America against itself. According to a lasting tradition, the American intellectual élite is America's severest critic, prosecutor, and scoffer. And this very fact is one of the mightiest sources of America's social and cultural vitality, for, in general, intellectual ferment constitutes a priceless element of renewal and progress. America's defender remains the simple man in the street, emotionally confused and rationally inept, lowbrow in his ambitions and predilections, unable to cope with complexities, helpless before the formidable dialectical challenge. Someone has to help him. What a tremendous task! The chore is immense, but so is the prospect of success.

VOLCANOLOGY

People who discuss social revolution in America generally do not take into account the obvious fact that, in one way or another, social revolution has been a constant factor in American reality since the nation began. It has never stopped—has only turned, with time, into a revolution on the installment plan, which is what all evolution is. Short periods of relative peacefulness are interrupted by some sort of unrest, whose regular appearance gives life here a certain insouciance about things that could easily bring any other country to the brink of bottomless failure. For someone who doesn't understand this phenomenon, volcanology might be a valuable study. It has found that the most disastrous eruptions are those of somnolent, supposedly inactive volcanoes. The active ones present little danger, and generate geysers that are useful in healing rheumatism.

THE HOLY PARADOX OF OUR TIME

Utterly exasperated by my primitive, stubborn refusal to approve either the ends or the methods of today's American revolutionaries, a charming and intelligent lady of the leftist persuasion said, "We fully understand and sympathize with the upheavals behind the Iron Curtain. We feel total empathy with the protest, the resistance, the insurgence against Communist tyranny. Our hearts, our best wishes, and our sense of justice are ardently with the Czech and Polish students, the Russian intellectuals, and all those persecuted and oppressed in the Red empire. Consequently, it is incomprehensible to me why someone like you, who comes from over there, doesn't *want* to understand us—our idealism and our revolution, our goals and our struggle to attain them."

"Madam, the expression in your eyes seems to me incomparable," I said. "I do not even try to look for a metaphor. Also, your way of using your fork and knife appears to me exquisite beyond comparison."

This brutal deviation from the subject was my sole means of escape. The lady was a complete human being except for one marginal trait: she didn't know how to respect her freedom. She would repeat, "But we want to enlarge our freedom, improve it." Unfortunately, this noble intention was to be realized, in her opinion, by ostracizing and slandering all those who happened to think in a different way. How could my arguments reach her power of reason? Today's American revolutionaries are the offspring of a civilization that firmly believes that almost everything should be permitted, because limitation equals the impoverishment or the repression of human rights. The present Eastern European and Russian revolutionaries are rebelling against a civilization built upon the principle that almost nothing should be permitted, because confinement enriches a human being and shapes him to a theoretically prescribed ideal. The two civilizations may be equally wrong, but within the Communist one the forces of opposition rise, logically, against a system that makes opposition impossible, whereas their Western counterparts revolt against a system that enables them to revolt. The first lose their lives or sacrifice their personal freedom in an effort to obtain what the second despise, trample on, and want to get rid of without bearing the consequences of their actions. The first yearn desperately for a sociopolitical arrangement that will assure their basic human dignity, whereas the second, having such an arrangement, are in the grip of an inexplicable obsession to destroy it and fall into a limbo of masochistic humiliation, in which they expect to find new human values.

My refined lady with the brilliant mind argued, "It's natural that the Russians and the Czechs should want to achieve what we have achieved in the way of fundamental liberties, and the output and distribution of goods, but *we* have to *move ahead*. We have arrived at a point where freedom is no longer freedom; therefore, we have to blow up the obstacles to new achievements." This is dialectical gabble, idealistic but also simplistic. The lady speaks from the point of view of one who has always been free and thus has no idea at all what the lack of freedom means. It is like discussing colors with a person born blind. She doesn't know and will never know that freedom is indivisible—that it has no shades or degrees but, rather, a oneness that determines its existence. It is or it is not; any attempt to modify that fundamental dichotomy deprives us of it. The lady and her fellow-revolutionaries ignore—or, at least, want to ignore—Giambattista Vico and his lessons of history: its circular principle, its spiral progress, and the simple fact that in sociopolitical relations no vacuum is possible. This is to say that whenever freedom regresses, subjugation and oppression follow. We may still be able to discover new chemical elements, construct an artificial cell, transplant organs, and erect a skyscraper on the planet Venus, but it is more than doubtful whether we can ever blend freedom and lack of freedom into one genuine moral value. This is the little holy paradox of our time, and I have never cared to ponder it at the dinner table.

But maybe I'm wrong. Maybe improvement is an idea of a higher order than liberty. When I came to this country, I thought New York buses a marvel. Now, after three years, I think them overheated in

winter, insufficiently air-conditioned in summer, and moronically sched-
uled. When I wait for a First Avenue bus for half an hour and then
four of them arrive together, in a row, I'm ready to march on City
Hall and execute no matter whom. In Communist Poland, in an analogous situation, I was more than happy if a bus arrived at all.

TOYING WITH NOTIONS

Youth, which a few years ago appeared on the national scene as a
new social class, building its own civilization, culture, ethics, and aesthetic, derives its ideology from the assumption that only newly created
values and criteria are valid, *de rigueur,* and worthy of being projected
into the future. Benefitting from the education and erudition provided
by its elders, youth formulates its thesis out of contempt for the past,
and especially for what have been regarded as the timeless imponder-
abilia that constitute the intellectual treasure and emotional muscle of
all who are not in the category of youth. Thus, avoiding conflict is
next to impossible. The conflict is unusually acrimonious not because
the two sides don't try to understand each other but because—maybe
for the first time in history—they're actually unable to understand each
other. Being loyal to my generation, I feel fully justified in accusing
young people unilaterally. They are guilty, not we. Their current catchword is improvement, but they do not really want improvement; they
want us to concede that they invented improvement as a concept. Which
is not true. From the dawn of mankind, *Homo* mastered the device of
improvement, in the cognitive as well as in the empirical sense. During
his stay on this planet, he has improved plenty of things around him, and
even a few things in him. My generation has been as busy improving as
any other, and we will never agree to let ourselves be deprived of what
we feel is the content of our lives. What keeps the current young generation so blessedly innocent as to be able to claim the invention of something that has always existed?

IGNORANCE AND TABOOS

People used to say, "The young are always right; time and history prove
that. They represent the inevitable future and are the annointed heralds
of an inevitable truth." These assertions are false. If only we dare doubt
them, they turn from the axiomatic into the absurd. Youth is sometimes
right and sometimes wrong, and history is filled with facts that prove
it. One has only to study the history. The nonsensical belief that youth
has a special mission to fulfill and is endowed with exceptional per-
ceptiveness stems from the period of *Sturm-und-Drang,* Johann Gottlieb
Fichte, German Romanticism, and its philosophy, which in the end led
to Nazism.

Producing taboos out of ignorance is as old as limestone, but neither the producers nor the helplessly worshipping customers are able to admit it, and they stubbornly proclaim each current shibboleth the last word in the human spirit of innovation and progress. Of late, the most oppressive taboo, apologetically idolized by many, has been that nothing should not be permitted. If everything is to be permitted, then the most rational and justified prohibition turns into an abuse that distorts human character and condones resistance. Art and theatre critics are, in our epoch, unusually busy fabricating and defending some of the most ludicrous taboos. They claim, for instance, that everything is permitted in terms of content and form, and then they wonder why everything around them seems to be so trashy. Having no real value to praise, they elevate artful gimmicks to their pantheon, and, blundering in the maze of their own errors, they have no choice but to mystify orders and qualities. Which is nothing but tinkering with taboos.

THE WORLD AND CHANGE

Does the world change? Certainly. But it changes less than it does not change. Even if it is pushed by force. Youth, which judges by appearances, takes pushing for change itself, and therefore believes the reverse to be true. It has always been this way—which proves the limited potency of change.

AMERICA AND CHANGE

The catchword "change" has lately acquired a mystical significance. I think we have reached the point at which America, having always been prone to rapid change, has to worry more about what to preserve and protect than about what to change. From its beginning, America has traditionally taken pride in its constant swift replacement of commodities and values with newer commodities and values. This swiftness has sometimes been quite embarrassing, for it has shown up a few things that the young American civilization tends to forget—that aging is *not* an ultimate negative, that things and concepts have a strange facility for reappearing on life's scene, and that the accumulation of time may turn out to be of enormous value in the spiritual as well as in the material sense. The American way of disintegrating things is so fast that the disintegration of substances brings with it an infinitely more dangerous disintegration of values. The culture of the last two hundred years has been permeated with a popular unwillingness to admit that preserved values and cultural motifs are more powerfully creative than elements of change. Honest research could rectify many such mistaken judgments.

To me, the endless search for the new seems somehow vulgar, but this is a strictly personal view. I have always preferred an old chair, an old overcoat, an old church, and a well-tested principle to new ones. I wonder why people who ceaselessly want something new don't see "new" as I do—as a concept from the realm of toys. The pyramids and the computer, printing and the H-bomb are mankind's toys, some of them dangerous or actually lethal. In spite of their superb complexity and their marvellous accomplishments, they have proved unable to remove from our shoulders even the lightest burden of disappointment. The struggle with passing time seems to me one of the most admirable features of humanness. An effort to overcome time and remain useful, beautiful, wise becomes a glory and a pride.

ETERNITIES

Walking, I passed a swelling group, young and excited, that was apparently trying to transform itself into a demonstration. Placards were being hastily produced and arranged. Covered with familiar nouns and verbs, they had about them an arrogant, belligerent multivocality, surely as instrumental in dividing people as in bringing them together. A couple attracted my attention; they were a classic embodiment of the ideas being promoted—painted and tattooed, decorated with all sorts of beads, dressed in a mixture of pseudo-Oriental modes with aggressive Cuban-Bolshevik overtones. Both were pale and by no means well scrubbed, and appeared exhausted, whether from starvation or ideology. She carried a baby in her arms. The infant, dismayed by the crowd, started to scream.

The girl tried to calm it with gentle words and hugging—unsuccessfully. Then she began lulling it. This was the same lulling movement of the female body that my mother used to apply to me, and that my grandmother surely applied to my mother, and that Eve probably used when she wanted to appease the exasperated Cain. I felt a little embarrassed. I hadn't thought about it before but, I suppose, had taken it for granted that the rebels would consider it beneath them to use such a traditional method. Now my ever-present anxiety about mankind's future was dissipating. How wonderful, I thought, if someone—let's say, a Supreme Intelligence—could take the whole group on His lap and cuddle them fondly. Maybe that is what they really need.

COMPLEXITIES OF TRANSPORTATION

If someone boarded an airy, convenient, and punctual bus on which we were being comfortably transported, and started having words with the driver, accusing him of feloniously lacking a bed of daffodils in the middle of the vehicle, we would be legitimately vexed. We would properly consider the person annoying and a little out of his mind. If some student demands at the universities have adequate logic and real value, some of them are as illogical as the daffodils, yet many people solemnly ruminate on them and are uncertain what to say or do about them. The students often claim that the bus is in fact not perfect and might be substantially bettered—which is true, for in the nature of things even the best existing bus can give way to a still better one. It's doubtful, however, whether blocking the aisle by planting some charming flowers there would enhance the quality of the bus, which, after all, is quite easily distinguishable from a garden. And a university, as someone has pointed out, is a place where those who know less come to get something from those who know more, and there is little chance of replacing this truth, however banal and unattractive, with something more appealing. Today, students want to determine what it is they should know. How they know what it is they should know, being unknowledgeable seekers of knowledge, is a mystery. Discussing it brings all of us to the stage of toddling.

A FANTASY

The tendency toward pervasiveness in American life is so immense that it often results in corrupting Evil (with all due reservations about the relativity of badness). The purchase by super-square executives in Madison Avenue shops of beads and amulets that were initially conceived as exorcistic equipment to be used against them, and the sporting of these objects at their suburban dinner parties, is only one example that stimulates reflection. This ambivalent power of corruption opens perspectives that seem to endow the American civilization with a messianic thrust. We can duly assume that in a short time even the most righteous and highly principled anti-capitalist revolution would here become an inexhaustible source of income and the basis for a healthy buildup of investment and industrial output. Let's take, for instance, barricades. Couldn't they be prepared in advance, in an appropriate number of sizes, styles, shapes, versions—the instant, the prefabricated, the frozen, and the do-it-yourself kind (with French, Spanish, Congolese, or Indonesian ornamentation), in individual and family sizes, just for couples, and for larger assemblages? Not to mention Molotov cocktails with factional New Left mix, modish rebel caps from all epochs . . .

PURE AMERICANA

Neither the cowboy hat nor the hot-dog stand nor "In the Chapel in the Moonlight" represents the purely American phenomenon of today, but, rather, social Dadaism—a radical movement without any popular roots, a new snobbery as a historical force. Dadaistic political sermons make up the folklore of this country. Everyone refers to the American people, but what is the American people? A people of wealthy workers?

The American working class—or, more classically, the proletariat—
turned, in the last two decades, into a classic middle class? It now
constitutes the only middle class in history that cannot be reproached
for *not* being a proletariat. According to the holy Marxist dogma, it
is dispossessed of the means of production; however, its countless members own stocks. What a fine field for the interplay of all kinds of snobbery, misplaced allegiances, biassed hatreds, and ridiculous adulation!

AMERICAN CENTURY

Voices are to be heard sounding a despondent note concerning America's
disappointing historical performance and consequent decline. America-
haters, both outside and inside the country, outdo one another in making
gloomy predictions and preaching America's inevitable failure. One of
them, a distinguished Briton, has said, not without *Schadenfreude*, "This
is not going to be the American century. Very few people are enamored
of the American way of life." The gentleman is perfectly right in expressing doubt about the future. This need not be said to be *going*
to be an American century, because it already *is* one, and has been
almost from its beginning. It became American not through cohorts
and legions, not through anything that rules the waves, not through
the exporting of a homemade revolution but through its glorious share
in the two most important wars of liberation that mankind has experienced, and its unheard-of position, in both, as the principal winner who
did not annex one single inch of the soil of its defeated foes. Neither
tanks and cannon and a constant readiness to use them nor an unlimited,
never-before-seen economic magnitude is what denotes an American
century, but, rather, an unprecedented civilizational influence upon the
rest of humanity. Hence the gentleman's grave error. To check how
wrong he is, he has but to look around his native England and recognize
how thoroughly Americanized it has grown during the last twenty-five
years—how many American words have become indispensable to his
native language, how many people from London, Glasgow, and Dublin
have opted for the American way of life. The objection that they make
this choice merely because America is richer and pays better wages
has no validity, for if one country is more affluent than another and
provides better rewards to those who work for it, this testifies to a
superiority that, if it was not achieved by conquest, must have stemmed
from the skills and the quality of its people and from its institutions.
However, resourcefulness and industriousness cannot explain the evident
fact that there exist few places on this planet where little boys do not
play cowboys and bigger boys do not sing rock and roll, where the
word "Hollywood" has never been pronounced or "Star Dust" hummed
or the New York skyline seen either on the screen or in illustrations.
No one forces humanity to watch American movies, listen to American

music, dance American dances, read American books, and wear American clothes. Nevertheless, all over the world these products of American civilization are best-selling items. If the gentleman were only aware of the piety with which some Europeans today listen to a ragtime tune totally forgotten in America, of how well acquainted they are with American history, of the fanatical curiosity with which they leaf through old American illustrated magazines, he would probably understand what the phrase "American century" means. In the Communist empire, as a matter of fact, people are persecuted for their craving for Americanism, and the persecution only intensifies the craving, endows everything American with greater magic, and gives names like Max Factor, Coca-Cola, and William Faulkner more content than the names of Lenin, Socialism, and Sholokhov. Charlie Chaplin's California and Gary Cooper's Wild West have become the world's most romantic landscapes for several generations on five continents, and countless millions have melted in tears at the end of "West Side Story," although no one sheds tears anymore on reaching the end of "Romeo and Juliet." As M. de Talleyrand once said, "I do not say it is good, I do not say it is bad, I say it is the way it is."

For me, the idea of an American century has a deeper meaning. We are now witnessing a strange exodus from Communist-dominated Eastern Europe. People are fleeing, inconspicuously but in very large numbers, from martyred Czechoslovakia; from Poland, held in a neo-Nazi grip; from lethargic Hungary. Many of them might do better on several continents that are ready to provide them with material opportunities infinitely superior to the daily hardship of American competition. Nevertheless, the most coveted prize in life's lottery is free entry into the United States. One can find among the arrivals from Eastern Europe political rascals who have devoted the past twenty-five years to besmirching America and its institutions, to lying about this country, to slandering it according to the most insolent and obscurantist Communist gospel. Yet it is here that they seek refuge. This act of providing enemies with shelter shines through the moral darkness enveloping our epoch and does more than anything else to bestow on it the title "American."

CONFESSION

When I was young, I hated oppressors, persecutors, and invaders. With the years, hatred turned into melancholy scorn. Today, I find it difficult to hate anything. Except conformism disguised as nonconformism.

ON PERSONAL SYMPATHIES

"Why don't you openly admit that you don't like revolutionaries?" a young radical student asked me.

"Certainly I don't like them," I said. "Indeed, human experience, accumulated through centuries, teaches us that the more ardent a revolutionary is, the more easily he turns into a ruthless self-appointed policeman. Policemen have to be hired, because only hired ones can be fired. Some time ago, I saw one of those superbly shallow French movies that pretend to know everything with not one single streak of incertitude. The film was a compilation of diverse emotions, psychological reactions, and actual events in the life of an aging Spanish revolutionary in exile. He was the embodiment of the ethical norms of the world's New Left, of its psychological penchants, its gustos, longings, predilections, and snobberies—he represented its arch-model, its ideal, its apotheosis. The man was handsome, well dressed, exhausted (he had fought against Fascism), frustrated (he hadn't defeated it), embittered, and contemptuous; he had sexual intercourse during the movie with two ladies, substantially different in appearance and age, and, more important, he continued to carry on an underground fight against Franco—an activity that he found virtuous and just as exciting. For me, however, the movie was cluttered with my mental follow-ups, because I could so easily imagine what would eventually become of the protagonist even if he were victorious. I saw too many of his kin in Eastern Europe—also Spanish Communist revolutionaries. With astounding facility, they skipped from their romantic barricades to the most callous and bloodthirsty secret-police activity, and their romantic countenances changed into the cruel visages of henchmen hunting and torturing those who were at odds with their Communist revolution. In hoary Europe, we have encountered at first hand some political peculiarities that young Americans seem unable even to guess at. For example, the perennial partnership between all the New Leftists in history and the perpetual Old Totalitarians. When the extreme right wins, many leftist intellectuals miraculously transform themselves into its faithful servants, becoming fascinated by victorious brute strength and taking neurotic delight in their self-abasement. When the extreme left wins, the rightist thugs form its muscle, enlisting in large numbers in the political police."

"It has been a long time since I heard an argument so clearly based on personal prejudice," the young student said.

"I know," I said, sighing. "No one finds it convincing except those who have seen revolutionaries *after* the revolution."

A PRETENDED WORD FROM W.S.

Nowhere, and at no time, could Caliban feel more *à l'aise* than among the intellectual rebels of our era. He would be accepted socially, adored by partygoers as an authority on hairdos and environmental conflict, and praised by subtle social critics for his seminal manuals of moral behavior.

OUR POOR, VICTIMIZED EGO

There is a universal outcry about our lost identity. We seem to be
submerged in a sociocosmic catastrophe of alienation, anonymity, and
loss of personal features. We are sentenced to dissolve in an apocalyptic,
mystical entity called, inventively, "the nameless, faceless crowd." The
destiny of today's man is to be on the sidelines, tossing acclaim to others.
As an American writer put it not long ago, he's got to be a fan. The
depersonalized world of our time generates in its womb a giant revolution against depersonalization.

A few questions arise. When was man's identity a social, economic,
political, or historical issue? Whenever the world wasn't filled with
anonymous creatures standing facelessly along the paths of history and,
according to circumstances, booing or cheering the others. Since its
dawn, mankind has been composed of namelessness, idleness, and an
effort to overcome both—with its elemental, single, anonymous, humble
component timelessly and devouringly watching either the gladiators
or the Popes or TV. The point is that the component himself has not
always felt nameless or devoid of identity, as some maintain he feels
now. And if he does, I doubt whether it's only TV that is to blame.

GUILT

A sociology professor told me the following story: "When researching
in Brooklyn, I came across and interviewed an old man in the vicinity
of Bedford Avenue. He was a Chassidic Jew who had survived Hitler's
concentration camp and had come here after the last war. He said to
me, 'My son, a student, arrives home each evening from his college
and begins a discussion with me. He challenges my spiritual peacefulness. He bids for my penitence—a fact that appears to me totally
incomprehensible. He calls on me to feel guilty for the Negro plight
of the last four centuries. I answer him that I understand very well
how horrible this plight was, because my whole family was bestially
murdered and I myself was forced to sleep in excrement and deprived
of the rest of humanness by my torturers. He says that this is the
past and has no more significance today. Then I say that I can't have
any feeling of guilt for something that neither I nor any of my ancestors
from Byelorussia had taken part in. He says that I am a wanton adherent
of the military-industrial complex. If he has in mind General Patton
and his troops, who liberated people from Dachau and Buchenwald,
I must proudly admit that I am. . . .' "

THE SENSE OF RESPONSIBILITY OF THE AMERICAN PRESS

We face now a more dangerous issue than that of the college students'
rebellion. It's the high-school revolt. The lower we descend, the more

complicated, brittle, and perilous are the elements that emerge, as the margin of rationality in the approach to responsibility shrinks. The natural belligerence, boisterousness, and rambunctiousness of high-school-age youth lead, with the addition of pseudo-politico-ideological argument and overtones, to a nightmarish buffoonery, and end with petty tragedies of mugged and knifed teachers. The role that the American information media play in this phenomenon is quite hideous. The so-called objective exposure becomes a display of staggering mindlessness. The *Times,* that bastion of American journalistic seriousness and correctness, carried a story about a high-school militant whose political enunciations indicated an acute mental disorder. The headline over the story: "——IS ORGANIZING A REVOLUTION AGAINST AMERICAN SOCIETY WITH THE SKILL OF A LITTLE LENIN." If this is what is meant by responsibility for the word, and a mature recognition of its consequences, I shudder to think what irresponsibility may be.

THE PRINCETON TALES

Not long ago, in Princeton—the site of a famous university—Americans convoked a strange gathering. A group of scholars invited scientists and intellectuals from all over the world to come and express themselves about America—its drawbacks, its limitations, its errors, its backwardness, its ineptitude in handling everything from world politics to cuisine. The invited Frenchmen, Englishmen, Greeks, and Eastern Europeans naturally accepted the invitation with alacrity—especially since they got free air tickets and luxurious accommodations and board—and started to pour buckets of hogwash on America with such eagerness that it aroused some doubts even among the courteous, attentive Americans, who wanted to learn something through their European colleagues' supposed knowledgeable impartiality and objectivity. One American remarked that perhaps it would have been fitting if the representatives of nations that had initiated two world wars, had built up and lost huge empires, and had been unable to manage their own economies had shown a little more restraint and modesty in criticizing and condemning. But this mild reflection only increased the scoffers' fervor. If someone in Communist Eastern Europe suggested a similar convocation, he would be put in jail for life. The French and the British would probably execute anyone who dared call into question their all-encompassing superiority and at the same time claim free meals and hotel accommodations. But in America the superstitious esteem for everything foreign has deep roots. The tradition derives from a nostalgic idealization of "the old country," where everything was better except personal poverty, or oppression. It is fully reflected in American literature and, later, in the movies, where an Eastern sage, a Russian maestro, an English aristocrat, a Hungarian violinist, an Austrian doctor, a German scientist, and a French perfumer were regarded a priori as commanding a pious reverence; their superiority constituted a dogma. I know of a professor from Eastern Europe with great financial nerve who has invented a simple but lucrative gimmick: He tells his students that everything within his discipline is better in Europe than in America. The American universities pay him large amounts of money for his keen insight into the matter.

THE PROFUNDITIES OF FASHION

In the youthful mind, the political consciousness is hopelessly intertwined with a feeling for fashion. Whole generations feel leftist or rightist because of the vicissitudes of vogue. Leaving aside the political fortunes of the black people in the South and the social fortunes of the blacks elsewhere in the country, hardly anyone could be termed politically oppressed, or repressed, in today's America—the young least of all. But it is extremely fashionable to *feel* politically oppressed. And if a sizable segment of a society thinks itself oppressed, a new reality is created, in which, though no fact of oppression exists, feelings of oppression do exist, and bloom. Popular fashion magazines come closest to sociocognitive discovery when they present models wearing groovy and comfortable dresses for an afternoon protest demonstration or some evening guerrilla activity.

CLOTHING AND REVOLUTION

In a society in which the pre-revolution revolutionaries proudly dress as revolutionaries, the need for revolution appears questionable.

AMERICAN ANTI-DREAM

Can America be ugly?

Of course. There are more than enough city blocks and other features of existence to prove the hideous, degrading possibilities of the American way of life.

Can American democracy be inhuman and oppressive?

Of course. One has only to peer into some Northern slums and Southern counties; the infamy of all man's subjugations is there, blatantly epitomized.

Can the American social structure be repressive, anti-progressive, and destructive?

Of course. De Tocqueville wrote about the ignominious tyranny of majority opinion, which can have the persecutive power of the Holy Inquisition.

Dissent and rebellion against these elements of Americanism have always been the nature and marrow of Americanism. They were and are deeply ingrained in the American consciousness. A mechanism whose purpose it is to warrant an unhindered defiance is peculiarly American; its intrinsic, privileged presence in American social and political institutions remains the cornerstone of their efficiency. The flexibility and extensibility of this mechanism is infinite—a fact that makes many young Americans think that its total destruction may be the proper solution. They underestimate its absorptive force and its skill at self-preservation. They also ignore the fact that they would become the first victims of its failure.

Today's young are no more and no less American than the prior generations. Americans are always seized by a strange awkwardness in handling their own brand of idealism. They liberate and feed other nations, which subsequently stone American embassies and libraries for not knowing how to be free or to nourish themselves. Idealisms are transmuted according to fleeting imponderables of history, and the current generation of Americans is trying to mold a *new* idealism, imbue it with living content, and make it superior to any earlier one. This is a beautiful attempt, notwithstanding its susceptibility to the same fate as every such attempt before it. A new sensitivity or intensity of emotion is always welcome, but it has to be protected against certain hypocritical smart clichés that can readily abuse and devastate it. If the young manage to improve our social morality and consequent modes of behavior, they may produce the greatest revolution of our time. Let us not forget, however, that Marx, Lenin, and Guevara tried to do the same thing, with catastrophic results. The young do rebel against plenty of things worth rebelling against, plenty of things that deserve hatred and rejection. But, oddly, even those who observe them most benevolently are not convinced they are always right.

PROGRESS AND REVOLUTION

Does revolution have an ingredient of progress and renewal?

I think so. Revolutions usually take place in lacklustre, shabby, worn-out settings—unhappy countries, overcrowded cities, rotten public edifices, slum neighborhoods—the decay (or ugliness or narrowness or cramped conditions) of which constitutes a legitimate reason for revolution. During the ensuing upheaval, the settings turn into shambles—or, at least, are sufficiently damaged to undergo extensive repair and painting once the revolution either is successfully suppressed or regrettably runs out of steam. I would call renovation a fair benefit of a revolution. This may be endangered only by the *victory* of the revolution. Under that condition, the shabbiness is meticulously preserved, to serve as evidence of the pre-revolutionary misery and hence as moral justification for having overthrown the system. Sometimes everything remains exactly as it was in the past but is declared better than before, with everyone being forced to repeat that such-and-such a house or street is bright and spacious, even though it is as filthy and cramped as it ever was.

THE NOSTALGIA OF WILTING IDEAS

"Isn't it frightening?" a concerned, law-abiding citizen said to me. "They are young, dynamic, rapacious. What can we do? We are helpless in the face of their voracious youth."

"I wouldn't say that," I replied. "Youth is their handicap and their weakness. History doesn't register any successful full-scale revolution of youth, by youth, and for youth. Revolutions have to be heterogeneous to succeed. It's impossible to make them without aged farmers and middle-aged housewives, and all kinds of people of all ages. Youth is too feeble a token to mobilize the forces necessary for an upheaval. Besides, time passes. A generation's revolution is always desperately vulnerable because of the generation's very transience. Before they know it, the revolutionaries will form a pathetic association of former worshippers of unfulfilled expectations."

ON COMMUNICATION

If the medium is the message, we are hopelessly disconnected. Communication is out. Even an exchange of ideas fades away. Words and ideas and concepts have lost their common value. "Freedom," "happiness," "objectivity," "tolerance," "love," "sense," "purpose," "guilt"—among many others—mean something different to the young from what they do to us who are not young. The contention over lack of identity is typical. People who think anonymity not an individual and psychological problem but a social and political one, related to all sorts of administrative powers, might be from another galaxy. It becomes almost impossible to determine whether by saying "lack of identity" the young may not mean "lack of influence," or to determine whether "meaning" doesn't equal "dominating" and "prevailing" in their minds.

Not everything is lost, however. "Disease," "death," "impossibility," "defeat," and "frustration," strangely, have the same sense for us as for them. If some of them insist that we cannot communicate even on these matters, let's just wait a few years.

THE MALAISE OF THE VOID

They are poor and helpless, the young, and hence desperate. They have to rely on trivial shams that we have already had time to investigate and classify as trivial shams, if not as criminal blunders, and they will have to pay for their blind devotion to slogans and half truths sooner or later, as many have paid before them. They are filled with lofty emptiness, which they take for a new, unique, noble social conscience, and which is sparsely furnished with a few smug commonplaces pre-fabricated by the mass media and coated with modish pseudo-intellec-tual Day-Glo paint so that they can pretend to be Ideas and Concepts. The young can't afford to tolerate criticism of either their theory or their practice, nor can they afford to yield to suasion, for their mental equipment is haphazardly constructed on the basis of comic-strip and TV science. The paltriness of their argumentation makes them unusually strong and self-assured, like many others who have focussed their la-mentably limited imagination not on what Socialism, democracy, justice, or morality is but on what it *could* or *should* be. Some of them speak constantly of all-encompassing compassions and guilts but are frightfully devoid of personal feelings. I have never noticed any of them revealing, during their press-sponsored harangues, the tiniest torment of ambiva-lence; not one of them, apparently, has ever felt an impulse to mention that in spite of his parents' bourgeois hypocrisy and ugliness he can't help loving them. My generation was spared that malaise of the void, because of our agony over a just war that we had to carry on, and then the chore of building a free society. This society was flawed, as everything human is flawed, but at least it eliminated, in its larger seg-ments, the risk of producing an undernourished youth, concerned only with making a living for a living's sake. It saved the youth of today from the abominations of opportunism—an act that eventually proved to be our unforgivable crime in youth's eyes.

LAW

Through the ages, law has been the best deterrent against human licentiousness, or crime. Laws can be limitlessly improved, but it's doubt-ful whether the principle of law as the chief instrument of communal existence can be improved. In recent decades, America has been experi-menting with the very notion of law, trying to replace it with a new sociopsychological approach. It has been a proud attempt to demonstrate that there is less injustice in America than anywhere else in the world. The results, however, have been rather meagre. Americans, in their van-ity, tend to forget sometimes that there must be as much suffering and injustice in America as everywhere else, because it is the human condi-tion that produces those things. The blame for which, of course, belongs not to America but to the human condition.

IDEOLOGY

There are people around us who proclaim revolution in a society in which the overwhelming majority is quite happy with—and, indeed, may even relish—the social status quo. They seem to forget the difference between a revolution and the *mise en scène* of a revolution. The latter requires just a bunch of passionate devotees and ambitious daredevils with a high-school education, and usually turns into a minor riot. The former must meet the demands and gain the approval and acceptance, conscious or unconscious, total or partial, of a large mass of people. If it does not, it swiftly changes from sublime loftiness into ugly slaughter. In a democracy, any preparation—both theoretical and actual—of a revolutionary stage setting is permitted and goes on in the open, whereas in a totalitarian state the revolutionaries-to-be are physically exterminated before they can assume their roles. But one should never confound a stage set—even a most expressive one—with real life. Every child who has been in a theatre even once gets a feeling for drama.

Any form of human awareness that is cut off from the cause-and-effect scheme is an inferior one. Many political movements of today appear to operate on the brainwashed, simplistic theory that it doesn't matter what existed before, what the reasons for action are, or what the results are going to be. Actually, the only legitimate reason for revolution, and its sole guarantee of success, is an inability of the existing social system to satisfy the needs of the social majority—either spiritual or material, or both. Any other conditions may justify only a putsch, or coup d'état, which in Western civilization traditionally exudes a bad smell. In spite of all its unprepossessing defects, the democratic capitalism of our century has revealed itself to be capable of satisfying not only material needs but also the whims of large segments of the population. Some accuse it of creating needs, but what's wrong with creating desires that in general are consistently satisfied? The democratic capitalism of our time means an enormous community that works to fulfill the needs of human beings. It is said that the greed for profit motivates its activities. What does that matter? The fulfilling of needs remains the only important thing. Watching this process in America, where it is carried on in a fascinating way, can become the purpose of one's life. Some scientists assert that the age of ideology is over, and there are certain signs that they are right. But meeting and fulfilling human needs still *is* an ideology. And how compelling it is to observe an ideology taking a physical shape without ruining lives, breaking bones and consciences, or establishing concentration camps. What a spectacle!

ASSORTED WORRIES

We have entered an age of insincerity all but impossible to detect. Sophisticated labels are invented: *"Umwertung aller Werte,"* or "disintegration of contents." As a matter of fact, values and concepts do not break down or perish; they become distorted, deformed, and degraded. The process of destruction affects only what is sensitive and can easily become biassed. But if whatever remains is strenuously attacked, it becomes tangled, and, consequently, loses its perennial usefulness for moral and social service.

The prophets of the currently In revolution claim that man, frightened by the impersonality and anonymity of existence, must revolt. But who feels that way? Certainly not the poor and underprivileged in this country. They crave much simpler delights than meaningfulness and identity. Social climbing and its material confirmation are enough for them. They neither feel bored by opulence nor call trouble alienation, nor do nuances of success make them unhappy. According to Lenin, fear, resignation, and decadence have always distinguished the outgoing classes, defending their doomed order. If he lived in today's America, his clean-cut analysis would grow blurred. If he wanted to remain brilliant and accurate, he would have to add lines about revolution as the pastime of the rich or as the opiate of the affluent and their children.

The *jeunesse dorée* was always counter-revolutionary, although an infinite number of good-family offspring tuned in on countless revolutions. Many bright individuals of aristocratic or middle-class descent helped to organize, shape, and carry out revolutions against their own classes. Never before in history, however, has a whole stratum of middle-class progeny, wealthy and also enraged, become the *sole* incubator of revolt against situations fatally intertwined with their ideals of thought and behavior. Lenin, of course, would recognize a suicidal trend in it, but this time perhaps he would not be believed by his followers. All the same, what name do you give to a call to action by those who are not oppressed and who do not defend anything that actually needs defense? Don't they understand that the validity of their protest and all its poignancy are inextricably interwoven with this country's established values and with the sociopolitical mechanism they are trying to destroy? What do they challenge? An order that takes pride in encouraging challenge? Which lack of virtue is revamped and accorded awesome consideration as a newly invented virtue? "Action is our words," proclaim the young, proud of their inventiveness. We who grew up in the thirties (I in Poland) can only smile, sadly. We know what this slogan means. For us, that is Fascism. The Nazi ideology emphasized action as an objective and independent good, and we know where it led. I remember the ravaged Jewish homes and massacred Jewish people whose desolation was caused by that sacred word "action." When a minority wants to impose its will upon a majority, the vocable "action" acquires some mystical gaiety and innocence. Its only sequel is dismal, monstrous injustice—also called tyranny.

A catastrophist would draw an unequivocal conclusion: In human hands, everything falls asunder and decays. Our good intentions are our doom. Psychoanalysis has attempted to improve us. Better understanding was supposed to make better men out of our children, but it ended with chaotic permissiveness and a new idolatry of spurious values. Our fake sublimation and suspiciously overzealous care for the characters and egos of entire generations brought about distrust, disenchantment, and appalling bitterness, of an intensity that passes all boundaries of logical concern. Our penetrating preoccupation with the spiritual and ontological health of our future fellow-men has resulted in a cry for revolution by those who have never been hungry, who have never worked for their living—who have never built anything, never sown and harvested anything. Our jealous quest for liberal impartiality and understanding, together with our intransigent worship of free expression, has brought us face to face with the hopeless abuse of these words and with those who say, "Our country is always wrong," although they have never contributed to any good in it.

Being an optimist, I think that if they haven't it's because they haven't yet had time.

TO RESTRUCTURE

The verb "to restructure" is on its way to becoming an important semantic figure in the near future. It is already quite fashionable in urban semi-philosophical debates. Like every chic term, it contains as much nonsense as euphemism. Many people are prone to overlook the fact that structure used to be the only categorical intangible element of an edifice. Isn't it simpler to operate with a less appealing verb, like "to demolish"?

MORAL SANITY

Man's crucial problem at present is how to deal with his own power of procreating and preserving life. Organization is the key to our future. And organization is becoming more complex and oppressive with each new billion of people on the planet. With the earth's population multiplying beyond all reason, humanity's big question is how we can live together. If we do not organize, our immensity will crumble us; we will suffocate under our own weight—smother in our madly increasing inability to perform functions. If we do not establish a complex system of coöperation, we will perish. Very different notions of social interdependence will have to emerge, and the world will have to accept them if it doesn't want to retrogress into unprecedented cruelty, the decay of the most valuable human instincts, and the end, for all practical purposes, of anthropocentric civilization. The childish grumbling of the common burgher against the growing role of bureaucracy becomes an elaborate philosophical rumination concerning life's depersonalization, the neomystical power concept, and dehumanized superstructures disposing of individual destinies. Now, once more, America steps to the front of the stage. With its multitude of diverse conflicts and its galactic variety of issues, and obsessed by its devouring passion for solving anything that seems insoluble, America becomes a lighthouse in the darkness of a century already known for its unsurpassed mechanization of murder. But America offers two antagonistic answers. One outlines the inevitable necessity of organizing *without* losing the sacrosanct sense of individual and social freedom. The other is simpler, and advises a revolution in order to destroy the existing state of things. When its partisans are asked "What about after the revolution?" they are usually unable to propose anything that hasn't already been tested by mankind, proved unbearable, and rejected as unfit. When it is pointed out that their suggestions have little relevance to our epoch's crucial problem, they answer that this can be solved by building up and imposing another superstructure, which naturally has to be much superior to the one destroyed, because they are going to construct it. Some of them feel more responsibility toward common sense and advocate Socialism. But Marxian Socialism has lost its chance to deliver any appealing answer. Fifty years of the Communist agglomeration of failures and crimes committed in the name of Socialism has removed the possibility of any hope from that direction.

All American liberties are founded upon the sage principle that people differ in every respect. Reality is composed of countless different elements, wherefore the only way to preserve a healthy society is to accept and observe the otherness of the other. This is also called pluralism. How it may work under the pressure of overpopulation we don't know. However, if we change only a few words and say "to recognize and accept the vestigial otherness even of the alike," we discover a transposed sense, which may prove useful, even priceless, under the coming conditions. It may sanction that moral sanity which we need in order to survive. For so-called moral insanity, inherent in so many human ideas and deeds, has been sufficiently discredited with the help of history, science, and the invention of printing, movies, and even TV so that it's wiser to be a little afraid of it.

CHINESE WISDOM

I don't think our epoch is stupider or more senselessly violent than any other. I don't think we face more insidious problems or venture into more precarious areas than other men have done. I think our time is an interesting one. And there is a Chinese curse that goes, "May God let you live in an interesting time!"

QUESTIONS FOR DISCUSSION AND WRITING

1. Although this essay is actually a series of individual vignettes and observations, it is nevertheless held coherently together by a central theme. Briefly, what is the main theme of this essay?
2. Comment on Tyrmand's analogy of the wheel and democracy and his conclusion that perhaps neither of them can or should be replaced by anything better.
3. What are your feelings about the woman Tyrmand talked to who was wealthy, well-groomed, and well-fed, and who said "I hate America"? Later, Tyrmand says "I shall never grasp how it happens that modest, over-worked, badly dressed underdogs adore this country and people who receive everything from it hate it." Do you agree with Tyrmand's general conclusion that revolution is "the pastime of the rich . . . the opiate of the affluent"? Explain.
4. Does this essay argue against revolution itself, or merely against what Tyrmand considers "thoughtless" or "pseudo-revolution"? In this regard, comment on Tyrmand's fear that revolutionaries can easily become "self-appointed policemen," and his criticism of American protestors because the consequences of their actions "can be annulled with fifty dollars bail."
5. Does the fact that Tyrmand came from Poland, and lived in a socialist country for twenty years, give him any special vantage point on what is currently taking place in America? Does it give more validity to his ideas? Or perhaps less? Explain.
6. Tyrmand says that "there must be as much suffering and injustice in America as everywhere else, because it is the human condition that produces these things." Do you agree? What is "the human condition"?
7. "Today, students want to determine what it is they should know," Tyrmand says. "How they know what it is they should know, being unknowledgeable seekers of knowledge, is a mystery." Can you explain this "mystery"?
8. To the lady who said that "we want to enlarge our freedom, improve it," Tyrmand rejoined that freedom "has no shades or degrees . . . It is or it is not." Discuss.
9. Some students have called this essay not only conservative but even reactionary. Others have maintained that it is essentially a traditional liberal point of view, similar to that of, say, Paul Goodman's essay in this section (p. 265). What is your opinion?

Lewis Chester
Godfrey Hodgson
Bruce Page

A Slight Case of Hubris?

"America's leadership must be guided by the lights of learning and reason—or else those who confuse rhetoric with reality and the plausible with the possible will gain the popular ascendancy with their seemingly swift and simple solutions."
——President John F. Kennedy, in a speech intended for delivery in Dallas on November 22, 1963

"It is an easy thing for one whose foot
Is outside of calamity
To give advice and to rebuke the sufferer."
——Aeschylus, *Prometheus Bound*

To apply to Lyndon Johnson as an individual the word *hubris* in its modern, dictionary-defined sense of "wanton arrogance" would be both abusive and unfair. But the word has an older and richer meaning. It was the term for the second stage in a progression which is perhaps the fundamental idea in the ancient Greek tragedy, a moral system as deep and as universal as the Christian cycle of sin, grace, and redemption, though a far less comfortable one. The Greeks believed that the danger of success was that it bred hubris; that hubris might lead to *nemesis*—divine retribution—and that nemesis led in the end to *ate,* total black destruction and annihilation.

It is worth pointing out that hubris, in their system, was not necessarily evilly motivated. On the contrary, the classic instance of hubris was the presumption of Prometheus, who stole the divine fire from heaven out of a wish to start mankind on the way to the Great Society. "In helping man I brought my troubles on me," he said as he lay chained to the rock and at the mercy of his enemies, and the titan from Texas was heard to make similar complaints in the privacy of the White House.

319

No: the sin of hubris lies not in any evil motives, but in a systematic conception of one's powers and one's place in the universe so proud, so presumptuous, and so erroneous that it can only end in disaster.

As a preliminary diagnosis, hubris might seem a strange name for the American malady at the beginning of 1968: a hysterical form of social hypochondria was more in evidence. From television and from the press, from every kind of expert and leader, Americans were inundated with an almost unprecedented torrent of gloom. Every kind of authority produced new reasons for believing that America had become what she was called by Nelson Rockefeller, scarcely the most radical of social critics: "the Afflicted Society." The New Left earnestly predicted the imminent establishment of Fascism; the Right foresaw decadence and mob rule. No prophecy and no denunciation was too wild for the new generation of black leaders; and yet even their antithesis, Senator William Fulbright, most urbane of conservatives, soberly warned that "unmistakably America is showing signs of that arrogance of power which has afflicted, weakened, and in some cases destroyed great nations in the past."

The politicians said that rarely had the country respected its President so little—and the polls bore them out.

The economists feared that the cost of the war and the persistent deficit in foreign payments would lead to devaluation of the dollar (technically, to an increase in the price of gold, which would amount to much the same thing) and to an eventual recession.

The sociologists described the failure of the War on Poverty and pointed out the appalling spread of pauperization in the midst of wealth.

Ordinary people worried over the alarming rise in the crime statistics and the actual alarming, though not quite so steep, rise in crime itself.

And moralists of every school threw up their hands at the vogue for marijuana, LSD, and other new fashions in escapism, and puzzled over the younger generation's lack of respect for their elders.

But two great problems above all were singled out as in some measure the cause of all the Republic's other troubles: the two downward spirals which became labeled for convenience, and sometimes, it seemed, with an almost affectionate familiarity, The War and The Cities.

There was good reason, in all conscience, for alarm on both counts. The war was killing more and more Americans. It was costing an astronomical amount of money. And it was beginning to do economic damage: from early 1968 it was noticed that, for the first time anyone could remember, peace was bullish on the Stock Exchange. Most important of all, as it turned out, the war was causing a massive rebellion among young people. The draft was so unpopular that a considerable number of young people were leaving the country and going to Canada or Europe—not a significant number in themselves but apparently, from the attention they attracted, enough to be psychologically wounding to a country that had always thought of itself as the last hope of troubled people from other parts of the world.

There was even more reason to be disturbed by the crisis in the relations between black and white Americans. At the beginning of 1968, the optimism of 1963—when Dr. King had a dream, everyone sang, "Black and white together, We shall overcome," and all that seemed needed for a second emancipation was an act of Congress—had been replaced by a mood of despair which could not be said entirely to lack foundation. In more than a hundred cities, black ghettos had exploded—from Watts in 1965 to Detroit in 1967—and it was generally assumed that each summer would be hotter than the last. What was more, it was getting harder and harder to dismiss these explosions as trivial incidents on the road to a solution of the country's oldest political problem, still less as the work of a handful of agitators. As the Kerner Commission was to say with shocking frankness at the end of February, there was a growing body of evidence that white racism was the cause of the new black militancy; and there was little reason to believe that the white majority was ready in practice to abandon the half-conscious assumption of white supremacy.

The majority of Americans, in short, approached the Presidential politics of 1968 with a strong, and simple, and unhappy picture of what was happening to their country. It was, in a catchphrase of the time, "being torn apart by the war and the cities." No one, it seems to us, can hope to understand what 1968 was about unless he accepts that, with infinite variations, that was the theme of the year for most Americans. But it also seems to us that the picture was not an altogether true one. It was at once too gloomy and too sanguine.

Both the War and the Cities were real enough, and bad enough. But the particular form in which these problems troubled so many Americans was not likely to last forever. There was every possibility that the situation would improve in Vietnam and that the cities would exhaust their anger and their energies in a futile eruption and then relapse into torpor; that people would then return with a sigh of relief to the mild complacency which is a far more natural state of mind for the most "successful" country in the world.

And that is exactly what happened. The escalation of the war did stop, and the peace talks began. The ghettos went up in one incandescent flare in April, and were then quieter than they had been for a long time. The United States triumphed in the Olympic Games. The gross national product went up seven per cent. Detroit had its best year ever, and so did the New York Stock Exchange. To crown it all, three American astronauts beat the Russians around the moon. Already, by the fall of the year, the jeremiads in the news magazines began to be replaced by self-congratulation, cautious at first and then gradually more confident.

Yet nothing that was achieved by the political process in 1968, it seems to us, did anything to heal what was actually wrong with American society. Vietnam and The Cities were not the disease. They were symptoms—real inflammations, but still effects, not causes. The disease was the whole complex of attitudes, traditions, interests, values, past choices, and hopes for the future which made it possible for the strongest country in the world to embroil itself in a cruel and futile war under the illusion that it was safeguarding the freedom of the world; and, at the same time, made it impossible for Americans to cut through the surface with realism and determination to get at the problems underneath at home.

The disease, in a word, was hubris.

We do not need to be reminded of the rebuke that Prometheus most deservedly hurled at the self-satisfied busybodies of the chorus. We know how much easier it is "for one whose foot is outside of calamity to give advice and to rebuke the sufferer." And, when we suggest that America's problem in 1968 stems from hubris, we are not striving to say something vulgarly abusive. We are using not the modern, but the old, tragic sense of the word. Hubris can spring from honorable pride in great powers and great achievements, and its motives may be as high as the improvement of mankind. We still think that when a society's perception of its mission rises too high above reality, there is the danger of nemesis.

It is certainly not hard to trace the failure both of the Great Society program at home and of the Vietnam adventure abroad to typically hubristic conceptions of America's unique power and mission.

The Great Society was not the most daring, but it was perhaps the most bellicose program of social reform in history. It was to be a *war* on poverty. Federal funds were to be "fired in" to pockets of poverty in what was known in Washington as "the rifle-shot approach." "This nation," Johnson had said at a dinner to raise funds for his 1964 election campaign, "this people, this generation, has man's first chance to create a Great Society. . . . No one will stop America," he warned grimly, "from wiping out racial injustice." On another occasion, he actually spoke of "throttling want." It was as if the President and the comfortable middle-class Americans who supported and helped to frame his program were intolerably affronted by the impudent persistence of poverty, rather than concerned at the condition of the poor.

The same initial burst of aggressive confidence characterized the 1963 and 1964 efforts of the Administration and, for example, the great foundations to destroy segregation and "achieve integration." The Congress did pass a long schedule of reform legislation, pieces of which—particularly those concerned with civil rights—are probably of historic importance. But it is fair to say that this program was sold more energetically than it was carried out and that it was, from the start, more aggressive than radical. The Administration's approach seemed curiously industrial.

A problem was identified: in this case, that there were too many poor people in the United States. Right. Let the problem be bulldozed out of existence. Experts were consulted and suggested "solutions." These suggestions were priced, and a carefully graduated "mix" of "programs" applied. Elaborate public-relations antics were directed where persuasion was thought necessary—to Congress; to the press, of course; even in certain instances to the proposed recipients, if they proved recalcitrant. Finally, quantitative estimates of the success of the program were proudly produced. Johnson's aide Joseph Califano was a great one for producing lists showing how many fewer poor people there were this year than at some earlier time.

But the point of social reform, of course, ought not to be to push *x* million people above some notional "poverty line." As poverty is relative, so there can be no useful "attack" on it that does not involve the effective redistribution of goods, services, and wealth. But redistribution hurts. It demands hard decisions. And these the Johnson Administration did not seem willing to make. Indeed, it is very doubtful whether the classes that exercise political power in the United States really want to abolish poverty or any other major social problem if it is going to mean paying a price that will hurt. And it is hubristic to think that you can conquer problems that have never been conquered before, however rich you are, if you are not prepared to pay a price to do so.

There are striking parallels between the failure of the Great Society— for, whatever particular successes it did achieve, it *was* a failure in terms of the original rhetorical claims made for it—and the failure in Vietnam. Each involved a refusal to make difficult decisions. This, we have suggested was the inherent, though concealed, weakness of the attractive doctrine of "limited war." And each was based on a premise that the United States was now so rich, so powerful, so omnipotent that it could do *without giving up any other desired goal,* whatever its President wanted to do. "The Johnson-Rusk policy in Asia," wrote Walter Lippmann, "is based on the assumption that two hundred million Americans, because they have a superior technology, can lead and direct the two-thirds of the human race who inhabit the continent of Asia. It cannot be done." He was perfectly right. But the very words, "It cannot be done," applied to a proposed policy of the United States, are regarded by too many of its citizens as tantamount to defeatism. "The impossible takes a little longer." The Johnson Administration thought nothing of proposing, *as a mere incident* in the military defense of South Vietnam, to impose an entirely exotic and imported social revolution. The Kennedy Administration proposed to export a social revolution to the whole of Latin America. And President Johnson not infrequently spoke as if his ambition was to make the whole world part of his Great, unhappy, Society.

One day in the spring of 1968, Senator Eugene McCarthy was asked whether he thought American foreign policy was imperialist. "Well, yes," he answered, "it is a kind of imperialism, but a new kind. It is almost a kind of ideological imperialism. It is an idea we seem to have of the world as our *imperium*."

It is almost certainly hard for Americans to appreciate the sense, not of arrogance, but of sheer unreality and fantasy, which their own view of themselves and of their place in the universe produces on the foreigner. A foreigner opens *Look* magazine, and he reads Eric Sevareid's opinion that "intelligent foreigners know that much of the world will be transformed in the American image. . . . They know that the struggle is really over—it is the Western way of living and doing, our way and the way of Europe combined, that the world wants." He turns in bewilderment to *Life* magazine, and—hoping, perhaps, for a respite from this messianism—turns to a pleasant little essay on jogging. But what is this? The author is describing the happy camaraderie "in heartland America," when one jogger meets another. "Charlie—corporate officer, community leader, man of substance and affairs, philanthropist, father of a Princeton man and another son on the way there—responds with a cheery wave and jogs on his way, caught up in the task of self-improvement and, *by tacit premise, the betterment of the world*" (our italics).

Such examples might seem too slight to found a thesis on. But they can be multiplied almost infinitely. Here, for example, is the peroration of a book by a professor of history at Harvard, Frederick Merk, *Manifest Destiny and Mission*. Professor Merk's thesis is that while manifest destiny was bad, "a truer expression of the national spirit" was a purer, more godly form of imperialism called mission:

> Manifest destiny, in the twentieth century, vanished. . . . Mission, on the contrary, remained alive, and is as much alive at present as it ever was. It is still the beacon lighting the way to political and individual freedoms. . . . It is still, as always in the past, the torch held aloft by the nation at its gate—to the world and to itself.

Or here is the chairman of the political science department at M.I.T., Dr. Ithiel de Sola Pool:

> The world has become a smaller place. In various ways we will all become more alike, and more like America. People everywhere want some aspects of American culture, such as automobiles, TV sets, refrigerators, and Coca-Cola . . . participant politics, civil liberties, social mobility, pragmatism, and a pacific orientation. . . . We can live safely only in a world in which the political systems of all states are democratic. . . . I predict there will be

a number of effective interventions in foreign crises in America's future.

(We have extracted three passages from Dr. Pool's contributions to a colloquy printed in the *Atlantic Monthly* in November 1968 and we have reversed their order. We do not think we have distorted the impression he gave that he considered the world an American *imperium*. That an educated man, let alone a professor of political science, can be under the impression that participant politics, civil liberties—or indeed the automobile—are either American inventions or American monopolies, passes belief.)

Last, here is the thought which Richard Nixon chose to leave before the American people in his last speech before the election of 1960:

> My friends, it is because we are on the side of right: it is because we are on God's side: [*cheers and applause*] that America will meet this challenge and that we will build a better America at home and that that better America will lead the forces of freedom in building a new world.

All nations live by myths, and there is nothing new about the myth of a God-given mission to "build a new world" in one's own image. The history of Europe in modern times can be written around the successive aspirations of its nation-states—Spain, France, Britain, Germany, Russia—to a universal "civilizing mission," to "make the world a better place" by making it more like themselves. Nor is the delusion specifically a heritage of European blood. Such pathetically weak states as Indonesia, Ghana, and India have all aspired to world leadership in the last few years.

But America is not pathetically weak. She is enormously, though not infinitely, strong. The real economic and military power the United States has acquired in the last twenty-five years makes the delusions both of an inherently better society at home and of a God-given universal mission abroad more plausible and therefore more dangerous. Nor is the temptation a new one for Americans. The historian Richard Hofstadter has pointed out that

> the American frame of mind was created by a long history that encouraged our belief that we have an almost magical capacity to have our way in the world, that the national will can be made entirely effective, as against other peoples, at a relatively small price. . . . Free security, easy expansion, inexpensive victories, decisive triumphs—such was almost our whole experience with the rest of the world down to the twentieth century.

All nations have their myths, and there is some merit in them as the bond of unity and the spur to effort. The danger, for a nation as for an individual, comes when the gap between rhetoric and reality becomes too wide. In an individual, such a gap between self-perception and reality is known as psychosis. A nation that indulges in too much self-glorifying rhetoric while unable to win a small war or to prevent deterioration in its social fabric is unlikely to be able to heal its real distempers.

ITEM: Americans cherished the myth that theirs is an anti-colonial, revolutionary tradition. Yet they found themselves with a quasi-colonial position in every continent, often with the advantages of possessing colonies without the responsibility of administering them. And they had become committed, almost without realizing it, to a global campaign to frustrate revolution.

ITEM: Americans "hold this truth to be self-evident," that the rights of Americans include the pursuit of happiness. Yet, by the beginning of 1968, an increasing number of them wondered whether they and their forebears had been intoning this sonorous promise with a muttered reservation: "except for black Americans."

ITEM: Americans believe with passionate and creditable intensity that their country offers a unique degree of social and economic equality of opportunity. Even one of the most radical social critics of America, Michael Harrington, has called America "the most radical country in the world," because "the worker on the assembly line has always known . . . that he is just as good as Henry Ford." Yet one of the few sociologists who has bothered to go and ask the worker on the assembly line, Ely Chinoy, found that "among the workers interviewed none spoke of any ambitions in the plant higher than foremanship. . . . 'For a fellow starting as an hourly worker,' " one twenty-four-year-old said, " 'there isn't much chance of going up there in the company. That's in the past now.' " Most Americans believe that the distribution of income in the United States "is the greatest social revolution in history," as President Eisenhower once said. The fact is that, though average incomes in America are very high by international standards (and have been since the eighteenth century), the distribution of wealth in America is noticeably top-heavy and has changed less than in most other countries. The lower half of the population received twenty-two per cent of the national personal income in 1964—which was just one per cent more than thirty years earlier. Some revolution . . .

ITEM: Americans believe that they are set apart from the rest of the world by far greater personal freedom and individualism. Yet more and more, in practice, their freedom and their individualism have been circumscribed by bureaucracy of many kinds—not just by George Wallace's Federal bureaucrats with beards and briefcases. Most of all, perhaps, the traditional American values are threatened by the bureaucrats of private business, with their building passes and their security checks, their credit ratings and their all-knowing computers, their consuming passion for judging a man as employee, customer, or debtor by his wife, his opinions, and his haircut. A man may cleave to his constitutional freedoms. But if he is to get the job, the house, the loan, or the credit he wants, if he is to register at a college or marry the boss's daughter, he learns that cautious conformity is safer than individualism. Far more than his cousin in Western Europe, he must learn to get his mind right.

There is another point. It is not only that the *content* of the American political creed, with its optimism, its faith in progress, its universality, tends to clothe the realities of politics with the cloak of rhetoric more than is acceptable in other cultures. There is also something in the *modus* whereby Americans receive their political ideas and information which encourages exceptionally shameless flights of rhetoric.

In the District of Columbia, in the summer of 1968, there had been so many robberies on the buses that the bus company decided to stop issuing change. Instead it announced that passengers who did not give the exact fare would be issued with "scrip" which would be useless for anything except bus rides and therefore not worth stealing. It was a sensible solution to a real problem. But the bus company didn't stop there. It posted on the sides of all its buses the following notice:

NO CHANGE GIVEN
TO SPEED YOUR RIDE
ONLY SCRIP ISSUED

"To speed your ride"! Whom did they think they were kidding? Americans have grown used to, and cynical about, and even perversely fond of the world's most preposterously audacious advertising. "The Springtime of a Woman's Life Should Begin at 55," says the ad for Information Incorporated. Who believes it? Yet who would pay for it if it had no effect? But—and this is the crucial point—Americans have come to get their information and their ideas about politics, especially in election year, from media that are deeply penetrated by the ethos and the techniques of advertising.

It is not just that Presidential candidates are "packaged" and "sold"— their words, not ours—by advertising professionals. It is not only that, whether citizens watch a serious documentary on urban problems or a candidate's speech on television, the political information is sandwiched between ads, so that it is psychologically all but impossible to switch the cynicism on and off in the right places. It is not just that the most serious political journalism, in the *New York Times Magazine* or *The New Yorker*, stretches like a lonely ribbon of gray between bright temptations to shop at Bergdorf Goodman or Van Cleef & Arpels.

Advertising itself has become permeated with politics, until the confusion is complete.

"If you're concerned about the times we live in," says the Equitable Life Assurance Company, under a display of slum pictures deliberately laid out to look like photo reportage, "so are we at Equitable." Thus the agony of the ghettos is made to sell insurance policies to the middle class. "Independence Day," proclaims the ad for Lewis & Thomas Saltz, gentlemen's outfitters, over a picture of the American flag, and then comes a little poem:

> This day of ours is full of sacred joy;
>> The proud glad moments weaving golden hours
> Which patriot souls, of purpose great, employ
>> To pledge ourselves anew with wakened powers.

Thus patriotism is twisted to sell English tweeds and Italian silks. The Army even pays for a full page in the trendiest copywriters' camp to sell war itself:

> Vietnam.
> Hot. Wet. Muddy. Perilous. To prove
> yourself here is to prove yourself
> to the world. No test is harder. No trial
> more demanding.
> But when a man serves here,
> he proves himself a man.
> To his Country. To himself.

Who believes advertising? Yes, but who is uninfluenced by it?

It can be argued, again, that this is not unique to America; that the difference in the audacity of advertising, is only a matter of degree or of time. But the difference of degree, at this point in time, seems to us to amount to a difference in kind. Certainly American advertising men themselves would be the last to deny that they have pushed the technique and the ambitions of their craft further than anywhere else in the world.

And so the great Bullshine Machine rolls forward, extending the field of fire for its shiny product from the advertising pages to the news columns, from skinless sausages ("oxygen intercepted") and mass-produced cakes ("like Grandma used to bake") to the personality of candidates and the great issues that divide society. The constant exposure to this shower of matter—half-true, untrue, or even true, but always simplified, always loud, always self-serving—induces a peculiar mixture of gullibility and cynicism that is close to neurosis. It is not an attitude that is well adapted for distinguishing between bullshine and brass tacks, rhetoric and reality.

QUESTIONS FOR DISCUSSION AND WRITING

1. How do the attitudes expressed in this essay differ from those in the preceding essay by Leopold Tyrmand?
2. Do the authors of this essay make a strong and convincing case for the idea of America being motivated by hubris? Why do they choose this classical word rather than "pride" or, as they say, "wanton arrogance"?
3. The authors assert that there are "striking parallels between the failure of the Great Society . . . and the failure in Vietnam." Explain their reasoning and whether or not you agree.
4. Does the fact that the authors of this article are English have any bearing on the validity of their views about America? Explain.
5. The authors quote Eugene McCarthy as saying that American foreign policy is "a new kind" of imperialism: "It is an idea we seem to have of the world as our *imperium*." Discuss McCarthy's comment.
6. Explain the following statement: "America is not pathetically weak. She is enormously, though not infinitely, strong. The real economic and military power the United States has acquired in the last twenty-five years makes the delusions both of an inherently better society at home and of a God-given universal mission abroad more plausible and therefore more dangerous."
7. Comment on the advertising and packaging techniques mentioned by the authors which simplify and glorify "the American Way," reducing it to a series of slogans. According to the authors, is such advertising the symptom or the cause of our problems? Explain.
8. If America does indeed suffer from hubris, what is the antidote?
9. If you believe that America does not suffer from hubris, explain why.

Irving Louis Horowitz

Is American Radicalism Possible?

Is a new radical movement possible in the United States? Of course, any movement called radical is possible. The burden of this question ought to be: Is a radical movement in this country imminent or feasible? Here the cliché answer is available: Anything is possible—even the re-definition of events to prove that we are in the midst of a radical move-ment right now. Indeed, some social scientists even say that Ameri-canism, socialism, and radicalism are united in a common enterprise to save the world from barbarism and/or Communism.

The possibility of redefining events to suit either our idiosyncrasies or our ideologies is ever-present. I will not attempt to answer whether a new radical movement in the United States is feasible, but only indi-cate the sort of definition of radicalism that makes sense for the children of the seventies—a definition that starts with civil libertarianism and civil disobedience, but does not end there.

Classical American liberalism has no future. Not so much because liberal aims are dead in America. This is a conjectural matter. It was already so in the twenties—in the times of Mencken, Veblen, Dewey, and Bourne; although through a clever manipulation of words and sym-bols, they were able to remain authentically American and liberal at the same time. This was generally true of pragmatism. But this domestic liberalism was made possible by the low stakes involved. If nativism, nationalism, and nervousness were always combined with radicalism in the past, this combination remained uncomfortable and disquieting, carrying with it a knowlege that such associations, like patriotism and flag-waving before them, were doomed to become symbols of the Right. This was inevitable, since it is always the authentic Right that is most adept at defending the national face and the national purpose. To be a radical is somehow to deny explicitly the existence of such a thing as a national purpose, and to repudiate face-saving as the basis of politi-cal decision-making.

330

There was always a suspect quality in the Left wrapping itself with the American flag. When the former head of the Communist Party, Earl Browder, pointed out that Communism was 20th-century Americanism—a statement uttered many times and in many forms—the Communist movement surrendered its claims to radicalism. Its entire postwar existence was embarrassed by federal claims of Communist un-Americanism, and absurd counterclaims (supported by absurd academics) of its pro-Americanism. Perhaps radicalism is doomed to a minority status, an Olympian ideology of those who think; but it can never be entirely destroyed or eliminated, as can political movements staking a claim to bigger and better Americanism. The radical defends the person against the movement. The radical defends the dissenter against the conformer. Above all, the radical assumes the risk and the liabilities of his position. Neither the Communist nor those engaged in similar movements could ever do this. To the bitter end, Communists engaged in "coalition politics"—as if the major parties even gave a damn!

Even at its most prosaic level, radicalism is tied to the future of the world rather than to the present of the United States. What separates the liberal from the radical is that for the liberal it is enough to demand a "war on poverty," while for the radical what is demanded is a concomitant "war on opulence." For the liberal, a call for a "revolution of rising expectations" is adequate, as if the economic world had an infinite elasticity and expansiveness in which all could gain and all could be content. The radical is less certain of this notion of infinite elasticity. In any event, he insists on a corresponding recognition of a "revolution of falling profits." In place of a consensus doctrine, the radical pushes for social demands with an assertion that some sector, group, some individual, must *pay* a premium for these social goods. In this sense, the radical posture is more tough-minded than that of the liberal. It insists that things desired have a price and a payoff; and that it is futile to disguise this fact in pollyannaish phraseology, or in demagogic appeals to yawning masses.

While Marx sometimes defended the interests of one nation against another, of Poland against Russia, of Spain against France, of France against Germany, or of the North against the South in the American Civil War, the principle was always the same—internationalism. It was *the rights of masses* against *the claims of classes*. This is one principle of Marxism that retains its full vitality. Support for the Third World, for Algeria against France, for Angola against Portugal, for the Congo against Belgium, for Ceylon against India, for Biafra against Nigeria, for Vietnam against the United States, must remain genuine—but always qualified, always tempered by international needs. This is the ethics of Marxism as a humanistic outlook; a political ethic that permits the differentiation of nationalism without at the same time committing us to a celebration. Not to take such a standpoint, to insist upon either full allegiance to one brand of nationalism or to a textbook internationalism, is to betray reality—to serve up the living ethic of Marxism to the dead soul of Marx. And this indeed is precisely what has taken place. Marx has been drowned in Western civilization programs—one more name added to Great Books courses. What is left after this process of intellectual castration is Marx the inept prophet rather than Marx the radical violator of the sacred cows of Western civilization.

What is radicalism today? In some measure it is an affirmation of negation, of stopping the machines. As Mario Savio, echoing the sentiments of Henry David Thoreau, put matters: "There is a time when the operation of the machine becomes so odious, makes you so sick at heart, that you can't take part; you can't even passively take part, and you've got to put your bodies upon the gears and upon the wheels, upon the levers, upon all the apparatus and you've got to make it stop. And you've got to indicate to the people who run it, to the people who own it, that unless you're free, the machines will be prevented from working at all."

What is Americanism today? In some measure it is the transformation of man into a fanatic nationalist and imbecilic purpose-finding patriot. As the President of the United States of America said in 1965, when addressing students from schools and colleges on a trip to Washington sponsored by the William Randolph Hearst Foundation: "I would like to see them [the students] develop as much fanaticism about the United States's political system as young Nazis did about their system during the War."

Perhaps someone astute in dialectical reasoning can synthesize these opposites of radicalism and Americanism. I cannot. Nor do I think the project worth undertaking. There is a limit to ecumenical sentiment; to sleazy efforts to liberalize Americanism and to conservatize radicalism. The history of the Soviet Union can be read as a gigantic contradiction between Marxism as a doctrine of liberation and Marxism as a metaphysics of enslavement. The choice in the Soviet Union was between radicalism and great Russian chauvinism. The Soviet leadership from Stalin to Brezhnev have chosen the latter. Can we for an instant imagine that the choice in the United States is somehow less urgent, or less significant? For an Evgenii Yevtushenko to become a radical meant for him to become a critic—ruthless and uncompromising—of Soviet life. For a C. Wright Mills to have performed a similar role in American life during the faded fifties meant the same "un-Americanism": abstention from voting; rejection of the Cold War; the exposé of militarization of the country. This is not a question of the *quality* of radicalism in America—this is an advanced question to which we are not yet entitled to give answers. It is a question of the sheer survival of radicalism.

Any meaningful definition of radicalism must not simply be an affirmation of retreatism but a set of propositions about the state of the world and what the individual ought to do about the world. It is an assertion that nations, like individuals, have the right to choose their own social system, whether they choose our way or not. It is a further assertion of the right of men to disaffiliate and dissociate if the original choice turns out to be sour. The first part is the tough part for the American ideology (and leadership) to accept; the second part is the tough part for the Soviet ideology (and leadership) to acknowledge.

The parameters of our modern world are not determined by either the words socialism or capitalism; but may just as readily be defined by the terms poverty-stricken and opulent, underdeveloped and overdeveloped, Christian and non-Christian, colored and white, etc. Such elements may be welded together at a critical moment in time, which is when revolutions are most likely to occur.

This appreciation of social change is still not radicalism. For a person to be radical means to deny the basis of his own superiority: to fight for blacks when he is white; to condemn Papal inaction when one is a Catholic; to urge land reform when one is a landlord, etc. That is why the poor and downtrodden can never be described as "radical"— what they do is "natural"—in keeping with their "interests." What the radical does is violate the canon of self-interest or national interest. He asserts a transcendent ethical principle. When Martin Luther King conducted a voter-registration drive in Alabama he acted naturally; when he denounced anti-Semitism he behaved radically.

The rationalist Marx was a radical, not because of his description of historical tendencies, long-run inevitabilities, majority interests (the downtrodden, the masses, the poor, etc.), but because at every critical moment he defended the ethics of internationalism against the facts of nationalism. The irrationalist Nietzsche took radicalism a step further. He asserted the antihistorical character of a moral act. The ability to perform heroically means the ability to fight for what may be a losing cause rather than for that which is rising. Cervantes' *Don Quixote* was more of a radical than any downtrodden character in literature: because Don Quixote violated his class to gain justice; he abandoned his wife to restore his sexuality; because he acted against his *interests* in the effort to recapture his *manliness*.

Why is Joseph Conrad's *Secret Agent* so superior to Victor Hugo's *Les Miserables?* It is because the anarchist professor in Conrad's novel is endowed with consciousness—with an understanding of the police inspector as his externalized self. Jean Valjean can only run, can only be chased, can only be reduced to permanent enslavement, since he searches only for permanent security. The radical alone can taste the abyss as he reaches for the heavens. The radical alone can feel the shame of defeat at the moment of his triumph. This is why radicalism is a 20th-century humanism. This is what transforms radicalism from sentimentalism, progressivism, liberalism, or any other fragmentary form of amelioration.

Thus it is given to the fortunate alone to behave radically, as distinct from those who behave naturally. As a white you can be radical; as Negro you behave naturally. As an American you can be radical in defense of Vietnamese independence; in Vietnam one behaves this way naturally. As a Christian or a Moslem you can be radical in defense of the Jew; as a Jew you can only behave naturally on the "Jewish question." As a rich man you can be radical with respect to land reform; as a peasant you can only behave naturally. To the extent then that self-awareness is a rare property in men, to that degree is radicalism doomed to a minority status, to an elite of those who transcend their particular egos. For every Evgenii Yevtushenko there are a thousand Ukrainian anti-Semites; and for every pacifist like A. J. Muste there are a thousand ready to take up arms. The search of radical politics has ended in collectivist demagogy. Politics to be radical must be anti-national, anti-Establishment, in short, self-negating—*anti-politique.*

It might be argued that this also defines reaction: the Negro who toadies up to white folks and uses chemicals to become white if possible; the General Khanhs who behave as if American troops should use napalm bombs on Vietnamese villagers; the Jew who turns anti-Semite; etc. The answer to this is complicated: In a sense, such reaction does indeed deserve to be labeled radicalism. The radicalism of the Right and of the Left are logically coincident; however, they are not coincident historically, or even in terms of psychological self-definition.

One never finds a Rightist using the phrase "radical of the Right." He howls to the contrary that he is a good American, that Birchism is 20th-century Americanism! There is no nobility in radicalism of such a posture. The Right is an appellation assigned to the Rightist, not one he wears. The radical of the Right is without consciousness of his extremism. He defends the "is," the present moment, even though this may mean a rolling back of time or a rolling back of other nations. The Rightist does not accept radicalism as a self-definition of the situation. Above all, the radical of the Right is not prepared to deny his interests in order to affirm his self. He is not prepared to empathize or to reverse roles. On the contrary, his is a position of pure egotism: of defending face, of saving territories that do not belong to him, etc. He has no transcendent principles. He perishes with his ego ideals in a final Götterdämerung of the American way.

The doubts that must plague those of us concerned with the future of radicalism cannot be settled by words alone. But at least we can underscore why it is one thing to speak of a radical man and quite another to speak of a political movement. We have too long institutionalized radicalism, and in this very process, castrated its meaning for individuals. The word radicalism can only be debased when it attaches itself to cheap political movements having ill-defined and prosaic ends. Look about the world and see how many absurdly conservative and historical political parties have employed the term "radical" in their titles. In such nations, the word itself creates a wry smile, like the word "liberalism" does in this country. Elsewhere in the world the notions of social action I have been talking of have had to run out from under the shell of the concept of radicalism—and find new linguistic expressions.

In the United States radicalism is still a word that carries thrust. Let us keep it that way—let us not debase it by affixing it to a concept of Americanism, yahooism, or rah-rahism. The "image" of radicalism should never be allowed to be used as a protective covering for the worst infirmities of modern civilization. It should remain a term of *marginal use,* and in this way retain its *central importance.* For a society *per se* to become or to remain radical would require of its main branches a flexibility and a willingness to appreciate its own inutilities rarely exhibited in a social system. Indeed the drive of a social system is toward structure and ultimately toward the maintenance of order. The same holds for political parties, whatever their ostensible persuasion or commitments. Individuals are better able to behave radically. They alone have the capacity to deny the necessity of what exists. They alone have the ability to call forth a scheme of the future as a judgment on the society of the present. Individualism has remained an exclusive preserve of the conservatives because Left-wing politicos have failed to face the fact that governmental bigness is an evil, and that solutions based on radical principles rather than radical people is a disease and not a cure.

This account of radicalism does not imply the sort of thundering totalism and intellectual noisiness that have become standard in the writings of professorial oracles. There is no intent here to prove that radicalism is the one and only role a person can perform; only that radicalism is a significant role. The relationship between radicals and revolutionists is a sorely neglected theme in political role performance. Rosa Luxemburg could perform as a revolutionist and as a leader of the Spartacists, of the German Left Socialist movement, but at the same time, she was able to function as a radical, as a critic of Lenin and of the dogma of proletarian dictatorship. This she did at a moment of revolutionary euphoria when serious thinking was at a premium. And it is her radicalism, after all, that is now best remembered. The same can be said of Eugene V. Debs, whose importance in the Socialist movement lay precisely in the fact of his being above the fratricidal struggles for control of the Socialist party apparatus. Debs was the radical man who at the same time was quite powerless with respect to the organizational aspects of American socialism. He was far less concerned with organization than was Daniel DeLeon. Yet, Debs alone emerged as the "ecumenical" figure for the Socialists. Examples of radicalism can be readily multiplied.

The point is clear enough. Radicalism entails a critique of organizational constraint. Yet revolution can only be made in terms of a theory of organization. This is why the two roles of radical and revolutionary, while they may coexist in the same person, give rise to a considerable amount of tension within the person and between the organization and the individual. If revolutionary man is driven to join forces with other advocates for rapid change, the radical man is driven to point out how limited these changes are in practice. The revolutionist, upon completion of his aims, seeks the fruits of victory; the radical is charged with the chore of seeking new vistas to conquer.

This cerebral radicalism suffers the defects of its virtues: Splendid isolation may result in a self-indulgent, happy alienation from worldly problems, in an intensified isolation from political struggles that would leave the practical world to the least capable people. Precisely what it is to "act radically" or to "act naturally" may be differentially seen. A Southern sheriff may see the struggle of Negroes for voting rights as the most "unnatural" thing in the world. And above all, this kind of radicalism, while "un-American," must appreciate the fact that a society exists that is flexible enough to absorb, if not to accept, such un-Americanism. These are surely major difficulties in the position outlined, and they require treatment. For the time being, I can only say that the problems of this radical communion are certainly no more insurmountable than the problems posed by any other doctrine. Indeed, it has the singular advantage of at least not transforming its declarations into directives.

I should like to conclude on a cautionary note: Radicalism is a posture, not a position. It may provide a style of life, but can never be a substitute for work. Radicalism cannot tell you the role of China vis-à-vis India in the developmental process of Asia. Radicalism cannot settle questions about the length of time it takes to make a transition from rural life to urban life. Radicalism cannot prove the merits or demerits of one or another form of economic investment. When radicalism is employed as a surrogate for social science, it becomes fanaticism—an uncompromising effort to replace substance with style. These limits being understood and expressed, radicalism can serve as a beacon light for measuring the distance between where we are and where we want to go— between the society and the utopia.

QUESTIONS FOR DISCUSSION AND WRITING

1. Horowitz' essay is largely a definition of "radicalism." Do you agree with his definition of it as a denial of a person's own basis of superiority? What does this statement mean?
2. According to Horowitz, what is the difference between "radicalism" and "liberalism"? Do you agree with Horowitz' contention that "Classical American liberalism has no future"? Discuss.

3. On p. 332, Horowitz quotes Mario Savio's definition of "radicalism," and President Johnson's definition of "Americanism." Then he says "Perhaps someone astute in dialectical reasoning can synthesize these opposites . . . I cannot." Can you? Or do you agree with Horowitz that perhaps it's not worth the trouble? If such a synthesis could be arrived at, verbally or politically, do you think it would contribute to solving America's problems? Explain.
4. Horowitz says that "We have too long institutionalized radicalism . . . solutions based on radical principles rather than radical people is a disease and not a cure." Comment.
5. In general, what is Horowitz' conclusion about the feasibility of an American radicalism? What is your own conclusion?

For Further Reading

Chester, Lewis, Godfrey Hodgson, and Bruce Page. *An American Melodrama: The Presidential Campaign of 1968.* New York: Dell Publishing Co., Inc., 1969. Paperback.

Graham, Hugh Davis, and Ted Robert Gurr. *Violence in America: Historical and Comparative Perspectives.* New York: Bantam Books, Inc., 1969. Paperback.

Harrington, Michael. *The Other America: Poverty in the United States.* New York: The Macmillan Company, 1962. Paperback.

Kotz, Nick. *Let Them Eat Promises: The Politics of Hunger in America.* Englewood Cliffs, N.J.: Prentice-Hall, Inc., 1970.

Mailer, Norman. *The Armies of the Night.* New York: The New American Library, Inc., 1968. Paperback.

————. *Miami and the Siege of Chicago.* New York: Signet Books, The New American Library, Inc., 1968. Paperback.

Oglesby, Carl, ed. *The New Left Reader.* New York: Grove Press, Inc., 1969. Paperback.

Spock, Benjamin. *Decent and Indecent: Our Personal and Political Behavior.* New York: McCall Books, 1970. Paperback.

Winick, Charles. *The New People: Desexualization in American Life.* New York: Pegasus (Publishers), 1969. Paperback.